How to Do Things with Fictions

How to Do Things with Fictions

JOSHUA LANDY

OXFORD
UNIVERSITY PRESS

OXFORD
UNIVERSITY PRESS

Oxford University Press, Inc., publishes works that further
Oxford University's objective of excellence
in research, scholarship, and education.

Oxford   New York
Auckland   Cape Town   Dar es Salaam   Hong Kong   Karachi
Kuala Lumpur   Madrid   Melbourne   Mexico City   Nairobi
New Delhi   Shanghai   Taipei   Toronto

With offices in
Argentina   Austria   Brazil   Chile   Czech Republic   France   Greece
Guatemala   Hungary   Italy   Japan   Poland   Portugal   Singapore
South Korea   Switzerland   Thailand   Turkey   Ukraine   Vietnam

Published by Oxford University Press, Inc.
198 Madison Avenue, New York, New York 10016

www.oup.com

Oxford is a registered trademark of Oxford University Press

Library of Congress Cataloging-in-Publication Data
Landy, Joshua, 1965-
How to do things with fictions /Joshua Landy.
      p.   cm.
Includes bibliographical references and index.
ISBN 978-0-19-518856-1 (cloth: acid-free paper)
1. Fiction—History and criticism. 2. Books and reading. I. Title.
      PN3335.L26   2012
      808.3—dc23   2011036654

For my parents

CONTENTS

Acknowledgments   xi

Introduction   3
    THIRTEEN WAYS OF LOOKING AT A FICTION   4
    FORMATIVE FICTIONS   8
    THE TEMPORALITY OF THE READING EXPERIENCE   11
    IN SPITE OF EVERYTHING, A ROLE FOR MEANING   14
    A POLITE WORD TO HISTORIANS   16
    THE VALUE OF FORMATIVE FICTIONS   17

PART ONE—CLEARING THE GROUND

1. Chaucer: Ambiguity and Ethics   23
    PRUDENCE OR ONEIROMANCY?   23
    A PARODY OF DIDACTICISM   25
    PREACHING TO THE CONVERTED   27
    THE ASYMMETRY OF "IMAGINATIVE RESISTANCE"   29
    VIRTUE ETHICS AND GOSSIP   33
    QUALIFICATIONS   34
    A GENUINE BENEFIT   37

PART TWO—ENCHANTMENT AND RE-ENCHANTMENT

2. Mark: Metaphor and Faith   43
    THE MYTH OF SIMPLICITY   43

FIVE VARIABLES, SIX READINGS   45

DELIBERATE OPACITY   47

THE VISION OF MARK   49

FROM HIM WHO HAS NOT   52

TO HIM WHO HAS   53

THE SYROPHOENICIAN WOMAN   55

THE FORMATIVE CIRCLE   57

METAPHOR AND FAITH   59

THEOLOGICAL RAMIFICATIONS   60

A PARABLE ABOUT PARABLES   61

GETTING IT WRONG BY GETTING IT RIGHT   62

CODA: THE SECULAR KINGDOM   63

APPENDIX: CHARLES BAUDELAIRE, "LE CYGNE"   65

3. Mallarmé: Irony and Enchantment   69

Part 1: Jean-Eugène Robert-Houdin   70

EXORCISMS AND EXPERIMENTS   70

SCIENCE AND WONDER   72

LUCID ILLUSIONS   75

Part 2: Stéphane Mallarmé   77

THE SPELL OF POETRY   77

SETTING THE SCENE   79

A REPLACEMENT FAITH   81

HOW TO DO THINGS WITH VERSES   82

A CORNER OF ORDER   83

THE MAGIC OF RHYME   85

A TRAINING IN ENCHANTMENT   86

A SEQUENCE OF STATES   87

POSTSCRIPT: THE BIRTH OF MODERNISM FROM THE SPIRIT
OF RE-ENCHANTMENT   89

PART THREE—LOGIC AND ANTI-LOGIC

4. Plato: Fallacy and Logic   95

A PLATONIC COCCYX   96

ASCENT AND DISSENT   97

THE DEVELOPMENTAL HYPOTHESIS   99

DUBIOUS DIALECTIC   101

PERICLES, SOCRATES, AND PLATO   105

THE *GORGIAS* UNRAVELS   108

THE USES OF ORATORY   111

WAS GORGIAS REFUTED?   114

SPIRITUAL EXERCISES   115

APPENDIX: JUST HOW BAD IS THE PERICLES ARGUMENT?   120

5. Beckett: Antithesis and Tranquility   124

Part 1: Bringing Philosophy to an End   125

ATARAXIA   125

ANTILOGOI   126

ONE STEP FORWARD   128

Part 2: Finding the Self to Lose the Self   130

AN IRREDUCIBLE SINGLENESS   130

RES COGITANS   131

SOLUTIONS AND DISSOLUTIONS   133

TWO FAILURES   135

"I CONFESS, I GIVE IN, THERE IS I"   136

NEGATIVE ANTHROPOLOGY   138

THE BECKETTIAN SPIRAL   139

AN END TO EVERYTHING?   140

Part 3: Fail Better   142

GLIMPSES OF THE IDEAL   142

TWO CAVEATS   144

CODA   145

Notes   147

Works Cited   225

Index   245

ACKNOWLEDGMENTS

My first book was the result of a failure to listen to some very sensible advice warning me not to focus on a single author. This second book is the result a failure to listen to some equally sensible advice in the other direction: whatever you do, don't spread yourself out over five countries and two and a half millennia. I'm not sure what that says about me—nothing good, at any rate—but it speaks volumes for the patience and generosity of my friends, who are still talking to me (and, I'm happy to say, still offering advice!) in spite of it all.

Many of those friends are colleagues of mine, both at Stanford—I think not only of my invaluable comrades in the Department of French and Italian but of those who, like Keith Baker, Russell Berman, Harry and Michele Elam, Amir Eshel, David Hills, Nadeem Hussain, Marjorie Perloff, Gabriella Safran, and Debra Satz, hail from elsewhere around the quad—and farther afield, not least among them André Aciman, Robert Alter, David Carrier, Katherine Elkins, Richard Kaye, Richard Moran, and Miguel Tamen. I have also been fortunate enough to come into contact with a series of extraordinary students. Let me just mention here Melanie Conroy, Joanna Fiduccia (whose miniature Mallarméan *Wunderkammer* I still treasure), Ben Hurlbut, Trina Marmarelli, Christy Pichichero, Matthew Tiews, Neil van Leeuwen (an expert on self-deception, in theory if not in practice), and Ben Wolfson (a mine of information on curious writings). There are too many more to list, but I hope even the ones I'm omitting here know how much they have enriched my work and my life.

I first came across Plato when I was in secondary school in England and had no idea what he was really up to. (Many, of course, would say I still don't.) My teacher, Peregrine Maxwell-Stuart, put everything he had into teaching at a level that was (I now see) completely beneath him, and fired more than one of us, in the process, with a lifelong passion for classical culture. It was probably because of this passion that, in 1992–93, I went to see Alexander Nehamas give the Sather Lectures at Berkeley, a decision that would ultimately prove life-changing for me. Although Alexander and I still don't fully agree on Plato, it is safe to say that I learned more about Plato from him than from anyone, not to mention about Nietzsche, postulated authorship, and so much else besides; the debt runs very, very deep. In writing up my thoughts on Plato, I also benefited tremendously from exchanges with G. R. F. Ferrari, Mark Griffith, Charles Griswold, Hans Ulrich Gumbrecht, Vanessa de Harven, Jonathan Lear, Anthony Long, Andrea Nightingale, David Roochnik, Jeremy Sabol, Patricia Slatin, Greg Watkins, and Allen Wood. What is more, six generations of Phil. 81 students have by now heard me musing about Plato (and Chaucer), and I've continually appreciated their more-than-musings back.

My interest in New Testament parables goes back to a transformative experience I had at Princeton working as a teaching assistant for Andrew Ford. Up till then I had unthinkingly accepted teaching as just an element among others in the academic's life; all of a sudden I came to see, from the palpable joy with which he went about his business, that it is the very core of what we do. I am not sure I would have pursued the career I did, let alone pursued it with such alacrity, had it not been for his example. Nor do I think I would have dug so deeply into the books we taught together, from Homer to the Gospels. My interest in the latter eventually led me to Robert Gregg, Tanya Luhrmann, David O'Connor, Bernard Reginster, Fred Rush, Susan Sebbard, Brent Sockness, and Manuel Vargas, each of whom provided invaluable feedback; and then Michael Petrin went to extraordinary lengths to help me improve my work, in what I have always considered an act of pure, unadulterated *caritas*.

Lanier Anderson, to whom we'll return in a moment, did me the enormous favor of forcing me, kicking and screaming, to teach Chaucer with him. I never looked back. I have extremely happy memories not just of that collaboration but also of taking the resulting ideas to Chicago, a place that, thanks to the brilliant and magnanimous Robert Pippin, became something of a home away from home for me. I learned a great deal from Pippin himself, as well as from Françoise Meltzer, Robert Morrissey, Thomas Pavel, Candace Vogler, and so many others, both within the Committee on Social Thought and without. Elsewhere I profited from the wisdom of Sandra Bermann, Stanley Corngold, Caryl Emerson, Stacie Friend, Sean Greenberg, Louis Menand, Gary Saul Morson, Elena Russo, Angela Sebastiana, Susan Stewart, Jennifer Summit, Tzvetan Todorov, Blakey Vermeule, and Michael Wood.

As for Mallarmé and Beckett, they remain (along with Proust) key examples of how little I can trust my own initial judgments on anything important. Tony Gande is to be commended for patiently attempting to pique my interest in French poetry, and Alison Finch for patiently attempting to pique my interest in Mallarmé more specifically. In recent years I have had many delightful conversations about modern enchantment with Michael Saler, someone who—by an amazing chance—happened to be at the Stanford Humanities Center, and working on astonishingly similar matters, while I was preparing my chapter on poetry and magic. An edited volume, a radio interview, and several memorable coffees at the Capoeira Café emerged from that. Equally enjoyable was my experience co-teaching Beckett with Adrienne Janus, thanks to whom, as well as to Manya Lempert, Govind Persad, Hervé Picherit, and Phoebe Prioleau, I was able to catch glimmers of light amid the Beckettian obscurity. Discussions with Eileen John and Martin Warner also helped tremendously, as did Akiba Lerner's persistent foragings for the perfect Rorty quotation.

Much of the work on this volume was completed at the Stanford Humanities Center. I wish to express my appreciation not just for the nine months of leave but for the opportunity to exchange ideas with Terry Castle and Kenneth Taylor and, a stunning bonus, to meet Jonathan Kramnick. I am indebted to him for all his comments; I am indebted, too, to Steffan Chirazi, Dan Edelstein, Jake Keklikian, and Bliss Kern for helping me tackle the exceedingly thorny issue of titles. (Dan, you win.) Rachel Cristy, Phil Galligan, and Eric Messinger performed valiant acts of research assistance; the irrepressible Anya Bershad produced the index; the indefatigable Liudmila Inozemtseva checked quotes and caught some embarrassing errors; Corrie Goldman was always in my corner; and Brendan O'Neill has been everything one could hope for in an editor.

A version of the Chaucer chapter appeared in *Art and Ethical Criticism*, edited by Garry Hagberg (Blackwell, 2008); what was to become the Plato chapter first saw the light of day in *Arion* 15 (2007); earlier states of the Mallarmé section came out in *Symbolism* 8 (2008) and in *The Re-Enchantment of the World: Secular Magic in a Rational Age*, the volume I coedited with Michael Saler (Stanford University Press, 2009); and a tremendously compressed stab at Beckett found its way into *The Blackwell Companion to Literature and Philosophy*, edited by Garry Hagberg (Blackwell, 2010). I am grateful to Garry, to Norris Pope, to *Arion*, to *Symbolism*, and to the presses for graciously permitting separate publication.

Above all I would like to thank Lanier Anderson, Alexander Nehamas, Thomas Pavel, and Angela Sebastiana, not just because they offered endless input and advice—which they did—or because they have shown me immeasurable *philia* (which they have), but because they constitute for me models of thinking well, writing well, speaking well, and living well. Their very existence in the world makes it a brighter, warmer, and more beautiful place to live in. And then there are my parents, Barry and Rosalind Landy, both of whom instilled in me from an early age a love of reading and a passion for knowledge, and whose happiness in my happiness has always been so moving. This book is dedicated to them.

How to Do Things with Fictions

Introduction

I don't try to make you believe something you don't believe, but to make you do something you won't do.

—Wittgenstein

Toni Morrison's *Song of Solomon* is one of my favorite books in the world, a novel I teach with as much regularity as enthusiasm. You can imagine my feeling, then, when a brilliant young student recently told me what she thought of it: "Morrison is pretty good," she said, "but she could have gotten to the point a bit quicker." Before you rush to condemn my student, let me say right away that it is not her fault; she is in the top 5 percent of the top 30 percent of the young people in the country,[1] she is bright and keen and dedicated, and (stated reservations notwithstanding) she likes Toni Morrison, which is greatly to her credit. But it is surely not Toni Morrison's fault either. (Morrison has repeatedly said that her novels are not recipes, that they do not have messages, and that they do not aim "to give [her] readers something to swallow.")[2] Rather, it is *our* fault, the fault of those whose job it is to tell people how to read. For some reason, we have systematically—albeit unwittingly—engaged on a long-term campaign of misinformation, relentlessly persuading would-be readers that fictions are designed to give them useful advice.[3] No wonder my student thought Toni Morrison took too long getting to the point. How else was she supposed to understand the hundreds of pages of apparently wasted space?

Things were not always so. We did not always tell our consumers of fictions that the aim of the exercise is to receive instruction, let alone instruction in the form of propositional content. By "propositional content" I mean an idea or set of ideas, expressible in declarative sentences; by "fiction" I mean a verbal performance in which the events depicted never happened, and in which everyone knows they didn't. If I believe the story I'm telling and you know it's false, I'm making a *mistake*; if you believe what I'm saying but I don't, I'm telling a *lie*; but if neither of us believes it, and if both of us know that neither of us believes it, then the chances are that I'm spinning a *fiction*.[4] Thus when Chaucer presents us with a talking rooster who quotes Macrobius and Virgil, he does so in full awareness

3

that there are no talking roosters, erudite or otherwise, and in full expectation that his audience feels the same way. Stories like these, whether told to disciples (Mark's Jesus),[5] circulated on scrolls (Plato),[6] recited aloud to a group of listeners (Chaucer),[7] read in private (Beckett), or performed on stages and screens, have been around for a considerably long time. And for about as long, many of their producers have been desperately trying to stop us mining them for "messages."[8]

Thirteen Ways of Looking at a Fiction

What else are we supposed do with fictions? Rather a lot, it turns out. Scores of accounts have been offered over the centuries, so many in fact that it is exceedingly difficult to compress them into manageable form. For the sake of simplicity, I am going to divide them into three main branches, which I will call the *exemplary*, the *affective*, and the *cognitive*. Those perched on the exemplary branch—people like Sidney, Scaliger, Racine, and Rymer[9]—have generally invited us to consider characters as models for emulation or avoidance (Be like that nice Samaritan! Don't be like those wicked tenants!). Let us leave Sidney and company sitting there for now; we will return to them in chapter 1. There is, however, a more sophisticated sub-branch, whose inhabitants consider the object of emulation to be not an element of content (the actions of the Good Samaritan, say) but a component of form. Fictions, they suggest, can serve as *formal models*, providing templates for structures we may import into our own experience. They may, for instance, show us how to impose narrative structure onto the diverse incidents that make up our life;[10] they may hint at the precarious armed truce we might strike between irreconcilable factions within our soul;[11] in some circumstances, they may even enable the transfiguration of the visible world.[12]

The second main branch, the affective, focuses our attention on what fiction does to or for our emotions. According to a first set of affectivists, including Percy Shelley and in more recent years Wayne Booth, Martha Nussbaum, Richard Rorty, and Lynn Hunt, fiction strengthens our capacity for empathy and hence our propensity to do good.[13] (Chapter 1 explains why this is over-optimistic.) According to a second set, who take their cue from Schopenhauer and thus ultimately from Kant's *Critique of Judgment*, the point of fiction is to permit us to take up a desire-free attitude to the world.[14] Since the objects depicted are not real, and since we know they are not real, we cannot want to *possess* them in any way; aesthetic contemplation thus becomes a foretaste of a certain kind of utopia, the utopia of eternal will-lessness.[15] (On one reading, Aristotle's notion of "catharsis" can be seen as referring to a similarly salutary reduction of emotion.)[16] According to a third set, finally, fictions are there neither to strengthen our empathetic connections to the world nor to weaken our appetitive connections but rather to stir up all kinds of feelings in us, feelings of joy, pain, yearning, sorrow, everything with which a human existence should, on some accounts, be full. Either by emotional contagion (the writer genuinely experiencing something and thereby causing us to experience it too)[17] or by sheer creative technique (the writer finding a form of words or images virtually guaranteed to do their work),[18] great novels and plays and films unleash a flood of sentiment in us. And that flood of sentiment is beneficial because it endows us with a richer inner life: since some of us—especially the blasé urbanites, says Wordsworth, anticipating Simmel and others[19]—have lost the capacity to register the full force of events, we need a mechanism for reconnecting us to affect. As Franz Kafka so beautifully puts it, "a book must be the axe for the frozen sea within us."[20]

We are left with the stoutest branch, the one that has produced by far the most offshoots and received by far the most attention in recent decades. Everyone on this branch—the cognitive—believes that in some way or other fiction grants us access to knowledge, and that increased knowledge is indeed the very point of our engagement with it. Where cognitivists differ is over the kind of knowledge ostensibly granted. Thus at one extreme we find people willing to see a work like *Romeo and Juliet* as giving us knowledge of the world at large; with a touch more modesty, a second group views it as delivering knowledge of a cultural moment; more modestly still, a third group takes it to convey something about its producer; and at the other extreme, it is deemed to reflect only on *us*, its appreciators. By way of concluding this excursus on theories of fiction, let us look a little more closely at the four cognitive approaches, starting with the last and working back.

If it is true, as Wordsworth noted, that our emotions are not always fully present to us, and that we periodically need assistance just to feel what we already feel, it is also true that our deepest *beliefs* are not always fully present to us, and that we need assistance just to know what we already know. Direct introspection not always being the most reliable route to self-knowledge, a *detour* is frequently required, and fictions of a certain kind provide, according to some, the most fruitful detour imaginable.[21] They serve as simulation spaces (Currie)[22] in which we may experiment with a variety of strategies without the costly consequences of adopting them in real life; they function as battlegrounds (Bakhtin)[23] in which different ways of living, grounded in different belief systems, come into conflict, offering themselves for our selective appropriation; they raise questions to which they give no answers (Barthes)[24], thereby inviting us to fill the gaps with responses of our own, and since those responses often derive from our deepest commitments, they may—so long as we are paying attention—end up revealing us to ourselves.[25] Fictions thus become, to borrow I. A. Richards's delightful phrase, "machines to think with," machines that assist us in becoming who we are.[26] Or in Friedrich Schiller's more sophisticated formulation, fictions assist us both in becoming something and, where necessary, in *ceasing* to be it, in softening the borders of the forged personality to allow for a new burst of expansion.[27]

Fictions, then, can bring about self-knowledge. But they can also, on many accounts, bring about knowledge of *others*. (According to Proust, indeed, it is precisely by doing the latter that they are able to do the former.)[28] Thus the novels of Toni Morrison convey to us her various intuitions, intuitions that even she would perhaps not have fully understood without having brought them to expression (Croce[29]); or, more broadly, they convey to us her deepest essence, her "perspective," the special way in which she sees the world.[30] Like all subjective experience (the *"qualia"* of philosophers), this is something that cannot be transmitted directly, in straightforward declarative statements. It can, however, be intimated via *style*, thanks to the particular inflection a writer places on an otherwise common language, in the unique metaphorical connections she makes, in the shape of the narrations she produces, in the combination of devices she deploys.[31] Literary language, being more heavily crafted than everyday speech, carries more readily the indelible mark of its creator.[32]

Hegelians, of course, feel somewhat differently. For them, what is revealed is not an individual temperament but a collective attitude, a "Zeitgeist,"[33] manifest either in ideational content or in formal technique.[34] (The "lifeworld" idea, to which Heidegger appeals in his Artwork essay, may well be a related concept.)[35] Even the Hegelians stop short, however, of positing an increase of actual knowledge about the world, this being the purview of our last group of theorists. Among these, finally, some regard fiction as granting knowledge by *acquaintance* (we learn what it is like, for example, to be a young African American in pre–civil rights Michigan[36]); some regard it as yielding knowledge by *revelation* (while it does not itself transmit any truths, the text is here taken to chip away at the barriers standing between us and epiphanic disclosure, thus functioning as a making-ready for Grace[37]); some, to recall, regard it as delivering *propositional* knowledge; and some regard it as providing a kind of sensory clarification. Rather than letting us know what we know (Carroll) or letting us feel what we feel (Wordsworth), here fictions are said to let us *see what we see*. They "defamiliarize" objects (Shklovsky), presenting them in new and unusual lights, not so that we may learn about them but so that we may simply perceive them at all—simply see them, for the first time, as they actually are.[38]

By my count, that makes over a dozen non-message-based theories, not to mention the ones I am missing, of the function of fiction. While I find one or two of them unpersuasive (the revelation view has always struck me as fanciful, and for reasons I will spell out in chapter 1, the empathetic and exemplary views do not seem to hold up), most are entirely plausible and some extremely compelling. And while claims of universality tend to be overblown—it is surely not the case that *all* fictions aim at defamiliarization, for example, or that *all* fictions aim at expression—it is generally possible, nevertheless, to find a work or two that fits each theory remarkably well, indeed that *needs* the theory in order to be fully

Theories of Fiction

1. Exemplary
   1.1. Characters (Sidney)
   1.2. Forms
       1.2.1. The shape of a life
            1.2.1.1. Synchronic (Richards)
            1.2.1.2. Diachronic (Nehamas)
       1.2.2. The transfiguration of the world (Nietzsche)

2. Affective
   2.1. Increase
       2.1.1. Empathy (Shelley)
       2.1.2. Other emotions (Wordsworth, Kafka)
            2.1.2.1. By contagion (Horace)
            2.1.2.2. By technique (Eliot)
   2.2. Decrease
       2.2.1. Desire (Schopenhauer)
       2.2.2. Fear, pity, and similar passions ("Aristotle")

3. Cognitive
   3.1. Knowledge of the world
       3.1.1. Propositional knowledge
            3.1.1.1. Of particulars (Lukács, Sartre)
            3.1.1.2. Of laws (Roche)
       3.1.2. Sensory knowledge (Shklovsky, Sontag)
       3.1.3. Knowledge by acquaintance (Feagin)
       3.1.4. Knowledge by revelation (Heidegger, Ricoeur)
   3.2. Knowledge of a Zeitgeist
       3.2.1. Via content (Hegel)
       3.2.2. Via form (Adorno)
   3.3. Knowledge of an individual
       3.3.1. Specific mental contents (Croce)
       3.3.2. Overarching perspective (Proust)
   3.4. Knowledge of oneself
       3.4.1. Closing (Iser, Carroll)
       3.4.2. Opening (Schiller)

4. Formative

appreciated. *Hamlet* is a notorious emotion-elicitor, *Madame Bovary* an in-triguing emotion-modulator,[39] *In Search of Lost Time* a monumental formal model for self-fashioning, *Song of Solomon* a powerful "machine to think with"; there is no shortage of fictions to prove almost every theory right.

We are left, in sum, with a good number of powerful and robust accounts of what happens to us when we read or listen or watch. But in many circles we just do not hear about them when novels and movies and plays are being discussed. We hear, instead, about propositional content. We hear that novels are mirrors, their function being to show us how the world is.[40] Or we hear that novels are oracles, their function being to deliver laws of experience, deep abiding truths about the world, "messages" about who we are and how we function and what we ought to do.[41] (Even the "deconstructive" school of criticism essentially belongs here, since its practitioners could not imagine literary artworks seeking to do anything other than send messages; *Jane Eyre* and *Effi Briest* become failed ef-forts at meaning, or better yet, "mean their own meaninglessness.") Either way, we hear that fictions can save themselves from utter futility only by being di-rectly educational, and that since education is their true task, they had better get on with it. That mind-set is surely what explains a best-selling writer's otherwise unaccountable complaint that with some novels "you have to read seven hun-dred pages to get the handful of insights that were the reason the book was written."[42] A seven-hundred-page novel written for the purpose of "insights"? With statements like these, is it any wonder my student feels the way she does about Toni Morrison?

Formative Fictions

It is time, I submit, to reclaim fiction from the meaning-mongers. The method by which fictions are currently being taught in high schools ("Spot the villain!") and evaluated in the public domain ("Find the message!")[43] has had a genuinely detrimental effect, not just on fiction but also, if I may say, on lives. The relent-less consolidation of a dichotomy consigning fiction to either blunt didacticism or utter insignificance has been bad, first, for critics, many of whom have clearly been tempted—against their better judgment, in some cases—to make room in their theories for the message idea[44] or, going in the other direction, to celebrate the glorious uselessness of fiction, its ostensible inability to yield anything beyond pleasure.[45] It has been bad, second, for writers, some of whom have ad-justed their work to the demand or at least felt the burden of its pressure.[46] It is bad, third, for their writings, which will gradually find less and less of an audi-ence: if you want to get people to read a novel or watch a play, assuring them that it is morally improving is not much of a winning strategy.[47] And it is bad, fourth, for (potential) readers, who are deprived of the *real* reward on offer from sustained engagement with substantial works of fiction. (They may, indeed, be positively *harmed* as a result of reading for the "message."[48]) Telling readers to mine fictions for instruction is a surefire way to put their actual benefits out of reach.[49]

All of us could do with returning to the wisdom of Wordsworth, Schopenhauer, and company, lovers of art who eschewed semantics in favor of pragmatics.[50] We could do, in other words, with ceasing to talk about what a text "says"—if indeed there is such a thing—and beginning to talk again about what it *does*. J. L. Austin is right: there are plenty of "things we can do with words" other than just transmitting propositional content.[51] (A fortiori, one wants to add, when those words happen to be the constituents of a literary artwork; hence my title, which refers at once to the kinds of attention we may bring to formative texts and to the kinds of impact they may have, in return, upon us.) It is true of course that fictions tend to be "about" something, and this "aboutness," as we will see in a moment, is an important part of their functioning. Still, aboutness is only one of their features, and (with exception made for hybrids like Proust's *Recherche*)[52] arguably not the most important. Fictions also give *form* to this aboutness; they instigate a *process* (an artwork, as John Dewey and others have noted, is not an object but an experience); and they have an *effect* that goes far beyond the mere delivery of information.[53] In Hans-Georg Gadamer's words, an artwork is not something at which we stare "in hope of seeing through it to an intended conceptual meaning" but is, instead, "an *event*."[54]

We should reinstate the pragmatic, then, and be careful while so doing to avoid falling into a second dichotomy, almost as crippling as the first: the moralizing dichotomy, according to which fictions are either morally improving or useless (and therefore, in the minds of some, positively depraving). That will be the subject of my first chapter, in which I offer reasons for seeing the three strands of moralizing discourse about fiction—the message theory, the empathy theory, the practice-space theory—as varying degrees of wishful thinking. The practice-space theory is the most compelling, and it may well be possible to use complex, detailed, and richly ambiguous works of fiction as venues for fine-tuning our skills of navigation through the labyrinth of moral life, but *pace* Martha Nussbaum, this process is far from automatic; it depends, rather, on a deep prior commitment to specific moral principles, as well as to the notion that the aim of fiction-reading is to strengthen them. Not only does moral improvement through fiction take place far less often than is widely suggested, but it is, in addition, not always to be desired. (Though regimes of reading can create conditions in which citizens look to fiction for moral guidance, the cost, as I will explain, far outweighs the reward.) Bakhtin-style clarification of what we already believe, a process that is morally neutral, is a more common and ultimately more beneficial result.

The way forward, as I see it, is to reinvigorate the pragmatic outlook in its broadly ethical, rather than narrowly moral, dimension.[55] And that is precisely what I aim to do in this book, by highlighting a way of thinking about (some) fiction that is not exemplary, not affective, and not, properly speaking, cognitive either. There is, I will claim, a set of texts that we might label "formative fictions," texts whose function it is to fine-tune our mental capacities.[56] Rather than providing knowledge per se—whether propositional knowledge, sensory knowledge, knowledge by acquaintance, or knowledge by revelation—what they give us is *know-how*; rather than transmitting beliefs, what they equip us with are *skills*; rather than teaching, what they do is *train*. They are not informative, that is, but formative. They present themselves as spiritual exercises (whether sacred or profane), spaces for prolonged and active encounters that serve, over time, to hone our abilities and thus, in the end, to help us become who we are.[57]

Take, for example, the parables in Mark, the subject of my second chapter. Why does Jesus tell so many of them? Is it, as is often said, in order to be more readily understood? In the book of Mark at least, nothing could be further from the truth. Here, Jesus speaks in parables precisely to *prevent* easy access to insight, even—shockingly—where such access might be the very key to salvation. "To you has been given the secret of the kingdom of God," he declares, "but for those outside everything is in parables; so that they may indeed see but not perceive, and may indeed hear but not understand; lest they should turn again, and be forgiven" (4:11–12). At the same time as keeping the outsider out, however, the parables are designed to bring the insider even further in ("to him who has will more be given" [4:25]). Engagement with parables, that is, offers the elect an *increase* in their talent, a higher level of "faith," where faith is closely related to abstract thought. For parabolic discourse presents the world around us as nothing more than a storehouse of metaphors: nothing we see is inherently significant, it implies, since the entire visible realm is merely a symbol for a higher plane of experience. At the end of the day, the parables' aim is not the straightforwardly didactic ambition of communicating a complex message in simple language; it is instead the formative desire to bring a restricted audience to a new way of hearing and speaking, and thus a new way of looking at the world.

Some eighteen hundred years later, sophisticated fictions are still being produced for the purposes of enchantment; the enchantment, however, is no longer always sacred in nature. In chapter 3 I present the joint case of stage magician Jean-Eugène Robert-Houdin and Symbolist poet Stéphane Mallarmé,[58] both of whom seek to re-enchant the world on strictly rational terms, both of whom see certain types of self-deception as indispensable to that end, and both of whom (crucially) understand that in order to maintain our necessary illusions—in order to preserve them, though we recognize them for what they are—we need to be skilled at adopting a rather peculiar state of mind. It is precisely that state of mind, a state of quasi-simultaneous conviction and distrust, that Robert-Houdin's tricks and Mallarmé's poems, with their paradigmatically proto-modernist reflexivity, require for their appreciation. To become skilled at handling modernist fictions (whether upscale or popular) is therefore, I argue, to strengthen our ability to re-enchant the world.

Having addressed two types of enchantment, one worldly and one otherworldly, I turn in my final section to two modes of reasoning. Chapter 4 examines the curious case of *Symposium* and *Gorgias*, Platonic dialogues whose protagonist offers arguments that are by turns dazzling and pitiful. Why does the character Socrates fall, at times, into the most elementary fallacies? It is, I propose, because the end goal for Plato is not the mere acquisition of superior understanding but instead a well-lived *life*, where living well is taken to involve being in harmony with oneself. For such an end, accurate opinions are necessary but not sufficient: what one crucially needs is a *method*, a procedure for ridding oneself of those opinions that are false. Now learning a method is a very different business from learning a set of ideas. It requires not just study but *practice*, and practice is precisely what Plato's dialogues, thanks to the layer of irony between author and protagonist, make possible. If we have a predisposition for detecting and are interested in resolving conflicts within a set of beliefs—if, that is, we instinctively posit logical consistency as a desideratum in life—then we stand to learn, when we read the dialogues, not only *what* to think, but also, and far more importantly, *how* to think.

Is it also possible (and desirable) to learn how *not* to think? For the ancient skeptics, early rivals of the Platonists, the answer was very much in the affirmative. As the skeptics saw it, the most pressing philosophical questions, none of which can ever be satisfactorily resolved, serve only to keep us awake at night. How, though, to escape their grasp? There is no forgetting them, since they lurk around the corner of every decision; nor will argument suffice, since argument is merely a continuation of philosophy. Once again, what we need is not a theory but a method, the method, in this case, of "antilogic," in which each claim is systematically juxtaposed against its opposite, together with evidence just compelling enough to allow the two of them to cancel each other out. In chapter 5 I read Beckett's trilogy—*Molloy, Malone Dies, The Unnamable*—as a latter-day work of ancient skepticism, a work that begins from the same premises (intractability), aims at the same telos (ataraxia), and employs the same devices (antilogoi) along the way. What the trilogy offers us, I claim, is not insight and not inspiration but the opportunity to detach ourselves from our desire for certainty and to achieve, for the first time, an enduring peace of mind.

The Temporality of the Reading Experience

Four (groups of) fictions, four opportunities for the fine-tuning of a capacity. In every case, it should be noted, the transaction has much less to do with content than it does with form (this is one of the reasons why only literary texts, and not just any type of writing, will do). Plato's dialogues would not function as training-grounds for reasoning were it not for the deliberate holes punched into the arguments; Beckett's novels would not function as training-grounds for ataraxia were it not for the relentless juxtaposition of claim and counterclaim; Mallarmé's sonnets would not function as training-grounds for lucid self-delusion were it not for the periodic self-reflexive gestures puncturing the mimetic illusion; the words of Jesus in Mark would not function as training-grounds for faith were it not for their heavy use of ostentatiously figurative language. For each capacity there is a specific formal device that corresponds to it, and accordingly a finite set of texts that serve as uniquely propitious training-grounds.

What is more, the transaction has less to do with content than it does with *process*. Message-based theories promise benefits that are the work of a moment (no wonder they have become so popular in our impatient age). The training of skills, however, always takes time. Formative fictions do their work gradually, sometimes indeed in imperceptible increments, and over a multitude of phases.[59] In the first, we simply begin reading or listening; we follow the plot; we reconstruct the scene; we decide whether we are engaged enough to continue. So far, so ordinary. When it comes to formative fictions, however, there is always a moment at which the stakes become apparent, a moment at which we realize that we are not just being told a story, a moment at which a crucial offer is put in front of us.[60] With Plato, for example, we read along for quite a while thinking that we are merely being given a view of life; it is only some way into the *Gorgias* (or perhaps while we are in the *Symposium*, or the *Parmenides*, or the *Protagoras*, or the *Phaedrus*—as with the parables, more than one story may be required) that the penny drops, that we notice just how poor some of the argumentation is, that we put this together with our picture of who Plato must have been to have been able and eager to write these dialogues,[61] and that we see what we stand to gain, at the cost of what effort. Each work, in other words, contains within itself a *manual for reading*, a set of implicit instructions on how it may best be used.[62]

Assuming that we accept the offer set before us by the manual, we are still only at the start of the second phase. Skills are burnished through repeated exercise, in a benevolent spiral: the more we are capable of, the more demanding our challenges can be, and the more demanding the challenges, the greater the impact on our abilities. Likewise, formative fictions invite us not to one but to several tests, tests of varying degrees of difficulty, our readiness to meet them steadily increasing as we go. Another way of putting this is to say that the second, potentially quite extended phase of reading places us within a special variant of the "hermeneutic circle."[63] We cannot understand a text as a whole without understanding its various parts, Friedrich Schleiermacher pointed out, but neither can we understand the parts without understanding the text as a whole. (What is the significance of the escaped criminal in chapter 1 of *Great*

Expectations? Scene-setting, character development, vital plot point? We will not be able to say for sure until we have finished the novel.) The result of this double bind is that we are forced, simply in order to take in each new element we encounter, to form a tentative hypothesis about the totality of the work. In turn, however, new elements cause us to revise our hypothesis, which in turn leads us to interpret new elements differently, which elements in turn generate new hypotheses, and so on, and so on.

In the *formative* circle, by contrast, we begin not with "pre-understanding" but with what one might call a "pre-capacity."[64] We must, that is, already be a little bit good at doing the thing in question: a little bit good at following trains of logic, a little bit good at handling figurative discourse, a little bit good at standing back from our attitudes, a little bit good at juxtaposing claim with counterclaim. It is this minimal aptitude that allows us to meet the text's first challenge—allows us, indeed, to *recognize* it as a challenge—and thus to begin fine-tuning our capacity. It is the fine-tuning, in turn, that allows us to do better with the next challenge, and so on through indefinite turns of the circle. To him who has will more be given, but only bit by bit.

Let me mention right away one important corollary. To derive the full benefit from Beckett's trilogy, we said, a reader must already begin with something to bring to the table, not just a shared set of concerns but also a certain degree of talent in the relevant domain. Now this means that the trilogy, like all formative fictions, is elitist. It is not elitist in any shallow sense; it does not discriminate on the basis of externals such as race, class, or gender;[65] but as we saw with the parables, it does distinguish between insiders and outsiders, and even as it rewards the former, it doggedly keeps the latter at the door. (Cultural egalitarians may take some comfort in the fact that each of us is excluded from *some* formative fictions, and none of us is excluded from all of them; there is, so to speak, a formative fiction for everyone.) Radically isolating, formative fictions always work on one soul at a time, even in such mass performances as the parabolic discourses of Mark's Jesus. Studiously meritocratic, they always exclude those who lack the relevant pre-capacity, those who cannot or will not decipher the manual for reading (reliably present, it is nonetheless deliberately discreet), and those who, having done so, are not willing to make the effort it calls for. Unlike certain theories of fiction, then, which consider its effects to be automatic, inevitable, "inescapable" (we will return to these theories and to that word in chapter 1), the approach shared by Plato, Mark, Mallarmé, and Beckett recognizes that some readers have what it takes to be benefited and others not; that there is always a choice to be made; that a text issues offers, not injunctions; and that it is less an obligation than a gift, one we are entirely free to leave unopened.[66] Formative fictions never force themselves upon us.[67] Without our active participation, they will not do their work.[68]

Nor, finally, does that active participation cease once we have closed the book. Formative fictions are texts that tend to be reread, texts indeed that reward rereading. (If fictions were nothing more than fancy delivery mechanisms for "messages," there would be little need to read them so much as once, and absolutely no reason to read them twice; one advantage of the formative theory is that it makes rereading more than a quirk of the eccentric.)[69] In some cases, too, the conversations we have with others about the text in question—reasoned argument with fellow Platonists, exchange of metaphors with fellow Christians, and so on—may provide further opportunities for the fine-tuning of our skills.[70] And then, at last, there are the delayed-release effects that slowly stretch out, like long tendrils, into the future of our life. The immediate impact of formative fictions is always subtle; their overall impact, if we take them up on their offer, is as diffuse as it is profound. Formative fictions begin from the assumption that there are, in life, no quick fixes.

In Spite of Everything, a Role for Meaning

In what I have said thus far, I have found it necessary to draw a sharp line between message-hunting, which has become the dominant approach in the wider cultural world, and the more agile way in which we need to approach formative fictions if we are to be benefited by them. The distinction is vital to formative fictions, which often include—as part of their "manual for use"—a warning that skills, unlike information, cannot be transmitted directly. (In the *Symposium*, for example, Socrates reminds Agathon that wisdom does not flow from one mind to another via osmosis.)[71] Still, it may be worth stating for the record that I am not taking up a position against *any* search for knowledge or *every* ascription of meaning.[72] Let us by all means worry over what a work of philosophy or a physics paper or a constitutional document is saying. And let us by all means strive to keep ourselves informed; knowledge, as Jefferson so rightly said, is essential to the functioning of a healthy democracy.[73] My point is simply that if truths are what one is after, fictions are the wrong place to start. Citizens who have been trained to seek messages in fiction, and conditioned to trust what they "learn" there, will pick up a lot of misleading, conflicting, and unsubstantiated theories, while in the meantime they are prevented from gaining access to what is actually on offer. (Similarly, by the way, citizens who have been trained to seek moral improvement in fiction may find themselves morally corrupted. Those of us who take morality seriously would do well to protect it against such dangerous habits of reading.)[74]

By way of a second qualification, I should note that some fictions fall under the category of literary-philosophical *hybrids*, combining strictly literary elements with a set of claims that are actually argued for, as opposed to just being baldly stated by a narrator or character or implied as the supposed inference from an imaginary sequence of events. Many of Plato's dialogues, in fact, work just this way: while some of the arguments are deliberately slipshod, with a view to prompting a rescue mission on our part, others are presented entirely seriously, with a view to us feeling their force. In such cases, what we should note is that teaching and training cannot *coincide*, cannot take place within the same series of words. When Socrates says Pericles was a bad politician, for example, we do not learn that Pericles was (or that the historical Socrates believed he was) a bad politician; nor, by taking authorial irony into account, do we learn the opposite, that Pericles was a *good* politician; we certainly do not learn that being a good politician in general comes down to improving the moral standing of one's fellow citizens. We learn, strictly speaking, nothing. We have other things to do besides learning.

My final and most important qualification is that attention to the semantic dimension—the text's "aboutness," even if not its "meaning"—is always indispensable. In cases, first of all, where the built-in instruction manual takes the form of assertions, our understanding of the assertions in question is obviously vital to the experience. (One thinks, here, of Plato and Beckett, as will become clear in their respective chapters.) With Plato, what is more, there is an additional reason to pay close attention to the semantic dimension: we stand to hone our skills of argumentation only if we make the effort to fill the holes and mend the faulty arguments, but we will not do that, most likely, unless we find the issues worthwhile.[75] There must, in other words, be a careful titration of irony, a studious balance between the closed and the open; formative fictions should leave *some* work for the reader to do, but not *all* the work, and they should offer rewards for progress made along the way.[76]

With Beckett, similarly, the questions being asked must be properly seductive, must have the proper feel of philosophical glue-traps, in order for the ancient-skeptical therapy to have a chance of taking place. With Mallarmé, where the training consists in the parallel processing of multiple referential dimensions, a base level of mimesis (here is a room, here are some tables, here is a window . . .) becomes more or less a necessity.[77] And with Mark, where what is at stake is a refinement of our ability to move from literal to figurative and back again, there has to be a literal level to start from, even if, as in most cases, that literal level is of minor interest. (The "meaning" of the Sower parable, for example, is that some people are not cut out to understand; hardly a revolutionary idea.) Here one almost wants to say, with T. S. Eliot, that the lure of "meaning" is a kind of ruse perpetrated on the reader, a way "to keep his mind diverted and quiet, while the poem does its work upon him: much as the imaginary burglar is always provided with a bit of nice meat for the house-dog."[78]

Whether for the sake of rectification (Plato), cancellation (Beckett), oscillation (Mallarmé), or allegorization (Mark), attention to the semantic dimension is thus always a requirement. It is, however, never the *point*. Far from being the aim of the entire exercise, ascertainment of a formative text's aboutness is only ever instrumental, only ever a stepping-stone on the way to a higher telos. And that means that it is possible to achieve entirely plausible readings of Marcan parables and Platonic dialogues *while having failed to use them correctly*; it is possible even to spend great lengths of time with them while seeing straight past the benefits they uniquely stand to confer; it is possible, in other words, to get it wrong by getting it right.

A Polite Word to Historians

Historians will no doubt have noticed, perhaps with some alarm, that the chapters in this book are not arranged chronologically. The choice is a deliberate one. I am attempting here to make a contribution to literary theory, not to literary history; the questions I am asking are questions to which history is only intermittently pertinent, often beside the point, and sometimes positively misleading. It is certainly relevant that reading practices and institutions of reading (or listening) have changed over the millennia, and—crucially, for my purposes—that we have the power to reshape them today. It is also relevant that the ancient Greeks made an intuitive distinction between fiction and nonfiction, that Plato founded an Academy, and that he was in direct competition with the Sophists. So too, it helps to know that the book of Mark was transmitted orally before being written down, that it was at one point the rival not only of Matthew, Luke, and John but also of the synthetic "Diatessaron," and that the Jewish homiletic tradition habitually employed sowing as a metaphor for preaching. And some light is shed, finally, by an awareness that many of Chaucer's contemporaries expected fictions to serve the needs of religious instruction, or that Mallarmé was writing against a background of widespread disenchantment among artists and thinkers.

When it comes to Beckett, however, my strong suspicion is that history is simply in the way, a dangerous distraction, a red herring at the very best. Beckett scholarship is in fact littered with critics, starting with Theodor Adorno, who wish to cast his most famous works as reactions to World War II.[79] Such readings are not just brutally reductive but also tangibly mistaken: by 1938 Beckett had already published *Murphy*, a novel whose protagonist sees himself as being trapped in a skull (107), is fascinated by permutations (96–100), cites Democritus and Geulincx (246, 178), engages playfully with Descartes (109), yearns for "will-lessness" (113), and strives for nothingness via mutual cancellation of contraries (246). The narrators of *Malone Dies* and the *Unnamable* list Murphy as one of their predecessors,[80] and they are right to do so: Beckett's manner may evolve,[81] but his core preoccupations remain untouched. Indeed his core preoccupations have remained untouched, so to speak, since the third century AD.[82] Beckett's questions are old ones ("Ah les vieilles questions, les vieilles réponses, il n'y a que ça!"[83]), and in response he offers us the same skills we have always required. All that has changed is the institutional situation—there are, today, no skeptical "schools"—and accordingly the mode of delivery.

The same is true for formative fictions at large. To be sure, they come into existence at a given moment, perhaps at a moment when the need is particularly pressing (where that is the case, history will enter our discussion). But when the urgency dissipates, the need has a way of enduring. Plato's Academy has long ceased functioning, yet skills of constructing and testing arguments continue to be of value. A century and more since Mallarmé, many of us still crave a means of re-enchanting the world. And the Christian way of having faith—need it be said?—maintains a powerful hold over the imagination of two billion believers, many of whom enjoy a less-than-detailed grasp of the historical context in which it arose.[84] This book is not a story but a typology. It does not seek to chart a progression from Plato to Mark, from Mark to Chaucer, from Chaucer to Mallarmé, and from Mallarmé to Beckett; it seeks, instead, to lay out a series of strategies for flourishing, all of which emerged at a specific juncture and for specific reasons but all of which, more importantly, remain live options today.

The Value of Formative Fictions

What I have laid out here is, then, a proposal for a theory of fiction; it is worth repeating, however, that it is not a proposal for a *universal* theory of fiction.[85] Just like the approaches I listed at the start of this introduction—cognitive clarification, emotional clarification, formal modeling, and the like—it applies only to *some* stories and plays and films, and even those stories and plays and films vary among themselves in fine-tuning disparate capacities via disparate formal devices. I take this restriction to be a strength, rather than a weakness, of the view. For one thing, it gives it a better chance of actually being right. (May not the best literary theories, in the end, be the ones of medium scope, embracing a plurality but not the totality of texts?) For another, it lends a certain deserved distinction to the films and plays and stories in question.[86] Not every work of fiction is a Parable of the Sower, a *Gorgias*, or a *Molloy*.

That said, there are plenty of additional formative fictions this volume does not have space to address in detail. (My principles of inclusion and exclusion: the main objects of study here are fictions that fall within my linguistic purview, that stand out as clear-cut cases of the formative mode, that serve different formative functions using different formal means, and to whose understanding, finally, I may hope to have something new to contribute.) Perhaps the clearest examples are the *Lehrstücke* of Bertolt Brecht, plays designed to be performed by amateurs, with the training taking place by way of participation rather than mere spectatorship; the infamous Brechtian *Verfremdungseffekt* (alienation effect) aimed to increase the players' ability to look critically in real life at what they saw around them, "so that nothing should appear immutable."[87] Relatedly, Jane Austen's *Pride and Prejudice* may well be inviting us, thanks to its liberal use of free indirect discourse, to practice stepping back from our sometimes over-hasty judgments.[88] (Free indirect discourse always situates us half inside a belief and half outside it.) And Gustave Flaubert's *Madame Bovary*, by contrast, could be seen as an affective variant of Beckett's trilogy, its shifting point of view fostering an aptitude for the juxtaposition, and thereby mutual cancellation, of our emotive investments.[89]

Then again, fictions set in relatively closed communities where appearances are at a premium (Lafayette, Austen, James, Woolf) often ask their readers to keep track of sources and to reconstruct nested beliefs (A thinks that B thinks that C is in love with her), thus granting them an opportunity to become cannier handlers of social information.[90] Kafka's stories, meanwhile, with their obvious call for allegorical interpretation, their teasing offer of clues, and their refusal to let any interpretive strategy fully pay off, seek to prepare us for a human condition that both demands and resists an attribution of significance.[91] Films like Fellini's *8½* and Charlie Kaufman's *Adaptation* follow Mallarmé in deploying reflexivity for formative purposes; Marcel Proust's convoluted sentences stretch the mind's capacity for keeping multiple hypotheses in play while imposing provisional order on a rich set of material; and Toni Morrison's *Song of Solomon*, that wonderful work from which we started, actually switches genre halfway through, encouraging an extremely important kind of mental agility.[92]

From Austen to Woolf and from Plato to Kaufman, the central literary device in every formative fiction corresponds not just to a specific readerly activity but to a particular top value (what Charles Taylor would call a "hypergood"). While Platonic irony is there for the sake of intellectual exercise, for example, intellectual exercise itself subserves a further end, namely the life of reason. In Mark, similarly, the telos of metaphor is a deeper faith, not merely a richer imagination; in Brecht the alienation effects are subtended by a vision of fruitful political engagement; and the same goes, mutatis mutandis, for the remaining practitioners we have discussed. To be sure, several of the capacities may be detached from their hypergoods and pressed into the service of a different, more comprehensive overall goal. Thus it is arguably a useful thing both to be able to see clearly and to be able to deceive ourselves when necessary (at *Gay Science* 110 and 344, among other places, Nietzsche suggests precisely that); and "dwelling in metaphor," as I explain in chapter 2, can bestow special satisfactions even on non-believers. No single recipe exists, however, for their combination, and no design will include them all. Plato's strategy for cultivating reason will simply not be relevant to the heirs of Beckett; Beckett's strategy for overcoming the self will leave Proustians (and Morrisonians) entirely cold; Brecht's political zeal will fall on deaf Flaubertian ears. In what follows, therefore, my task is to present a series of case studies, not to propose a formula for happiness. There are many authentic ways of being, and this book does not seek to privilege one over another. It issues only conditional imperatives: if you stand in need of skill X, it says, then book Y (or book Y's very close counterpart) is the one you should be spending time with.

At the same time, we could phrase the imperative more forcefully: if you stand in need of skill X, you really should be spending time with book Y. And the converse imperative—if you are reading book Y, you really should be reading it for X—is just as (conditionally) binding. Where the formative theory applies, in other words, it is the only viable account; there is, I submit, no other explanation that makes sense of the relevant text's various features, that truly captures how they work and what they are for, that makes them fully available to us. They *can* be read differently, and indeed often *are* read differently, but such (mis)reading comes, as I see it, at a serious cost. The formative theory is the only one that affords a reason for these texts being the way they are, an explanation for why writers with philosophical (or religious) fish to fry have sometimes chosen to place them in literary frying pans. It is also the only one, I like to think, that provides a satisfactory rationale—beyond mere pleasure, and outside of moral improvement—for our continued attachment to them, for the fact that we find it so worthwhile to spend considerable amounts of time in their company. In a way, then, what I am offering here is a defense of the literary, partial perhaps but no less spirited for that. If all we needed were "messages," the delivery mechanisms would be dispensable; my brilliant but impatient student would be absolutely right. If what we need is training, however, then process is essential, and if a particular kind of process is essential, then form is essential. For certain purposes, the right formative fiction is exactly what we need.

Early in this introduction, we saw that fictions offer a variety of benefits to their eager consumers. Training is only one such benefit, and it takes place in only a relative handful of texts. Works that clarify are more prevalent than works that train; and works that do nothing very much, whether through lack of ambition or lack of skill, are more prevalent than either. Still, that rare gift may well be of the greatest value. Aristotle is surely right that living well is a matter of acting well, and that acting well requires much more than having the correct beliefs, including—I would add—the correct beliefs about ourselves.[93] What we need is "virtue of character," and virtue of character comes from habit, not from insight. (Indeed insight will only be possible in the first place if the ground has been prepared by habits.)[94] In other words, meeting the demands of life requires *above all* a range of semi-automatic responses that we have cultivated by means of repetition. Even, then, if they are few and far between, and even if their readers do not always take advantage of them, formative fictions may nonetheless be the most important fictions there are.

PART ONE

CLEARING THE GROUND

1

Chaucer

Ambiguity and Ethics

Prudence or Oneiromancy?

Men shal nat maken ernest of game.
—The Miller, in *"The Miller's Tale"*

Imagine you are a professor teaching Chaucer's *Canterbury Tales* to a group of undergraduate students, and that today's class is on "The Nun's Priest's Tale." You summarize the plot for them, to remind those who have bothered to do the reading what the gist of it was, and to give the rest a graceful opportunity to escape with their dignity intact. There is a rooster, you say, named Chauntecleer, who dreams he is carried off by a fox. When he wakes up, he tells his wife, Dame Pertelote, that he is in grave danger, since dreams are—as is well known—portents of things to come. She, however, will have none of it: far from predicting the future, she retorts, dreams merely testify to the digestive system of their maker, so that what Chauntecleer needs to take is not preventative action against predators but only (she does not mince words) "som laxatyf."[1]

Pertelote fails to persuade her husband, but a vigorous bout of lovemaking drives the dream clear from his mind, and he wanders out into the yard, where, sure enough, he finds a suitably hungry fox lying in wait for him. Being as wily as any self-respecting fox should be, Daun Russell asks Chauntecleer to sing for him with that beautiful voice of his, and to close his eyes in order to concentrate better; being as susceptible to flattery as one might expect from a puffed-up rooster, Chauntecleer readily acquiesces, allowing the fox to snatch him up in his mouth and start bringing him home for dinner. Chauntecleer is saved, you remind the students, only by his own native wit: turning the fox's trick against him, he convinces Daun Russell to crow (no pun intended) triumphantly—at which point, the fox's mouth being open, Chauntecleer makes his escape.

Now imagine that you go on, feeling generous with your wisdom, to point the moral of the story—so generous, indeed, that you offer two separate morals, in two distinct speeches. "Chaucer's story is highly instructive," Speech A begins. "It warns us against being like that silly rooster who closes his eyes and begins to sing, seduced by the fox's flattery, indifferent to the danger of his situation. We learn from the story to be more prudent in our own lives. Chaucer is writing not just for fun but to help his audience become better and happier people." Speech B starts and ends similarly, but runs somewhat differently in between: "Chaucer's story is highly instructive. It warns us against being like that silly rooster who ignores the prophetic significance of his dream, and thus rushes headlong into the yard where the fox is waiting for him. We learn from the story to accept oneiromancy in our own lives. Chaucer is writing not just for fun but to help his audience become better and happier people."

My suspicion is that you could quite easily convince your students of proposition A (the prudence moral), but that you would have a much harder time convincing them of proposition B (the prophecy moral). They furiously scribble notes at first, then surreptitiously start to put their pens down. Why? What is the difference between the two claims? Is it that the story adequately proves we should be more circumspect, but somehow does not adduce enough evidence to show that we should be more credulous? Surely not. If anything, it is the other way around: the one and only piece of "support" for the prudence moral is a ludicrously fictional scenario in which a talking fox captures a talking rooster by convincing him to sing with his eyes closed (can this story really "prove" anything other than the claim that if you happen to be a talking rooster, you should beware of talking foxes, talking foxes tending to be particularly seductive?), whereas the argument for dream interpretation, which draws its strength from ancient tradition, is so extensive that it occupies more than a quarter of the tale. In the course of a scene occupying 173 lines out of the story's 626, Chauntecleer cites no fewer than eight authoritative stories, at least some of which—those that come from the Bible—Chaucer's listeners, and indeed many of your students, could reasonably be expected to take seriously. Here are three of those exempla, concerning Daniel, Joseph, and Andromache, respectively:

> And forthermore, I pray yow loketh wel
> In the Olde Testament, of Daniel,
> If he held dremes any vanitee.
> Reed eek [also] of Ioseph, and ther shul ye see
> Wher dremes ben somtyme (I sey nat alle)
> Warninge of thinges that shul after falle.
> . . . .
> Lo heer Andromacha, Ectores wyf,
> That day that Ector sholde lese his lyf,

She dremed on the same night biforn,
How that the lyf of Ector sholde be lorn [lost]
If thilke day he wente into bataille;
She warned him, but it might nat availle;
He wente for to fighte nathelees,
But he was slayn anoon [immediately] of Achilles.
(361–82)

It might, of course, be argued that it is quality, rather than quantity, that counts. Chauntecleer could produce eighteen or eighty or eight hundred classical sources without advancing the cause of the prophecy moral an iota; one simple fable of a fox, by contrast, suffices to show how important it is to be cautious. The dream narratives prove nothing, however copious their number, because they are all invented. Whereas the farmyard narrative . . . But is the farmyard narrative not every bit as invented as the Homeric account of Hector's last night on earth? Why do we ascribe to it any greater corroborative power?

Perhaps we should talk in terms of the *vraisemblable* rather than the *vrai*. Perhaps, that is, we are swayed by the fable because it, or at least its translation into the human realm, seems plausible to us—people behave this way in everyday life, even if roosters do not—whereas the dream narratives, having no basis in real-world events, leave us utterly cold. Yet there is a serious problem with the antithesis thus phrased, and that is that *we have already assumed the very thing we set out to prove*. We say that the story fails to convince us that dreams are prophetic because it offers, as its only evidence, a series of tales that do not seem likely; but the reason such stories do not seem likely is that dreams are not prophetic. In circular fashion, "The Nun's Priest's Tale" convinces us only of what we already believed before we began to read it. Which means, strictly speaking, that it convinces us of nothing at all.[2]

A Parody of Didacticism

The [*Nun's Priest's*] *Tale* could only have been written for a medieval audience which looked at life seriously. . . . If we turn to the poetry, we can see that it is of a kind which could only proceed from a fine moral concern.
                      —David Holbrook, *"The Nonne Preestes Tale"*

The bell rings (or rather, since such bells only ring in movies, the end of class is announced by a tumultuous relocation of papers from desk to backpack), and you move on to your graduate seminar, where you explain what just happened. You have, you admit, failed to convert any of your students to oneiromancy.

They have learned three things at most: (1) that *you* believe dreams to be prophetic; (2) that *you* believe you can use a tale by Chaucer as evidence (just as, within the tale, Chauntecleer thinks he can draw on stories from Homer); and (3) that Chaucer may possibly have thought so too. They have *not* learned (4) that they have any reason to accept the view themselves.[3] You have, in other words, only succeeded in convincing your students of your own insanity. They have responded to your second harangue the way a non-believer would respond to the claim that Genesis, with its injunction from God to be fruitful and multiply, constitutes a cast-iron argument against birth control: few people wish to rule their lives on the basis of a work they take to be made up.

You do, of course, have a number of rather lupine graduate students in the seminar, and one of the very shrewdest (let us call him Daun Bertrand Russell) raises an ingenious objection. "The prudence moral," he argues, "is borne out by the story, whereas the prognostication moral is not. It just so *happened*, on this occasion, that a dream matched up to reality; rash behavior, on the other hand, *necessarily* proved costly, such being the way of the world. Chaucer probably meant moral A, but was surely too sensible to stand behind moral B." Has Bertrand bested you? Not necessarily. You do not even have to play devil's advocate and pretend, on behalf of the oneiromancers' union, that dreams match up to reality more often than not. You merely have to remind Bertrand that rashness is not always a bad thing. Sometimes, to be sure, it is good to look before one leaps; but he who hesitates is also, at other times, lost.[4] As Picasso put it, surprisingly aptly for your purposes, "to draw, you must close your eyes and sing."

Bertrand now falling silent, Dame Erica Auerbach, a graduate student who knows her literary history, directs us to the story's postscript:

> But ye that holden this tale a folye,
> As of a fox, or of a cok and hen,
> Taketh the moralitee, goode men.
> For Seint Paul seith that al that writen is,
> To our doctryne it is y-write, y-wis.
> (672–76)

"As a good medieval Christian," opines Erica, "Chaucer could not possibly have told stories unless he thought they were in some way edifying."[5] You feel tempted to ask her for the moral of "The Miller's Tale," but content yourself with making two points. First, Saint Paul is, as Chaucer and his readers know perfectly well, referring to holy scripture, not to writing in general.[6] And this is only reasonable, since if "*al* that writen is," from litanies to laundry lists, yielded equally valuable lessons, the value in question would be pitifully small. Second, when the Nun's Priest exhorts us to take the "moralitee," we are placed in something of a quandary: *which one* does he mean? Is he referring to the prognostication moral? The prudence moral? The downbeat moral that "ever the latter ende of joye is wo" (439)? The upbeat moral that, thanks to God's justice, "mordre wol out" (286)? The fatalist moral that "destinee . . . ma[y] nat been eschewed" (572)? Or, finally, the charming moral that the advice of women should not be heeded (490–93), since "*mulier est hominis confusio*" (398)?[7]

All of these morals can surely not be true at once. The confident claim of divine justice stands in tension with the more pagan, pessimistic wheel-of-fortune discourse;[8] more importantly, neither of the two quite squares with the instigation to forethought. We cannot possibly take the Nun's Priest seriously, and indeed he himself is perhaps not speaking seriously, when he blames not only Chauntecleer (for his lack of prudence) but also Pertelote (for her failure to believe in dreams) and even destiny (for its relentlessness)—

> O destinee, that mayst nat been eschewed!
> Allas, that Chauntecleer fleigh [flew] fro the bemes!
> Allas, his wyf ne roghte nat of [paid no heed to] dremes!
> (572–74)

—as though any room for belief and prudence could be left over once destiny has extracted its due.

Dame Erica is right about one thing: medieval audiences expected the stories they heard to have easily detachable, easily assimilable morals. And the Nun's Priest duly obliges his (and by extension Chaucer's) audience. He just obliges a little too much. Like the hawker of panaceas, he oversells his product, claiming for it every virtue imaginable—with the result that we trust it less than if he had only promised to cure a single ill. "The Nun's Priest's Tale" is, in fact, a *parody* of didacticism, a story that reminds us how extraordinarily easy it is to draw edifying lessons from any narrative. As long as our listeners already subscribe to a particular piety, they will happily consider a story to illustrate it, indeed consider it to emerge automatically from the story, as the only possible inference; they will, under certain circumstances, go so far as to consider the story all the evidence it needs.

Preaching to the Converted

> This was a murie tale of Chauntecleer.
> But by my trouthe, if thou were seculer [layman],
> Thou woldest ben a trede-foul [rooster] aright.
> For if thou has corage as thou hast myght,

Thee were nede of hennes, as I wene [think],
Ya, moo than seven tymes seventene.
                    —Harry Bailly, in *"The Nun's Priest's Tale"*

Fictions, you are forced to conclude, preach to the converted alone. Since they offer no substantiation for their implicit claims,[9] they are powerless (by themselves) to shake our deeply held convictions. It is always open to us to dismiss them as fantastical.[10] The fact that an author is capable of portraying roosters as able to talk, for instance, does not even mean that *one* rooster is able to talk, let alone that the *typical* rooster is able to talk; while a real-life example is at least proof of possibility (if not prevalence), a fictional example is proof of absolutely nothing.[11] If we happen to have already seen talking roosters, we will accept the accuracy of the depiction; if we have not, we will reject it, and (if we choose) everything that follows from it. In neither case will our minds have been changed.[12]

The Nun's Priest must know this, for otherwise he would not pretend that his story is a true one, and worthy *on those very grounds* (as the punctuation indicates) of careful moral attention:

> Now every wys man, lat him herkne me:
> This storie is also [as] trewe, I undertake,
> As is the book of Lancelot de Lake,
> That wommen holde in ful gret reverence.
> (444–47)

Someone is, of course, joking here—since we are aware of the Nun's Priest's feelings with regard to women,[13] we can infer what kind of reverence *he* has, or at least should have, toward "the book of Lancelot de Lake"; either he is trying to trick his employer, the Nun, into taking the fable as fact and, equally foolishly, into "tak[ing] the moralitee," or Chaucer is mocking his inconsequence—but what is clear is that *everyone takes true stories to be more convincing than fictions.* The Nun's Priest knows it, and Chaucer must know it too, however medieval he may be. Far from depicting cases of conversion-by-exemplum, Chaucer has a way of presenting us with characters who do *not* learn from stories, characters like Chauntecleer himself. After reciting his endless catalog of ancient anecdotes, designed to impress upon Pertelote the seriousness of his plight, what does Chauntecleer do? He saunters out into the yard and starts singing with his eyes closed.[14]

No one learns anything from "The Nun's Priest's Tale." Those who agree that we should be prudent already thought so before they read it; those who disagree are likely to be as little affected as is the Wife of Bath by her husband's harangues.[15] It is not even the case that we learn *this* from "The Nun's Priest's Tale"[16]—not even the case, that is, that we learn how ineffectual fictions are as a tool for conversion. "The

Nun's Priest's Tale" is a parody of didacticism, but true to its own implicit principles, it fails to teach so much as the impotence of literary instruction. Had it done so, there would surely not exist today the voluminous and intensely earnest bibliography of devout interpretations, reading it as an allegory of the Fall,[17] an allegory of the Church,[18] a positive exemplum (via the frugal widow who opens and closes the tale),[19] or a negative exemplum (via the rooster).[20] "The Nun's Priest's Tale" is a story that fails to prove even its own futility—and which, in so doing, vindicates itself.

The Asymmetry of "Imaginative Resistance"

> CHARLES: You can't expect much sympathy from me, you know.
> I am perfectly aware that your highest hope was to murder me.
> ELVIRA: Don't put it like that, it sounds so beastly.
> —Noël Coward, *Blithe Spirit*

Human nature is a strange thing. We know how blissfully immune we are to the influence of artworks whose underlying worldview departs from our own (am I really likely to become a con-man after watching *The Sting*? an advocate of whaling after reading *Moby-Dick*?), and yet we carry on recommending films and novels and plays and poems to friends we consider in dire need of inner change. "Read this," we say, "it will make you see things differently" (by which of course we mean "it will make you see things my way"). Perhaps we give a copy of *Candide* to one who is laboring under the delusion that God works in the world. Perhaps she returns the favor by forcing us to read some C. S. Lewis. The two of us end up, like the positivist and the priest in *Madame Bovary*, as firmly entrenched in our positions as we ever were before. We should all just come out and admit it: "morally improving" is merely a compliment we pay to works whose values agree with ours.

Such a view is not likely to be widely shared in the age of the "ethical turn." Quite the contrary, substantial quantities of time and journal space have recently been dedicated to assessing the precise ways in which literature contributes to a better society. Some (like Richard Rorty) have argued that literary texts foster empathy with an ever-widening circle of human types, gradually bringing more and more of "them" under the designation "us."[21] Others (like Gregory Currie) have suggested that literary texts serve as spaces for "simulation," in which we imaginatively apprehend the probable consequences of certain decisions, indeed of certain overall value systems, and as a result learn what it is that we want to do—which, by a magic that betrays a degree of residual Socratism, turns out to be what is objectively *good* to do.[22] Or, finally, the simulation is said to fine-tune our moral decision-making capacity, so that we are better equipped to notice and respond to subtle claims on our moral attention (this is Martha Nussbaum's position).[23]

In almost all cases, the salutary effect on readers is presented as automatic, inevitable, "inescapable" (to use a term as beloved of Wayne Booth as, in related contexts, of Charles Taylor)—as though novels were so many bricks with which to hit recalcitrant unbelievers over the head, in hopes of shaking their skepticism loose. Thus for Booth, "all of our aesthetic judgments are inescapably tied to ethics" (1998:378–79); when we read, we are "inescapably caught up in ethical activity" (1998:374).[24] And for Nussbaum, similarly, "the [novelistic] genre itself, on account of some general features of its structure, constructs empathy and compassion in ways highly relevant to citizenship" (1995:10).[25] In particular, works like Dickens's *Hard Times* positively oblige us, whether we like it or not, to become better people: "it is impossible to care about the characters and their fate in the way the text invites," according to Nussbaum, "without having some very definite political and moral interests awakened in oneself" (1999:278).

Good literature, in short, simply leaves us no choice but to be improved by it. Bad literature, on the other hand—and this is a striking asymmetry in many moralist positions—*has no effect on us whatsoever.*[26] We are all blessed with what has been dubbed "imaginative resistance": when presented with a fictional world in which, say, murder is good, we find ourselves unable (Hume) or at least unwilling (Gendler) to imagine it; by consequence, the work will fail to move me as it wishes, and thus come up short not only ideologically but also aesthetically (Walton).[27] As Tamar Gendler puts it, "I have a much easier time following an author's invitation to imagine that the earth is flat than I do following her invitation to imagine that murder is right."[28] Is this correct? First of all, we might object that to use such a beastly word (as Noël Coward might put it) is already to stack the deck, since "murder," unlike "killing," is a moral term. What if we called it, say, "taking care of"? What, in other words, if we consider the case of Mafia fiction, in which the very worst thing one can do is to report crimes to the police, and the very best thing one can do is, at times, to "take care of" an unarmed human being, someone whose only blemish is, perhaps, to have reported crimes to the police?

It is a fascinating fact about certain Mafia movies, and virtually all outlaw movies,[29] that they perform an imaginative "re-evaluation of values" *without us resisting in the slightest.* (Mummy movies, incidentally, have a related effect: when the ultra-rationalist—the one who insists loudly that there is no such thing as mummies—is the first to be strangled to death, we feel no sorrow, since obviously he should have known better. For the duration of the movie, we are people who would rather spend time with believers in the paranormal than with seekers of fact; we are people whose firm conviction it is that to base one's judgments on logic and empirical evidence is to merit extermination.)[30] And perhaps this attitude, which we could term "imaginative inertia," is the standard case.[31] Far from resisting the different, sometimes opposite, values of the fictional world, we positively delight in trying them on for an hour or two, like a carnival costume. Even works like *Hamlet*, which do not depart quite so radically from our everyday worldview, nonetheless require us to imagine not only that ghosts exist but also that it is proper to avenge murder with murder, indeed that it is a positive moral failing to leave a killer alive.

Figure 1.1. The skeptic, before. From *The Mummy*, directed by Terence Fisher (London: Hammer Film Productions, 1959).

Figure 1.2. The skeptic, after.

Those who follow Kendall Walton's lead in understanding mimetic fictions as games of make-believe are surely in the right; what they often overlook, how-ever, is the fact that players of such games take on *roles* in order to play them. (The four-year-old who pretends that her doll is a baby, for example, also pre-tends that she herself is a parent.) We do not enter the fictional world as tour-ists, anthropologists, passive spectators of the strange goings-on; instead we are granted temporary citizenship.[32] We share its values, operate within its rules, define heroism and villainy by the standards that apply there—not, or at least not exclusively, by those that hold in our home-world.[33]

At all events, any honest account of the aesthetic experience must be sym-metrical. If I am virtuous, then I will certainly resist the promptings of Sade to rape and torture; but if I am vicious, then I will just as strongly resist the urgings of Dickens to do unto others what I would have done to myself, or to be kind to escaped convicts, or to embrace (heaven forfend) the Christmas spirit. Perhaps I will resist Dickens *even if I am good* (which is to say, even if I share the values his texts appear to be endorsing). After all, there is something about sanctimonious fictions that makes one either burst out laughing—"one must have a heart of stone," Oscar Wilde famously remarked of *The Old Curiosity Shop*, "to read the death of Little Nell without laughing"—or respond with indignation.[34] In my more Dostoyevskian moments, I do not consider it impossible for previously well-meaning readers to become just a little bit immoral, out of spite.[35]

Conversely, while absorption in *Goodfellas* does not make me into a mafioso, since the persona I send into the fictional world is disconnected from my ordi-nary self, it must be added that absorption in *Clarissa* does not make me into a paragon of patience, and for analogous reasons.[36] Indeed, one of the most se-ductive pleasures such wholesome fictions offer us is the satisfaction of being, for an hour or two, supremely equitable, unbendingly thoughtful, unadulterat-edly righteous. "How good I was! How just I was! How satisfied I was with myself!" writes Diderot about the experience of reading *Clarissa*, and one won-ders if there might be a modicum of wry Diderotian irony in the third exclama-tion.[37] The version of ourselves that we send into Richardson's world is indeed unerringly noble, uncompromisingly idealistic. The pleasure we derive is that of being on the side of the angels, making (for once) categorical judgments, un-qualified by the nuances and objections required in day-to-day existence; like the pleasure of hissing the villain at the pantomime, it is a fantasy of clarity, a form of escapism for the morally obsessed. It may even be a profoundly narcis-sistic sentiment—the sentiment of utter uprightness—brilliantly disguised as altruism. We convince ourselves that we are doing the world a favor by reading *Clarissa*, while the only person for whom any favors are done is us. For when we put *Clarissa* back on the shelf, we return to being the very same earthbound, pragmatic, exception-making individual we were before.[38] (Perhaps we are even *less* likely to make a positive contribution to society, having purged ourselves of all benevolent emotions in our favorite armchair.)[39] If we cannot be harmed by fictions, then we cannot be improved. Fictions, to repeat, preach only to the converted.

Virtue Ethics and Gossip

> SOCRATES: And a just man does just things, I take it?
> GORGIAS: Yes.
>
> —Plato, *Gorgias*

It is, perhaps, for this reason that theorists of moral improvement tend inadvertently to argue against their own position. Thus when Richard Posner reports having enjoyed Dickens's *Hard Times* for entirely non-moral reasons— a feat utterly inconceivable, as we saw above, in the eyes of Martha Nussbaum— the latter responds, curiously enough, by summoning Dickens from beyond the grave to castigate the obdurate judge. "Well, Judge Posner," the resurrected Dickens scolds, "you are not a very valuable member of society" (1998:360). Deep down, Posner's resistance to ethical criticism is really "an assault on political egalitarianism"; deep down, "insisting on taking his stand with works that keep him at a distance from the demand of the poor and the weak" is just a way to evade "the claim of a painful reality" (1998:344, 361). Now leaving aside the question of whether someone who has devoured all those improving novels by Dickens and James could be expected to rise above such ad hominem attacks,[40] Nussbaum's rejoinder stands at least as an acknowledgment that Posner *has not been affected by his reading*. And if Dickens does not succeed in converting those who, like Posner, ostensibly *require* moral improvement, what good does he actually do? Those who, like Nussbaum, are already benevolent egalitarians will remain so; those who, like Posner, enter as self-indulgent aesthetes will depart unchanged.[41] Tacitly, Nussbaum is admitting Posner's point.

The moralists have, after all, only shaky empirical evidence at hand to suggest that well-intentioned art actually makes a difference in how people act.[42] Such theorists, who wish nonetheless to find moral value in the experience of reading, are reduced to positing some kind of effect on the inner structure of the mind, one that (conveniently and mysteriously enough) fails to translate into measurable everyday praxis. Thus Nussbaum, under pressure, says that she is only talking about "the interaction between novel and mind during the time of reading" (1998:353). Since, on her view, the mere fact of recognizing subtleties in the interpersonal world constitutes "moral conduct" all on its own, we can score virtue points *simply by (correctly) reading a Henry James novel*,[43] even if we return the next day to running the plantation.

There is something pleasantly Greek-flavored about the approach, implying as it does that goodness refers to a state or shape of the soul, rather than the decisions to which it gives rise. Still, even the Greeks insisted on proof through action: in Plato's *Gorgias*, for example, Socrates and Gorgias clearly agree that a man behaving badly is a man who lacks virtue, however much they disagree about whose fault it is. With such doubts nagging at her, perhaps, Nussbaum quickly seeks to take back what she conceded to Posner, writing—a mere two pages after having localized our increase in virtue to the period we spend with a book in our hand—that "the activities of imagination and emotion that the involved reader performs during the time of reading . . . strengthen the propensity so to conduct oneself in other instances."[44]

Yet the fact is that there is nothing whatsoever to prevent us from taking an intensive, vigorous, sustained, detailed, painstaking interest in the entanglements of other lives while remaining entirely remote from the moral fray. This intensive, vigorous, sustained, detailed, painstaking yet detached interest even has a name: it is called gossip. And as irony would have it, the very work Nussbaum considers the archetype of morally improving fiction—Henry James's *The Golden Bowl*—features a gossip of world-class caliber. If, as Nussbaum claims, "the activities of imagination and emotion that the involved reader performs during the time of reading are not just instrumental to moral conduct [but] are also examples of moral conduct" (1998:355), then Fanny Assingham, who spends all day every day picking apart in thought and conversation the predicament of her friends, has surely clocked up enough instances of moral conduct to earn herself a niche on the portal of Notre-Dame.

A clear reductio ad absurdum of Nussbaum's position, the Fanny Assingham case shows, if it shows anything, that a fascination with interpersonal niceties need not fuel any concern for our fellow human being; fine awareness, to phrase it in Jamesian terms, is no guarantee of rich responsibility. We do not have to be a vicious anti-egalitarian in order to read *Hard Times* for non-moral reasons. On the contrary, that is probably the way *most* of us read it. Like Fanny Assingham, we are infinitely curious (even pruriently so) about the lives of others, whether fictional or actual; if, as Nussbaum correctly states, Fanny stands as a model for the reader,[45] this is because her interest is just as amoral as ours, not because ours is just as moral as hers.[46]

Qualifications

> Oh! children, see! the tailor's come
> And caught our little Suck-a-Thumb.
> —Heinrich Hoffmann, *"The Story of Little Suck-a-Thumb"* (*in*
> *Slovenly Peter*)

What, however, about the very chapter you are now reading? Did it not begin precisely with a fiction, a made-up scenario (two classrooms) with made-up characters (Daun Bertrand Russell, Dame Erica Auerbach)? And did I not intend to affect your views on the basis of it? It has sometimes been argued that the examples used in philosophical arguments are miniature fictions, and so, conversely, fictions are nothing but extended philosophical examples, perfectly serviceable as tools for securing conviction. The comparison is misleading, however: one only needs to imagine trying to have my little classroom fantasy published in the *New Yorker* in order to register the vast distance between literary fictions and philosophical examples. The latter tend, first of all, to be as general as possible, dispensing with details (if I told you about Erica's interests, it was just for fun; and you know nothing about what she looks like, where she comes from, or what her ambitions are). Second, they hew with obsessive tenacity to the way in which events (are taken to) unfold in the real world.[47] Philosophical examples must begin in self-evidence—in situations, that is, on whose plausibility almost all readers will readily agree—in order to elicit intuitions supporting controversial hypotheses. Literary fictions, by contrast, add in such elements as drama and surprise.[48] Their endings tend, furthermore, to have an appropriateness (consider the denouement of "The Nun's Priest's Tale," a traditional case of the trickster tricked) rarely to be met with in real life.[49]

Let us say, then, that philosophical examples (like mine) are types of fiction—but nonliterary fiction—that can be used to summon intuitions. Let us also add that it is entirely possible for a philosophical author to compose a serious treatise, full of claims and arguments, and then encompass it in a fictional frame (by attributing it, say, to a character, perhaps with an exotic name like Zarathustra). Parmenides' poetic treatise on Truth and Opinion is a case in point, beginning as it does with an account of a mythical journey before launching into intricate metaphysical disquisitions.[50] There are even (and this would be a third concession) borderline phenomena, hybrid works that combine the imaginative world-building of literature with the argumentation of philosophy. (Proust's *Recherche* is one example, and Sartre's *Nausée* might be another, but James's *Golden Bowl* would most definitely not constitute a third.)[51] In such cases, I would suggest that we do indeed learn from novels, *but only insofar as they are philosophical*: only, I mean, insofar as they deploy convincing chains of reasoning (as, for instance, does Roquentin when he contends that "adventure" is a structure we impose on the sequence of events).

Finally, we should acknowledge that even canonically literary fictions can be used as tools of education, *as long as they are backed up by the sanction of an external authority*. I said above that your putative students may have derived from your lecture the idea that you and Chaucer share a belief in the prophetic power of dreams. Now if, in addition to believing this, your students are also sufficiently misguided to take you (and/or Chaucer) for an *expert* on such matters, they may change their minds on that very basis. The story may then serve them as a vivid reminder, a mental image helping them to remember how important dreams are. It seems to me that edifying children's literature works in just this way. What children learn is that it is good *according to their parents* to share their toys, keep their thumbs out of their mouths, and resist eating the gingerbread walls of rustic houses in the woods, and that *according to their parents* unpleasant consequences will necessarily follow should they do otherwise.[52] The children respond by adjusting their behavior in the direction of the parents' implicit agenda (or indeed, if they are old enough and self-willed enough, in exactly the opposite direction).

Without such sanction, mind you, the outcome is completely unpredictable. You might think that La Fontaine's fable *Le corbeau et le renard*, the tale of a crafty fox who tricks an arrogant crow out of his cheese by persuading him to sing, inevitably encourages its young readers to be a little less vain; you would, however, be mistaken. Rousseau was shocked to discover that eighteenth-century pupils (who were so well acquainted with the poem that they could recite it from memory) spontaneously identified with the *fox*, taking the poem as a handy reminder that if you wish to steal, it helps to use fake praise.[53] And I daresay the same would have been true if the story had featured a vain rooster, named Chauntecleer perhaps, instead of a vain crow. Even your students might—who knows?—have read it as advocating flattery and deception, were it not for the fact that, fortunately enough, they have you there to reveal the deep oneiromantic truth to them.

Now your students may, given a list of recommended readings, start concluding on their own—that is, without specific confirmation from you each time—that it is good to help the poor (*Hard Times*), or to avenge murder with murder (*Hamlet*), or to throw strangers out of railway carriages (*Les caves du Vatican*). Indeed, numerous literature courses at universities around the country assemble sequences of novels, penned by representatives of unquestionably deserving groups, with a view to conditioning students into taking each novel as an object lesson in empathy for the group concerned. Those who run such courses, we might say, are not merely training their students (to be better moral agents) but also training them *in how to be trained*, teaching them how to learn. (We could call this higher-order instruction "meta-training.") Just as we inform our children not only that Beijing is the capital of China but also that such facts can be found in the encyclopedia, so we may inform them not only that they should share their toys but also that answers to other ethical dilemmas are to be found in fables.

But telling our children, our students, and our citizens to go to the movies for moral instruction is a serious mistake. For anyone who can be converted to a view by a fiction can be converted *out* of it by a fiction. If *The Iliad* is enough to talk me into setting honor above life, then *The Odyssey* will be enough to talk me into doing the reverse.[54] If "The Nun's Priest's Tale" makes your students prudent during week one of your survey course, then *The Open Road* will make them reckless by week ten. (Just so, rhetoric was sufficient to convince the Athenians to slaughter all the men on Mytilene, and rhetoric was sufficient—mere hours later—to make them change their minds.)[55] Our culture is full of competing values, and of stories to "prove" any one of them;[56] conversions through fiction are simply not reliable. We are breeding a generation of what Harry Frankfurt would call "wantons," easily swayed from one well-meaning but unnuanced value judgment to the next. We are on our way to producing a nation of Madame Bovarys.[57]

A Genuine Benefit

"Why, some people may lose their faith by looking at that picture!"
—Prince Myshkin on Holbein's *The Body of the Dead Christ*, in
Dostoyevsky, *The Idiot*

It will be tempting for some on both sides to conclude, in horror or delight, that literature, if it has no edifying function, has no function at all. Indeed, part of what is troubling about the moralist line is that it so frequently sets up a stark "with us or against us" opposition. If novels are not morally improving, then they are morally depraving, or at best frivolous—which, as it turns out, still means pernicious. "Some works," writes Nussbaum, "promote a cheap cynicism about human beings, and lead us to see our fellow citizens with disdain. Some lead us to cultivate cheap sensationalistic forms of pleasure and excitement that debase human dignity. Others, by contrast, show what might be called respect before humanity" (1999:274). In other words, there are only three choices: improve, corrupt, or distract (and by distracting, "debase human dignity"). Pleasure, on this view, is not something humans can justifiably seek in between helping little old ladies across the road. It is, instead, a *diversion* from a little-old-lady-helping that should, by rights, constitute our full-time occupation. Aesthetic pleasure—which, like all pleasure, is inherently sinful, not just amoral but immoral—can just about become acceptable if it subserves the end of edification;[58] otherwise, whether sought by readers or offered by authors,[59] it is a positive shirking of our responsibilities to humankind.[60]

We would probably do well to preserve a space for reading without ulterior motives. (Perhaps it could even be argued, for the benefit of the irretrievably utilitarian, that society *requires* such amoral pleasures, as a "pressure valve" for pent-up self-directed or antisocial energies.)[61] But there is also a third way, in between hedonism and moralism, a way in which fiction can aid our emotional growth without turning us all into social workers. For while novels only tell us what we already know, and only convince us of what we already believe, *that very process may be indispensable*. As Posner puts it, "If you don't already sense that love is the most important thing in the world, you're not likely to be persuaded that it is by reading Donne's love poems, or Stendhal, or Galsworthy. But reading them may make you realize that this *is* what you think, and so may serve to clarify yourself to yourself" (1997:20).[62] Literature, in short, helps us to find our *own* values, which *may* turn out to be moral values such as rich responsibility, but which may just as well turn out to be, say, an individualist (and other-sacrificing) perfectionism. Fiction cannot edify, but it can clarify.[63] Wayne Booth is right that literary works can stand to us in the same relation as friends. But few of us today ask our friends to treat us as Aristotelian φίλοι would, or as Job's so-called "friends" (is this a rare case of irony in the Old Testament?) treat him: far from expecting them to repeat indefinitely how mired in sin we are, and enjoining us to meet an abstract, universal standard, we prefer them to invite us to be who we are.[64]

A work of narrative art can be a true friend of ours when, first, its background scheme of facts and values is close enough to our own, so that it makes sense to speak of a simulation shedding light on the intuitions of our real-world self.[65] A second, and absolutely vital, precondition is that it be axiologically *complex*. If it is to spur us to serious reflection on our attitudes, then it must challenge us by placing at least two of our values into conflict, allowing each to assert its claim on us, rather than simply reinforcing one of them (in imagination) and making us feel, like Diderot, how astonishingly good and just we are. The most useful texts are the *Antigones*, not the *Clarissas*;[66] however tempted we are to use purportedly "improving" novels as electrodes with which to jolt the misfiring neurons of the benighted, we should remember that those works which try hardest to change us are those which succeed the least.[67] It is, perhaps, no coincidence that certain segments of the population place a premium on artworks that generate lengthy discussion, rather than those that proceed from incontestably noble moral principles.[68]

We might even—my last, and most expansive, compromise proposal—be able to put a subset of axiologically complex works to edifying purposes. Nussbaum is surely right that fully moral behavior requires not only an adherence to general precepts but also an attention to nuances that tend to escape the latter's grasp. (This is why her contribution to moral philosophy has been so important.) And she is surely also right that a certain kind of engagement with a certain kind of text can fine-tune our capacity for such attention, acting as a moral obstacle-course, training us to navigate the treacherous road conditions and sudden swerves of real life. Her suggestion, finally, that the most important type of knowledge I gain from my reading is know-how, not propositional (or even experiential) knowledge, is equally welcome. *I must, however, be good already in order to use texts in the way she prescribes.* I must be predisposed to moral improvement, and indeed must come to the text *for* that, at least among other goals.

Literary texts, in other words, *can* make us more finely aware and more richly responsible. But they will do so only if we want them to.[69] If we are not already virtuous, they may leave us unaffected, or even enable us to render ourselves still more grossly obtuse and still more richly irresponsible than we were to begin with. (Any theory with pretensions to adequacy must, to repeat, be symmetrical.) If we come in with murderous desires, then literary texts may offer us new and exciting ways of killing people; while fictions do not, I think, turn good people into criminals, there is nothing to stop them inspiring *specific* crimes in nefarious appreciators. Simulation, by helping us to plan, may assist us in implementing any altruistic schemes we happen to have, but simulation may also assist us in implementing a successful bank heist, a successful kidnapping, or a successful cull of spotted owls.

Back in your classroom a week later, you address the crowd of sleepy undergraduates, retracting what you said last time about dreams. Literary texts do not teach us anything, you say, unless it is who we are as individuals. While they may occasionally permit the honing of a capacity for fine-grained concern, they do so only in certain cases, and only for those rare readers who seek moral improvement wherever they go. Such readers may even end up, who knows, taking some "moralitee" from "The Nun's Priest's Tale." As the Nun's Priest's hilarious antics remind us, one can, if one wants to, find a moral in just about anything.

PART TWO

ENCHANTMENT
AND RE-ENCHANTMENT

Mark

Metaphor and Faith

The vision of Christ that thou dost see
Is my vision's greatest enemy. . . .
Thine is the Friend of all Mankind;
Mine speaks in parables to the blind.
                                    —William Blake, *"The Everlasting Gospel"*

The extraordinary power of the New Testament owes a great deal to the deeds and events it reports, from the miraculous birth of Jesus to his prodigious wonders, his tragic death, and his glorious resurrection. It also owes a great deal to the revolutionary ideas—simplicity privileged over resplendence, faith over ritual, forgiveness over retribution—that it transmits to future ages. But it surely owes just as much to the specific *style* in which these pronouncements are delivered. In particular, it derives from the profusion of *parables*, those mysterious miniature fictions that so captured the imagination of Jesus's earliest listeners. If Mark is to be believed,[1] Jesus never made a speech without using a parable:[2] he may well not have been the inventor of the genre,[3] but he was almost certainly the first to make it the core of his pedagogical practice, spinning story after curiously gripping story. I want to argue here that this is not an arbitrary decision, and that the literary form employed by Mark's Jesus, far from being a mere ornament, is in fact indispensable to his project. The choice of genre turns out to have profound implications for, and indeed to be in the service of, the kind of life to which he is summoning his followers; profound implications not just for *what* they believe but even for *how* they believe. Without fiction, I will suggest, there would be no true faith.

The Myth of Simplicity

Why does Mark's Jesus place a fictional form at the center of his practice?[4] In recent years, one popular answer has been that parables are more effective, rhetorically speaking, than plain speech.[5] Since Jesus is talking to ordinary folk, not an audience of trained theologians, he must pitch his sermons accordingly: rather than dealing in abstractions, he must bring his ideas down to earth, make them concrete by appealing to everyday activities and familiar situations; he must reduce the unknown (say, the kingdom of God) to the known (say, a good harvest); he must, in the words of John Calvin, "represen[t] the condition of the future life in a way that we can understand."[6] Under such circumstances, metaphor and related devices become the perfect resource.[7] In addition, the parables "make [Jesus's] discourse more vivid," as John Chrysostom puts it, "leav[ing] a deeper impress on the mind than abstractions."[8] And finally, the parables are *persuasive*. Implicit arguments by analogy,[9] they ask the listener to accept that if something can be true of human love (such as disproportionate excitement at a prodigal's return), then it is reasonable to think it true of divine love; or that if something holds for plants (we don't understand their growth, but it happens nevertheless), then it may also hold for God's plan. Striking, straightforward, and convincing, parables ostensibly serve the rhetorical function of winning converts to the cause.[10]

Is it really true, however, that parables take something complicated and make it simple? Consider, for instance, the Parable of the Sower (Mark 4:1–25),[11] which, since it forms the core of my argument, I will quote in full.

Again he began to teach beside the sea. And a very large crowd gathered about him, so that he got into a boat and sat in it on the sea; and the whole crowd was beside the sea on the land. And he taught them many things in parables, and in his teaching he said to them: "Listen! A sower went out to sow. And as he sowed, some seed fell along the path, and the birds came and devoured it. Other seed fell on rocky ground, where it had not much soil, and immediately it sprang up, since it had no depth of soil; and when the sun rose it was scorched, and since it had no root it withered away. Other seed fell among thorns and the thorns grew up and choked it, and it yielded no grain. And other seeds fell into good soil and brought forth grain, growing up and increasing and yielding thirtyfold and sixtyfold and a hundredfold." And he said, "He who has ears to hear, let him hear."

And when he was alone, those who were about him with the twelve asked him concerning the parables.[12] And he said to them, "To you has been given the secret of the kingdom of God, but for those outside everything is in parables; so that they may indeed see but not perceive, and may indeed hear but not understand; lest they should turn again, and be forgiven." And he said to them, "Do you not understand this parable? How then will you understand all the parables? The sower sows the word. And these are the ones along the path, where the word is sown; when they hear, Satan immediately comes and takes away the word which is sown in them. And these in like manner are the ones sown upon rocky ground, who, when they hear the word, immediately receive it with joy; and they have no root in themselves, but endure for a while; then, when tribulation or persecution arises on account of the word, immediately they fall away. And others are the ones sown among thorns; they are those who hear the word, but the cares of the world, and the delight in riches, and the desire for other things, enter in and choke the word, and it proves unfruitful. But those that were sown upon the good soil are the ones who hear the word and accept it and bear fruit, thirtyfold and sixtyfold and a hundredfold."

And he said to them, "Is a lamp brought in to be put under a bushel, or under a bed, and not on a stand? For there is nothing hid, except to be made manifest; nor is anything secret, except to come to light. If any man has ears to hear, let him hear." And he said to them, "Take heed what you hear; the measure you give will be the measure you get, and still more will be given you. For to him who has will more be given; and from him who has not, even what he has will be taken away."

Imagine that you are a first-century dweller of Palestine, and that you hear only the parable (verses 3–9), without the explanation.[13] What do you make of it? You understand, presumably, that Jesus is not simply recounting an actual event he has witnessed; you recognize it as a fiction, one that symbolizes something beyond itself. Clearly *something* is at stake beyond mere sowing and reaping. But what? You may be assisted by the tradition, in the Jewish context, of sowing used as a metaphor for preaching;[14] still, you could be forgiven for feeling deeply confused, just as Jesus's own disciples clearly are, as to what exactly to make of things like paths, thorns, and stony ground.

Now imagine that you hear the explanation provided by Mark's Jesus. Those on the wayside are skeptics; the thorns are temptations and distractions; the stony ground is the soul of the half-hearted adherent; and the good soil is the soul of the true believer. Everything is clear now. But that's precisely the problem. What the parable ostensibly conveys is *already* straightforward, and extremely easy to swallow, *without* the story that supposedly serves to "clarify" it. Were these ideas really so hard to understand that they needed dressing up in narrative garb? Were they so controversial as to require special argument? The reality, it seems to me, is precisely the opposite of what is generally claimed:[15] far from taking something complicated and making it clearer, the parables take something transparent and render it incomprehensible.[16] In our era, Jesus could have made a successful career as a literary theorist.

Five Variables, Six Readings

Mark's explanation has become so standard by now that it is hard for us to hear the Sower as its original audience must have done. We today are tempted to feel not only that the explanation goes without saying—that we would infer it on our own if it were absent—but that it is entirely *sufficient*, dispelling every last ambiguity, to such an extent that the disciples' incomprehension becomes itself incomprehensible. In fact, however, the parable leaves a number of crucial questions open, and exegeses have accordingly varied wildly across the centuries, with multiple variables combining to form a plethora of possible permutations.[17] To start with, the Sower may be either *eschatological* (concerned, that is, primarily with end-time and the "kingdom of God") or *ethical* (concerned primarily with the believer). If ethical, it may give priority to *quantity* of believers or to *quality* of adherence; if eschatological, it may be discussing the present or the future; and if the future, it may consider the prospect it talks about to be secure or at risk. Either way, is its mood positive (focusing on what will go right) or negative (focusing on what will go wrong)? And is it a statement (perhaps even a statement that human agency is irrelevant) or a call to action (implying that human agency is all-important)?

Some have argued that the parable is fundamentally eschatological in character, its focus falling squarely on the harvest (rather than on the sower or the soils). Of these exegetes, the first subgroup sees the parable's function as that of communication: it *teaches* us, they say, that the kingdom of God is an enigma, apparently uncaused, arriving suddenly and mysteriously.[18] This is a view that is *informational, eschatological, positive, future-oriented*, and *passive* (humans being powerless to affect the outcome). A second subgroup, by contrast, reads it as telling us that the kingdom is *already here* (still informational, eschatological, positive, and passive, but present-tense: here, the "sowing" has taken place in the past).[19] And a third subgroup finds *consolation* in the parable, which supposedly reassures us that that in spite of all setbacks, the kingdom will come (here the approach is consolatory, eschatological, positive, future-oriented, and passive).[20] This faction further subdivides into those who believe success will be measured in number of adherents—each seed standing for a person, the hundredfold harvest standing for a hundred individuals—and those who believe success will be measured in strength of commitment (here, each seed stands for an idea sown in a single soul, the hundredfold harvest for a healthy inner flourishing).[21]

The trouble with all these views is that they emphasize the happy outcome, whereas the parable itself dwells at least as much on the various forms of failure, setting three scenes of sterility against a single scene of fruition.[22] We find, therefore, a second main category of interpreters, namely those who take the parable's focus to be on the *soils*. Of these, a first subgroup sees the parable as conveying knowledge, telling us that not everyone will understand, be converted, and be saved,[23] while a second subgroup views it as an incitement to action; the parable, on this reading, is about *you*, not about *them*.[24] Both approaches are ethical and negative, but whereas the first is informational, future-oriented, and passive, the second is hortatory, present-oriented, and volitional.

By my count, that makes a total of six schools of thought (not even allowing for Cadoux's suggestion that the parable is really focused on the *sower*, and represents Jesus's apologia for his practice of preaching to all and sundry[25]). Nor are they mutually compatible, since one cannot think both that we must take urgent action and that human action is irrelevant. Bultmann is surely right to express bemusement: "Since, in my view, the Kingdom of God was not thought of, either by Jesus or the early Church, as a human community, there can be no talk of its 'growth.'. . . Or has it to be interpreted in relation to the individual?: do not despair if there seems to be little result from your labour. . .? But no-one is able to say whether the meaning is just the reverse, viz. a warning against the evil that poisons the heart" (1963:200). "No-one is able to say"; can Jesus's original audience really have been expected to fare any better?

Deliberate Opacity

As Mark presents it, Jesus's original audience did *not* fare better. To the apparent irritation of Jesus—"Do you not understand this parable? How then will you understand all the parables?" (4:13)—even the disciples revealed themselves to be completely at a loss. Later, too, "his disciples asked him about the parable. And he said to them, 'Then are you also without understanding?'" (7:17–18). Indeed quite generally the disciples appear to have required a translation on each and every occasion: "privately to his own disciples he explained everything" (4:34). But if the disciples could not understand the parables, then how on earth could the common or garden Palestine-dweller expect to be enlightened by them?

Worse still (from the point of view of the rhetorical theory), when the disciples ask Jesus why he speaks in parables, the answer is not comforting. "For those outside," he says, "everything is in parables; so that they may indeed see but not perceive, and may indeed hear but not understand; lest they should turn again, and be forgiven" (Mark 4:11–12). This is an astonishing statement on the part of one who, by the standard account, strives for the salvation of all. The fact that the disciples fail to understand is not an accident, and not just a measure of their own shortcomings, but a deliberate strategy on the part of the master. Mark's Jesus is quite unequivocal: the function of the parables is to *prevent people from understanding them*, so that they will not convert to the correct belief, so in turn that they will not attain salvation. It is, in short, the very opposite of what Calvin and so many others have argued through the centuries.

So shocking is this statement, in fact, that some have preferred to think Mark's Jesus never made it. (May the reader forgive me, and/or skip the next section and a half, but I have to deal here with a number of widespread and deeply entrenched counter-positions.) If one understands the word ἵνα (*hina*) correctly, they insist, what Jesus says is merely "*with the result that* they may indeed see but not perceive,"[26] or—given that the "see but not perceive" segment is a quotation from Isaiah[27]—"so that *the prophecy should be fulfilled which states that* they may indeed see but not perceive."[28] And if one understands the word μήποτε (*mḗpote*) correctly, what Jesus says is not "*lest* they should turn again" but rather "*for otherwise* they would turn again"[29] (or perhaps, following an even more desperate interpretive gambit, "*unless* they should turn again"[30]). In short, Mark 4:11–12 really means something like "you insiders are lucky enough to understand the mystery of the kingdom of God, but to outsiders it all seems impossibly mysterious, with the unfortunate result that they see without perceiving and hear without understanding; otherwise they would surely convert, and their sins would be forgiven." Thus is the dangerous sentence rendered harmless, to everyone's considerable relief.

The problem, of course, is that the reading is heavily forced. If Isaiah 6:10 were merely a *statement*—"the heart of this people *will become* fat, and their ears *will become* heavy"—then it might perhaps be reasonable to think that Mark 4:11 is citing Isaiah in the way Matthew does so often, "that it might be fulfilled which was spoken by the prophet."[31] But Isaiah 6:10 is not a prediction. It is a command. "*Make* the heart of this people fat, and *make* their ears heavy, and *shut* their eyes": the three imperatives render it much harder to square the friendly reading of Mark 4:11 with the passage it is quoting, whether from the Hebrew or the Aramaic.[32] Further, the gentle reading does not account for what has just happened in Mark 4. Jesus, recall, has told a story *that no one understands*, neither the crowds nor the disciples nor even the Twelve.[33] Does it make sense for him then to suggest that what he is saying is inherently clear, but that it just so happens that some people cannot understand it? That his stories merely *seem* like parables (i.e., riddles) to the uninitiated, but are in fact completely straightforward?

And finally, the innocuous reading does not cohere with much of what happens elsewhere in the book of Mark. It does not cohere, first of all, with the disciples' need for a translation every time Jesus produces a parable. It fails to account, second, for Jesus continually withholding that translation from the crowd, those poor unfortunates who, on the gentle theory, are simply not blessed with sufficient understanding. It runs up, third, against Jesus's firm policy of keeping his identity a secret.[34] When the priests, scribes, and elders ask him what authority he has to preach, he answers the question with a question (Mark 11:27–33); whenever he performs a miracle, he issues instructions to keep it quiet;[35] when Peter identifies him as the Christ, "he charge[s] them to tell no one about him" (8:30); and when he is transfigured, "he charge[s] them to tell no one what they had seen, until the Son of man should have risen from the dead" (9:9). And it has a hard time, most importantly, explaining the fact that Jesus refuses to do miracles for those who are not already believers. "The Pharisees came and began to argue with him, seeking from him a sign from heaven, to test him. And he sighed deeply in his spirit, and said, 'Why does this generation seek a sign? Truly, I say to you, no sign shall be given to this generation'" (Mark 8:11–12). Jesus has the option of being clear—giving the priests a direct answer, letting the disciples spread his fame, performing miracles before unbelievers—but deliberately chooses, in each of the three cases, to make it difficult for people to understand, and hence to be converted, and hence to be saved.

The Vision of Mark

Those who do accept that Mark's Jesus considers himself a deliberate obscurantist tend to dismiss this as an idiosyncrasy on the part of Mark.[36] After all, they reason, *Matthew* sees things differently; on Matthew's account, Jesus does not speak in parables *so that* [ἵνα] people will not understand, but rather *because* [ὅτι] people do not understand; Jesus, that is, speaks even more clearly than he would otherwise, since he knows his audience are not experts. Here is the passage in question:

> And he answered them, "To you it has been given to know the secrets of the kingdom of heaven, but to them it has not been given. For to him who has will more be given, and he will have abundance; but from him who has not, even what he has will be taken away. This is why [διὰ τοῦτο] I speak to them in parables, because [ὅτι] seeing they do not see, and hearing they do not hear, nor do they understand. With them indeed is fulfilled the prophecy of Isaiah which says: 'You shall indeed hear but never understand, and you shall indeed see but never perceive. For this people's heart has grown dull, and their ears are heavy of hearing, and their eyes they have closed, lest [μήποτε] they should perceive with their eyes, and hear with their ears, and understand with their heart, and turn for me to heal them.'" (Matt. 13:11–15)

Matthew, it would appear, gives us a Jesus who wishes to reach everyone, and indeed *attempts* to reach everyone, failing only because of the regrettable obtuseness of his listeners. And so the book of Matthew departs from the eccentric Mark.[37] Or does it? While Matthew's version amends the ἵνα, it preserves the equally troublesome μήποτε, as well as the rather inegalitarian "to him who has will more be given . . . but from him who has not, even what he has will be taken away" (Matt. 13:12).[38] (Indeed the opening of verse 12—*this is why* [διὰ τοῦτο] I speak to them—connects the choice of genre directly to that inegalitarian policy: I speak to them in parables, Jesus is saying, *because* it is right to give more to those who have and to take away from those who have not.)[39] And just like Mark, it portrays the parables as unintelligible even to the disciples, requiring explanations that Jesus reserves for their ears alone, keeping the crowd, once again, fully in the dark.[40] In fact, Jesus goes so far here as to single out one of the Twelve—not just "those who were about him *with* the twelve," as in Mark 4—for special chastisement. "But Peter said to him, 'Explain the parable to us.' And he said, 'Are you also still without understanding?'" (15:15–16). None of this should happen, if indeed the point were to make matters as clear as possible.

There remains one last resort for those uncomfortable with the idea of a secretive, hermetic, deliberately obscure Jesus, and that is to say that Matthew and Mark *both* have it wrong. After all, each was written a minimum of forty years after the death of the historical Jesus,[41] and each draws on two layers of oral tradition—an initial layer that transmitted the acts and deeds of Jesus as faithfully as possible across the generations, and a second layer that attributed to him various statements he did not make but which the early church may have wished he did—as well as adding its own contribution, if only in the ordering of the various elements.[42] (Since the mere act of placing old items in new contexts can immediately alter their perceived meaning, this contribution is an extremely important one.) The word of Jesus may be divine, but it is transmitted via human mouths and hands.

Why not say, accordingly, that Matthew is right about the stated purpose of the parables but wrong about what actually happened, and Mark simply mistaken about everything? In reality, perhaps, the parables were perfectly clear at the time; once the original context (the famous *Sitz im Leben Jesu*, or situation in Jesus's life) was forgotten, however, the parables began to *appear* obscure, and after people had been repeating obscure stories to each other for a while, curious theories arose to explain their existence.[43] The Sower parable may well be the authentic word of Jesus, but the allegorical interpretation (the seed is the word, the thorns are temptations, etc.) and the claim of deliberate opacity ("that they may indeed see but not perceive") are an invention of the early church, and the arrangement—including the insertion of the *logion* "to him who has . . ."—is all down to Mark.[44]

All of this is perfectly plausible. But it is not categorical. It is, at the very least, not *obviously* the case that the parables were transparent when first uttered: the precedent of the Hebrew משל (*mashal*)—a word generally translated as "parable"—shows that there was already a long tradition of oracular pronouncements wielded by prophetic figures by the time of Jesus.[45] In the end, there is no real way to adjudicate definitively between the claims, to determine for certain what the historical Jesus actually said and actually did.[46] We have only the writings of contemporaries like Josephus, which say almost nothing; the letters of Paul, which do not offer direct quotation; and the Gospels, which were put into written form starting some time after 70 CE, a full forty years after the death of Jesus. Some, like the members of the Jesus Seminar, have attempted to assign to each *logion* its own degree of probability, but absolute confidence will forever elude us.[47]

My own analysis makes no claim to have it right about the historical Jesus. It claims, instead, to have it right about Jesus *as he is portrayed in Mark*. Rather than trying to offer a new theory as to what the historical Jesus said, meant, or intended to do, I am trying to explain what *Mark* is trying to do, and why so many have found that Gospel so gripping. Whatever Jesus himself may have been up to—and we can, to repeat, never know for sure—a certain group of early Christians clearly found it deeply inspiring to think of him as an enigmatic figure, as one who routinely concealed his identity and who spoke to the multitude in mysterious ways. And it seems to me that we are at liberty to feel similarly inspired today.

This last point is worth stressing. While I am eager to do justice to the findings of biblical scholars—over the past two centuries, their tendency has increasingly been to emphasize the gap separating Gospel depictions from the historical Jesus—and while I feel (for reasons I will spell out more fully below) that nonbelievers can and should find powerful inspiration in the Marcan parables, still I feel that practicing Christians have, if anything, the most to gain from the vision of Mark I am putting forward here. To be sure, many Christians today would reject the biblical scholars' distinction between the historical Jesus and Mark's portrayal of him. But there is, in fact, nothing un-Christian about such a separation; if anything, its enforcement is a way of taking the book of Mark more seriously. For it allows us to consider Mark as a totality, as a profound and coherent meditation on the essence of Christianity, rather than as a mixture of fragments, some to be trusted and others rejected as inauthentic. (Every Christian has, after all, to make a rather difficult choice: given that the four canonical Gospels present markedly differing accounts, she must either discard parts of each so as to be able to accept other parts as historically accurate or consider each text as a whole, at the risk of distancing its contents from her vision of the historical Jesus.)

To many nowadays who grew up hearing Bible stories in Sunday school, the differences among the canonical Gospels may be easy to overlook. Even those for whom these differences become salient may yet consider them elements it is their duty to ignore, minor glitches to be repaired, unfortunate but inevitable and ultimately remediable artifacts of an all-too-human transmission of the divine Word. In reality, however, Christians have every reason to *treasure* the distinctiveness of the separate scriptures. For in forming their canon of holy texts, the church fathers did not retain just one of the evangelists and discard the rest, as they could easily have done; nor did they opt for something like the "Diatessaron," a very popular second-century attempt to synthesize all four into a single consistent text; instead, they deliberately chose to preserve the individual contributions of Mark, Matthew, Luke, and John. In other words, the canon developed as it did precisely because believers considered it preferable to have four distinct Gospels rather than a single, definitive account of Jesus's life.

If, then, the focus of my investigation will be the specific contribution of Mark, rather than any speculation about the historical Jesus, this will, I believe, be in keeping with an important (albeit sometimes neglected) aspect of the Christian tradition.

I hope, therefore, to be able to speak at once to three very diverse communities. To biblical scholars, I seek to offer what may be a modest addition to the extraordinary sum of knowledge they have accumulated. To secular humanists, I seek to offer not just fresh insight into the beauty of the Christian faith but reflections of universal application on the subject of metaphor. And to believing Christians, I seek to offer a new way of understanding their Christianity. Just as Van Harvey argues that we can still see Jesus as "a normative possibility of human existence" even if we do not know whether the historical Jesus himself actually lived it,[48] so too, I want to argue, we can see *Mark's* Jesus as a normative possibility of human existence, whether or not it conforms to the historical record. The Jesus we find in Mark points the way, I believe, to a deeper and richer Christian life.

From Him Who Has Not

Mark's Jesus really does say, then, that he speaks in parables in order not to be understood. And his practice really does bear this out: starting from relatively simple concepts, Mark's Jesus spins stories around them so opaque, so uncertain in application, as to surpass the understanding of his own closest followers; far from injecting clarity, vividness, and persuasiveness into difficult and controversial material, he willfully complicates the straightforward. While this may or may not be what the *historical* Jesus had in mind, it is certainly true of the Jesus that we find in Mark. It is, moreover, *consistently* true of that Jesus; assembled from multiple sources as it may have been, Mark has the feel of a powerfully unified document,[49] conveying through the incomprehension of the disciples, the refusal to give signs, the refusal to explain to the masses, and the insistence on secrecy a single overarching vision. (Whoever authored or redacted it, one wants to say, knew exactly what he was doing.) And above all, it is *appealingly* true of that Jesus. Mark's vision must have been deeply inspiring for the early Christian communities that produced and propagated that Gospel, and it remains, I think, a live option for believers today.

It is a live option for believers today to share Mark's vision of a Jesus who spins parables that most listeners do not understand, that they are not *meant* to understand, and that do not contain much to understand in the first place. We too may regard the parables not as spreading the word to the widest possible audience but, on the contrary, as designed to *restrict* its transmission, to make sure it reaches only those who are worthy of it, to carve up the audience into insiders and outsiders (with no guarantee, fascinatingly, that the disciples will end up on the inside[50]). We too may see the parables' function as that of *driving people away*. It is no coincidence that Mark deploys the rather disquieting *logion* "to him who has will more be given; and from him who has not, even what he has will be taken away" in the context of the parables: it is the parables themselves that do the work, that are *designed* to do the work, of taking away "even what he has" from "him who has not." Which is to say, it is the parables that—precisely by being obscure—repel the casual listener, generate irritation and disdain, and eradicate the modicum of interest that he or she once had.

The parables thus turn out to be a mechanism for dividing the audience into two parts, the haves and the have-nots, the people who are comfortable with— perhaps even intrigued by—the mysterious operation of inscrutable tales and the people who are rebuffed by their impenetrability; those, in other words, who stand a chance of becoming insiders and those who are doomed to everlasting exclusion. (There is, of course, a bit of a determinist flavor here.)[51] Or to be more precise, the parables are a mechanism for dividing the audience into *four* parts: true adherents (the good soil), no-hopers (the wayside), and backsliders both temptable (the thorns) and dauntable (the stony ground).[52] The stony-grounders, recall, "when they hear the word, immediately receive it with joy," yet "have no root in themselves, but endure [only] for a while" (Mark 4:16–17). A stony-grounder is that most dangerous of false friends, the lukewarm adherent. Parables keep such friends at arm's length; they avert the cheap conversion, which is not reliable; they ensure that the souls they save *remain* saved. They readily sacrifice quantity for the sake of quality.[53]

Or to be even *more* precise, the parables are a mechanism for dividing the audience indefinitely, not just bisecting it into insiders and outsiders, and not just quadrisecting it into four different soils, but splintering it into as many segments as there are hearers, isolating each individual in a bubble of autonomous choice. The parables require *work*, a kind of work that—unlike mere interpretation— nobody else can do in our stead.[54] For Mark's Jesus wishes every soul to participate in its own salvation;[55] he is not interested in mass conversions, in demagoguery, in indoctrination, in coercion, in peer pressure, or in group psychology (if one seed yields a hundred stalks, these stalks are not separate believers but a harvest of faith within the heart of a single adherent). Mark's Jesus is not out to redeem the world en masse but to save one soul at a time.

To Him Who Has

Mark's Jesus makes an offer to everyone, but he is well aware that not everyone will wish to accept it, and he has no desire to save people, as it were, in spite of themselves. (That is why he performs miracles only for those who already believe,

and reserves explanations for those who already know his vision of the world.)
His aim is not quantity but quality; rather than attracting a world full of superficial adherents, he strives for a narrow clique of the deeply committed, and the
parables are his way of ensuring it. They are there to keep the unworthy at
the door, "lest they repent"—lest, that is, they make a cheap conversion, for the
wrong reasons and (quite possibly) without the conviction necessary to sustain
it in the face of competing promises and trials of faith. The parables are a crucial
test,[56] one whose failure has permanent consequences.

There is, however, still more to them than that. Recall that in addition to
taking away from him who has not even that which he has, they are supposed to
give something additional to him who has. What, then, can we expect to receive
if we are fortunate enough to pass the test? Across the ages, by far the most
widespread answer has been *knowledge*: we gain, it is said, an understanding of
the kingdom (that it grows secretly, but with indirect signs of its arrival); lessons
on how we are to live (that we should be vigilant, that we should share our wisdom, that we should stand together);[57] mystical insight into that which defies all
expression;[58] or, finally, some highly specific information, tailored precisely to
the needs of a given reader at a given moment in time. This last view is that of
the allegorists, according to whom the parables, along with the Bible more generally, are so many coded messages, ready to be deciphered by right-minded
interpreters. To get a sense of the results, consider the Good Samaritan parable
from Luke (10:30–35) as translated by Augustine:

> A man [Adam] was going down ["falling"] from Jerusalem [Eden: Jerusalem is
> the heavenly city] to Jericho [mortality: the moon, *yareaḥ*, waxes and wanes],
> and he fell among robbers [the Devil and his minions], who stripped him [of his
> immortality] and beat him [by persuading him to sin], and departed, leaving
> him half dead [i.e., only half knowing God]. Now by chance a priest was going
> down that road; and when he saw him he passed by on the other side. So like-
> wise a Levite, when he came to the place and saw him, passed by on the other
> side [the Old Testament is of no help]. But a Samaritan [Jesus: *shomer* means
> "guardian"], as he journeyed, came to where he was; and when he saw him, he
> had compassion, and went to him and bound up his wounds [restrained his
> sinfulness], pouring on oil [hope] and wine [exhortation to work fervently];
> then he set him on his own beast [belief in Christ's incarnation] and brought
> him to an inn [the Church], and took care of him. And the next day [after the
> resurrection] he took out two denarii [this life and the afterlife] and gave them
> to the innkeeper [Paul, who works for a living so as not to be a burden on his
> brethren], saying, "Take care of him; and whatever more you spend, I will repay
> you when I come back." (*Quaestiones evangeliorum* 2.19)

The allegorical approach to the parables, which has much in common with the
Straussian approach to Plato that we will meet in chapter 4, enjoyed a surprisingly

long life—having begun with church fathers like Clement and Origen of Alexandria, continued with Augustine, and found new impetus in the Middle Ages under Bede and Gregory, it had a major proponent as late as the nineteenth century in the form of Archbishop Richard C. Trench[59]—but has by now, thanks in good measure to the work of Adolf Jülicher, almost entirely disappeared from the hermeneutic landscape. It has, after all, become a dogma of biblical hermeneutics that, as Aquinas puts it, "nothing necessary to faith is contained under the spiritual sense which is not elsewhere put forward by the Scripture in its literal sense";[60] and surely the function of the parables cannot merely be to transmit obscurely what is elsewhere stated in plain speech.

But *all* of the knowledge-based theories are in fact problematic. For the parables are designed not just to give us more, but to give us more *of what we already have*, more indeed of what allowed us access to the parables in the first place.[61] And knowledge is simply not a fit candidate to fill this role. The disciples, one assumes, have more knowledge than anyone about the kingdom and about the right way to live, yet they, as we have seen, are completely mystified by the parables. The parables must therefore require, and sustain, something different.

Here, then, is the riddle that Mark sets before us: what is it whose possession is both required and strengthened by the parables? What is it that both grants us entry into the parabolic world and emerges stronger as a result of the experience? What exactly is it that he who has, has; and that he who has not, has not?

The Syrophoenician Woman

The answer, it turns out, is to be found in the tale of the Syrophoenician woman.

> And from there he arose and went away to the region of Tyre and Sidon. And he entered a house, and would not have any one know it; yet he could not be hid. But immediately a woman, whose little daughter was possessed by an unclean spirit, heard of him, and came and fell down at his feet. Now the woman was a Greek, a Syrophoenician by birth. And she begged him to cast the demon out of her daughter. And he said to her, "Let the children first be fed, for it is not right to take the children's bread and throw it to the dogs." But she answered him, "Yes, Lord; yet even the dogs under the table eat the children's crumbs." And he said to her, "For this saying you may go your way; the demon has left your daughter." And she went home, and found the child lying in bed, and the demon gone. (Mark 7:24–30)

At one level, the Syrophoenician woman story is a reasonably standard miracle account: anguished mother pleads for intervention, Jesus acquiesces, child is cured.

But at another level, there is something deeply strange about the sequence of events. Why does Jesus give way, having at first refused? It is, to my knowledge, the only time in Mark that an ordinary individual persuades Jesus to change his mind. To put it the other way around, why does Jesus refuse, if he is later going to accede to the request? What has changed between the start and end of the episode?

It is not that Jesus has suddenly become aware of the Syrophoenician woman's belief in his capacity to perform miracles. To be sure, such belief is a precondition in other contexts for Jesus's willingness to exorcise demons and cure diseases. But the Syrophoenician woman *already* possessed it—if not, she would hardly have "fallen down at his feet" and "begged him to cast the demon out of her daughter"—and yet that was not enough to convince Jesus to make an exception for her as a non-Jewish woman, a "dog" among "children." If he grants her petition, it is not because of something she believes but instead because of something she *says*. "For this saying you may go your way": what saves the Syrophoenician woman's daughter are the words "Yes, Lord; yet even the dogs under the table eat the children's crumbs." How can this be explained?

It is, I think, quite simple: the reason Jesus changes his mind is that the Syrophoenician woman *uses a metaphor*.[62] Without missing a beat, she responds to Jesus's use of figurative language with some figurative language of her own, picking up his canine image and sending it back to him under a new application. In so doing she vastly outstrips the performance of the disciples, who, far from composing their own improvisations, show themselves to be tone-deaf even as mere passive recipients: when Jesus warns them to "beware of the leaven of the Pharisees," they think—delightfully—that he is complaining of their failure to bring bread (Mark 8:15–16). In Matthew's version, Jesus ascribes their obtuseness to a lack of faith ("O men of little faith [ὀλιγόπιστοι], why do you discuss among yourselves the fact that you have no bread?" [16:8]); in Matthew's version of the Syrophoenician woman, conversely, he ascribes the woman's linguistic finesse to a surplus of faith ("Then Jesus answered her, 'O woman, great is your faith [μεγάλη σου ἡ πίστις]! Be it done for you as you desire'" [15:28]).[63] What makes the difference between faith and non-faith, in this very special sense—and, I want to say, between "having" and "not having"—is the ability to turn a trope at the drop of a hat.

The Syrophoenician woman deserves special treatment because she is someone who "has," where to "have" means to be able to translate literal language into figurative language and figurative into literal. Better yet, it means being able to operate exclusively on the figurative level; like a fine poem, a parable is meant not to need paraphrase, indeed to *resist* paraphrase.[64] Whereas "the essence of prose is to perish," says Paul Valéry, to be "entirely replaced by the image or impulse that it stands for," poetry "is expressly made to be reborn from its ashes and to become once more, over and over again, what it has just been."[65] The true insider is supposed never to return to earth, never to turn poetry into prose, never to crush the lyricism with paraphrase: he or she is supposed, like the Syrophoenician woman, to operate exclusively on the higher plane, to live among symbols, to glide easily from image to image. Our response to a parable should not be translation, let alone allegorical exuberance (which is, after all, just translation run amok), but the production of figurative language of our own.[66]

The Formative Circle

"To him who has will more be given": in Mark, one has to come in with a little in order to go out with more. Now this, to some extent, is a version of Rudolf Bultmann's justly famous notion of *Vorverständnis*, or "pre-understanding."[67] On Bultmann's hermeneutic theory, it is always necessary to start from at least a vague intuition of what a given text means and what purpose it serves; without that, interpretation could simply not get off the ground. The vague intuition guides our reading of the text, subsuming various features under itself and providing a way to resolve certain ambiguities; but as we encounter elements that flatly contradict it, we refine our initial hypothesis, and then use our newly refined estimate to guide interpretation as we go forward. We end up in a "hermeneutic circle" (fig. 2.1), or perhaps more accurately a hermeneutic *spiral*, since our reading gradually becomes more and more sophisticated, more and more attentive to the text, more and more competent to explain its various facets.

Here, however, one wants to say that what separates "those outside" from "those inside" is less an intuition—however vague—about what the parables mean than a raw, nonintellectual feeling of their power. It is, one wants to say, nothing other than a sensitivity to figurative language, a tendency to be gripped by metaphors. This is something that disciples Simon and Andrew clearly do not lack. "And passing along by the Sea of Galilee, he saw Simon and Andrew the brother of Simon casting a net in the sea; for they were fishermen. And Jesus said to them, 'Follow me and I will make you become fishers of men.' And immediately they left their nets and followed him" (Mark 1:16–18). Immediately they left their nets: Simon and Andrew do not have to think twice, for a man who is capable of moving so quickly from literal to figurative fishing is instantly going to grab their attention. (Whether they will then go on to rival the Syrophoenician woman or show blank incomprehension at figurative language is another matter; the disciples may not ever achieve full proficiency, but they have *pre*-proficiency in abundance.)

We should speak, then, not of a pre-understanding but of a pre-capacity, and not of a hermeneutic circle but of a *formative* circle (fig. 2.2). For what we have to begin with, and what is refined in the process, is less an interpretive hypothesis than a cognitive capacity—the capacity to appreciate, receive, and produce

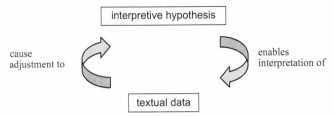

Figure 2.1. The hermeneutic circle

metaphoric discourse.[68] As in the hermeneutic circle, so here one must begin with something: the wayside cannot magically become good soil; "the right use of metaphor," as Aristotle says, "cannot be learnt," being a "token of genius" (*Poetics* 1459a). But as in the hermeneutic circle, so here what one came in with is also enhanced in the process.[69] To him who has will more be given.

It is not, then, just a matter of a simple yes or no, a welcoming or an exclusion, insider or outsider status, Saul or Paul. Rather, initiation admits of *degrees*. A series of levels is already suggested by the progression from stony ground (weakly plants) to thorns (strong but ill-fated plants) to good soil,[70] but it comes out most strongly in what Mark's Jesus has to say about the ideal listeners, with their three separate verbs: "those that were sown upon the good soil are the ones who *hear* the word and *accept* it and *bear fruit*" (Mark 4:20). First comes hearing, which is to say being intrigued by metaphorical discourse, sensing hidden depths (this, presumably, is the stage of Andrew and Simon); next comes accepting, which is to say a facility in decoding metaphorical discourse, in understanding it without assistance, in readily translating the figurative into the literal; and then there is bearing fruit, the more active capacity to translate in the other direction, indeed to operate exclusively on the figurative level, and thus to produce figurative language of one's own.

That is how it is possible to receive more of what one already has. Those who "have not" (those, that is, who have a tin ear for metaphor) are kept at arm's length by the parables, alienated, driven even further away from their opportunity for access; but for those who "have"—those who are already intrigued by (or indeed comfortable with) figurative discourse—the parables are a means to even greater mastery. The parables are not message, not warning, not consolation, not instigation. Their primary purpose is not the transmission of information, whether directly ("Be the good Samaritan") or indirectly ("Adam fell from Eden"). They do not teach by means of their content; instead they train by means of their form. They are what allow the transformation of stony ground into good soil, the shift from enthusiasm to proficiency, from proficiency to creativity. They are what turn a novice into a true son of God.

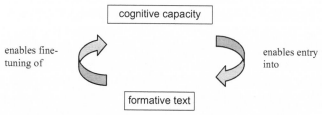

Figure 2.2. The formative circle

Metaphor and Faith

But what does figurative language have to do with salvation? Why is it, in fact, that the Syrophoenician woman's easy handling of metaphor is enough to convince Jesus that she has what it takes (that, as Matthew phrases it, she has faith)? Why is it that the crucial test of insidership comes in the form of parables? The answer, I think, is that parabolic discourse, by presenting the world around us as a storehouse of metaphors, implies in its very form that nothing we can see, hear, smell, taste, or touch is inherently significant—that everything visible and audible and sensible merely serves as a possible symbol for something higher, something intangible, something spiritual.[71] That, after all, is how Jesus himself so frequently uses language, rebuking Andrew and Simon (as we saw above) for being actual anglers when they could be fishers of men; responding, when asked where his family is, that his true brothers and sisters are those around him;[72] telling the rich to lay up treasures in heaven rather than treasures on earth.[73] Jesus habitually rejects the literal meaning in order to press for a figurative sense, which is to say that he habitually rejects immanence in order to press for transcendence. Spiritual aptitude is inexorably tied to a particular way of seeing the world, which in turn is inexorably tied to a particular way of speaking; salvation depends on our ability to think parabolically, to dwell in metaphors, since to dwell in metaphors is to consider the entire sensory realm as a shadowing-forth of a higher plane of experience, and thus to see the world from God's point of view.[74]

I am not speaking here of the particular point of view of *Jesus* as he considers his mission on earth.[75] Nor am I suggesting that Jesus is attempting to convey a beautiful but inarticulable vision through the *specific* metaphors he uses, through the unique connections among individual concepts (as would be in keeping with Proust's powerful theory of figurative language). Rather, my thought is that it is the parabolic mode *in general* that does the work of gradually shifting the listener to a higher plane. It is a literary form, surprising as this may be, that does the work of turning fringe adherents into genuine insiders, by allowing them to reconfigure their epistemic stance (to rewire their neurons, as today's brain scientists might say). Metaphor is not a luxury here, not an embellishment but a requirement. And fiction too is a requirement. For if metaphor reduces the physical to the mere ground term of an image (nothing but a "vehicle," in I. A. Richards's terminology), parable reduces temporality to a mere vehicle of transformation, to a discardable ladder into extratemporal enlightenment.[76] Time becomes non-time, the temporal gives way to the eternal. The one who truly "has," the one who is expert in the spinning of parabolic discourse, understands his or her narratives as taking place outside of time; which is to say, he or she sees the world *sub specie aeternitatis*, as though (again) with the eyes of God.

Theological Ramifications

It is sometimes said, especially by "crisis theologians" like Rudolf Bultmann, that Paul's Epistles and John's Gospel depart radically from the vision of life proposed by Jesus himself.[77] But as Van Harvey points out (445), the parables (at least, I would add, in Mark) show Jesus to be entirely with Paul in seeing salvation as redemption from bondage to the temporal, or with John in saying "My kingdom is not of this world" (John 18:36).[78] John, Paul, and Mark actually present a united front in suggesting that what is called for is a move away from the body and toward the soul. The only difference is that Mark understands, much more than his successors, that language is the best place to start: that by habitually making the leap from literal to figurative, in full awareness that this is what one is doing, one trains one's mind to pass from letter into spirit, from immanence into transcendence, from human concerns to the point of view of God. Mark's Jesus does not have to say explicitly, as John's Jesus does, that the leap itself is the telos. His consistent use of the parable form is as eloquent as any direct statement.

At the same time—and this would be a second corollary of the hypothesis advanced so far—the leap, which is a leap into a *higher* world, should not be confused with a leap into a *future* world. Most readers of the Gospels assume, understandably enough, that when Jesus refers to the "kingdom of God," he is thinking of a state of affairs yet to come, to be brought into being by God. (This is the "consequent eschatology" position.)[79] Others, insisting that Jesus must have made a substantial change to the nature of experience even on his first coming, conclude that the kingdom has been set underway but not completed. (This is the "inaugurated eschatology" theory.)[80] For a third group, however, the kingdom is *already here*.[81] Advocates of the "realized eschatology" model see Jesus as offering not a later life of consolation and reward but a *present* life shot through with the divine. In Luke, famously, Jesus says that "the kingdom of God is in the midst of you" (γὰρ ἡ βασιλεία τοῦ θεοῦ ἐντὸς ὑμῶν ἐστιν) (17:21); in Thomas, that "the Kingdom of the Father is spread out upon the earth, and men do not see it" (113); "it will not," he adds, "come by waiting for it" (ibid.). What the parables offer is a growing detachment from worldly care that could easily become an end in itself, that would not require a glorious finale in order to be counted a redemption of humankind. The kingdom of God is now, is here, is spread out upon the earth, and all we have to do is to enter it—which is to say, to move up into it (perhaps the reason we do not see it is that it is, so to speak, above our heads)—by training ourselves to look down upon sensory phenomena. All we need, in other words, is parabolic proficiency.

A Parable about Parables

If the Sower means anything, then, it means that the kingdom is available immediately—but only to some, and only at a price. It is available to those who are able to hover above the earth, seeing everything from God's point of view, but withheld from everyone else; it is restricted not to those who know the truth, or to those who hold the right beliefs, but to those who possess the necessary *skill*, that talent the Syrophoenician woman is naturally blessed with, the three-tiered capacity to "hear," "accept," and "bear fruit." And the parables are the whetstone on which to hone that skill.

The parables help those who can appreciate the power of figurative discourse to become people who can *follow* it, and help those who can follow it to become people who can coin fresh metaphors of their own. They require metaphoric competence, as a "pre-capacity," but also reward active listeners with *increased* metaphoric competence (rather than with allegorical or epiphanic revelations), in an endlessly rising "formative spiral": *to him who has will more be given.* As for those who lack even the faintest interest in metaphor or the willingness to work for their salvation, and who are therefore liable to make faint-hearted adherents, they will be repelled by the parables' (otherwise unnecessary) opacity and drift away from what might have saved them. *From him who has not, even what he has will be taken away.* Thus do the parables make the sacrifice of quantity for the sake of quality, for the sake, that is, of a circumscribed community of true believers, full-fledged citizens of the kingdom of God.

All of which is to say that the Sower is a meta-parable, a parable about parables, a parable that only indirectly concerns the kingdom of God, being focused, rather, on the ability to handle figurative language.[82] (It is no wonder that the general discussion about the utility of parables comes up, in Mark, immediately afterward.) It is also a self-enacting parable: not merely a story about sorting listeners into an in-group and an out-group, it is a story that *does* sort listeners into an in-group and an out-group. If you understand what "to fall on good soil" means, then the parable has fallen on good soil; if, conversely, you do not understand what "stony ground" means, then you are the stony ground. (If you do not even care, then you are the wayside, and heaven help you.) The Parable of the Sower casts its own seeds, letting the resulting harvest reveal, as well as amplify, the quality of the soil. By their fruits, to coin a phrase, shall ye know them.

Getting It Wrong by Getting It Right

It might be tempting to say that our journey is at an end, our work complete. Now we grasp what the Sower means; now we have solved the riddle; now we understand the "message" that Jesus was trying to transmit to us in that rather unusual way of his; now we can rest easy, having fulfilled our task and earned our salvation. This, however, would be a very costly mistake, its price the loss of our ticket into the kingdom. For it is only *practice*, and not knowledge, that can gain us entry. To be sure, it is important to understand—but only instrumentally, only as exercise, and only (in the specific case of the Sower) as a way to gather what it is we are supposed to do in the first place. Meaning is just a stepping-stone, not the destination.

For some two thousand years, readers have pored over the parables, producing endless explanations, taming their raw power with interpretive ingenuity. In a sense, of course, such interpreters are doing what is called for, since to reach the second stage of parabolic talent is to be able to "receive" a metaphor with success. Yet in another sense they are doing the *opposite* of what is called for. For by imposing a literal reading, by attempting (in many cases) to pass it off as the only possible construal, and—above all—by presenting the propositional upshot as the *point* of the parable, they accustom their listeners to rely on authoritative paraphrase rather than wrestling with the parable for themselves (a task that Mark's Jesus clearly calls on each individual to do unaided); they condition everyone to think that the telos is understanding, rather than the state of mind that parabolic interpretation contributes to fostering; least of all do they help, a fortiori, to spur the all-important *creation* of parabolic discourse on the part of the community. With the best intentions in the world, they deprive their congregation of the key to the kingdom.[83]

The situation here is (to anticipate slightly) very much the same as the situation in Plato. Just as it is entirely possible to fix the arguments in a Plato dialogue without understanding that the *point* is to fix the arguments in a Plato dialogue, so too it is entirely possible to understand the parables as metaphors without understanding that the *point* is to understand them as metaphors. In both cases, the choice is a disastrous one, one that sacrifices the most important thing the text has to offer; in both cases, the mistake has been made millions of times over thousands of years; and in both cases, the selectiveness of the text—allowing the unworthy to fall, so to speak, by the wayside—has made the error not only conceivable but highly likely. In both cases, in short, one can get it wrong by getting it right.

It might be asked: why, if this is so, does Jesus explain at all? Why tell the disciples what the Sower means and how it works? Indeed, why does Mark compound the problem by inserting the "he who has" logion here? And why am I compounding it still further by attempting to spell out the entire process? Are all three of us not failing in our duty to preserve the mystery of the parables and thus allow them to do their work? The answer, I think, is no. Before Mark's Jesus launches into his translation of the Sower, he asks the disciples, "Do you not understand this parable? How then will you understand all the parables?" (Mark 4:13). The point is not that the Sower is easier than all other parables; the point is that it teaches the *method*. Without understanding the Sower—which is to say, without understanding what parables are and what we are supposed to do with them—we, like the disciples, will be perpetually out of our depth. Jesus is not doing all the work for them; he is just priming the pump, explaining one parable in the hope that they will go on to interpret the rest for themselves ("how then will you understand all the parables?") and, of course, spin metaphoric stories of their own. So too, Mark primes the pump for us, his readers. And so too, I hope, this chapter primes the pump for contemporaries who have been led to consider Mark outlandish. In an odd way, the repeated failure of the disciples proves that Jesus's aid was not excessive, just as the repeated misreading of the parables has proven that *Mark's* aid was not excessive. For all the help we have been given, each of us is still in the same situation as the disciples, faced with beautiful and mysterious sayings and challenged to make sense of them, without imagining for a second that sense is all we need.

Coda: The Secular Kingdom

I hope to have persuaded Christian readers that a huge amount is at stake in what one does with the parables, and that there may be much to be gained by going beyond mere comprehension. But should non-Christian readers care, for more than just anthropological reasons? I believe that they should. For it seems to me that there is a remnant of Mark in our abiding love for figurative language. To be sure, people no longer read a great deal of lyric poetry these days, but comedy still relies heavily on innovative metaphors, and so do banter and slang (consider such wonderful coinages as *couch potato, wallflower, airhead, mall rat, beanpole, bookworm, gumshoe,* and *scatterbrain*). Why are we so fond of imagery? It is not, I think, because it permits insight into the renamed objects: certain scientific metaphors, like "solar system" for atomic structure, may well be heuristic fictions, but I am really not sure we stand to learn anything more about a "bookworm" by thinking of her as an invertebrate inside a dictionary. Nor is it for its persuasive power (again, we probably *already* think someone is a bookworm, but still delight in hearing the term), or for its explanatory power, or for its ability to convey the inexpressible inner world of an individual speaker (in the cases listed, the pleasure lingers when the original coiner is forgotten).[84] There's a sheer joy in metaphor that resists such utilitarian explanations; we enjoy it for its own sake, heedless of cognitive or rhetorical gain.

The reason, I want to suggest, is that there is something over and above the local deployment of metaphors for strategic or aesthetic purposes, and that is what we might call a *figurative state of mind*. If we move from coining the odd metaphor every now and then to cultivating a generalized love for the figurative—if we come to *dwell* in metaphor, as Emily Dickinson would say[85]—then our stance toward existence becomes subtly but powerfully shifted: the world becomes less concrete and more abstract, less impersonal and more humanized, its components less monadic and more interconnected. And as everything we see begins to point sideways to what is like it, rather than backward to what preceded it or forward to what follows, we find ourselves released from the tyranny of time.[86]

Such, to take one example, is the extraordinary power of Baudelaire's poem "The Swan," a poem whose very core is pitiless temporality. In the wake of Haussmann's renovations of Paris, Baudelaire's speaker no longer recognizes what he sees about him; his heart is unable to adjust to the rate of change; modernity, which presents us with one change after another in an endless, dizzying flow, has left him bereft, unmoored, an exile in time.[87] He feels like a swan trapped in the dry city, far from its "native lake." He feels like Andromache, ripped from her home in Troy. He feels like Victor Hugo, stuck in Guernsey. He feels like an African woman in Paris, one whose ancestors, we assume, were forcibly displaced to France. Comparison piles on top of comparison, with increasing levels of generality and increasing rapidity of pace; at poem's end, it is no longer a question of individual figures but now of orphans, of captives, of sailors (like Philoctetes) abandoned on an island, of "those who quench their thirst with tears," and indeed—the poem's final words—of "many more besides." What is stunning, however, is that after a while the comparisons no longer deepen the melancholy but, on the contrary, begin to alleviate it. By situating himself within a network of exiles united across the miles and the millennia, the speaker has ingeniously lifted himself out of time, and thus out of modernity, and hence, in a way, out of the very predicament these exiles are helping him lament.

There is, then, a secular variant of the Marcan vision. It too demands of us a pre-capacity, in the form of an ability to appreciate striking metaphors. It too grants more to "those who have," with appreciation sliding into production, production gradually becoming *instinctive* production, and brief forays into the figurative giving way to a dwelling in metaphor, until finally the entire world begins, as Baudelaire puts it, to feel like a mere warehouse of images.[88] It too comes at a cost; it too requires the privileging of constant practice over punctual acts of comprehension; but it too offers us the key to a kingdom. And even that secular kingdom is worth the high price of admission.

Appendix

Charles Baudelaire, "Le Cygne"

À Victor Hugo

I

Andromaque, je pense à vous! Ce petit fleuve,
Pauvre et triste miroir où jadis resplendit
L'immense majesté de vos douleurs de veuve,
Ce Simoïs menteur qui par vos pleurs grandit,

A fécondé soudain ma mémoire fertile,
Comme je traversais le nouveau Carrousel.
Le vieux Paris n'est plus (la forme d'une ville
Change plus vite, hélas! que le coeur d'un mortel);

Je ne vois qu'en esprit tout ce camp de baraques,
Ces tas de chapiteaux ébauchés et de fûts,
Les herbes, les gros blocs verdis par l'eau des flaques,
Et, brillant aux carreaux, le bric-à-brac confus.

Là s'étalait jadis une ménagerie;
Là je vis, un matin, à l'heure où sous les cieux
Froids et clairs le Travail s'éveille, où la voirie
Pousse un sombre ouragan dans l'air silencieux,

Un cygne qui s'était évadé de sa cage,
Et, de ses pieds palmés frottant le pavé sec,
Sur le sol raboteux traînait son blanc plumage.
Près d'un ruisseau sans eau la bête ouvrant le bec

Baignait nerveusement ses ailes dans la poudre,
Et disait, le coeur plein de son beau lac natal:
«Eau, quand donc pleuvras-tu? quand tonneras-tu, foudre?»
Je vois ce malheureux, mythe étrange et fatal,

Vers le ciel quelquefois, comme l'homme d'Ovide,
Vers le ciel ironique et cruellement bleu,
Sur son cou convulsif tendant sa tête avide,
Comme s'il adressait des reproches à Dieu!

II

Paris change! mais rien dans ma mélancolie
N'a bougé! palais neufs, échafaudages, blocs,
Vieux faubourgs, tout pour moi devient allégorie,
Et mes chers souvenirs sont plus lourds que des rocs.

Aussi devant ce Louvre une image m'opprime:
Je pense à mon grand cygne, avec ses gestes fous,
Comme les exilés, ridicule et sublime,
Et rongé d'un désir sans trêve! et puis à vous,

Andromaque, des bras d'un grand époux tombée,
Vil bétail, sous la main du superbe Pyrrhus,
Auprès d'un tombeau vide en extase courbée;
Veuve d'Hector, hélas! et femme d'Hélénus!

Je pense à la négresse, amaigrie et phthisique,
Piétinant dans la boue, et cherchant, l'oeil hagard,
Les cocotiers absents de la superbe Afrique
Derrière la muraille immense du brouillard;

À quiconque a perdu ce qui ne se retrouve
Jamais, jamais! à ceux qui s'abreuvent de pleurs
Et tettent la Douleur comme une bonne louve!
Aux maigres orphelins séchant comme des fleurs!

Ainsi dans la forêt où mon esprit s'exile
Un vieux Souvenir sonne à plein souffle du cor!
Je pense aux matelots oubliés dans une île,
Aux captifs, aux vaincus! . . . à bien d'autres encor!

The Swan

To Victor Hugo

I

Andromache, I think of you! That little river,
Poor, sad mirror in which once gleamed
The immense majesty of your widow's sorrow,
That false Simois which swelled with your tears,

Has suddenly nourished my fertile memory,
As I was crossing the new Carrousel.
The old Paris is no longer (the form of a city
Changes faster, alas! than the heart of a mortal);

Only in my mind's eye do I see that whole camp of stalls,
Those piles of rough-hewn capitals and of pillars,
The weeds, the huge stone blocks turned green by puddle water,
And, shimmering in the windows, the cluttered bric-a-brac.

There a menagerie once used to sprawl;
There I saw, one morning, at the hour when beneath the
Cold, clear skies Labor arises, when road-menders
Drive a dismal storm into the silent air,

A swan who had escaped from his cage,
And, rubbing the dry paving-stones with his webbed feet,
Dragged his white plumage along the uneven ground.
Beside a dried-up gutter the creature opening his beak

Nervously bathed his wings in the dust,
And said, his heart full of his beautiful native lake:
"Water, when will you rain down? when will you strike, thunder?"
I see that unhappy bird, strange and fateful myth,

Toward the sky sometimes, like man in Ovid,
Toward the sky so ironic and cruelly blue,
Lifting his eager head on his twisted neck,
As though he were aiming reproaches at God!

II

Paris is changing! but nothing in my melancholy
Has shifted! new palaces, scaffoldings, stone blocks,
Old *faubourgs*, everything for me becomes allegory,
And my dear memories are heavier than rocks.

Thus before this Louvre an image afflicts me:
I think of my great swan, with his crazy gestures,
Ridiculous and sublime, as exiles are,
And gnawed by an unremitting desire! and then of you,

Andromache, fallen from the arms of a great husband,
Mere livestock now, under the hand of proud Pyrrhus,
Bent over an empty tomb in ecstasy;
Widow of Hector, alas! and wife of Helenus!

I think of the negress, emaciated and consumptive,
Trudging through the mud, and seeking with haggard eyes
The absent palm trees of proud Africa
Behind the immense wall of fog;

Of whoever has lost what can never be found again,
Never! of those who quench their thirst with tears
And suck at Sorrow as at a good she-wolf!
Of scrawny orphans withering like flowers!

So in the forest where my mind takes its exile
An old Memory calls with a full horn-blast!
I think of sailors forgotten on an island,
Of the captive, the vanquished! . . . and many more besides!

3

Mallarmé

Irony and Enchantment

The world is disenchanted. One need no longer have recourse to magical means in order to master or implore the spirits, as did the savage, for whom such mysterious powers existed. Technical means and calculations perform the service.

—Max Weber

Third Law: Any sufficiently advanced technology is indistinguishable from magic.

—Arthur C. Clarke

"Whether science can furnish goals of action after it has proved that it can take such goals away and annihilate them": this, insists Nietzsche, is "the thorniest question of all."[1] What, indeed, is left when science has disenchanted the world? At one time we considered rainbows mysterious phenomena, divine perhaps in origin (Iris's scarf, God's covenant), but then science came along and taught us about prismatic refraction.[2] We used to believe that the cosmos had—as its etymology suggests—an intrinsic, humanly apprehensible order, with the earth set firmly at its center; after Copernicus, we think differently. And though we fondly imagined for a while that we were placed on the planet for a purpose, we now know that our evolution involved a considerable degree of contingency, and might just as well not have happened at all.[3] Little by little, science has stretched its tentacles into more and more corners formerly occupied by religion and myth.[4] It has removed the persuasion that there is something beyond what is offered by the evidence of our senses; it has uprooted the conviction that things are what they are, and where they are, for a reason; it has eradicated mystery, order, and purpose—and in their place, it has put nothing at all, simply leaving a gaping void. Can science, then, redress its own wrongs? Can it restore mystery and wonder to experience? Can science itself re-enchant the world it disenchanted? Or if not, what can?

Nineteenth-century answers to Nietzsche's question were varied. Many, of course, refused so much as to feel its force, either because they had never relinquished their beliefs—it is still the case today that thoroughgoing disenchantment affects precious few, even in the "enlightened" West—or because, at the other extreme, they did not see the need to replace them. (These, and not Christians as is commonly thought, are the target of Nietzsche's madman who, in *The Gay Science*, urges his fellow atheists to face the consequences of the "death of God.")[5] Others, however, took the task very seriously. Nietzsche himself sought to restore a sense of purpose to life, even if this purpose had to be invented and autotelically endorsed by each individual; Jean-Eugène Robert-Houdin, the stage magician, disclosed a mystery at the heart of science; and Stéphane Mallarmé, the magician of words, offered his intricately crafted miniature masterpieces as both models of and training-grounds for a new principle of order. The burden of the present chapter will be to explain how Robert-Houdin and Mallarmé, two self-described magicians, helped pull off the greatest trick ever performed in the modern age: nothing short of the re-enchantment of the world.

Part 1: Jean-Eugène Robert-Houdin

Exorcisms and Experiments

It might, at first glance, seem counterintuitive to begin with Robert-Houdin. After all, his chief achievement is to have turned the rejection of supernatural forces and the exposition of frauds into a staple of stage magic. Robert-Houdin called himself a *prestidigitateur*, not a *magicien*; his handbills spoke of illusions (and "experiments"), not of enchantments; he dedicated volumes (*Les tricheries des Grecs dévoilées*, 1861, and *Les secrets de la prestidigitation et de la magie*, 1868) to the unmasking of ancient and modern humbuggers; and he was even employed by the French government in 1855 to reproduce each of the feats performed by the Marabout sorcerers, like a latter-day Moses, so as to forestall an impending coup in Algeria.[6] In short, Robert-Houdin made good on his determination, explicitly stated in the 1858 autobiography *Confidences d'un prestidigitateur*, "to offer new experiments divested of all charlatanism" (159). And his successors followed suit, quite literally in fact. In the wake of Robert-Houdin, more or less every magician adopted sober evening dress, and more or less every magician took a swipe at something while on stage, whether past impostors, present spiritualists, or even his own tricks.[7]

The demolition of lingering belief in actual sorcery became, thanks to Robert-Houdin, a primary function of the magic show at large. For belief did continue to linger, with three factors jointly responsible for its dogged persistence. First of all, there was the charlatanism Robert-Houdin was complaining about: even at the end of the eighteenth century, conjurors like Andrew Oehler and Giovanni

Pinetti were claiming, letting it be known, or simply not denying that their feats required divine or diabolical intervention. Giovanni Pinetti's antics brought condemnation from Henri Decremps in the form of a treatise, *La magie blanche dévoilée* (1784); some fifty years afterward, Jean Julia de Fontenelle found it necessary to publish a book under the same title, this time exposing Louis Comte.

The second factor was education. In rural Switzerland, during the second decade of the nineteenth century, Louis Comte was set upon by townspeople armed with cudgels who wanted to burn him alive; Comte escaped, appropriately enough, by ventriloquizing the voice of a demon, causing his terrified assailants to scatter.[8] And in Cornwall a decade later, Antonio Blitz was "arrested and brought before the magistrate of the borough, a Colonel Tremain, and openly charged with being engaged in the 'Black Art'" (Blitz, 36). "The poor Cornish miners," he explained, "looked upon me as a being not all of human make" (Blitz, 37).[9]

The third and final contributor to the survival of superstition was, perhaps surprisingly, Christianity. While the French legal system had long since abandoned witch trials, an edict of Louis XIV in 1690 decreeing that the relevant criminals were merely guilty of fraud,[10] the eighteenth century witnessed a powerful counter-Enlightenment reaction inside and outside the country. A. Boissier's *Recueil de diverses lettres au sujet des maléfices et du sortilège* (1731) and Antoine Daugis's *Traité sur la magie, le sortilège, les possessions, obsessions et maléfices* (1732) both reaffirmed the existence of real enchanters, as did the abbé Fiard's *De la France trompée par les magiciens et les démonolâtres du dix-huitième siècle*, published—hard to imagine—in the nineteenth century (1803). Meanwhile, the Vatican, having enacted the Inquisitorial Code of Pasquelone in 1730, helpfully offering a definition of magicians (as those who cause other human beings to be possessed by demons) so as to facilitate their prosecution, went on in 1795 to put the legendary Cagliostro on trial as "a freemason, a heretic, and a sorcerer." (Under torture, Cagliostro confessed.)[11] The Vatican's Code actually remained on the books until 1870, prompting Stéphane Mallarmé—only slightly behind the times—to speak in 1893 of "practices that the preservation, at the papal court, of a law intended to defeat them indicates to be alive and well."[12]

It is, of course, unlikely that *all* nineteenth-century clergymen, and *all* nineteenth-century country-dwellers, gave credence to the idea of diabolical possession. Reported cases may, on occasion, have been the product of a tacit alliance between members of the church who did not believe in it and members of the uneducated classes who did not believe in it either. In 1816, for example, a young woman, having become pregnant, understandably chose to blame her condition on supernatural forces; a Jesuit, equally happy to connive with her in this, exorcised her demon, who, it seems, "ended up stationing itself in the young lady's *pudendum*."[13] The "exorcism" took place on regular occasions for several days—until, one assumes, they finally caught him at it.[14] Nonetheless, plenty of priests and preachers were willing to take the matter extremely seriously, to the point of putting itinerant performers in the dock. In 1826, the ecclesiastical court of Exeter charged Antonio Blitz with "deceiving honest people by base acts, and tempting them to look for riches, by giving themselves over to his master,—the arch-enemy of mankind"; a Manchester clergyman, for his part, called Blitz "a necromancer—at war with religion and morality" (Blitz, 34, 85). And perhaps we should be less astonished at such attitudes, which many Christians today consider almost inconceivably archaic, than at the fact that they ever died out. For as Augustine notes in *The City of God* (21.6), "such marvels we cannot deny without impugning the truth of the sacred Scriptures we believe": the cost, for the Church, is nothing less than the rejection of Deuteronomy 18:10–12, in which God lays out punishments for practitioners of the secret arts, and of Mark 5:1–20, in which Jesus transfers demons from man to pig (to cite only one example from the New Testament).[15]

Thus the cleric preached, the uneducated trusted, and the charlatan profited, all the way into the middle of the nineteenth century. Nor were the *educated* classes entirely immune to mystification.[16] Blitz met with the same behavior in London as he did in Exeter and Cornwall: "even here," he writes, "there were many to be found with the same feelings of credulity, as ignorant respecting my character, and profession, and performances, as were those in the most remote and benighted districts" (38). In 1830s England, according to Charles Mackay (2:188–89), it was not just the poor that summoned witch doctors to cure diseases inflicted by the Devil, but also "ladies who rode in their carriages." And Robert-Houdin himself, toward 1846, fell victim to an "elegant" female visitor who considered him an actual necromancer.[17] Looking suitably tragic, a veil covering her fine features, this young woman begged him to help her take revenge on a wayward spouse; when Robert-Houdin vociferously denied any connection with the forces of darkness, she simply changed tactics and pulled out a knife. She would not leave until Robert-Houdin had taken down a dusty book from a high shelf, stuck a pin in a candle, and mumbled an impressively incomprehensible incantation. He should, presumably, have checked in advance to see that she had nothing up her sleeve.

Science and Wonder

Robert-Houdin may have played the part when his life was at stake, but as we have seen, he generally considered himself an active force for *dis*enchantment, a champion of enlightenment in its continuing struggle against credulity. And so his theater seems, to repeat, an unlikely place to look for answers to Nietzsche's "thorniest question." Did its audiences not split down a simple fault line, that of

THE ETHEREAL SUSPENSION

Figure 3.1. Robert-Houdin's most famous "experiment." From *Memoirs of Robert-Houdin.*

the mid-century at large, with faith (in traditional religion, ancient magic, or recent options such as spiritualism) on the one side and doubt (originated by science, reinforced by prestidigitation) on the other? Were believers, like the dagger-wielding avenger we just met, not free to preserve their beliefs, and skeptics their skepticism, throughout the performance? These questions are, it turns out, not entirely rhetorical. To understand why, we need to consider the trick that made Robert-Houdin's reputation when he debuted it in October 1847, the one for which he was best known and most widely copied: the Ethereal Suspension.

Imagine a forty-one-year-old Jean-Eugène Robert-Houdin, dressed in the evening wear he is in the process of making de rigueur, accompanied on a simple and well-lit stage by his six-year-old son Joseph, and starting to spin out his patter "with all the seriousness," as he put it, "of a Sorbonne professor." "Gentlemen," he begins, "I have just discovered a new, truly wondrous property of ether. When this liquid is at its highest degree of concentration, if a living being breathes it, the body of the patient becomes in a few moments as light as a balloon."

This exposition being complete, I proceeded to the experiment. I placed three stools on a wooden bench. My son climbed onto the one in the middle, and I made him stretch out his arms, which I held up in the air by means of two canes, each of which rested on one stool.

Then I simply put an empty bottle, which I carefully uncorked, under the boy's nose. . . . My son immediately fell asleep, and his feet, having become lighter, began to leave the stool.

Judging the operation a success, I removed the stool, so that the child was no longer supported by anything except the two canes.

This strange equilibrium already elicited great surprise among the audience. The surprise only grew when I was seen removing one of the two canes and the stool which supported it; and finally it reached its peak when, having raised my son to a horizontal position by means of my little finger, I left him thus asleep in space.[18]

What matters here is not that Robert-Houdin succeeded in creating the illusion of levitation, however influential the trick may subsequently have been. What matters is, instead, that Robert-Houdin presented it as a miracle of *science*, with himself acting the role of *professor*, and his performance gaining the feel of an *experiment*. "In 1847," he would later explain, "the insensibility produced by inhaling ether began to be applied in surgical operations; all the world talked about the marvellous effect of this anaesthetic, and its extraordinary results. In the eyes of many people it seemed much akin to magic" (1859:214; cf. Lamb, 34). In order to be enthralled, then, audience members did not have to believe that Robert-Houdin possessed mystical powers, or even that he was particularly skillful. They had only to believe in the mysteries of science.[19] And believe they did: many of them, misled by a combination of Robert-Houdin's patter, a smell of ether coming in from offstage, and their own faith in pharmacology, took Robert-Houdin to be actually etherizing his son every night, and wrote to scold him for this appalling mistreatment (1859:215).

Robert-Houdin's befuddled patrons have, it seems to me, unwittingly furnished a partial answer to Nietzsche's question. Science *can* re-enchant the world, after having so mercilessly disenchanted it. For modern science, when presented in the right way, can itself be awe-inspiring.[20] And performers like Robert-Houdin, even as they demystified old superstitions, were simultaneously replacing these with new sources of enchantment—indeed disenchanting *by* re-enchanting. Like Antonio Blitz, Robert-Houdin could have said that his performances had as their aim "to remove the long-prevailing impressions attached to the history of magic, by demonstrating to the mind that the rapidity of the hand, and the mechanical inventions of the nineteenth century, were more wonderful in effect than the mysteries of the ancient magicians" (Blitz, 86).[21]

Mid-century prestidigitation was a legerdemain in which what was taken away with one hand was simultaneously restored with the other.

Nietzsche, of course, asked for more than just wonder; he asked "whether science could furnish goals of action." The answer, surprising as this may seem, was again in the affirmative for a segment of Robert-Houdin's audience. One year after the first performance of the Ethereal Suspension, Ernest Renan addressed Nietzsche's question head on, in *L'avenir de la science* (*The Future of Science*). "Since science has barely appeared up till now except in critical form," he wrote, "people do not imagine that it can become a powerful motive for action. That will change, however, as soon as science has created in the moral world a conviction equal to that which religious faith once produced" (74, my translation). And four years after that, Auguste Comte published an actual "Catechism of Positive Religion," offering a new God, a new faith, a new Providence, a new way of explaining the world, a new type of immortality, a new (grounding for) morality, a new set of rituals, and even a prayer, to be repeated "whilst placing the hand in succession on the three chief organs of love, of order, and of progress."[22] Flaubert's Homais, with his absurd devotion to science, is often seen as a caricature; this, however, is only because those on whom he was based, like Ernest Renan, were already caricatures of themselves.[23]

Lucid Illusions

We could sum everything up by saying that in mid-nineteenth-century France, religion, science, and magic stood in a curious relationship to one another, as though in a circular relay race. Religion remained stubbornly tinged with magic; magic, for its part, became increasingly scientific; and science took on, for some at least, the appearance of a new religion. As a result, in performing his onstage "experiments," Robert-Houdin was simultaneously contributing to the disenchantment of the world—attempting, via the non-illusionistic aspects of his performance, to extirpate the residuum of superstition—and to its re-enchantment, both via wonder and via the nascent hope in science itself as a "motive for action."

Yet even this précis is not entirely accurate. What we should say, rather, is that when Robert-Houdin performed his experiments, he contributed to the re-enchantment of the world via the *illusion* of wonder and the *illusion* of science itself as a motive for action. For the "ether" in his bottle was, let us not forget, nothing more than air. To be sure, Robert-Houdin wafted the scent of ether across the theater, and a *part* of the audience—the Renan type—must have taken the act for an actual experiment, just as a second part of the audience (children, Fiard-style clergymen, and dagger-wielding noblewomen) must have taken it for a palpable demonstration of diabolical dealings. But for every believer (in science or religion) there was a thoroughly urbane and disabused spectator, interested only in besting the magician by refusing to be duped; and for every cynic, last and most importantly, there was an "*homme d'esprit*," an individual who asked for nothing more than to be deceived by an artful prestidigitator. "The ordinary man," explained Robert-Houdin,

> sees in conjuring tricks a challenge offered to his intelligence, and hence repre-
> sentations of sleight of hand become to him a combat in which he determines
> on conquering. . . . The clever man [*l'homme d'esprit*], on the contrary, when he
> visits a conjuring performance, only goes to enjoy the illusions, and, far from
> offering the performer the slightest obstacle, he is the first to aid him. The
> more he is deceived, the more he is pleased, for that is what he paid for.
> (1859:92–93)[24]

In other words, the capacity crucially required for the full appreciation of a magic show—that which separated the "ordinary man" from the "*homme d'esprit*"—was, in Robert-Houdin's estimation, the capacity to let oneself be deceived, knowingly and willingly. (As would be said about one of Robert-Houdin's immediate successors, "he deludes the most watchful spectator, [even] as he lucidly explains, 'that is how it is done.'")[25] Demon-hunting clerics and dagger-wielding noblewomen did not possess this capacity, since in their eyes magic was simply a reality; adherents to the religion of science did not possess it either, since for them the miracle of *science* was real; and cynics lacked it just as thoroughly, since, as they saw it, being deceived was the worst imaginable fate. Only those who were beyond universal cynicism had what it took to allow their world to be re-enchanted by Jean-Eugène Robert-Houdin. Only those spectators who, with a mental agility equal to his manual dexterity, were ready to don and doff their lucidity repeatedly throughout the show could respond appropriately to the Ethereal Suspension: could respond, that is, by entertaining the conscious fantasy that science "can resolve for man the eternal problems whose solution his nature imperiously demands," indeed that science "can become a powerful motive for action." What Robert-Houdin required was, so to speak, an ethereal suspension of disbelief.[26]

Robert-Houdin sought out, and sought to create, such spectators not just because they helped him (by actively contributing to the illusions) but also because he felt able to help *them*. For his performances did not merely require the capacity for (quasi-) simultaneous conviction and distrust; they also of-fered the opportunity to *hone* that state of mind, to reinforce an aptitude for detached credulity—that very aptitude which would make it possible for everyday life to be re-enchanted. In the Ethereal Suspension, Robert-Houdin provided his audience with a *model for the construction of a belief system that recognizes itself as illusory*: even science can be a religion, he seems to have been hinting with a sly wink to those in the know, if you lucidly wish to believe it one.

Part 2: Stéphane Mallarmé
The Spell of Poetry

If, as I have suggested, Robert-Houdin viewed nineteenth-century France as insufficiently enlightened, as being in need at once of magical demystification and of new, non-magical strategies for re-enchantment, then later developments surely proved him right. On January 3, 1893, nearly fifty years after Robert-Houdin first took to the stage, the abbé Joseph-Antoine Boullan died suddenly at the age of sixty-eight. What was the cause of death? According to the medical establishment, Boullan had suffered a simple heart attack.[27] But according to some members of his sect, a splinter group of the decidedly unorthodox Church of Carmel,[28] foul play had been involved—indeed, metaphysical foul play. For only a few years earlier, the co-founder of the French Rosicrucians, Stanislas de Guaïta, had written to Boullan in threatening terms, condemning him to "death by the fluids" for misusing cabalistic rites.[29] So had de Guaïta murdered Boullan by magical means?

Some otherwise highly intelligent individuals believed that he had. In the pages of the *Gil Blas*, Jules Bois directly accused de Guaïta of having cast fatal spells on Boullan. "It is now an incontestable fact," wrote Bois; "the abbé Boullan, who has just died suddenly in Lyon, was struck down by invisible wrath and criminal hands armed with occult thunderbolts, with formidable and unknown forces." One day later, in the *Figaro*, Joris-Karl Huysmans came out in support of Bois, adding that the Rosicrucians were trying to kill him too (one can only speculate that his *"pâte à exorcisme,"* a present from Boullan, had spared him the same fate). "They have done everything they could," said Huysmans, "to harm yours truly! Every evening, at the precise instant when I am about to fall asleep, I receive . . . how shall I say? . . . fluidic punches on my skull and on my face. I would like to think that I am quite simply the victim of false sensations . . . caused by the extreme sensitivity of my nervous system; but I am inclined to think that it is well and truly a case of magic. The proof is that my cat, who for his part is hardly likely to be a hallucinator, is gripped by spasms in the same way and at the same time as me."[30]

In the light of such strong and public statements, and of the duels that ensued,[31] Stéphane Mallarmé decided that something needed to be said. Mallarmé was, after all, a friend of Huysmans: Duc Jean des Esseintes, protagonist of Huysmans' 1884 novel *A rebours*, ranked Mallarmé above all other living poets (219–23); a year later, Mallarmé returned the favor by dedicating a poem to des Esseintes (kindly overlooking the latter's fictional status). Mallarmé's article for *The National Observer*, published on January 28, 1893 and entitled "Magie," was not so friendly. Here Mallarmé chided both Huysmans and Bois for continuing, at the very end of the nineteenth century, to believe in the medieval world of wizards and enchantments. He did, however, make a crucial concession to the lovers of magic. For while it is true that spells and sorcerers do not exist in the real world, he argued, still they are to be found in poetry, indeed they are the very source and substance of poetry. "There is a secret equivalence," wrote Mallarmé,

> between the old procedures and the Spell that poetry continues to be. . . . To evoke, in a deliberate obscurity, the unspoken object, by means of allusive words, never direct, reducing themselves to an even silence, constitutes an effort close to creation, one that gains plausibility by confining itself within the sphere of the idea. Now only the idea of an object is put in play by the Enchanter of Letters, with such aptness, to be sure, that it dazzles, in the eye's imagination. The line of verse, that incantatory stroke! Who will deny me a similarity between the circle perpetually opened and closed by rhyme and the rings in the grass made by fairy or magician?[32]

Poetry, that is, resembles magic by setting up a protected space—in the case of poetry, that delimited by end-rhymes—and by using it in order to create something out of nothing. The difference is that poetry evokes the *idea* of an object (presumably its essence, since ordinary language already evokes its concept), whereas magic ostensibly brings forth an *actual* object. Like an alchemical combination of solutions, a poem's words yield clear silence, with *idée* as their by-product. Poetry thus remains what it has been since its origins: incantation. Poetry has the power to re-enchant the world.

Most of us would presumably agree with Mallarmé in denying the existence of the paranormal and insisting on a diagnosis of natural causes for the ill-fated Boullan. But what of the claims about poetry? What would it mean, exactly, for poetry to be magical? If poetry were to re-enchant the world, it could surely not do so by *communicating* something: in a disenchanted world, there can (ex hypothesi) be no enchanting truths. A redemptive poetry would have not to *say* something but to *do* something, to do by saying. Or rather, it would have to permit *us* to do something by its means, just as books of spells permit their users to transform friends into gods and foes into frogs. And in that case it would have to say something after all—namely, what the spell is, what it is for, and how it is to be used. Redemptive poetry would, then, be an effective spell, complete with instructions for its use.

Setting the Scene

Mallarmé's most famous sonnet is, I wish to argue, just such a spell.

Ses purs ongles très haut dédiant leur onyx,	Her pure nails very high dedicating their onyx,
L'Angoisse, ce minuit, soutient, lampadophore,	Anguish, this midnight, upholds, a lamp-carrier,
Maint rêve vespéral brûlé par le Phénix	Many an evening dream burned by the Phoenix
Que ne recueille pas de cinéraire amphore	And gathered by no funereal urn
Sur les crédences, au salon vide: nul ptyx,	On the credenzas, in the empty room: no ptyx,
Aboli bibelot d'inanité sonore,	Eradicated knicknack of sonorous inanity,
(Car le Maître est allé puiser des pleurs au Styx	(For the Master is gone to draw tears from the Styx
Avec ce seul objet dont le Néant s'honore).	With that sole object in which Nothingness takes pride).
Mais proche la croisée au nord vacante, un or	But near the vacant window to the north, something gold
Agonise selon peut-être le décor	Twists in agony according perhaps to the decor
Des licornes ruant du feu contre une nixe,	Of unicorns hurling fire against a nixie,
Elle, défunte nue en le miroir, encor	Her, the naked corpse in the mirror, while, in the
Que, dans l'oubli fermé par le cadre, se fixe	Forgetfulness enclosed by the window, immediately
De scintillations sitôt le septuor.	The septet of scintillations comes to fix itself.

Let us begin by trying to understand what is going on in these fourteen lines. (I must here crave the patience of readers unfamiliar with Mallarmé, assure them that perplexity is the natural initial state, and promise them that the gains will reward their investment.) At first, second, and third glance, Mallarmé's midnight sonnet appears irremediably (and notoriously) opaque: submerged beneath a torrent of scintillating, cadenced, harmonious phonemes, we hear plenty, see nothing, and understand still less. The speaker must know where (and when) we are, and pretends to assume that we do too, since he deploys, perhaps exasperatingly, any number of definite articles and demonstrative adjectives—*the* Master, *the* room, *this* midnight, *that* object—but the result is, if anything, an even greater sense of confusion. The actors in the drama are in the main mythical or semi-mythical figures (the unicorns, the nixie), some of which even command a capital letter (the Phoenix, the Master, Anguish, Nothingness). And the background consists in part of objects that do not exist (no amphora, no "ptyx") and in part also of objects whose connection to elements in the real world is uncertain (the "ptyx" again, the "something gold" [*un or*], the "forgetfulness" [*l'oubli*]). Gradually, however, our eyes grow accustomed to the darkness, as one or two items begin to detach themselves from the void. We receive with gratitude a handful of concrete, present, everyday nouns dispensed from the second stanza onward, reassuring fragments of a tangible scene, stable landmarks by which we may hope to find our way.

We can see, at least, that we are in a room (*salon*, line 5). We can also see that the room, otherwise empty (*vide*, 5), contains three things: (1) tables (*les crédences*), (2) a mirror (*le miroir*), and (3) a window (*la croisée*; see lines 5, 12, and 9 respectively). And then, as illumination spreads over the scene, it transpires that each of these objects is the site of further entities, this time more ethereal, whether vanished, hallucinatory, or intangible. The tables once housed a ptyx (whatever a ptyx is: we sense we will have to suspend that question for the time being); the mirror seems to contain the image of a dead nymph (*nixe*, 11), murdered by unicorns, as in a medieval legend; and a septet of scintillations is suddenly forming within the frame of the window (*le cadre*, 13). Since it is midnight—this may be the only piece of solid information retained from stanza one—we may reasonably assume that the scintillations are stars, and that the septet is a constellation. And since the nymph is in a mirror, we may even speculate that she is the reflection of something, presumably of these very stars, there being no other source of light.

If we make it thus far, we have arrived at Mallarmé's own synopsis of the "subject" of his poem: "An open night window, . . . no furniture, except the plausible outline of vague console tables, the warlike and dying frame of a mirror hung in the back, with its reflection, stellar and incomprehensible, of the Great Bear, linking this dwelling, abandoned by the world, only to the sky."[33] And we may be emboldened enough to return to the enigmatic opening stanza, still relying on our spatial sense alone. We may not know *what* the nails of Anguish are, but we can tell *where* they are, namely "very high" (*très haut*, 1). We may thus begin to perceive a gradual downward movement in the first part of the poem, from a point of maximal elevation to the depths of Hades via the intervening empty room; and a counterbalancing movement back up in the second part of the poem, from Hades (implicitly) to the room and thence up to the stars, to the shimmering septet of scintillations. And we may begin to conclude, quite reasonably, that the fingernails are not merely as high as the stars but *identical with* the stars; the pure nails of Anguish in the first line *are* the gleams that appear in the mirror of the final line. *Ses purs ongles très haut* and *le septuor*, so closely related in sound, turn out to be one and the same.[34]

And just as the downward spatial movement of the first half is counterbalanced by the upward movement of the second half, so too, we notice, the *temporal* structure presents us with a pair of mirror images. The quatrains begin at midnight, before flashing back to evening dreams (*maint rêve vespéral*, 3); the tercets, for their part, open with empty skies (*croisée . . . vacante*, 9) and conclude with the sudden emergence of a constellation. (This, indeed, is the force of the word "immediately" [*sitôt*, 14]: our attention is drawn to the fact that the appearance of stars is an *event*.) On either side of the Master's removal from the room, which occupies the very center of the poem (lines 7–8), we perceive a matching pair of incidents given in opposite spatial, temporal, and indeed evaluative order, like two panels of an almost symmetrical diptych.[35] To the left, a lofty constellation preceded by an anguishing death by fire; to the right, an agonizing death by fire followed triumphantly by stars.[36]

A Replacement Faith

If, then, we wish to find an allegorical meaning in the sonnet—and all the capitalized nouns are loudly urging us to do so, albeit only as a temporary measure, as a stepping-stone toward an overall appreciation of the poem—we must clearly start here, from this twice-told tale: *a nymph dies in fire, and a constellation is born.* The flavor is clearly Ovidian, and there may in fact be a direct, if partial, allusion here to the story of Callisto, a beautiful nymph turned by Jupiter into the constellation Ursa Major, after having been changed into a bear by a jealous Juno[37] (this would account for the stars appearing *immediately* following the death of the nymph [14] and for them appearing in a *north*-facing window [9]).[38] But since Mallarmé's incinerated *nixe* is the counterpart of the incinerated *rêve* in the first panel of the diptych, we should rewrite the story as follows: a *dream* dies and a constellation is born.

We can go further. Based on the contrastive *encor que* (12–13) in the second half of the poem—unicorns kill the nixie, *yet* the constellation appears—and based on the dual action of Anguish in the first half, literally holding up stars and figuratively upholding murdered fantasies, we can infer that the constellation not only follows but somehow *replaces* the dream. And the poem is generous enough to offer us, at strategic intervals throughout the first three stanzas, further indications as to how to understand the latter. For the tables are not just tables, or *consoles* as they were in the 1868 version, but *crédences*, connoting faith; the window is no mere *fenêtre*, but instead a cruciform *croisée*;[39] each lost dream is a *rêve vespéral* (as in vespers), not just a *rêve du soir*; Anguish is not just holding up its nails but, like a lamp-carrier in a sacred ritual (*lampadophore*), dedicating (*dédiant*) them to the night. And so we should rewrite again: what the constellation replaces is *religious* faith, faith in what Mallarmé, after describing an epiphanic night one year before writing the first version of his sonnet, called "that old nefarious plumage, fortunately floored, God."[40]

If a constellation is capable of replacing religious faith, this is because a constellation is more than simply a collection of stars. It is a set arbitrarily carved out from among the dense cluster on view, deemed to belong with each other and not with the rest; a set, furthermore, on which a *shape* has been imposed, by a doubly bold act of human intervention into the non-human world.[41] What before was chaos now comes forth as order; where contingency reigned, now there is a certain internal necessity, as each point of light has to be just where it is for the posited shape to hold. The constellation confers upon each of its members a raison d'être, and all by an act of human will. Unlike the theological *kosmos* it replaces, then, a constellation is *an ordering that tacitly admits its own arbitrariness*.

Once we recognize this, we can see that the poem is actually a three-act drama of enchantment, disenchantment, and re-enchantment.[42] First there is faith in an external source of transcendence, in a suprahuman agency capable of delivering an oracular pronouncement that would make sense of everything; then the death of such dreams, as sunset gives way to darkness; and finally the emergence of a new, secular, minor-key affirmation, a principle at least of structure and necessity, even if meaning has been lost.[43] Like Nietzsche, Mallarmé leaves us with the hope that "one can endure to live in a meaningless world," as long as one "organizes a small portion of it oneself."[44]

How to Do Things with Verses

As I suggested earlier, however, merely to *say* this would not be to re-enchant the world. Mallarmé's poem must also do what it says, enact the organization of which it speaks. It must, in fact, live up to its earlier title, "Sonnet allégorique de lui-même" ("Sonnet allegorical of itself"),[45] by working a spell and, at the same time, indicating how the spell operates, showing where to look in order to see the results of its magic. And that, it turns out, is exactly what the poem does. It is indeed its own allegory—not just an allegory of poetry in general, nor yet an allegory of Mallarméan poetry, but an allegory of *itself*—in that its surface stands for its depth, which is to say, in that its visible drama stands for what the poem is quietly doing behind the scenes. For just as the visible drama presents the demise of old forms of enchantment (superseded evening dreams, archaic spirits) and their replacement by newly-forged patterns (the septet of stars), so too the action of the poem operates by preliminary destruction of the reader's anticipated expectations and subsequent compensation in the guise of immaculate formal perfection.

Based on our prior encounters with lyric poetry in general, and with the sonnet form in particular, we may well expect "Ses purs ongles" to offer insight into nature (what the night sky looks like, say, when poetically seen), into the poet's soul (what powerful emotions look like when they are "recollected in tranquillity"), or at the very least into the poet's mind (what experience looks like when filtered through the lens of genius). Not so, however. There is barely any description here (in fact, a fair amount of space is devoted to what is *not* present: no funereal urn, nothing in the "vacant" window, only credenzas in the otherwise "empty room"). There is also no mention of love affairs, either celebrated or mourned; nothing about the difficulty of writing (despite what one line of interpretation has advanced);[46] indeed, not so much as a first-person pronoun.[47] The "master" has left the room—which is to say, the poet has become impersonal. ("I am now impersonal," Mallarmé famously informed his friend Cazalis, "and no longer the Stéphane you have known, but a capacity the Spiritual universe has for looking at itself and developing itself, through that which was me.")[48] If there is a subject here, it is something like the transcendental subject, not reducible to any particular observer; just as the tears well from the Styx rather than the Master's eye, so the anguish is not Mallarmé's in particular but capital-A *Angoisse*, an aspect of the human condition at large.

It is not, mind you, that the poet is *entirely* absent, as a number of critics have suggested.[49] Mallarmé's oft-quoted statement to the effect that "the pure work implies the elocutory disappearance of the poet, who cedes the initiative to words"[50] is actually somewhat misleading. For the poet's presence is in fact directly on show here, in the telltale qualifier "perhaps" (*peut-être*, 10); clearly *someone* is looking at this scene, otherwise there would be no one to doubt what is being witnessed.[51] More importantly, the words are not simply allowed free rein to generate infinite connections, all equally arbitrary, among themselves.[52] On the contrary, the poet's control is, as we are about to see, so vice-like in its grip as to be felt on every line. What is missing, then, is not the poet per se but the individual *personality* of the poet. Gone is the suffering or exultant lyrical subject of Romanticism. Gone are the elaborate thought processes of Baudelairean verse. What we find instead is an impeccable structure enclosing almost nothing, "an empty sonnet, reflecting itself in every way":[53] no divine voice from beyond the poem, just a manmade principle of order meticulously imposed upon chaos.

A Corner of Order

And manmade order is absolutely ubiquitous. We have already seen how the events in the poem find themselves neatly mirrored from one panel to the other. But the highly unusual rhyme scheme forms its own brace of mirror images, again preserving the pairing while reversing the polarity (the *-yx* rhymes become "feminine," the *-or* rhymes "masculine," in the second half of the poem).[54] The poem's visual dimension even motivates its overall form. It has to be a sonnet, that is, so that it can contain twice seven lines—a quatrain plus a tercet set outside, in the realm of the real stars; a quatrain plus a tercet set inside, in the realm of the reflections—just as the scene it depicts shows us seven stars reflected in a mirror.[55]

Indeed everything, one wants to say, has its immovable place in this poem; everything is exactly what and where it has to be. The starlight *has* to precede darkness in the first half and follow it in the second; the tercets *must* begin low, the quatrains high. The tables, as we saw above, have to be *crédences*, the window a *croisée*, the fingernails *dedicated* to the night. The unicorns must be unicorns, rather than, say, griffons, because the unicorn is related to the real-life oryx, and "oryx" is the only possible combination of the poem's two ubiquitous rhymes.[56] So too the ptyx can be nothing else if it is to be a container and to rhyme as fully as possible with Styx (as well, presumably, as summoning to religious minds the *pyx*, container for the Eucharist).[57] And then, the second line of the quatrains calls to mind the second line of the tercets—not only is *agonise* a near-anagram of *Angoisse*, but each is followed by the identical phoneme [sə]—just as the third calls to mind the third, "*feu . . . nixe*" almost bringing a departed *Phénix* back to life.[58]

This general principle of overdetermination builds, as it happens, to a stunning climax. The poem's concluding clause—"se fixe/De scintillations sitôt le septuor" (literally, "there fixes itself of scintillations immediately the septet")—is tortured by hyperbaton, that is, by rearrangement of the normal syntactic order, with the express purpose of keeping *scintillations* before *sitôt* and *sitôt* before *septuor*. For only in this way will the last two lines count out, almost subliminally, the appearance of seven stars in the sky: *cadre* (quatre), *scintilla-tions* (cinq), *sitôt* (six), *septuor* (sept).[59] By the time we reach the final word, we are more than prepared for it. We know, of course, that it has to rhyme in *-or*. We know that it must point again to the constellation of stars evoked in line 1; and it makes sense for the constellation to have seven stars, in part because of the Callisto allusion, in part because only a reflected constellation of seven stars can stand, allegorically, for a sonnet. But then *septuor* is itself a word of seven letters, indeed of seven *distinct* letters; as septet, it connotes music, another manmade form indifferent to content, and thus picks up on the sonorous vacuity of the abolished *ptyx*; and it sends us, for good measure, all the way back to the beginning, since every last phoneme of *le septuor* is contained within those of **ses purs ongles très haut**.[60] No other word would do anywhere near as well.

In all these cases, a word ends up (at least) doubly motivated, finding itself at the locus of contact between two (or more) intersecting lines. As though each term were the solution to a cryptic crossword clue,[61] we know it is right—we know it is the only possible choice—not merely because its meaning is appropriate but also because its phonetic substance fits. Every single piece of the Mallarméan world acquires an aura of indispensability, almost inevitability, not because it captures adequately some mystical truth about the world, or some emotive truth about the poet,[62] but because it *is the only logical outcome of a self-imposed puzzle*. It gains legitimacy by virtue of its place within the poetic system, rather than (just) by virtue of what it points to outside it; each element, as Proust would put it, receives its raison d'être from all the others.[63]

The Magic of Rhyme

In other words, the poem forms a magic circle from within which all contingency is banished. That is what Mallarmé means, in "Magie," when he speaks of the magic circle opened and closed by rhyme: if the first rhyme-word appears random ("opening" the circle), the second becomes necessary ("closing" it), and—strikingly—*ends up imparting a type of retrospective necessity to the first.* There is, a priori, no reason why Mallarmé should use the word *onyx* rather than, say, *opale* at the end of line 1, but once *onyx* is in place, *Phénix* makes sense, *Styx* appears obvious, and *ptyx* itself somehow feels as though it belongs, even before we know what, if anything, it means. (It is almost as though, in Mallarmé's famous and disingenuous remark, the word had been generated ex nihilo "by the magic of rhyme.")[64] But then in turn *Styx, ptyx,* and *Phénix* force us, on rereading the poem, to accept *onyx* as the one and only possible choice of initial rhyme. Rhyme, as Mallarmé puts it, repudiates chance.

And rhyme, though of primordial importance for Mallarmé, who often knew the ends of his lines before he knew anything else, is synecdochic for aesthetic practice more generally. Literature at large is nothing other than the relentless elimination of chance, the construction of a protected space over which randomness has no hold. The real world is full of haphazard, happenstance objects, people, events; the created world, by contrast, is one in which everything has a necessary place. And ordinary *language* is made up of haphazard, happenstance *words*, whose connection to ideas is in every case contingent—"next to *ombre* [shadow]," Mallarmé famously complains, "*ténèbres* [darkness] isn't very dark; what disappointment in the face of the perversity that confers on *jour* [day] and *nuit* [night], contradictorily, a somber tone for the one, a bright for the other!"[65]—whereas poetic language is made up of *lines*, units designed precisely to compensate for this insufficiency. The line of verse, a "total word, new, outside of language, almost incantatory," overcomes the arbitrariness inherent in the separate terms.[66] Thus Mallarmé's sonnet does not merely *speak* of constellations; it *is* a constellation, a manmade imposition of order onto an unruly universe. To immerse oneself in "Ses purs ongles" is, for a space, to breathe a different, and purer, air.

To put it another way, to immerse oneself in "Ses purs ongles" is to live, for the first time, in a world of soundlessness. In the ideal poem, we recall, "allusive words, never direct, reduc[e] themselves to an even silence." For, paradoxical as it may seem, silence is never a given; silence is, instead, always to be *created*. While there is, admittedly, such a thing as a stillness that precedes poetry, this stillness is full of virtual noise, of competing hypotheses and capricious speculations. After poetry, by contrast, "chance having been defeated word by word, without fail the white space returns, gratuitous a moment ago, certain now, in order to conclude that nothing [lies] beyond and to authenticate the silence."[67]

The Stygian hush that follows poetry is authentic, unlike the uneasy peace preceding it, because the former has been produced by a form of speech that expressly targets noise, canceling it out. Chance must be defeated word by word.
Music, which might at first appear to have the edge over poetry, since from
start to end it is purely abstract, reveals itself to be poetry's inferior for precisely the same reason. Content cannot simply be avoided; it must be *destroyed*.
Just as we can reach an idea of nothingness only by continually imagining
objects and then their absence[68]—which is exactly what happens when we are
presented with the nonexistent amphora and the nonexistent *ptyx*—so too all
false hopes, all evening dreams, all personal feelings must be summoned in
order to be eliminated one by one, leaving just silence, white space, and absolute order.[69]

A Training in Enchantment

Does this count, however, as a genuine re-enchantment of the world? It could
easily be argued that replacing the world is hardly the same as re-enchanting it.
Quite the contrary, it might seem that we are being offered a mere *evasion* from
the world, a refuge within a cosmos that is perfectly ordered but that does not
exist. Perhaps poetry leaves the world itself just as it is; perhaps the latter's in-
adequacies become, if anything, only the more glaring as a result of our immer-
sion in an ideal environment. (This is, after all, Nietzsche's wholesale verdict on
two-world systems.) Wherein would reside the superiority of such escapism over
earlier forms of illusory enchantment?

The answer is, first of all, that the sonnet does more than produce an alternative world. It provides, at the same time, a set of implicit instructions for
bringing aesthetic ordering techniques to bear on the *real* one. The sonnet does
not offer itself as a lesson on the truth of existence—does not seek to teach us
that, say, God is dead—but offers itself, instead, as a literary training-ground.
Rather than gaining a set of *facts* about human life, we stand to learn a *method*
for coming to terms with them, a method for projecting a network of interrela-
tions onto the raw data of experience. ("Things exist, we do not have to create
them; we have only to seize the connections among them," writes Mallarmé,
"and it is the threads of these connections that form verses and orchestras.")[70]
Our engagement with a microcosm in which the threads are drawn together as
tightly as they can possibly be is, at least potentially, a training for re-engage-
ment with the macrocosm, for an engagement in which we ourselves may find
and invent the links, forging a world that, *even though each of its elements remains
untouched*, suddenly acquires order, and thus suddenly becomes livable.[71] We
should, in other words, understand Mallarmé's entire project of overdetermination as a figure for the importation of apparent necessity into objects and events
in the extrapoetic universe; if, like Mallarmé, we experience "a rather cabalistic

sensation"[72] on repeating the poem to ourselves, it is not just by virtue of being transported to another realm. The spell works, if we wish it to, on ours as well.

What is more, there is something *sublime*, in the Kantian sense, about the experience of "Ses purs ongles." In the space of a mere fourteen lines, comprising exactly one hundred words, Mallarmé has set up a network of such complexity that it feels almost impossible for any reader to hold all of its filaments in his or her head at once—let alone for any writer to have deliberately produced them.[73] We are overwhelmed by the cosmic magnitude of this tiny poem. And the author-figure we are forced to postulate in order to account for its effects is something more than human, something more than the empirical Stéphane Mallarmé, burning the midnight oil in Tournon. Our universe is enriched by contact with an intelligence of a different order from ours.

A Sequence of States

We should not forget, however, that Mallarmé has promised more than just this for his poetic magic. Out from the silence of absolute necessity, against the background of constructed darkness, something luminous and musical is supposed to emerge, something that Mallarmé, in his article on magic, calls the idea of an object.[74] Like the constellation, it shimmers (*scintille*) before our credulous gaze. And indeed, something more than order attaches to Ursa Major after we have made "Ses purs ongles" our own. From now on, we will see it differently: no longer as a collection of bright objects in the night sky, but as the symbol for poetic hope, for the capacity of the human imagination to re-enchant the world by giving it an arrangement of our own making. The constellation turns, so to speak, into the symbol of symbolism; the stars, having already been granted structure, now acquire a *meaning* into the bargain. Mallarméan poetry becomes a formal model for the imposition not just of form but of *idea*.

Perhaps we will even start to imagine these stars sending such signals on their own initiative, fixing *themselves* in the mirror (the middle voice of line 13), as though they really did incarnate the nymph Callisto. Perhaps, in other words, we will begin to believe, animistically, that enchantment is something we may discover in the world around us, not something we are required to create. This, as the "Magie" passage clearly indicates, would of course be an illusion ("cela scintille, à *l'illusion* du regard"). Yet it would be an illusion that we could sustain *even in the face of the knowledge that it is one*.[75] And that brings us to the final, and most important, function of Mallarmé's poem, the function that requires us at last to address the enigmatic *ptyx*.

What exactly *is* a ptyx? The question has been hotly debated,[76] in a way and to an extent that is frankly baffling. For Mallarmé makes it quite plain, in "Le mystère dans les lettres," that obscure lyrical works must be ultimately intelligible, the guarantee of intelligibility being *syntax*.[77] And the syntax around *ptyx* is, in fact, decisive. From the conjunction in line 7 (*car*) and the demonstrative adjective in line 8 (*ce*), we can be absolutely sure that the ptyx is identical with the object used to draw water from the Styx. Whatever it is, then, it must be capable of holding liquid (which would rather rule out Graham Robb's "writing tablet"[78]). But we can also tell that its absence is logically linked to the absence of funereal urns; the lack of urns and the lack of ptyx are, after all, connected by a colon ("gathered by no funereal urn . . .: no ptyx"). It is not just that there is no urn *and* no ptyx, as it would be if the two were separated by a semicolon. Instead, it is that ptyxlessness *explains* urnlessness. And this can happen only if the two are identical. No urns *because* no ptyx: ptyx, in this poem at least, is simply a synonym for urn.[79] Syntax guarantees intelligibility; the context of the poem is, and is designed to be, sufficient, without recourse to any Greek lexicon.

We are left, in short, with a word that has a clear meaning, but one given entirely by the surrounding context. And stranger things are to follow:

Sur les crédences, au salon vide: nul	On the credenzas, in the empty room: no
ptyx,	ptyx,
Aboli bibelot d'inanité sonore . . .	Eradicated knickknack of sonorous inanity . . .

An extraordinary set of shifts takes place here within the space of twelve words, shifts not in plot or even in meaning but in *the way the poem is to be read*, shifts not in *what* words mean but in *how* they mean, indeed in *whether* their function is to mean at all. The stanza begins reassuringly, with solid, familiar, and present objects (credenzas). But this referential use of language gives way to what we might call an *anti*-referential use of language: *nul ptyx*, two words whose effect is at once to summon and to banish the same mental representation. And from there we move, even more daringly, to what is almost a *non*-referential use of language, the assonance in "aboli bibelot" being so rich that it is barely possible to hear a meaning underneath the flow of sounds. "Aboli bibelot" is practically nonsense poetry; it can be understood, to be sure, but what it says is redundant (we already know the ptyx is not there), and its powerful harmonies simply drown out sense.

Nor do we stop here. Instead we end up in a *self*-referential use of language. It is not the *object* ptyx that is of "sonorous inanity"; it is instead the *word* "ptyx," a word that functions semantically as a placeholder, but fits the rhyme scheme perfectly.[80] Or perhaps it is the phrase "aboli bibelot" that is sonorously inane, for reasons we have just given; perhaps the second half of line 6 refers to nothing other than the first half of line 6. Either way, reference to the external world is suspended, and our attention is further divided. We imagine perceiving real objects; we imagine perceiving the absence of objects; we hear the musicality of consonant phonemes; and we catch the poem in the act of producing those phonemes. Our oscillation between states—an oscillation continually repeated as the poem forces us to reread it multiple times—is, if we use the spell correctly, a training in the two skills that make life bearable: generating fictions, and persuading ourselves that they are true.[81]

Postscript: The Birth of Modernism from the Spirit of Re-Enchantment

The ultimate function of Mallarmé's poetry, then, is identical to that of Robert-Houdin's magic performances: what it offers us is an opportunity to *hone our capacity for lucid self-delusion*. For Mallarmé, there is nothing beyond the world we know—"certes, n'est que ce qui est" (to be sure, there is only what is)—yet at the same time no escape from the need to believe that there is something more.[82] We human beings require illusions in order to live, and the only dignity left us is the capacity to choose our own illusions, and to acknowledge them for what they are. "Yes, I know," wrote Mallarmé to Cazalis,

> we are but vain forms of matter, yet quite sublime for having invented God and our soul. So sublime, my friend! that I wish to offer myself this spectacle of matter, conscious of being and yet frenetically throwing itself into the Dream that it is able *not* to be, singing the Soul and all those similar divine impressions that have accumulated in us since the dawn of time and proclaiming, before the Nothing that is the truth, these glorious lies![83]

We are back, once again, in the three-part drama of re-enchantment. We began with belief in the "divine impressions" accumulated over the millennia of early human history; we had a moment of insight, suddenly seizing the truth in ourselves ("vain forms of matter") and in the world around us ("Nothing"); finally, however, we rejected even this rejection, understanding that the illusion is evidence not just of our credulity but also of our *creativity*,[84] that God and the soul are therefore not just lies but *glorious* lies, and lies—most important of all—of which we can and should be *conscious*, even as we believe in them. Mallarmé's key intuition is that a maximally constructed, maximally self-conscious poetry is the ideal site for spiritual exercises in this domain. It is by reading such writings, by spending time in their world, that we may hope to develop the capacities we have for seeing our own world as orderly, while taking a distance, at the same time, from any given structure we impose.

One of the defining features of modernist (including "postmodernist") literature is its tendency toward "reflexivity," toward the establishment and simultaneous undermining of referential illusion,[85] in comic and non-comic genres alike. Thus James Joyce, after giving very believable life to Molly Bloom, has her beseech him in the middle of her monologue "O Jamesy let me up out of this"; Marcel Proust constructs an extraordinarily elaborate fictional world, only to let a narratorial voice announce that "everything has been invented by me in accordance with the requirements of my demonstration"; on the first page of Gide's *Paludes*, the narrator blithely mentions that he happens to be writing a novel called *Paludes*; M. C. Escher depicts a pair of hands, each impossibly drawn by the other; close to the conclusion of Samuel Beckett's tragedy *Endgame*, Hamm announces "I'm warming up for my last soliloquy"; Eugène Ionesco's king, in *Le roi se meurt*, is told he will die "at the end of the play"; Bertolt Brecht's actors deliberately show that they are actors, rather than attempting to disappear behind the characters they are playing; Italo Calvino's novel *If on a Winter's Night a Traveler* begins "You are about to begin reading Italo Calvino's new novel, *If on a winter's night a traveler*"; and so on, and so on.[86] Serious, representation-undermining self-reflexivity, which until then had been something of a rarity (the German Romantics had theorized it, but few major works had instantiated it in recognizable ways[87]), now becomes the dominant literary mode.[88]

But why? So far three main theories have been advanced, which I shall call the *symptomatic*, the *strategic*, and the *informative* hypotheses. According to the symptomatic hypothesis, reflexivity in modernist literature is simply a sign of authorial self-doubt, itself in turn an index of a more general cultural tendency toward self-consciousness: when subjects of knowledge become increasingly aware of their own activity as knowers, as well as of the objects known, it is inevitable (so the symptomatic account runs) that literary artifacts should be infected with the same disease.[89] On the strategic view, by contrast, reflexivity is something deliberately, not unconsciously, deployed by writers, and something deployed precisely as a strategy for *bypassing* the critical spirit of the age. Legitimately anticipating skepticism on the part of the average reader, authors permit themselves a moment of pathos by preemptively ironizing it, or at least by ironizing almost everything else. Only one who, like Proust's narrator, has treated love and friendship with the utmost suspicion has the right to move us by recounting the death of his grandmother.[90] For we no longer trust naive, spontaneous outbursts of enthusiasm; what we trust is, instead, the passion of a cynic.

In a second variant of the strategic approach, self-reflexivity is seen as a way of *controlling* the critical spirit. Consider the predicament of Denis Diderot, author of *Jacques le fataliste*, one of the most reflexive works of the eighteenth century (rivaled perhaps only by its forebear, *Tristram Shandy*). There is a voice within Diderot that loudly pronounces free will to be an illusion, since humans are a part of nature and since nature is ruled by iron laws of cause and effect. Another voice, however, just as firmly maintains that this cannot (and had better not) be true. The result: "I fume at being entangled in a devilish philosophy that my mind cannot keep from approving and my heart from denying."[91] Who, then,

actually speaks for the conflicted Diderot in *Jacques*? Is it the fatalist title character? The latter's voluntarist master? Or the narrator, who repeatedly insists on
his freedom to tell whatever story he likes? The answer is that it cannot be any of
them—not least because none of them even speaks (unequivocally) for himself:
the ostensibly fatalist Jacques is incapable of sticking to his beliefs, the ostensibly voluntarist master behaves like an automaton, and the ostensibly free-
wheeling narrator is fully controlled by Diderot. On the contrary, the novel as a
whole is what enables Diderot precisely *not* to take a stand, to identify himself
neither with the cynical voice within him that declares all action to be determined in advance nor with the credulous voice that proclaims a continuing faith
in the *libre arbitre*, but instead with the observer who coolly and amusedly registers the internal debate. In cases of intractable inner conflict, when it is impossible to synthesize both positions and just as impossible to jettison either, the
choice is between denial and a smiling ascent to Olympian detachment; Romantic
irony is the only road to equanimity.[92]

It is also, to draw on the third and final variant of the strategic view, a path to
freedom. Not just freedom from inner division, and not just freedom from excessive emotion, but freedom from everything that we are and everything we
have been. "We must rise above what we love and be able to destroy in our
thoughts what we adore," writes Friedrich Schlegel, for "whatever does not annihilate itself is not free."[93] Why? Because freedom, when understood as Gidean
disponibilité—the capacity to do anything at any time—requires a thoroughgoing unmooring of commitments.[94] If I am to be completely *disponible*, it is not
enough for me to stand clear of my attachments to religion, family, state, and
community: I must also stand clear of my own most cherished achievements,
beliefs, and capacities. I must, in short, attain freedom from *myself*. And thus
Romantic irony, as a disparagement of the very work to which so much energy
and love is being devoted, becomes, in some hands, a strategy for liberation.

In spite of the power of the strategic hypothesis in its three variants—
Romantic irony as means to smuggle in emotion, to stand clear of division, to
remain infinitely *disponible*—the most prominent hypothesis today is no doubt
the *informative*, which holds that the function of modernist reflexivity is to *tell
us something*. Thus Malcolm Bradbury and James McFarlane, in their authoritative book on Modernism, define the latter as "a new era of high aesthetic
self-consciousness and non-representationalism, in which art turns from realism and humanistic representation towards style, technique, and spatial form
in pursuit of a deeper penetration of life" (25, my emphasis). In other words, reflexivity permits the discovery, and subsequent transmission, of something that
had not been seen before. And that something is usually taken to be what Astradur Eysteinsson calls "the social 'fabrication' of reality,"[95] or what Patricia Waugh
calls the "fictionality of the world." As Waugh puts it, self-reflexive works
"explore the possible fictionality of the world outside the literary fictional text"

(2); "in showing us how literary fiction creates its imaginary worlds, metafiction helps us to understand how the reality we live day by day is similarly constructed" (18–19).[96] Just as we allow ourselves to believe in the existence of Pip, Estella, and Magwitch while reading *Great Expectations*, so we allow ourselves to believe in the existence of our life and everything it contains. A self-reflexive text like *Paludes*, on the other hand, continually reminds us that it is made up—and by so doing asks us to see that the same is true outside the novel.[97]

Stéphane Mallarmé would, it seems to me, reject the premise that the world is a fiction. "Les choses existent" ("things exist"), he is entirely happy to acknowledge. For him as for Nietzsche, the problem with life is, if anything, precisely the opposite: reality is *all too real*; deadly truths are all too easy to come by. What we need in response is not a mechanism for seeing through illusions but, quite the contrary, a technique for producing and sustaining them. And it is this technique, as I have argued, that readers stand to practice when they engage with Mallarmé's writings. These writings undermine the referential illusion they set up not because they reflect, willy-nilly, a tide of self-doubt, and certainly not because they have something important to tell us about the "fictionality of the world"; they do not even have as their primary function the removal of Mallarmé from his own inner divisions, however powerful a byproduct this may be. No, the explanation for Mallarméan reflexivity does not reside in the informative hypothesis, or in the symptomatic, or in the strategic. Rather, Mallarméan reflexivity must be understood as *formative*, as designed to offer practice in an increasingly vital skill. It is no coincidence that aesthetic self-consciousness becomes dominant just when philosophy begins to recognize the inescapability of "necessary illusions" (Nietzsche, Vaihinger, and company); poems like "Ses purs ongles," novels like *Paludes*, drawings like *Tekenen*, and plays like *Endgame* are *training-grounds for lucid self-delusion*, for the tenacious maintenance of fantasy in the face of the facts. They are what makes possible the re-enchantment of the world.

PART THREE

LOGIC AND ANTI-LOGIC

4

Plato

Fallacy and Logic

Schrecklich ist die Verführung zur Güte!
(Terrible is the temptation to do good!)
— Bertolt Brecht, *The Caucasian Chalk Circle*

What does it mean to apply the principle of charity to works like the *Symposium* and the *Gorgias*? Not, I would like to suggest, what is usually assumed. Generations of scholars have spent thousands of hours constructing elaborate defenses for the statements made therein by Socrates—that punishment is good for the criminal, that Pericles was a bad politician, that Socrates was a good politician, that desire always implies lack, that pleasure always involves pain, that rhetoric requires no skill and imparts no benefits, that we are irresistibly drawn to those activities we know to be good for us—as though this were the way to do justice to Plato. To be sure, if we were dealing with treatises, it would be only fair to construe the various arguments in as compelling a manner as possible. But since we are dealing with dialogues, and with an author who never speaks in his own voice, I would propose that we apply a *literary*[1] principle of charity. While the philosophical principle of charity urges us to assume that the ideas in a text are true until proven otherwise, the literary principle of charity states that it may, under certain circumstances, be more generous to assume that some of them are false, obviously false, known to be false, *designed* to be false. Ironically, the attempt to be charitable in the first sense can easily lead us to be unkind in the second; the "charitable" scholars risk turning Plato into a lesser mind.

When it comes to the *Symposium* and the *Gorgias*, as I hope to show here, many of Socrates' key claims simply cannot and should not be saved. In the *Symposium*, Socrates treats Agathon to a display of manifest sophistry, and then goes on to make a speech whose central presupposition is defeated by the very existence of Alcibiades, a walking counterexample. In the *Gorgias*, Socrates deploys premises Plato gives us every reason to reject, and concludes with a tirade whose length and whose bitterness bespeak despairing *ressentiment* rather than magisterial wisdom. Should we say, to be charitable, that Socrates' arguments are good *simpliciter*, or good when properly understood, or good when slightly amended, or good enough for his interlocutors, or good enough for the ancient Greeks? We should not. No appeal to Socratic irony, no deployment of the developmental hypothesis, no amount of tinkering will redeem them. Charity consists, here, in cutting them loose, in refraining from the temptation to attribute to an author the views of one of his characters. Charity consists in understanding the role of fiction in the project of a thinker whose aims are formative as much as informative, and for whom philosophy is above all a way of life. It consists, in other words, in understanding the function of bad arguments in excellent works of philosophy.

A Platonic Coccyx

The irruption of a drunken, unruly Alcibiades into the singularly placid thinking-party of the *Symposium* has presented aficionados of Plato's philosophy with a bit of a puzzle. What need is there for any more discussion, once Socrates has finally revealed the ultimate truth about Eros and the good life, simultaneously synthesizing and transcending all previous contributions, bringing the dialogue to a tidy and powerful conclusion? Doesn't the final speech, which Socrates will subsequently call a "little satyr play" ($\sigma\alpha\tau\nu\rho\iota\kappa\acute{o}\nu \ldots \delta\rho\hat{\alpha}\mu\alpha$, 222d),[2] feel somewhat anticlimactic, not to say bathetic, or at least as otiose and awkward as a vestigial appendage? What are we to do, in short, with this Platonic coccyx?

Some have reacted by pretending it does not exist: one eighteenth-century English translation surreptitiously omits the Alcibiades section, stopping at Stephanus page 212a,[3] and so do at least two critical studies of the *Symposium*.[4] Others have sought to account for it by saying that it completes the dialogue, proving that Socrates' theories are fulfilled in his praxis, since he *incarnates* the ideal lover, as well as just describing him. What once looked like a threat to the dialogue's coherence now starts to look like a necessity: "there *had* to be a concluding part," writes Paul Friedländer, "in which the ascent to the heights would be depicted in the reality of actual life" (3:28, my emphasis); "this apparently accidental after-thought," adds Theodor Gomperz, "is the true root from which the whole work sprang" (394).[5] Many have since agreed that "Plato's chief purpose in this speech is to show us that Socrates put into practice the morality implicit in Diotima's theory" (Dover, 164); "its main purpose is to present to us a vivid portrait of Socrates as the perfect exemplar of Eros" (Bury, lx); "Socrates confirms the value of inner beauty" (D. Frede, 410n23); "Socrates emerges as the star example of the philosophic lover" (Santas 1988:15); "in the *Symposium* the great lover in the spiritual sense is Socrates himself, as we learn from Alcibiades' speech" (Burnyeat, 55).[6] As a corollary, the scene purportedly serves to exonerate the historical Socrates from charges brought against him, whether of "indulging in impure relations with his disciples" (Bury, lx) or of corrupting the youth in other, less sexual ways. (Socrates cannot have made Alcibiades vicious, Plato is taken to be suggesting, because Alcibiades was vicious to begin with.) Thus, according to R. E. Allen, "Plato's portrait of Socrates in the *Symposium* is a powerful defense of Socrates" (1984, 2:106); "the entire work," Richard Patterson concurs, is "Platonic praise of Socrates" (212).[7]

I will leave aside the question of how a dialogue that is made up, using an imaginary "Alcibiades" to defend an equally imaginary "Socrates," can vindicate a historical person. (Suffice it to add that if Gregory Vlastos is right, and the Socrates we see in the dialogue is massively distinct from the Socrates we hear about in Alcibiades' speech,[8] the issue becomes even more complicated.) For now, I just want to ask how the *Symposium* could ever be considered to place Socrates, even the *character* Socrates, in an entirely favorable light. For what Alcibiades actually does is to undermine—merely by existing—a key premise of the speech in which, so generations of Plato scholars have agreed, we learn what Plato has to teach us about love, goodness, and philosophy. His function in the dialogue is not to confirm Socrates' claims but, on the contrary, to place them in doubt; it is to raise questions that are not answered; it is to generate effects that a straightforward treatise, like the works of Aristotle, could never hope to produce.

Ascent and Dissent

Consider, first, the Ascent from desire to philosophy, so memorably described by Diotima at the end of her speech, and so heartily endorsed by Socrates in statements bookending it.[9] A man[10] may start out desiring a particular boy, the story runs, but he will soon become aware that the beauty of all boys is the same, and hence become a lover of beautiful bodies in general (210b). Next he will realize that souls are even more beautiful than bodies, and find himself transformed as a result into a lover of beautiful souls (even those housed in not-so-beautiful bodies). From his new vantage point on the third rung of the ladder, he will perceive that the beauty of souls is the same as other types of beauty—that of customs and, especially, that of knowledge—and accordingly end up a lover of knowledge (210c). Finally, recognizing that all such things (bodies, souls, customs, knowledge) are beautiful by virtue of partaking in a common essence, the Beautiful itself, he will blossom into an admirer of Beauty (210d). Forsaking "human flesh [and] any other great nonsense of mortality," he will direct his devoted gaze (θεᾶσθαι) and his desire for union (συνεῖναι) away from the beloved and onto the Form, remaining its companion for the rest of his natural life.[11]

What is striking here is not just the fact that the Ascent requires us to leave the beloved behind—a thought chilling enough to have provoked straightforward, text-denying disavowals from conciliatory interpreters[12]—but also the fact that absolutely nothing is needed, beyond the mere apprehension of our error, in order to move us up from one level to the next. As soon as we perceive (intellectually) that we are mistaken, and that what we really love is, say, not the beauty of bodies but the beauty of souls, we will automatically surrender our initial desire and enthusiastically embrace a new one.[13] Even before we reach the highest plane of enlightenment, that vision of Forms which allows us to understand what beauty actually is in itself, and which thus confirms our local insights to have sent us on each occasion in the right general direction, we find ourselves irresistibly driven by reason. In short, according to the uncompromisingly intellectualist Socrates of the *Symposium*, a calculus of desiderata is entirely sufficient to motivate action.

What, then, can possibly be holding Alcibiades back? Why is Alcibiades not on the stairway to virtue? His calculus of desiderata is just as it should be, and even finds itself expressed in impeccably Socratic idiom. Socrates, he laments,

> makes me admit that my political career is a waste of time, while all that matters is just what I most neglect: my personal shortcomings [ὅτι . . . αὐτὸς ἔτι ἐμαυτοῦ μὲν ἀμελῶ], which cry out for the closest attention. So I refuse to listen to him; I stop my ears and tear myself away from him, for, like the Sirens, he could make me stay by his side till I die. Socrates is the only man in the world who has made me feel shame. . . . I know perfectly well that I can't prove he's wrong when he tells me what I should do; yet, the moment I leave his side, I go back to my old ways: I cave in to my desire to please the crowd. My whole life has become one constant effort to escape from him and keep away, but when I see him, I feel deeply ashamed, because I'm doing nothing about my way of life, though I have already agreed with him that I should. (216a–b)

Not merely susceptible at an instinctive level to the erotic attraction of philosophy, Alcibiades also seems to understand fairly well both its means (refutation, agreement) and its ends (care of the self [ἐπιμέλεια ἑαυτοῦ]),[14] and senses that such care is far more important than any political activity. And he has only to *suppose* Socratic conversation to be good for him, if the implicit psychology of the Ascent (or indeed the explicit philosophy of the *Protagoras*) is correct, in order to lose all temptation to stray from the master's side. By rights, he should be a philosopher by now. But he is not one. And the explanation for this fact could not be simpler: like most of us, he knows what he should be doing, but he enjoys doing something else. While his reason informs him of his duty, the irrational parts of his soul (drives toward sex on the one hand, glory on the other) sing a different, and louder, song. As Alcibiades himself says so eloquently, he caves in to desire.[15]

In short, Alcibiades disproves Socrates' speech not by arguing against it (he has, after all, not heard it) but *merely by existing*.[16] For those readers who pay attention only to what is explicitly stated, the *Symposium* says that progress is merely a matter of increased awareness. But for those who are alive to characterization, the dialogue *shows* that increased awareness is, on Plato's view, far from being sufficient. Alcibiades forms a direct counterexample to one of Socrates' key premises, simply by being the living, breathing, drunkenly staggering incarnation of motivational conflict that he is.[17] His very existence constitutes proof positive that Plato (who is, after all, his creator) understands something Socrates does not—that motivational conflict is part of human nature—and hence that Socrates is not, contrary to a belief that remains extraordinarily widespread, Plato's spokesman in the *Symposium*. Alcibiades' function is to put us on notice that there is a fundamental flaw in the picture of love as sketched by Socrates,[18] a gaping hole that nothing in the dialogue can fill.[19] That, and not posthumous vindication, is the primary raison d'être of his speech.

The Developmental Hypothesis

Socrates is, of course, famous for advocating new forms of life, forms that few are willing to adopt. Here, however, what he is asking us to do is not to *act* differently but instead to *believe* something that flies in the face of empirical evidence. Indeed, the idea in question, this most counterintuitive of intuitions, is not even one to which Socrates himself subscribes in all of Plato's dialogues. Thus in the *Phaedrus*, a work often considered the *Symposium*'s thematic companion piece, the course of true love does not run so smooth. Far from drifting lightly up the ladder of love, the *erastes* there finds himself continually subject to temptation, even after being vouchsafed that precious vision of the Forms which constitutes the highest level of the Ascent. Notice how Socrates, having divided the soul into three parts—a "bad horse" (presumably desire), a "good horse" (quite possibly the spirited component),[20] and a "charioteer" (very likely reason)—describes what happens when a man lays eyes on a beautiful boy:

> When the charioteer sees that face, his memory is carried back to the real nature of Beauty, and he sees it again where it stands on the sacred pedestal next to Self-control [μετὰ σωφροσύνης]. At the sight he . . . has to pull the reins back so fiercely that both horses are set on their haunches, one falling back voluntarily with no resistance, but the other insolent and quite unwilling. They pull back a little further; and . . . one horse . . . bursts into a torrent of insults as soon as it has caught its breath, accusing its charioteer and yokemate of all sorts of cowardice and unmanliness for abandoning their position and their agreement. Now once more it tries to make its unwilling

partners advance, and gives in grudgingly only when they beg it to wait till later. Then, when the promised time arrives, and they are pretending to have forgotten, it reminds them; it . . . forces them to approach the boy again with the same proposition; and as soon as they are near, it drops its head, straightens its tail, bites the bit, and pulls without any shame at all. The charioteer is now struck with the same feelings as before, only worse . . . and he violently yanks the bit back out of the teeth of the insolent horse, tongue and jaws, sets its legs and haunches firmly on the ground, and "gives it over to pain." (254b–e; cf. *Phdr.* 246a–b)

Nothing could be more different in tone from Diotima's Ascent than this breathless, bloody battle. One imagines Diotima's lover arriving at the top of his ladder without having broken a sweat; the horse-drawn human of the *Phaedrus* is, by contrast, battered and bruised by the time he arrives—if indeed he ever arrives—at the blissful, sex-free union (256b–c), his "charioteer" having been required to punish his "dark horse" for repeated, possibly incessant, certainly forceful attempts to commandeer the vehicle.

Scholars have responded to the discrepancy in two main ways. One group tries to reconcile the *Symposium* with the *Phaedrus* by claiming that they are complementary, showing us different aspects (or filling in different details) of the same overall theory.[21] The other group, perceiving the futility of such efforts, invokes the now-standard *developmental hypothesis*,[22] explaining that Plato's philosophy, like that of most thinkers, must have evolved as he went along. Among other things, Plato began in his "middle period" to countenance the existence of multiple components within the soul—the charioteer and horses that, in the *Republic*, are also known as τὸ λογιστικόν, τὸ θυμοειδές, and τὸ ἐπιθυμητικόν[23]—and, as a consequence, the possibility of motivational conflict. Freedom from temptation became the province of the perfected philosopher, of the one who has scaled Diotima's ladder all the way to the realm of eternal Forms, and ceased belonging as an automatic birthright to any given individual. Indeed, the τελέως φιλόσοφος had to be born with a philosophical nature (*Rep.* 375e), a "talent for philosophy" (*Phdr.* 252e) that, in addition, had been refined by training, over and above the mere acquisition of superior knowledge.[24]

Now since the *Symposium* falls, on most chronologies, early in the middle period, scholars have tended to conjecture that Plato's understanding of human nature was still relatively rudimentary at the moment of its composition, and that he, like his character Socrates, still considered a glimpse of higher things sufficient to turn lust into philosophy.[25] On the face of it, the developmentalist approach does not sound entirely far-fetched. But when we also learn that these same scholars tend to assume that the *Republic* is *the very next dialogue Plato wrote* (with the *Phaedrus* following not far behind),[26] things begin to look a little strange. Are we really to believe that Plato, as it were overnight, converted wholesale from a unitary conception of the psyche—entirely constituted, or at least entirely motivated, by reason—to a sophisticated tripartite picture of the soul, with an awareness of the difficulties this poses and even a three-ingredient recipe for their attenuation (nature, nurture, knowledge)? Given that Alcibiades incarnates motivational conflict, wouldn't it make more sense (be less "expensive," as philosophers put it) to think of Plato as already implying something in the *Symposium* that he will have Socrates state explicitly in the *Republic*?[27]

The metaphorical bill is even higher for those who reject the developmental hypothesis and yet remain wedded to the belief that Plato would never knowingly allow Socrates to make a mistake. Such writers are forced to perform intellectual acrobatics in order to reassure us that the Ascent makes perfect psychological sense just as it is,[28] and that it is Alcibiades' own fault if he fails to profit from his association with Socrates.[29] They rarely stop to ask whom, exactly, Socrates *should* improve if not the ones who stand in greatest need of improvement;[30] or to acknowledge that a program of treatment would be well advised to start with people as they actually are (people like Alcibiades) as opposed to assuming that people are already almost perfect (like the man on the ladder). Theirs, I would argue, is an act of misplaced interpretive charity. Rather than expending infinite amounts of energy construing Socrates' claims in the most convincing way possible, adding a qualification here and a modification there,[31] they would do better to extend their charity to *Plato* and to accept that composers of dialogues have every right, and perhaps every reason, to make a protagonist fall on his face in order to serve their own literary and formative purposes.

Dubious Dialectic

We should really be ready for Socrates to lose his footing during the Ascent speech. For what immediately precedes it—the sole and only piece of live Socratic dialectic in the *Symposium*[32]—is a piece of argumentative logic so palpably, profoundly, and multiply flawed as to make the head spin. Here is the essence of the exchange, Socrates speaking first, Agathon second:

> "Wouldn't Love have to be a desire for beauty, and never for ugliness?"
> He agreed.
> "And we also agreed that he loves just what he needs [i.e., lacks] and does not have."
> "Yes," he said.
> "So Love needs beauty, then, and does not have it."

"Necessarily," he said.

"So! If something needs beauty and has got no beauty at all [τὸ ἐνδεὲς κάλλους καὶ μηδαμῇ κεκτημένον κάλλος], would you still say that it is beautiful?"

"Certainly not."

"Then do you still agree that Love is beautiful, if those things are so?"

Then Agathon said, "It turns out, Socrates, I didn't know what I was talking about in that speech."

". . . Don't you think that good things are always beautiful as well?"

"I do."

"Then if Love needs [i.e., lacks] beautiful things, and if all good things are beautiful, he will need [i.e., lack] good things too."

"As for me, Socrates," he said, "I am unable to challenge you. Let it be as you say."

"Then it's the truth, my beloved Agathon, that you are unable to challenge," he said. "It is not hard at all to challenge Socrates." (201a–c)

However cooperative Agathon may be as an interlocutor, it should surely be obvious to any minimally alert reader—even at an intuitive level—that there are serious problems here. For in order to establish the thesis that Eros is utterly un-beautiful and un-good, Socrates is actually making the following six claims:

1. Love is a desire for beauty.
2. We lack whatever we desire.
3. Love lacks beauty. (By syllogism, from 1 and 2.)
4. Love has no beauty at all.
5. Good things are beautiful.
6. Love lacks good things. (Ostensibly by syllogism, from 2 and 5.)

Socrates has, it seems to me, entirely failed to prove (a) that love lacks all beauty, (b) that love even lacks the specific type of beauty it is interested in, or (c) that love lacks goodness. There is, first of all, no justification for leaping from (3) to (4).[33] Love may lack *some* beauty, but we need not conclude from this that it lacks *all* beauty, that it is in no way (μηδαμῇ) beautiful. To translate into the world of human individuals (taking "love lacks beauty" as a Pauline predication[34]), an attractive woman could very easily desire an attractive man: the woman would lack, as it were, the specific beauty of the man, while possessing beauty in her own person.[35] Second, there is no reason to imagine that we are unable to desire what we already have. To extend our example, a woman could continue to desire a man even after a love affair has begun between them; she could, in other words, desire not to obtain a beauty she lacks but to preserve a beauty she already has.[36] And how do we know about this possibility? *Because*

Socrates himself raised it, a little earlier in his conversation with Agathon. "Whenever you say, *I desire what I already have*," he cautioned, "ask yourself whether you don't mean this: *I want the things I have now to be mine in the future as well*" (200d). What is more, he is about to define Eros, in Diotima's name, as a desire for something it already has: "In a word, then, love is wanting to possess the good forever" (206a).

Just as strikingly, and even more immediately, the Diotima speech undermines the more general claim that love lacks all beauty. The entire onus of its first part is, after all, to cure Socrates of his extremism, his tendency to view things as either totally *f* or not *f* at all:

> So I said, "What do you mean, Diotima? Is Love ugly [αἰσχρός], then, and bad [κακός]?"
> But she said, "Watch your tongue! Do you really think that, if a thing is not beautiful [καλὸν], it has to be ugly [αἰσχρόν]?"
> "I certainly do."
> "And if a thing's not wise, it's ignorant? Or haven't you found out yet that there's something in between wisdom and ignorance?" (201e–202a)[37]

Why, if Socrates has already been effectively taught by Diotima at some unspecified date in the distant past, does he continue now to act as though there were nothing in between, as though something is either utterly beautiful or completely devoid of beauty?[38] Has Socrates, in his eagerness to put Agathon to the elenctic sword, forgotten what Diotima taught him, both about the in-between and about continued possession? Diotima's position is far more sophisticated than the "truth" Socrates uses to berate Agathon; while it may at first appear as though the Agathon elenchus presents us with Socrates' mature views and the Diotima flashback with the route he took in order to acquire them, we should probably ignore the stated chronology and read the sequence from 201a to 202a as a more or less continuous argument, steadily moving toward increased refinement and plausibility.

Finally, it is straightforwardly illegitimate to extrapolate from "love lacks beautiful things" and "all good things are beautiful" to "love lacks good things." Socrates is clearly assuming that since all good things are beautiful, all beautiful things are good;[39] he is, in other words, committing the fallacy of the undistributed middle, the one that consists in inferring from "all As are B" to "all Bs are A." To feel the full force of its fallaciousness, we need only imagine it filled in with some everyday examples. While I may acknowledge, for instance, that all people named Mike are men, I may not wish to conclude from this that all men are named Mike; and while I may recognize that all dogs have four legs, and also that my cat has four legs, I may be equally reluctant to accept that my cat is a dog.

Now there are those who would object at this point that the term "undistrib-uted middle" postdates Plato by several centuries, and that Plato was a lowly ancient who could not be expected to understand such logical niceties.[40] Just because there was no word for it, however, does not mean that such an elemen-tary mistake could not be seen for what it was. And it would in fact be very strange if Plato had been unaware of it, since he has his characters quarrel about it on at least two separate occasions, not just Socrates against Euthyphro—

> it is then not right to say "where there is fear there is also shame," but that where there is shame there is also fear, for fear covers a larger area than shame. Shame is a part of fear just as odd is a part of number, with the result that it is not true that where there is number there is also oddness, but [it is true] that where there is oddness there is also number. . . . where there is piety there is also justice, but where there is justice there is not always piety, for the pious is a part of justice (*Euthyphro* 12c–d)—

but even Protagoras against Socrates (note the role reversal):

> SOCRATES: Then what do you mean by courageous men? Aren't they those who are confident?
>
> PROTAGORAS: I still hold by that.
>
> SOCRATES: Then . . . the most confident [θαρραλεώτατοι] are the most cou-rageous [ἀνδρειότατοι]? . . .
>
> PROTAGORAS: You are doing a poor job of remembering what I said when I answered your questions, Socrates. When I was asked if the courageous are confident, I agreed. I was not asked if the confident are courageous. If you had asked me that, I would have said, "Not all of them." (*Prot.* 350b–d)[41]

Plato knows full well that "all As are B" implies only that *some* Bs are A (that B is a subset of A), and not that *all* Bs are A. He has Protagoras argue it against Socrates, and Socrates against Euthyphro, and us—so it seems to me—against Socrates in the *Symposium*, where Agathon is too witless to do the job himself. Socrates' "proof" for love's lack of goodness cannot be sustained. And in general, his so-called refutation of Agathon falls apart so fast and in so many different directions that it is hard to know which way to turn in order to avoid the falling rubble.

We receive no warning, mind you, from the vast majority of Plato's inter-preters, so intent are they on assuring us that the building is structurally sound, and that the troubling claims listed above—(a) that love lacks all beauty, (b) that love lacks the specific type of beauty it is interested in, (c) that love lacks goodness—are at worst tiny scratches on a rock-solid foundation. On point (c), as I just mentioned, we are told that the undistributed middle was not a fallacy yet; on point (b), we are told that love could not possibly be the desire for continued possession of beauty;[42] on point (a), we are told (i) that Socrates is not really saying that love is completely lacking in beauty, (ii) that a handsome lover is still ugly inasmuch as he is a lover (whatever this means), and/or (iii) that beauty is fundamentally one, on Socrates' view, so that to lack part of it is to lack it entirely.[43] As if that were not enough, we are told (on all points put together) that Socrates is merely exposing a conflict within Agathon's views, not presenting any of his own.[44] There is no shortage of defenses for the elenchus. Almost everyone, a surprising number of otherwise critical readers included,[45] has found a way to read it as a glorious victory for Socrates and his superior intellectual abilities, the perfect lead-in to an equally flawless speech about love, philosophy, and the life well lived.[46]

Pericles, Socrates, and Plato

Many and sophisticated are, as we have seen, the ruses readers have adopted in order to clear the fictional Socrates of charges actually or potentially pressed against him. The last-mentioned, Socratic irony, is usually sufficient for commentators to extricate themselves from particularly sticky situations: Socrates, they contend, doesn't actually *endorse* the offending view (e.g., that love lacks all beautiful things) but merely repeats the view of his interlocutor, in such a way as to bring out its incompatibility with other views that the interlocutor also holds (and which Socrates endorses no more than he did the first). Socrates' aim is simply to reduce the interlocutor to confusion (ἀπορία), so that he will admit his ignorance—"a reward we could not fairly be dissatisfied with" (*Tht.* 187c)—and perhaps, if confusion is anything like wonder, set him, in addition, on the road to philosophy (*Tht.* 155d). In other words, Socrates is both the "torpedo fish" that renders its victims numb and the "gadfly" that goads them to action. (For the "torpedo fish," see *Meno* 80a–b, 84a–b, and Irwin 1979:122–23; for the "gadfly," see *Apol.* 30e.)

Now while there is something generally apropos about all of this, I am not convinced that it applies to the point-counterpoint with Agathon, at the end of which Socrates insists—without the slightest compulsion to do so—that what has defeated Agathon is the *truth*: not Agathon's own admissions, not Socrates' cunning, but just the way things actually are. And even if Socratic irony did explain the Agathon elenchus; even, indeed, if it accounted for the curiously smooth Ascent, which we could perhaps, if desperate, ascribe to the statedly sophistical Diotima;[47] still, no amount of Socratic irony could ever save Socrates from what happens in the *Gorgias*. For here, in the context of an increasingly heated debate with Callicles, Socrates makes a rather peculiar argument about the great statesman Pericles:

> At first Pericles had a good reputation. . . . But after he had turned [the Athe-
> nians] into "admirable and good" people, near the end of his life, they voted to
> convict Pericles of embezzlement and came close to condemning him to
> death. . . . Shouldn't he . . . have turned them out more just instead of more
> unjust, if while he cared for them he really was good at politics? . . . But Pericles
> certainly showed them to be wilder than they were when he took them over,
> and that toward himself, the person he'd least want this to happen to. . . . And
> if wilder, then both more unjust and worse. . . . So on this reasoning Pericles
> wasn't good at politics. (*Gorg.* 515e–516d)

Pericles, that is, cannot have been a good politician, for good politicians make
their constituents just, and just individuals do not seek to harm those who have
improved them. Far from being a good politician, indeed, Pericles was not a good
citizen (ἀγαθός . . . πολίτης, 515d), a fact we could infer directly from his unfortunate fate, Socrates strenuously insists, even if we knew nothing else about
him.[48] The argument is already somewhat problematic in itself (all the more so
if, as Irwin claims, it is historically inaccurate[49]), but notice what happens when
we add the following claim:

> SOCRATES: It wouldn't be at all strange if I were to be put to death. Would you
> like me to tell you my reason for expecting this?
> CALLICLES: Yes, I would.
> SOCRATES: I believe that I'm one of a few Athenians— . . . the only one among
> our contemporaries—to take up the true political craft and practice the
> true politics. This is because the speeches I make on each occasion do not
> aim at gratification but at what's best. They don't aim at what's most
> pleasant. And because I'm not willing to do those clever things you recom-
> mend, I won't know what to say in court. (*Gorg.* 521d–e)

In arrogating to himself the role of "true politician," Socrates is professing to
be a person (indeed the *only* person) who sets about raising the moral level of his
fellow Athenians, and therefore, presumably, an excellent citizen.[50] Yet if there is
one thing we know about him—and just in case we had forgotten, Socrates inadvertently reminds us, in the very words he uses to frame his assertion[51]—it is
that those fellow Athenians are about to put him to death.[52] By his own argument, then, Socrates is even less successful (and even worse a citizen) than Pericles: if *almost* being put to death makes someone a poor statesman, surely being
handed an actual jar of hemlock must promote one into the class of world-beat-
ing political failures.[53]

The Pericles section is a work of unparalleled Platonic brilliance. It is as though
Plato set himself the challenge of making an otherwise ruthlessly logical and un-
blinkingly astute character condemn himself out of his own mouth, over the

space of a mere seven Stephanus pages. How could Socrates, the arch detector of inconsistencies, possibly fail to notice that a set of statements he himself is producing generates an intolerable contradiction? Simple: make him respond to a question on a separate topic, and make him respond with emotion. Have Callicles taunt him with the entirely accurate prediction that his disdain for worldliness may land him in trouble one day. Have Socrates rise to the bait, telling Callicles with unusual ressentiment that it is Callicles who will be the one in trouble come the afterlife (526e–527a) and that he, Socrates, is *proud* of his incapacity to please the crowd. He, Socrates, tells the truth, not what people want to hear; no wonder they do not like him. Callicles may not notice that Socrates has unwittingly offered Pericles a defense, but we do. "On your own admission," a resurrected Pericles could say, "people do not like those who seek to improve their condition. How are you now going to use my fate as evidence against my civic virtue?"

Once again, Plato is setting before us a collection of mutually inconsistent views and—just as Socrates would, under comparable circumstances—forcing us to choose among them. Here are the three main claims:

1. Good citizens will always be loved by those they try to help. (Pericles, who was nearly condemned to death, must ipso facto have been a bad citizen.)
2. Socrates is likely to be (and, as we know from independent evidence, actually was) condemned to death.
3. Socrates, the one true politician in Athens, is an excellent citizen.

To repeat, Socrates clearly believes each of these statements; we are not dealing here with a case of Socratic irony. (Even if he did not believe 1 and 3, he could hardly imagine them to be *Callicles'* views: despite his casual agreement at 516c, Callicles has no interest in the moral improvement of citizens, and it is unlikely that he feels particularly warmly about Socrates' "political" activities.) But since, by syllogism, what follows from (1) and (2) should be the *contrary* of (3), Socrates is not entitled to all of them.

Which one shall we then discard? Plainly not (2), which is a historical fact; and presumably not (3), which feels plausibly Platonic; instead the untenable claim must be the idea that good intentions will always be rewarded. After having impugned Pericles on the basis of an unrealistically optimistic view of human nature, finally Socrates, when his own reputation is at stake, is revealing himself capable of a more earthbound one: *it is not always a teacher's fault if the pupil turns out badly.*

And why, after all, should Socrates *not* subscribe to this eminently sensible position? His counterpart in the *Theaetetus* is fully willing to acknowledge that there have been

> many cases where people . . . thought that I was no good. They have then proceeded to leave me sooner than they should, either of their own accord or

through the influence of others. And after they have gone away from me they have resorted to harmful company, with the result that what remained within them has miscarried; while they have neglected the children I helped them to bring forth . . .; finally they have been set down for ignorant fools. (*Tht.* 150d–e)

Surely no reasonable person would blame Socrates for what happens to such rogue disciples, any more than she would blame him for the fate of Alcibiades,[54] or fault philosophers generally for the waywardness of their followers ("it's inevitable that the greater number are vicious . . . [but] philosophy isn't responsible for this" [*Rep.* 489d; cf. 539b–c]). Surely the *Gorgias* Socrates is right that his own merits may go unrewarded: as his counterpart says in the *Meno*, pandering sophists are much more likely than demanding philosophers to be adored by their charges, for all the corrupting ambitions of the one set and the ennobling ambitions of the other.[55] Yet if Socrates *is* right, then Pericles may yet deserve the lofty reputation he enjoys among Athenians; the conspiracy against him (such as it was) may have been every bit as unmerited as the conspiracy against Socrates will be. Socrates' critique of politicians does not hold up. Neither, accordingly, does his critique of sophists, who

do this absurd thing: while they claim to be teachers of excellence, they frequently accuse their students of doing them wrong, depriving them of their fees and withholding other forms of thanks from them, even though the students have been well served by them. Yet what could be a more illogical business than this statement, that people who've become good and just, whose injustice has been removed by their teacher . . ., should wrong him—something they can't do? (*Gorg.* 519c–d)

It is true, of course, that attributing injustice to the just would be illogical. But Socrates is being disingenuous here. He knows as well as Callicles that "teachers of excellence"—even those who really do seek to make their charges upright individuals—may not succeed. Between his first and second sentence yawns a vast abyss, the abyss of agency, susceptibility, and errant desire.

The *Gorgias* Unravels

Notice, now, what happens next. Not only does Socrates' tacit admission, in his rancorous retort to Callicles, play havoc with the attack he launched, a mere two pages earlier, on sophists at large; it also throws us all the way back to the start of the dialogue, placing in doubt what appeared at the time to be his victory over Gorgias. It reveals Socrates' whole argument, which has seemed to hold up under pressure from three separate interlocutors, to have been built on the flimsiest of foundations. It shows, to change the metaphor, that one sustained pull on the Pericles thread is enough to make the entire dialogue unravel in our hands.

Difficult as it is to summarize such a rich and complex text, I propose that we view the dialogue as *a systematic challenge mounted by Socrates, point for point, against Gorgias's apologia for rhetoric*. Socrates refuses to accept anything Gorgias says on behalf of his profession: first, that it is a craft ($\tau\acute{e}\chi\nu\eta$), consisting in the learnable and teachable skill of turning persuasive speeches on legal matters (449b, 449e, 454b); second, that it is often used for the good of others, inveigling patients to take their bitter medicine, for example (456b), or cities to invest in costly military defenses (455e); and third, that it benefits the orator himself, by giving him the power to gain pleasure and avoid pain (452d–e).

Socrates begins by characterizing rhetoric as a mere "knack" ($\acute{e}\mu\pi\epsilon\iota\rho\acute{\iota}\alpha$, $\tau\rho\iota\beta\acute{\eta}$) (462c, 463b, 465a). If it were a craft, he reasons, then it would know and impart the truth about its subject matter, and since its subject matter is justice, orators and their students would necessarily be just (460b–c); but as we know, students are often unjust, sometimes toward their very benefactors (456d–457c, 461a). As for its ostensible social utility, the nearly tragic case of Pericles proves that orators who convince their fellow-citizens to build long walls and stronger ships and the like are clearly not helping in the ways that count.

The remainder of the dialogue (on this admittedly schematic rendition) consists in Socrates' repeated assault on the idea that oratory is advantageous for the orator. Are the rhetorically talented happier than the rest of us? No, declares Socrates, because pleasure is not in itself a good; only *beneficial* pleasures are potential contributors to our happiness, and oratory is of no assistance in helping us to distinguish these from their detrimental counterparts (500a). Nor does it help to appeal to the criteria of respect and power. No one admires orators (466b); further, those who are in a position to have innocents thrown in jail do not really have power, since power is the capacity to achieve what is good for us, and acting unjustly is *bad* for us, more harmful to the perpetrator than it is to any victim. This must be so, for (a) whatever is shameful ($\alpha\grave{\iota}\sigma\chi\rho\acute{o}\nu$) is either painful or harmful (474d–475a); (b) committing injustice is shameful; (c) committing injustice involves no physical pain; ergo (d) it must involve harm (475a–c). And then, in order to rule in a democracy one must please the people, which in turn involves becoming *like* the people, sacrificing our autonomy in the process.[56] Finally, we should recall that in the afterlife we will lose our body and become pure soul (524b), which means that the soul is the most important possession we have; and since souls will then enter a perfect system of rewards and retributions, with those of philosophers (like Socrates) faring well (526c) and those of tyrants, orators, and hedonists (like Callicles) faring badly (526e–527a), it is good for us, while embodied, to be good.[57]

Now Socrates' argument on the first point, about crafts and knacks, is highly problematic. If something is a craft, contends Socrates, it will necessarily turn its students into practitioners of the relevant expertise. A man who has learned carpentry is a carpenter; a man who has learned medicine is a doctor; "and, by this line of reasoning, isn't a man who has learned what's just a just man too?" (460b). The answer, of course, is no. In each case, the training makes apprentices *capable* of practicing the relevant skill, but nothing requires them actually to do so. They may choose to make tables, to be sure, but they may also choose *not* to make tables, and—most significantly—they may choose to make *bad* tables. For *those who are good at acting well are also those who are good at acting badly*. (Who says this? None other than Plato's Socrates, in *Hippias Minor* and in the *Republic*.)[58] What is more, students of oratory are supposed to learn not only what is just but also what is unjust (454b).[59] If a craft makes people into practitioners of the knowledge it gives them (as Socrates purports to believe), then oratory could be a craft that teaches (among other things) injustice; the ungrateful behavior of certain students would be no strike against its effectiveness.[60]

One might respond that these are subtle objections, so subtle that they escaped Plato's attention (although, as I have noted, he shows himself fully cognizant of them elsewhere). A first-time reader might easily be forgiven, therefore, for imagining, as does Friedländer,[61] that Socrates has straightforwardly defeated Gorgias. She might equally be forgiven for supposing, as does Irwin,[62] that if Socrates has made a mistake, it is also *Plato's* mistake; or, again, for joining Kahn[63] in the belief that Socrates is merely reproducing Gorgias's own views, hiding behind his habitual ironic mask. But once we reach the Pericles section, things really should change dramatically. It should, at this juncture, become clear to each and every reader that Socrates' premises are flawed; that Plato is aware they are flawed; that they are Socrates' own premises, not merely borrowings from the worldview of his interlocutor; and taking all in all, *that Plato deliberately has Socrates fail to defeat Gorgias*.[64]

Certain readers may, in fact, begin to detect Plato's ironic strategy in advance of the Pericles section. For in the surrounding, more general debate about hedonism, Plato has Callicles state not only that the good life consists in indulging a maximally abundant and maximally intense set of appetites, but also that such indulgence paradoxically requires *courage*. "The man who'll live correctly," urges Callicles, "ought to allow his own appetites to get as large as possible and not restrain them. And when they are as large as possible, he ought to be competent to devote himself to them by virtue of his bravery [ἀνδρείαν] and intelligence" (492a); "this isn't possible for the many," he adds, "because of the shame they feel" (ibid.). At times, that is, we may feel ashamed to satisfy a certain craving—to eat, say, a tenth slice of chocolate cake—but must dauntlessly overrule the voice in our head that tells us to put our fork down. In order to make our hedonism complete, we must resist, as Brecht would put it, the temptation to be good.[65] And so, while Callicles merely speaks of the motivational conflict that Alcibiades incarnates, and while the particular species of motivational conflict varies, arguably, from one dialogue to the other, the *Gorgias* replicates to perfection the overarching structure of the *Symposium*.[66] For if Callicles knows that humans are sometimes subject to temptation, surely Plato does; if Plato does, then his spokesman should too; if Socrates behaves here as though there were no such thing as motivational conflict,[67] then he is not acting as Plato's spokesman, any more than does his counterpart at Agathon's banquet.[68]

The Uses of Oratory

Ever the consummate non-spokesman, Socrates has signally failed to carry the first point against Gorgias and rhetoric. Even the (absurd) possibility that rhetoricians might concern themselves with the moral welfare of their charges is, astonishingly, not ruled out by Socrates' elenchus, still less the (entirely reasonable) possibility that rhetoric teaches justice, in the sense of a body of information about the law. (It should always be borne in mind that the closest contemporary analogue to oratorical training is law school.) And the collapse of the Pericles argument also brings Socrates' *second* criticism, that orators are never of any help to other people, down with it. Since we need no longer hold Pericles to the extraordinarily high standard of making the Athenians both virtuous and grateful, a standard to which no one would dream of holding Socrates, we are free to return to the customary assessment of his contribution. Pericles did indeed help the Athenians, at least temporarily, by convincing them to make short-term sacrifices for long-term gains; and he showed himself, in the process, perfectly able to "pick out which kinds of pleasures are good ones and which are bad" (500a).[69]

We are left with a third and final charge, namely that rhetoric is of no use to the orator himself. Here the quality of Socrates' "proofs," whose very profusion bespeaks a doubt in the persuasive capacity of each, varies considerably from one to the next. Thus the claim that orators are never held in high esteem (οὐ νομίζεσθαι) is what hardened Platonists would call a "deliberately misleading paradox" (cf. Irwin 1979:137) and what others would call a barefaced lie;[70] the posit that power in a democracy requires self-abasement is clearly question-begging;[71] and the extreme position that, not content with subordinating pleasure to virtue as an inferior good, denies all intrinsic value to the former is unlikely to move an average virtue-seeker, still less a hedonist.[72] Socrates' main hope resides in the argument that what goes by the name of power is not worth having, *and this argument is vitiated from the start by the very same presupposition that defeated his first and second challenges to rhetoric.* For in order to make his case that the purportedly mighty (like Archelaus of Macedonia) never achieve what they want, Socrates has to rely on the assumption that they do not actually want to enrich themselves and their friends, harm their enemies, and always remain safe from prosecution; what they want deep down, he imagines, is "the good," i.e. that which will, over the long term, have done them the most benefit.[73]

It is already tendentious to assert that we do not want things we know to be bad for us. However much I may now regret my decision, and however clearly I suspected it to be a bad idea at the time, I ate that tenth slice of chocolate cake because I *wanted* to; perhaps indeed I ate it in part *because* I knew it was bad for me (even fourth-century Aristotle knew of such perverse desires).[74] It is yet more problematic, however, to add that what is really good for us is to behave justly. My acts of injustice must, as we saw above, be harmful, since they are not painful; but why must they be harmful to *me*?[75] Conversely, it must be good for my acts of injustice to be punished, but why must it be good for *me*?[76] The mistake becomes obvious when, later in the dialogue, Socrates describes the fate awaiting Archelaus and his kind. "From among those who have committed the ultimate wrongs and who because of such crimes have become incurable," says Socrates, "come the ones who are made examples of. These persons themselves no longer derive any profit from their punishment, because they're incurable. Others, however, do profit from it" (525b–c; cf. *Phd.* 113d–e).[77] If punishment benefits bystanders, then punishment need not be good for the culprit in order for it to be, in general, a good thing.[78] And so, by analogy, iniquity need not be bad for the one who commits it in order for it to be, in general, a bad thing. Archelaus need not be harming himself by having his enemies executed, and he is certainly not harming himself by seeking to avoid retribution. Given that, as an incurable, he stands to derive no benefit from his own punishment, should we not say that when he protects himself, he is doing exactly what he wants?[79]

Socrates' reasoning is bad enough here, but worse is to follow. If it is good for an individual to be punished, he continues, then it is good for him to turn his friends and family in to the authorities (480b–c; reprised at 508b).[80] Are we not in the presence of a classic reductio ad absurdum? Polus certainly seems to believe so: "I think these statements are absurd [ἄτοπα], Socrates, though no doubt you think they agree with those expressed earlier" (480e). And Polus is right. Socrates' claims are entirely consistent with those he has been adducing; their patent absurdity should make us reconsider the soundness of those that led up to them. So, too, should the final corollary, that "if [an] enemy did something unjust against another person, . . . he should scheme to get his enemy off without paying what's due" (480e–481a). For if punishment is good for me, then surely escaping punishment is bad for me, and helping other people escape punishment is bad for them; and if it is bad for them, then it constitutes an injustice, *and Socrates should not be advocating it*.[81] To put it another way, the only people who would maliciously strive to protect their enemies are people who already believe that injustice is bad for the perpetrator—and those people would, ex hypothesi, not have the malice necessary to embark on such an undertaking.

That Socrates fails to convince Polus (who, as we just saw, cries foul) or Callicles (who asks whether Socrates is joking) is immediately apparent. It is, however, still more salient at the end of the dialogue. For what, other than desperation, could possibly lead a staunch advocate of rapid question and answer, in whose eyes a handful of sentences strung together constitute a reprehensibly "long style of speechmaking" (449b),[82] to a fire-and-brimstone tirade filling almost five Stephanus pages (523a–527e)? And what else would reduce the famously passionless advocate of rationality to a policy of sending his interlocutor to hell?[83] Socrates does not even content himself with saying, in a general way, that all hedonists will be punished somehow or other in the afterlife. Instead, he targets Callicles directly: "I take you to task, because you won't be able to come to protect yourself when you appear at the trial and judgment I was talking about just now" (526e). Further, the torments he promises are equally specific, and are, in fact, *a direct response to Callicles' earlier taunts.*

> CALLICLES: As it is, if someone got hold of you or of anyone else like you and took you off to prison on the charge that you're doing something unjust when in fact you aren't, be assured that you wouldn't have any use for yourself. *You'd get dizzy, your mouth would hang open* and you wouldn't know what to say. . . . Socrates, "how can this [philosophy] be a wise thing, the craft which took a well-favored man and made him worse," able neither to protect himself nor to rescue himself or anyone else from the gravest dangers . . .? Such a man *one could knock on the jaw* without paying what's due for it. (486a–c, my emphasis)
>
> SOCRATES: When you come before that judge, the son of Aegina, and he takes hold of you and brings you to trial, *your mouth will hang open* and *you'll get dizzy* there just as much as I will here, and maybe *somebody'll give you a demeaning knock on the jaw* and throw all sorts of dirt at you. (527a, my emphasis)

To be sure, the myth of an after- (or pre-, or inter-) life ruled by a system of fitting rewards and punishments is found elsewhere in Plato (see esp. *Rep.* 614b–621d, *Phdr.* 248c–249c, *Phd.* 63b–82a, *Phd.* 110b–114d), and it is entirely conceivable that Plato himself entertained such a notion. That, however, is not to say that it is deployed in a convincing manner in the *Gorgias.* Socrates should have mentioned it much earlier, while trying to convince Polus that injustice is bad for the agent: the latter view immediately follows, and indeed *only* follows, within a two-world framework. (Even if it could be established that injustice harms the soul without recourse to such a framework, it would still remain to be shown that the health of the soul always outweighs the flourishing of the body.) He should have restricted himself to a short statement (or, conversely, allowed his interlocutors to discourse at equal length). And most importantly, he should have kept his statement free from personal *ressentiment*. The conclusion of the *Gorgias* offers us the spectacle of a human, all too human individual who has been stung by a failure to convince, not one of a demigodly philosopher calmly laying out the truth.[84] And if, as Kahn believes, "it is the extraordinarily seductive power of [Plato's] portrait of Socrates that helps to make so many of us sympathetic . . . to the philosophical claims of these dialogues" (1983:120; cf. 1996:146), could it not also be the case that the repellent power of that same portrait—one which, as Nehamas has pointed out, makes his execution credible[85]—puts the rest of us on guard against his philosophical claims?

Was Gorgias Refuted?

Astonishing as it may seem, Gorgias's sales pitch has remained entirely unscathed, for all the objections that have been thrown at it over the course of the dialogue. Rhetoric is still free to have a central subject matter (the law), to be a teachable and learnable skill, to provide a power that is good for the orator, and to help the orator's friends and fellow-citizens take their literal or figurative medicine (Cooper 1999:41); in spite of Socrates' relentless onslaught, Gorgias has every right to persist in the conviction that oratory is (1) a craft (2) of benefit (a) to the orator and (b) to other people. And we, the readers, have every right to do the same. For over and above the fact that Socrates' arguments are not, as Allen surmises, fundamentally sound, it has to be added that they are not even flawed in ways that would admit, as Irwin thinks, of subsequent correction.[86] Their key posit, that doing injustice is bad for the doer, depends on a belief in a life after death, and *such a belief could never be produced by means of argumentation*. Accordingly, Socrates has not changed Callicles' mind, *knows* he has not changed Callicles' mind—the present tense of his concluding exhortation gives him away[87]—and indeed *could* never change the mind of a Callicles.[88]

From the outside, it may seem quite natural to expect the pleas of a crusader for justice to fall on a hedonist's deaf ears, the two positions being, as Alasdair MacIntyre would say, "incommensurable."[89] Yet from the inside, Socrates' defeat sets up a final and devastating contradiction, a contradiction between what he promises and what he delivers. Unlike such "early" dialogues as the *Euthyphro*, in which the elenchus serves merely to reduce an overconfident interlocutor to a (salutary) confession of ignorance, the *Gorgias* presents a Socrates who endows it with a *constructive* capacity. "If there's any point in our discussions on which you agree with me, then that point will have been adequately put to the test," he tells Callicles; "*mutual agreement will really lay hold of truth in the end*" (487e, my emphasis). Absolute knowledge may still elude our grasp, that is, but when a position has survived repeated challenges, we can begin to feel confident about it, so confident indeed that we are liable to call it a "truth" (Vlastos 1991:114)—much as we might, after several years of victories, start calling an athlete "unbeatable." And the superior advantage of suffering wrongs over inflicting them is, in theory, just such a "truth":

> SOCRATES: Among so many arguments, this one alone survives refutation and remains steady: that doing what's unjust is more to be guarded against than suffering it. (527b)
>
> SOCRATES: These conclusions, at which we arrived earlier in our previous discussions are, I'd say, held down and bound by arguments of iron and adamant . . . for my part, my account is ever the same: I don't know how these things are, but no one I've ever met . . . can say anything else without being ridiculous [*i.e., without self-contradiction*]. So once more I set it down that these things are so. (508e-9a)

The challenge Socrates issues to Polus—"if I don't produce you as a single witness to agree with what I'm saying, then I suppose I've achieved nothing worth mentioning" (472b–c)—must be understood on precisely these terms. Since the other-cheek-turning stance has, in Socrates' experience, proven to be the *only* consistent set of attitudes, he feels supremely confident that Polus will become "ridiculous" (καταγέλαστος) should the latter try to propose anything different; indeed in a sense Socrates *must* convince Polus and the others in order for his "elenctic certainty" to remain intact, in order for his pet convictions to remain undefeated in combat.[90] It is striking, therefore, that Socrates does not in fact produce Polus, still less Callicles, as "witness" for his position, with the result that he has, by his own standards, achieved nothing worth mentioning (Nightingale 1995:82). Even as he wrote the *Gorgias*, the dialogue that lays out in the fullest detail what it would mean to subscribe to a positive proof by elenchus, Plato must have known that it could not be done.[91] He must have known that the elenchus can only ever establish the mutual incompatibility of two beliefs, and never indicate which one is the culprit.[92] The long-winded, ill-tempered, highly rhetorical performance at dialogue's end is the most eloquent possible evidence of its failure to do anything more.

Spiritual Exercises

The holes in Socrates' logic are so numerous, so broad, and so manifest that it is a wonder anyone ever took him for the mouthpiece of a brilliant and original thinker. An unprejudiced reader should, it seems to me, react either by considering Plato a blundering fool (on the assumption that he stands firmly behind his character) or by regarding him as an exceptionally sophisticated literary craftsman (on the assumption that he does not). Yet the vast majority have seen neither clumsiness nor genius of the relevant variety, and it remains standard, even to this day, to consider Socrates as having scored a resounding victory over the antagonists of the *Gorgias*, just as it remains standard to consider Alcibiades, in the *Symposium*, as providing nothing but confirmation of Diotima's ladder-of-love theory. By the time of the *Symposium*, the 1995 *Oxford Companion to Philosophy* tells us, "one can now be quite confident that the views put into his [Socrates'] mouth are Plato's own views" (Bostock, 684); the Diotima speech, concurs a 1999 *Cambridge Dictionary of Philosophy*, represents "Plato's theory of erotic passion" (Kraut, 711). "Since Aristotle himself treats the middle and late dialogues as undissembling accounts of Plato's philosophy," it continues, "we are on firm ground in adopting the same approach" (ibid., 713).[93]

But is the ground really so firm? It is true that Aristotle appears to have turned a singularly deaf ear to Platonic irony. This does not mean, however, that there is no such thing; for all his privileged position as Plato's student, Aristotle is not the final authority on the Platonic corpus. Indeed, there seems to be some tension between his overall reading method on the one hand and, on the other, his famous reference to a stock of "unwritten beliefs" that, he suggests, Plato made available to initiates but never committed to papyrus.[94] What is more, subsequent generations of Platonists, even within the Academy, saw the dialogues as evincing a type of skepticism, a philosophy that withholds its firm assent from any particular standpoint (Cooper 1997:xxiii). The Seventh Letter may not be authentic, but the very fact that it was once *thought* to be authentic, so that Plato was widely held to have kept his most important beliefs to himself and his friends (letter 7, 344c–d), speaks volumes on post-Aristotelian reception. Nor is that reception entirely surprising, given Socrates' famous and striking remark in the *Phaedrus* that "a written discourse on any subject can only be a great amusement . . . no discourse worth serious attention has ever been written [down]" (*Phdr.* 277e). According to Cooper (ibid., xxiv), the skeptical view prevailed within the Academy for two hundred years, until Antiochus of Ascalon reduced Plato to the status of systematic philosopher in the first century BCE; perhaps one day soon scholars will look back on the two millennia that have since passed as a rather extended interregnum between two periods of genuine contact.

In the meantime, Plato scholarship presents a curious amalgam of disparate positions. Some interpreters continue to push the esoteric-doctrine doctrine, elevated to more recent prominence by Leo Strauss and his followers;[95] others, in increasing numbers, make a case for the importance of Platonic irony; everyone else carries on treating the claims and arguments put forth by Socrates as items to be understood and emulated, perhaps sometimes amended, certainly always adopted. Plato's desire to leave critical space between himself and his purported mouthpiece is routinely covered up, denied, or simply not imagined as a possibility. My first point in conclusion is that Platonic irony is real, and widespread; in particular, the *Symposium* and the *Gorgias*—quite possibly the *Protagoras* too[96]—are deeply impregnated with it, so much so that their proper appreciation absolutely depends on taking it into account. My second point, a corollary of the first, is that the traditional developmental theory is flawed. Dialogues like the *Gorgias* (and the *Protagoras*) already gesture toward the complex psychology of the *Republic* and the *Phaedrus*: the shift, if there was one,[97] took place earlier than is usually thought.

If, however, the *Symposium*, *Gorgias*, and *Protagoras* are heavily laden with Platonic irony, and if that irony has nevertheless gone unnoticed by the vast majority of readers, should we not admit that the dramatic gulf between construction and reception bespeaks a marked deficiency on Plato's part? On the contrary. By allowing so many to miss the point of the dialogues in question, Platonic irony has not failed but rather fulfilled its primary function, that of *audience partition*. (This is my third point, one that sends us back to our discussion of parables in chapter 2.) While every other text "rolls about everywhere, reaching indiscriminately those with understanding no less than those who have no business with it, and it doesn't know to whom it should speak and to whom it should not" (*Phdr.* 275e), Plato's writings divide their recipients into three separate groups, driving some people away by giving the impression of irremediable incompetence, encouraging others to attend only to the words of Socrates, and offering the happy few, finally, an opportunity to go beyond the mere accumulation of knowledge.[98] Fourth point: over and above *teaching* us, Plato's dialogues have the capacity to *train* us. If we have a predisposition for detecting and are interested in resolving conflicts within a position—if, that is, we instinctively posit logical consistency as a desideratum in life[99]—then we stand to learn not only *what* to think, but also, and far more importantly, *how* to think.[100]

Like mathematics textbooks, Plato's dialogues (the irony-rich among them, at least) provide us both with models and with *exercises*, sample arguments being accompanied by problems for us to solve by ourselves. The *Gorgias* shows us, through Socrates, how to perform a reductio ad absurdum (Callicles and the catamites);[101] it also invites us to go on and find the reductio in Socrates' own position (Polus and the exonerated enemy). And just as it indicates what it would look like to detect a hidden tension within a collection of convictions (when Socrates appears to defeat Gorgias), so it makes room for us to bring such a technique to bear on Socrates (when his Pericles harangue puts that "defeat" into question). Similarly, the *Symposium* enables us to try out our capacity for recognizing an undistributed middle when we see one ("love lacks good things"), and for noticing a counterexample when it is thrust before our eyes (Alcibiades, incarnator of motivational conflict). The test cases are not always inherently significant: it does not matter whether we know what nineteen times eleven comes to, what the exact definition of a statesman is, or why Pericles was quite a good one after all.[102] What matters is our ability, in general, to multiply one number by another, to collect and divide, to locate holes in an argument. What matters, in other words, is the *method*; and a method, unlike a set of facts or ideas, can only be acquired through practice.[103] It can only be acquired, by consequence, when the ostensible mouthpiece makes mistakes. Point five: *training and teaching are antithetical aims*; at the precise moment in a text where one is taking place, its counterpart is necessarily absent.[104]

That is not to say, of course, that the dialogues as a whole have no theories to impart. On the contrary, all kinds of suggestions put forward by Socrates (and by analogous figures in dialogues like *Sophist* and *Politicus*) must be taken extremely seriously. Indeed, many of them—that there is a distinction between apparent goods and true goods, for example, and that it is vital to be able to tell the two apart (*Gorg.* 464a); that it is important not merely to live but to live well (*Crito* 48b); that to live well is to lead an examined life (*Apol.* 38a), giving the right kind of attention to one's soul (*Phd.* 82d); that the right kind of attention crucially involves setting the soul in order (*Soph.* 228b); that setting the soul in order requires the elimination of false belief and the overcoming of motivational conflict (*Phdr.* 253c–254e); that the elenchus can take us part of the way, by identifying tensions within our stock of commitments and by arousing us from our introspective slumbers (*Apol.* 30e); that rhetoric and sophistry are of no assistance here (*Gorg.* 500b); that speech is superior to writing in such contexts (*Phdr.* 276a); that any aptitude can be used for ill as well as good (*Meno* 88a–b); that the fully virtuous individual layers knowledge and training over an innate disposition to uprightness (*Pol.* 310a); that intermediary states do exist (*Symp.* 201e–202a); and that written texts risk falling into the hands of those who have no business with them (*Phdr.* 275e)[105]—are, as will have been evident, critical to my overall approach. It is just that their transmission is not the sole ambition or function of the dialogues.

While the more active manner of using the dialogues is not forced upon the reader (if it were, audience partition would be sacrificed), it is nonetheless encouraged. Clues as to their formative potential are planted right in the dialogues; each contains an inset *manual for use*, a coded set of instructions on how it may be employed for the purposes of training. (Such would be my sixth point.) In the *Gorgias*, our guide is the reaction of the interlocutors, with Polus's suspicion of a hoax, for instance, alerting us to the presence of a reductio in the vicinity. In the *Symposium*, positive hints are joined by cautionary tales. Not only does Plato have his protagonist say "it is not hard at all to challenge Socrates" (201c)— though Socrates is no doubt being ironic here, Plato is also being ironic at his expense[106]—but he puts on stage the very incarnation of a wrongheaded attitude toward philosophy, in the persons of Apollodorus and Aristodemus.

Front-runners in the relay team that leads us back to the thinking-party, these two have no reason to be in the dialogue other than the fact that they show us how *not* to be a "lover of Socrates" (Σωκράτους ἐραστής, 173b). While Aristodemus slavishly imitates the master's habit of going barefoot (173b, 220b), Apollodorus, who has spent the last three years "ma[king] it [his] job to know exactly what [Socrates] says and does each day" (173a), triumphantly parrots the credo about knowing his own ignorance and spending his hours in dialectic:

> I used to think that what I was doing was important, but in fact I was the most worthless man on earth—as bad as you are this very moment. . . . My greatest pleasure comes from philosophical conversation, even if I'm only a listener. . . . I'm sorry for you and your friends because you think your affairs are important when really they're totally trivial. Perhaps, in your turn, you think I'm a failure, and, believe me, I think that what you think is true. But as for all of you, I don't just *think* that you are failures—I know it for a fact. (173a–d)

The smug, self-satisfied Apollodorus, with his arrogance of humility, and the superficial imitator Aristodemus, with his affectation of asceticism, should immediately put us on notice: in order to profit from what follows in the *Symposium*, it is not sufficient to understand what is being said.[107] It is a mistake to think that we can improve ourselves merely by sitting all day at the feet of the master, soaking up information by osmosis, as though "wisdom were like water, which always flows from a full cup into an empty one when we connect them with a piece of yarn" (175d–e). However illuminating the master's sayings may be, simply memorizing and repeating them will not do, any more than will the emulation of his mannerisms. As Michael Frede has pointed out (1992b:216), even the acquisition of a perfect and complete set of true beliefs would not necessarily help, because it could easily coexist, judging by the characters in Plato's dialogues, with a parallel set of *false* beliefs. We could never extirpate the latter, indeed could never so much as discern their presence, without the method. What the method gives us is a principled way to justify our beliefs, to the degree to which justification is possible; what it gives us, above all, is a way to live in harmony with ourselves, a way to introduce consistency into our soul. It is this consistency to which, I believe, everything else is instrumental[108] in a philosophy that (seventh and final point) presents itself as a way of life as much as, or more than, a set of theoretical doctrines.[109]

It is in part because philosophy has largely ceased thinking of itself as a way of life, and has reconceived its mission as one of theory-generation, that the *Symposium* and the *Gorgias* are so routinely read without any attention to Platonic irony. We encourage our students to focus almost exclusively on what Socrates says (in, say, the Ascent speech), on the grounds that what Socrates says is what Plato means, and that what Plato means is what we stand to learn by reading his texts; we save sophistications, if at all, for advanced courses, as though the proper use of the dialogues were not the very first thing one should be told about them. In so doing we respond to a contemporary cultural bias which decrees that every book is valuable for its "message," not for its transformative potential. There is nothing, however, that obliges us to follow the trend. Each of us is free to apply a literary principle of charity, and to gain, in the process, the capacity to use Plato in the way he would have wanted: as a stepping-stone, that is, on the way to perfection.

Appendix

Just How Bad Is the Pericles Argument?

So as not to get bogged down in too many details, I presented my case against the Pericles argument rather rapidly, and it might seem that I have left myself open to an obvious objection.[110] Many, I think, would deny that Socrates has inadvertently tarred himself with the same brush as Pericles, since Socrates, unlike Pericles, is at least attempting to turn his fellow Athenians into better people.[111] Whereas Pericles merely pandered to the Athenians, providing them with what they already (thought they) wanted, Socrates aims at their transformation, inviting them to change their sense of what is truly valuable. Perhaps he does not succeed, but he does *try*—his heart, we would say, is in the right place—and that is surely enough to grant him, unlike Pericles, the status of good citizen.

Most of us would, no doubt, be willing to accept that the kind of assistance Socrates offers is superior to the kind of assistance provided by Pericles. To be sure, it is not at all clear that Socrates can *prove* its superiority in a non-question-begging way; still, everyone is entitled to a few axioms, and if Socrates had contented himself with saying what my imaginary objector says on his behalf— "maybe I will fail, but at least I am trying, and what I am aiming at is the true improvement"[112]—there would be no suspicion of Platonic irony in this part of the *Gorgias*. We might still disagree with the ideas put forward, but we would take ourselves to be disagreeing with Plato, as opposed to surmising that something strange and interesting is going on.

The reason some of us *do* think something strange and interesting is going on is that Socrates does *not* content himself with those very reasonable statements. Instead he decides to dub Pericles a bad citizen, offering as sole evidence the fact that Pericles came close to being executed. If the citizens turned against Pericles, says Socrates, that is a sure sign that he failed to improve them; and if he failed to improve them, that means he is a bad citizen. End of story. There is no talk here of trying or not trying: for Pericles' ultimate fate to count singlehandedly as evidence of his shortcomings, what he was *attempting* to do must necessarily remain irrelevant.[113] Unfortunately for Socrates, the very same logic can easily be used to show that *he* was a bad citizen (arguably worse than Pericles, since he was actually executed). If Socrates had been a good citizen, then the Athenians— "it necessarily follows"! (515d)—would have become better under his care; if the Athenians had become better, then they would not have condemned him to death. But of course they did condemn him to death, in a court case spearheaded by a man who, within the world of Plato's dialogues, had been exposed to Socrates' claims and methods.[114] So Socrates cannot have been a good citizen.

It is, perhaps, even worse for Socrates than that. In discussion with Callicles, he makes a big point—covering an entire Stephanus page and then some (514a–515c)—of how important it is to vet people before permitting them to undertake public works, whether building houses or tending to souls. "We'd have to check, wouldn't we, whether we've ever built a work of construction . . . and whether this structure is admirable or disgraceful," insists Socrates; "if we could point out . . . either none at all or else many worthless ones, it would surely be stupid to undertake public projects" (514b–c). "Wouldn't it be truly ridiculous," he continues, "that people should advance to such a height of folly that, before producing . . . successful results in private practice . . . they should attempt to 'learn pottery on the big jar,' as that saying goes, and attempt both to take up public practice themselves and to call on others like them to do so as well?" (514d–e) Again, this is an odd thing for Plato to put into the mouth of Socrates, given that Socrates does not convert anyone to philosophy in the early dialogues: not Gorgias, not Polus, not Callicles, not Alcibiades (see *Symposium*), not Nicias (see *Laches*), not Euthyphro (see *Euthyphro*). . . not, in short, a single interlocutor.[115] On the basis of Socrates' own argument, then, his apparently heroic undertaking of "the true political craft" strongly risks appearing "ridiculous," not to say the "height of folly."

To repeat, nothing I have said implies that Socrates is mistaken in considering his efforts more noble than those of Pericles. It is just that some of the *arguments* he offers for doing so are astonishingly weak. He should not be saying that it is ridiculous for someone who lacks notable private achievements to take up public service, since this claim inadvertently casts a shadow over his own thoroughly admirable endeavors. He should not be saying that popular revolt ipso facto constitutes evidence of a leader's shortcomings, since this claim rebounds immediately upon his own case. (One imagines a sharper-witted Callicles telling Socrates that people who live in glass houses shouldn't throw stones.) And he should not, all things considered, be saying that Pericles is a bad citizen.

Socrates' categorical repudiation of Pericles is all the more shocking when we consider the respect he accords to doctors, a respect so great that Socrates proudly compares himself to one when describing his mission to the Athenians.[116] Doctors are admirable because they aim at the good rather than at the merely pleasant: paying no heed to how a particular medicine may taste or to the pain of a procedure, they focus exclusively on the long-term health of their patients. They thereby perform a valuable service and so, presumably, earn the right to be called good citizens, in spite of the fact that their concern is entirely for bodies, without the slightest thought for the state of a patient's soul. Pericles, however, was acting in a remarkably similar way. In persuading the Athenians to build the walls and dockyards, he was asking them to set aside short-term comfort for the sake of long-term security.[117] (Far from gratifying a preexisting desire, Pericles' proposals met with strong initial resistance.)[118] The walls and dockyards thus constituted a sacrifice of the (physically) pleasant for the sake of the (physically) good, in exactly the same way that a medical operation requires a sacrifice of the (physically) pleasant for the sake of the (physically) good. Pericles behaved like a doctor. Why not consider him admirable, then, within the limits of his self-assigned task?

Is it, perhaps, because walls and dockyards—and presumably also temples like the Parthenon[119]—are mere "trash," as Socrates would like us to believe (519a)? Such an assessment is at best wildly controversial, and certainly not shared by any of Socrates' interlocutors here. Is it because such accomplishments are simply irrelevant to the role of a good politician, politics being exclusively concerned with souls?[120] Again, Gorgias and company are unlikely to agree.[121] It is conceivable, I suppose, that they might include the improvement of souls (under their very different definition![122]) within the job description of politician, but they would surely never consider it a politician's sole concern. For them, and doubtless for most of us too, the construction of effective military defenses counts as a genuine achievement. Perhaps donkey-herders are expected to make their charges more docile; that does not mean, however, that politicians have to set themselves an analogous target.[123]

What Socrates *should* have said, of course, is that Pericles accomplished some public projects of genuine significance, but that he did not undertake (in a serious way) the more important task of improving souls, a task to which he himself, Socrates, has been dedicating his life, while remaining uncertain of how much impact he might have. Pericles was on balance a good citizen, to be sure,[124] but Socrates is a better one. A poor reception should have no retroactive impact on our assessment of the "politician": what counts is the attempt to direct citizens toward the genuine care of the soul. It is not a public servant's fault if he or she is repaid with ingratitude.

This is an eminently sensible position, and one that (as I mentioned above) concords with statements in the *Theaetetus* (150d–e), the *Republic* (489d, 539b–c), the *Phaedo* (90c–d), and elsewhere. It does, however, come at a cost. We must be willing to relinquish some of the charges Socrates levels against Pericles, including the claim that he was a bad citizen. We must also be willing to relinquish some of the charges Socrates levels against unpopular politicians in general.[125] Finally, and most importantly, we must be willing to relinquish some of the charges against rhetoricians. For just as the bad behavior of students does not (on its own) discredit a teacher of philosophy, neither does the bad behavior of citizens (on its own) discredit a statesman, nor that of budding orators a master rhetorician.[126] The Pericles argument is so weak, and its ramifications within the dialogue so devastating, that a mind as sharp as Plato's can only have deployed it strategically, inviting his reader to detect its fallaciousness and to see how many others collapse along with it.

5

Beckett

Antithesis and Tranquility

The three novels Beckett wrote in French between 1947 and 1949—*Molloy*, *Malone Dies*, and *The Unnamable*—are notoriously difficult works of fiction. Any one of them levies a tremendous interpretive burden on its reader. Even within a given volume, a single sentence can prove genuinely daunting; indeed, a mere fragment need not prove that much easier. Take the following 98 words, extracted from a forbidding 2,284-word monster, and indented for greater clarity. Can we make any headway at least in them?

we would seem to know for certain . . .	il semble enfin acquis . . .
that it has not yet been our good fortune	qu'il n'a pas été possible
	jusqu'à présent
to establish	de déterminer
with any degree of accuracy . . .	avec certitude . . .
if it's I who seek,	si c'est moi qui cherche,
what exactly it is I seek,	ce qu'au juste je cherche,
find,	trouve,
lose,	perds,
find again,	retrouve,
throw away,	jette,
seek again,	cherche à nouveau,
find again,	trouve à nouveau,
throw away again,	jette à nouveau,
no, I never threw anything away,	non je n'ai jamais rien jeté,
never threw anything away	jamais rien jeté
of all the things I found,	de tout ce que j'ai trouvé,
never found anything	jamais rien trouvé
that I didn't lose,	que je n'aie perdu,
never lost anything	jamais rien perdu
that I mightn't as well have thrown away,	que je n'eusse pu jeter,

if it's I who seek,	si c'est moi qui cherche,
find,	trouve,
lose,	perds,
find again,	retrouve,
lose again,	reperds,
	cherche encore,
seek in vain,	ne trouve plus,
seek no more . . .	ne cherche plus. . .[1]

Let us at least understand the question correctly: when I speak of making head-way I am asking not what Beckett's words *mean*, but what they are *for*. The most widespread assumption has, I think, been that the two questions can be answered simultaneously, since the function of Beckett's words is the transmission of information; Beckett, the story goes, is *telling* us that there is no ground for epistemological certainty ("it has not yet been our good fortune to establish . . ."), just as he *instructs* us elsewhere that free will is an illusion, *shows* that Descartes is wrong, and helps us *learn* that the self is in language.[2] (We are on familiar terrain here, having seen scholars make similar pronouncements with regard to Chaucer, Plato, and Mark.) Or at the very least, Beckett is *expressing* something, putting on display his deeply fractured soul, riven between affirmation and negation ("no, I never threw anything away") and at tortured grips with the insufficiency of speech.[3] Both of these approaches take it for granted, however, that the what-for question can and need only be answered with relation to the writer, whereas it must also be answered, as Beckett is well aware, with relation to the reader.[4] What do Beckett's texts do for *us*? Why do we, some of us at least, willingly put ourselves through them?

Part 1: Bringing Philosophy to an End

> For in me there have always been two fools, among others, one asking nothing better than to stay where he is and the other imagining that life might be slightly less horrible a little further on. . . . And these inseparable fools I indulged turn about, that they might understand their foolishness.
>
> —Beckett, *Molloy*

Ataraxia

The answer can only be, I think, that readers of Beckett are suffering from the same disease as Beckett's characters, in search of the same recovered health, and eager to undergo the same rehabilitation. (Incidentally, this may also explain why many do *not* take pleasure in Beckett's texts: these are presumably the healthy, or at least the unhealthy in different ways.) The novels are not arguments—who in their right mind would infer from the existence of a confusing story to the conclusion that life in general is absurd?—and not expressions (why would we care so deeply about yet another complaint at the limitations of language?), but *courses of treatment* waiting to be undergone.

Now health here, let me add, means tranquility; the disease is philosophy; and the treatment is nothing other than the trilogy itself. "To know nothing is nothing," writes Molloy, "not to want to know anything likewise, but to be beyond knowing anything, to know you are beyond knowing anything, that is when peace enters in":[5] the ultimate telos of Molloy's quest is not his mother, not knowledge, and not even himself, strictly speaking, but *peace*. It is the calm of a mind that is beyond the reach of any external disturbance, the composure of a soul at one with itself, in a word the "ataraxia" of the ancient Greeks. (Beckett's Watt, titular protagonist of an earlier novel, deemed himself capable of "ataraxy," and Molloy goes so far as to consider it his natural, if fragile, condition.)[6]

And this means that Molloy, like most of Beckett's heroes, is not just a skeptic but an *ancient* skeptic.[7] For him, that is, epistemological questions—questions about what can and cannot be known and with what degree of certainty—are secondary, merely instrumental to the primary goal of ataraxia, freedom from disturbance, enduring peace of mind. If he puts in question who he is, what he seeks, what he finds, what he throws away, and so on, it is not in order to express his inability to know, let alone to convince others that they too are at a loss; rather, he is deploying doubt *strategically*, in the service of a stable equanimity. Thus Beckett, who agrees with his characters on at least this much, departs from the post-structuralist critics who so often claim him for their own: the telos here is neither the exposure of error nor the advent of political utopia but a resolutely personal silence.[8]

Antilogoi

Peace of mind is, of course, easier wished for than achieved. Tranquility is not our natural state: chattering incessantly, the brain can be silenced only at the cost of immense effort. Any number of intractable worries keep us awake at night, with philosophical questions in particular—who are we really? is free will an illusion? is there a God? what is the relationship between mind and body?—tending to tantalize us, both by their genuine importance and by their apparent susceptibility to resolution,[9] even though they merely serve, in the end, to distract us from the business of living.[10] "The chief malady of man," Beckett would agree with Pascal, "is restless curiosity about things he cannot know."[11]

Once down the path of reflection, we lose all hope of calm. And we become, in addition, very hard to cure. It may well not be enough to *want* to stop, to *decide* to cease ruminating; thinking is, in its own special way, a form of addiction, and the will is a notoriously weak opponent. Nor is it possible to *argue* ourselves into stopping. "If we wish to philosophize," Aristotle was delighted to point out, "then we must philosophize; and if we wish not to philosophize, then we must [still] philosophize; in either case, therefore, we must philosophize."[12] Which is to say, the idea of arguing oneself out of philosophy is simply a contradiction in terms. (This is another reason, incidentally, why Beckett's aim cannot simply be to *tell* us something: for the aim he has in mind, information is of no assistance.)

No, the sole solution is to inveigle the intellect into abdicating of its own accord, out of sheer despair.[13] It must somehow form the impression not only that it does not know but also that it *cannot* know the thing in question; it must become persuaded, as we saw above, that it is "beyond knowing anything."[14] Otherwise, the temptation to address the unanswered questions, the dim intuition that certainty is somewhere to be had, will always be a danger. And in order to achieve this state of affairs, we must bring before it *opposite hypotheses* in answer to every question that arises, the equal plausibility of which will induce it to suspend judgment indefinitely.[15] "You announce, then you renounce, so it is, that helps you on, that helps the end to come";[16] you indulge the two fools within yourself, as Molloy would put it, until both of them give up.[17]

Now all of this is straight out of the skeptical playbook.[18] For skepticism, as Sextus Empiricus defines it, "is an ability to set out oppositions among things which appear and things which are thought of . . ., an ability by which, because of the equipollence [$\dot{\iota}\sigma\sigma\theta\acute{\epsilon}\nu\epsilon\iota\alpha\nu$] in the opposed objects and accounts, we come first to suspension of judgment [$\dot{\epsilon}\pi\sigma\chi\acute{\eta}\nu$] and afterwards to tranquillity [$\dot{\alpha}\tau\alpha\rho\alpha\xi\acute{\iota}\alpha\nu$]."[19] As Sextus realized, it is never a matter of showing that a particular theory (or even series of theories) cannot work: refutation, which always leaves room to switch to a new angle of attack, is just not demoralizing enough.[20] What we need is an impossible choice between two opposing hypotheses. *Antilogoi* are what begets *epoché*, and *epoché* is what begets *ataraxia*; in Beckettian terms, "find again, lose again, seek in vain, seek no more."

Resignation, then, is an achievement, not a starting point. Nothingness is not a state that preexists objects and beliefs but is instead a product of their mutual cancellation.[21] (Thus Murphy's senses "found themselves at peace. . . . Not the numb peace of their own suspension, but the positive peace that comes when the somethings give way, or perhaps simply add up, to the Nothing.")[22] And silence—the true silence, "the silence not of vacuum but of plenum"[23]—is not a given, but requires, just as in Mallarmé, to be *made*. If one speaks, indeed, it is only in order to bring speech to a close: "when all goes silent, and comes to an end, it will be because the words have been said, those it behoved to say."[24]

Is Beckett's ideal achievable? The narrator of *The Unnamable* has his doubts. "Can one," he asks, "be ephectic otherwise than unawares?"[25] Is it possible, in other words, to *know* that one is suspending judgment, given that suspension of judgment requires (by definition) the absence of knowledge?[26] Is it possible, as Molloy puts it, "to know you are beyond knowing anything"? If not, then the game of thinking can never reach a conclusion. Still, Moran allows himself to dream of it—"to be literally incapable of motion at last, that must be something! . . . your memory a blank! *And just enough brain intact to allow you to exult!*" (140, my emphasis)[27]—and it gains some plausibility, I think, from the fact that there is something it *feels* like to know. It is the experience of a quiz show contestant with her finger on the buzzer: she has to know *that* she knows before she knows *what* she knows. There is something it feels like to know that we know. And correspondingly, there is something it feels like to know that we don't know. And so we can, if we are lucky, bring thinking to an end after all.

One Step Forward

Beckett does depart from the ancient skeptics in one important way.[28] The quotation from which we started speaks, to be sure, of the abdication of the intellect; still, the self-correction here yields not uncertainty but *certainty*, to such an extent indeed that the sentence continues to build on the newly acquired foundation.[29] Does the speaker throw things away? Perhaps not. Is it even he that searches? Perhaps not. But *somebody* searches, somebody finds, somebody loses—this much is repeated—and, most important, somebody seeks no more. To speak technically for a moment, our sentence fragment begins with an *epanorthosis* (i.e., revision: "throw away again, *no, I never threw anything away*") but shifts to *anadiplosis* (a new clause opening with the last phrase of the previous: "I never threw anything away, *never threw anything away of all the things I found*").[30]

In a similar example—

and again the tiny silence,	et à nouveau l'infime silence,
and the listening again,	
for what,	
no one knows,	aux aguets
a sign of life perhaps,	d'on ne sait quoi,
that must be it,	un signe de vie,
a sign of life	ça doit être ça,
escaping someone,	un signe de vie
and bound to be denied if it came,	qui échapperait à quelqu'un,
that's it surely . . .	qu'on nierait s'il venait,
	c'est sûrement ça . . .
(372)	(*I,* 142–43)—

the narrator's first instinct is to doubt ("no one knows"), but this doubt is itself doubted,[31] a new hypothesis is put in place ("a sign of life perhaps"), and the new hypothesis is tested, affirmed, and even developed (the anaphoric "a sign of life escaping someone . . ."). Elsewhere, we frequently find a narrator refining rather than rejecting his initial statement, gradually reaching a level of conceptual precision that satisfies him. Thus Molloy: "at the end there were two recesses, no, that's not the word . . . I entered one of the alcoves, wrong again . . . I crossed the alley into the other chapel, that's the word" (60–61).[32] This modicum of success is far more common than one might imagine.[33]

In fact, the trilogy's forward line is continually being interrupted—indeed increasingly interrupted: one of the sentences in *The Unnamable* boasts more than five hundred commas—not only by backtracking (the retraction of a hypothesis) or by horizontal shifts (the proposal of a new hypothesis) but also by what one might call a movement *down*, down toward a refinement or qualification[34] of the original hypothesis, and it is this vertical motion that allows the discourse to regain its momentum. Beckett's prose does not move in a straight line, to be sure, but it does not run in endless circles either; instead it describes a steady *spiral*, gradually reaching down into the essential, out into the knowable.[35]

Contrary to appearances, then, not everything remains uncertain.[36] We know, to start with, that there is a consciousness (whoever it may belong to and wherever it may be). We know, in addition, that there is suffering, both physical and mental. There is the impression of solitude (actual or metaphorical), of imprisonment within the walls of one's body. There is a desire to improve the situation, whether by altering it or by ending it. There is a voice, or at least the impression of one (we might speak at least of *phenomenological* certainties, even where epistemological certainties are lacking). There is a relentless *fascination* with just such issues: existence, identity, knowledge, space and time, expression, the obstacles between individuals, the pain of life, the desire to end, the will to continue, the limits of one's power to affect things. And then, of course, there is the doubt itself; of that much, surely, there is never any doubt.

From the juxtaposition of one proposition with its opposite, we may draw four possible conclusions. We may judge, first, that proposition A is true; second, that proposition B is true; third, that both are true at different times or in different ways; or fourth, that we cannot know. Now any one of these conclusions is equally valuable from the point of view of Beckett's characters, so long as it bears the stamp of finality. To decide that it is A or that it is B is less of a cause for celebration than it might appear: this knowledge is merely instrumental to ataraxia, to an end of our concern about the question. "But once Watt had grasped, in its complexity, the mechanism of this arrangement . . . *then it interested him no more*, and he enjoyed a comparative *peace of mind*, in this connexion."[37] Conversely, however, to decide that one does not and cannot know the answer is less of a cause for dismay than it might appear: from the point of view of ataraxia, knowledge of ignorance is just as good as knowledge simpliciter.[38]

Thus Beckett's text is constantly moving in two directions at once, forward into corollaries of premises already posited, backward to test or reject those premises. Regressing and advancing by turns, it relentlessly pares away to the essential, builds another layer upon that foundation, finds that layer flimsy, knocks it down, builds another, and so on and on. Eventually, every question will either have been solved or have been dissolved.[39] Eventually, we can hope at least to know what can be known, and to know of everything else that it cannot; to know, in other words, the limits of our knowledge, and thereby, at long last, to bring philosophy to an end.[40]

Part 2: Finding the Self to Lose the Self

> One is what one is, partly at least.
>
> —Beckett, *Molloy*

An Irreducible Singleness

For most philosophical issues, the treatment is simple enough (conceptually speaking, at any rate): juxtapose competing claims, feel the "equal force" of each, and let them cancel each other out. But when it comes to the question of who we are, the treatment turns out to be far more elaborate. In part this is because the temptation is particularly intractable, an itch it is almost impossible not to scratch ("but my dear man," says a rather imperious voice in *The Unnamable*, "come, be reasonable, look, this is you, look at this photograph, and here's your file . . . at your age, to have no identity, it's a scandal").[41] In part it may be because all other cures depend on this one, since without some minimal locus of known consistency, we cannot be sure of having overcome philosophy (we might otherwise worry that it was merely a *part* of us—or an earlier, discarded self—that thought it had done so). And in part, surely, it is because the matter itself is so convoluted. Even leaving aside changes over time, which appear to vex Beckett somewhat less than they did Proust,[42] we still find ourselves faced with an extremely difficult set of problems. What, if anything, is the core of our identity? And how, if at all, can it be known?[43]

If one thing is clear, it is that whatever can be taken away from us without causing us to be a different person cannot form part of our self-definition. Possessions, for example—bicycles, knife-rests, sucking-stones, all the objects that Malone so carefully lists—are liable to be misplaced without the slightest effect on the core personality. Vocations, too, are dispensable, and become less and less important in Beckett's writing as it circles more and more tightly around the true self: whereas Murphy works as a psychiatric nurse, Watt as a servant, and Moran as an agent of some kind, Molloy, Malone, and Mahood have no job to speak of (assuming, of course, that one does not count serving inadvertently as a restaurant sign). We are neither what we own nor what we do for a living.

Our nationality, likewise, is external to us: like Beckett himself, Beckett's characters are Irishmen who speak impeccable French and who mark time by Bastille day, the Transfiguration, and the Assumption,[44] even though they refer to the Mayor of Cork and the Bank of England and hail from places like Bally.[45] There is no suggestion here of "identity" in what has become today its most widespread usage, namely membership in a social, national, racial, or ethnic group. Such groups, in Beckett, are nothing more than contingent clusters of resolutely solitary individuals; even a group of two is after all merely a "pseudo-couple."[46] Each of us is, as Molloy would put it, in a jar, our soul—to borrow a different metaphor from the same character—on an elastic, ready to snap back at any moment from every outward stretch (296–97).[47] And thus the presence of other people, far from offering community, merely confirms the prison of our subjectivity. To see a man and a woman side by side on a Jack Yeats canvas, says Beckett, is to receive "a kind of petrified insight into one's ultimate hard irreducible inorganic singleness," to see "two irreducible singlenesses & the impassable immensity between."[48]

Family is no exception. As narrator, Molloy considers turning to his mother for an understanding of his existence—"if I'm ever reduced to looking for a meaning in my life, you never can tell, it's in that old mess I'll stick my nose to begin with"[49]—and it may even have been for this (in addition to money) that, as character, he initially set out on his quest; he is, however, clearly mistaken. There is no meaning to be found in "that old mess," and it is significant, I think, that the narrator of *The Unnamable* "remembers" the decision in a strikingly different way: "I'm looking for my mother," he says, "to kill her."[50] Our personal origins are ultimately as irrelevant as our communal origins, our communal origins as our vocation, our vocation as our possessions. In none of these are we anywhere to be found.

Res Cogitans

What, then, about the body? It might seem, at first glance, a bit more promising as a guarantor of personal identity. I am always where my body is, and no one else occupies the same space at any given instant: could not a minimal definition of myself be *whatever it is that has been where I have been* over the course of my life? Not quite. The problem is that, on Beckett's view, the body can undergo significant changes without the sense of self being profoundly affected.[51] Molloy remains Molloy, for example, in spite of losing the use of his legs; it is indeed a general feature of Beckett's characters that they tend to combine remarkable mental agility with extensive bodily decay, "the soul," as the trilogy's last narrator puts it, "being notoriously immune from deterioration and dismemberment."[52] My hands, in the words of Molloy, are not mine; far from *being* me, my feet take *orders* from me, from the incorporeal something that I cannot help feeling I am.[53]

We are, then, most centrally a mind, a "thinking thing" (*res cogitans*), as Descartes so memorably put it. Or rather, we are *part* of a mind. For once we begin applying the same criterion to the contents of the mind, we find—contra Descartes, now—that many of these will need to be discarded from our definition. Memories fade, and yet, short of senility, we still remain who we are (none of us recalls everything that happened in the past twenty-four hours, let alone the past twenty-four years).[54] Beliefs and desires change ("Hard to believe I was ever that young whelp. The voice! Jesus! And the aspirations!"[55]). Drives conflict with one another (one thinks here of the will to go on and the will to end, those twin impulses that, in so many of Beckett's characters, vie perennially for control). If we take the reduction to its logical limit, we are left with a vanishingly small kernel. Nor can that kernel ever be seen, since it is precisely what always does the seeing. "All my senses are trained on me," says Malone, "I am no prey for them" (186): when I look, that is, I see "me"—the conglomeration of detachable parts—and never the "I" that constitutes my core identity.[56]

There is, in other words, a serious epistemological problem. And there is also an ontological problem, one that is, if anything, even more intractable. Let's say I am to be identified with (part of) my mind, as our amended Descartes suggests. There remains the fact that *communication takes place between mind and body*. From one direction, as we saw above, the mind appears to issue orders that the body understands and obeys. From the other, the body—in the form of the senses—delivers information to the mind, information that may not always be accurate but that the mind frequently feels itself incapable of having invented. If mind and body are indeed separate, how can such two-way interaction be possible? If not, am I a different person every time something happens to my body? Every time I catch cold? Every time a strand of hair changes color? Every time a single cell is replaced?

Descartes' own solution, notoriously, was to posit an agency responsible for the mediation, in the form of the pineal gland.[57] This, however, merely displaces the question. Is the pineal gland made of matter? If so, then it has no point of entry into the mind, and we will need an additional gland to deliver the messages. If not, then it can receive no signals from the body, and we will need an additional gland to communicate the orders. Either way, the same problem will affect the second gland, causing the need for a third gland, and so ad infinitum. How then can the mind ever have received information from the body? That, on one reading, is what the narrator of *The Unnamable* is asking himself early in his narration:

> I can see them still, my delegates [*i.e.*, *Molloy, Malone*, etc.]. The things they
> have told me! About men, the light of day . . . But when, through what chan-
> nels, did I communicate with these gentlemen? Did they intrude on me here?

No, no one has ever intruded on me here. Elsewhere then. But I have never been elsewhere. . . . What puzzles me is the thought of being indebted for this information to persons with whom I can never have been in contact. Can it be innate knowledge? Like that of good and evil. This seems improbable to me. Innate knowledge of my mother, for example, is that conceivable? Not for me.[58]

How does the speaker know what he knows? Some of it, including abstract concepts such as good and evil, could (if Kant is right[59]) be part of the standard-issue furniture of the brain, but knowledge of particulars—knowledge, for example, of what his mother is like—requires empirical data gathered in the world. Now he cannot have gathered this data himself, being unable to venture out, and so he must have received it from his "delegates," the senses. Yet he and they have never met, and can in principle never meet. How is the conundrum to be resolved?[60]

One suggestion that Beckett's characters periodically entertain is that the apparent interaction between mind and body is in fact a magic trick performed, everywhere at once and billions of times per second, by God. As "occasionalists" Malebranche and Geulincx present it, each time our senses perceive something, God places a notion of it in our mind at exactly the same moment; each time our will decides something, God moves our body at exactly the same moment.[61] Alternatively, God has set up from the very beginning a coordinated system of mental and corporeal events, the famous "preestablished harmony" of Leibniz. It is not clear, however, that either view can really be taken seriously by such professional skeptics as Molloy, Malone, Mahood, and company. So where does that leave us?

Solutions and Dissolutions

It leaves us, I would like to say, with one problem that may be solved and one that may only be dissolved. The interaction problem is and remains a mystery; all we can do is shrug it off, which is exactly the approach adopted by Beckett's characters. With admirable breeziness and cheery insouciance, Molloy tells us that "at a given moment, *pre-established if you like, I don't much mind*, the gentleman turned back."[62] As for Murphy, even more delightfully, he

> felt himself split in two, a body and a mind. They had intercourse apparently, otherwise he could not have known that they had anything in common. But he felt his mind to be bodytight and did not understand through what channel the intercourse was effected nor how the two experiences came to overlap. He was satisfied that neither followed from the other. He neither

thought a kick because he felt one nor felt a kick because he thought one. . . .
Perhaps there was, outside space and time, a non-mental non-physical Kick
from all eternity, dimly revealed to Murphy in its correlated modes of consciousness and extension, the kick *in intellectu* and the kick *in re* . . . However
that might be, Murphy was content to accept this partial congruence of the
world of his mind with the world of his body. . . . The problem was of little
interest. (*Murphy*, 109)

Here is Murphy beginning from the premise that mind and body are separate; raising the objection that if they were *totally* separate, his mind would
not even have an idea of his body, and the very issues would not arise in the
first place; trying out an empiricist hypothesis à la Locke (my senses feel a
kick therefore my mind thinks "kick"); trying out an idealist hypothesis à la
Berkeley (my mind thinks "kick" and invents the apparent evidence of my
senses); trying out a metaphysical hypothesis à la Leibniz (thanks to God,
who created all events at the beginning of time, there is a preestablished
harmony between my ideas and my perceptions); and finally rejecting each
and every one of them, dismissing the problem as "of little interest." We do
not know, we cannot know, we do not need to know. (I should add, in case
this seems unnecessarily defeatist, that there is no sign of the mind-body
debate being resolved any time soon, in spite of the hyperbolic claims of certain materialists.)

With the epistemological problem, by contrast, progress *can* be made, albeit only partial and only via an elaborate set of steps, steps to which the
remainder of the present section will be devoted. The opening pair—step one,
seek yourself in the external world; step two, fail—may well come as little
surprise. (Not only does Molloy never see his mother again, but there is no
sense that it would have helped if he had, no sense that sticking his nose into
"that mess" would have revealed "a meaning in [his] life.") The third, by contrast, is a bit more unexpected: *enjoy* the failure, *which turns out to be a kind of
success.*

In order to understand this, let us consider once again Sextus Empiricus.
"Men of talent," Sextus writes, "troubled by anomalies in things and puzzled as
to which belief they should rather assent to, came to investigate what in things
is true and what false, thinking that by deciding these issues they would become
tranquil." "Being unable to do this," he continues, "they suspended judgment.
But when they suspended judgment, tranquillity followed as it were fortuitously,
as a shadow follows a body."[63] In other words, having begun from a desire to set
their minds at rest by solving all puzzles and explaining all anomalies, thinking
persons find themselves unable to decide between two equally compelling theories; they give up; and lo and behold, irony of ironies, they attain the peace of
mind they set out to achieve.

So too with Molloy, who is at his happiest when he is derailed from his pursuit and lies down in a ditch ("this ditch. How joyfully I would vanish there, sinking deeper and deeper under the rains") or sinks into a lawn: "my life became the life of this garden as it rode the earth. . . . Yes, there were times when I forgot not only who I was, but that I was, forgot to be."[64] And so too with Moran, who experiences a "growing resignation to being dispossessed of self."[65] The quest in both cases leads to failure, but failure in both cases leads to abandonment, and abandonment to unexpected peace.

Two Failures

Unfortunately, however, such peace is as precarious as it is thoroughgoing, as slender as it is deep. Neither Molloy nor Moran is permitted to dwell indefinitely in his literal or metaphorical ditch, sinking deeper and deeper under the rains; instead, each is called upon to produce a written account, as if (though this is only implicit) a voice in their head were prompting them to imagine that selfhood can still be had, if not through the outside world then at least through writing, through introspection, through narrative.[66] This is step four, the confessional step, the one which operates on the Rousseauist assumption that in the teeth of self-division and inauthenticity, something like a unified essence of personality may yet be dragged from the wreckage of a life, precisely in its recounting.

But can the recounting of a life really reveal who I am? Not in the world of Beckett. At best, as we saw above, such a recounting puts the *me* on display—that set of contingent, exchangeable characteristics—leaving the *I* entirely out of the spotlight. And at worst, it distorts the narrative even of that "me." For stories have a way of imposing a spurious order on the events they contain. And so instead of relating our own existence in such a way as to make it cohere as a totality, we frequently end up inventing a *character* whose life makes sense; if our story hangs together, this is only because it is not really *our* story. Step five, then: fail again. Invent while trying to remember. "I invented my memories," admits the narrator of *The Unnamable*, "not one is of me."[67]

Yet once more the failure stunningly reverses itself. Did *Molloy* turn out, in spite of its narrator's best efforts, to be a fiction?[68] Well, so much the better. Malone not only acknowledges the fact ("then it will all be over with the Murphys, Merciers, Molloys, Morans and Malones"[69]) but embraces it, *deliberately* choosing to tell stories, safe in the knowledge that they are exactly that.[70] "I began again," he writes, "with a different aim, no longer in order to succeed, but in order to fail."[71] Step six: fictionalize. To be sure, if autobiography is fiction, then any attempt to depict the self will at the same time, necessarily, be an evasion of self; but if it is an evasion of self, is it not precisely the thing we were looking for in the first place? If failure is the goal, then will not failure, paradoxically, be a form of success?

It will—or rather, it would. For even such failure cannot be accomplished. "I wonder if I am not talking yet again about myself," laments Malone. "Shall I be incapable, to the end, of lying on any other subject?"[72] "You think you are inventing," echoes Molloy, "you think you are escaping, and all you do is stammer out your lesson, the remnants of a pensum one day got by heart and long forgotten."[73] "All these stories about travellers, these stories about paralytics," concurs the final narrator, "all are mine."[74] Even in one's wildest flights of fancy, a narratorial or authorial persona still persists. Step seven, then: inadvertently betray the truth. If the Molloy-style failure was to invent when trying to remember, the Malone-style failure is remembering when trying to invent. And failing to succeed and failing to fail both seem equally inescapable.[75]

"I confess, I give in, there is I"

One last time, however, failure daringly mutates into its opposite. If the stories are actually about me—if they end up, in spite of my conscious intentions, with an unmistakable *air de famille* ("Mahood's old tales," notes the final narrator, "are all alike"[76])—then perhaps I can learn something about myself from them after all, regardless of their unreliable content.[77] Perhaps I can *work back from what I have done to knowledge of who I am*, the way Beckett's characters frequently infer from their own actions to what their motivations must have been ("I preferred the garden to the house, *to judge by the long hours I spent there*"; "I *must have needed my mother, otherwise why this frenzy of wanting to get to her?*"[78]). Just as in Proust, so in Beckett self-knowledge is available not by introspection but by what might be termed self-sleuthing, self-espionage, taking oneself by surprise. Step eight: work back from the style of what one produces, from those endless stories that bear the identical imprint of one's deepest disposition, to what that disposition must be in order to have inspired them.[79]

Can this be right? Can there really be a self in Beckett? Does the narrator of the third volume not repeatedly insist that it is not he speaking, and indeed that he does not exist? Yes, the narrator does indeed say such things. But we should not believe him. As he himself ultimately admits, "there must be someone," and since there is no one else, that someone must be he;[80] to doubt one's existence is, after all, simultaneously to affirm it.[81] To say "it is not I talking" is already to posit the existence of an *I* separate from the statements one happens to make. And to say "it is not I talking" is also, it must be added, to be doing some talking. For even if *some* of what the narrator is saying has been dictated to him by a Voice, surely *this*—the statement that everything is dictation—is not itself dictation. Surely the affect of distaste for the dictated words comes from a separate source,[82] the same source that, when it borrows clichés from a preexistent stock of language, takes particular pleasure in deforming them ("there are some irons in the fire, *let them melt*").[83]

There *is* an I, then, and it *is* speaking, in spite of what the narrator may some-times allege. He periodically denies his own existence, to be sure, but then so does the speaker in Beckett's play *Not I*, a work in which it is absolutely explicit that the denial is a lie, a self-protective reflex designed to shield against self-recognition ("she began trying to . . . delude herself . . . [that] it was not hers at all . . . not her voice at all" [219]). He denies his existence, yes, but this may just be out of confusion: "when I think of the time I've wasted with these bran-dips, beginning with Murphy, who wasn't even the first, when I had me . . . within easy reach . . ., rotting with solitude and neglect, till I doubted my own existence, and even still, today, I have no faith in it, none, so that I have to say, when I speak, Who speaks."[84] After so many failed efforts, so many misguided attempts to seize the self by means of narratives that turned out to be fictions, demoraliza-tion has set in, a creeping disbelief in the very existence of the thing so vainly sought for; that does not mean, however, that it was never there.

Indeed, a certain knee-jerk pessimism is typical in general of this character's approach to life. At every turn, the negative hypothesis comes first, only fol-lowed belatedly by the positive. What, for example, can be said of the real silence?

what can be said of the real silence,	que dire du vrai silence,
I don't know,	je ne sais pas,
that I don't know what it is,	que je ne le connais pas,
that there is no such thing,	qu'il n'y en a pas,
that perhaps there is such a thing,	qu'il y en a peut-être,
yes,	oui,
that perhaps there is,	qu'il y en a peut-être,
somewhere,	quelque part,
I'll never know.	je ne le saurai jamais.
(408)	(*I*, 203)

Here as almost everywhere, the initial instinct is to put everything in doubt (what can be said of the real silence? I simply don't know). But the first wave of wariness recedes just slightly across the sand of thought, leaving behind it a thin strip of certitude (I know at least that I don't know; I *do* know what can be said, which is that I don't know anything about it). And then the second wave recedes a little further, revealing an attitude that is negative but specific (I can at least say that it does not exist). And as the third wave departs, it uncovers the most positive claim of all: yes, the real silence *does* exist.

This movement, this slow, painstaking, continually interrupted crawl in the direction of hard-won certainty, is, I think, symptomatic of the novel as a whole. And so it is no surprise that the narrator finally comes out and says, a couple of dozen pages before the end, "there is I, yes, I feel it, I confess, I give in, there is I."[85] For all the Beckettians who have so gaily claimed (on the author's behalf) that there is no self, it has to be pointed out that the narrator himself ends up strongly suspecting its existence, that he wonders whether his earlier denials have been the result of confusion, and that there is a real suggestion that "it's not I" has just been wishful thinking, as it so clearly is in *Not I*.[86] Full-blown self-hood, as we know, is something not given but achieved;[87] it must be added, how-ever, that full-blown *non*-selfhood is also something not given but achieved. Postmodern skepticism is too light, takes too easily for granted (in theory, at least) that the self is an illusion, to be dispelled by the mere snap of one's philo-sophical fingers.[88] Beckett, by contrast, knows that the self is all too real, its gradual dispersion the task of a lifetime.

Negative Anthropology

For Beckett, then, the ultimate goal is an enduring peace of mind, a lasting respite from nagging philosophical questions; to such ends, it is sufficient to dissolve those questions that cannot be solved; in both cases it is more a matter of patient endeavor than of punctual insight; and though such solving and dissolving is particularly complicated in the case of selfhood, the self being both stubbornly present (contra Hume, contra Malone) and stubbornly elusive (contra Rousseau, contra Moran), some knowledge about it may none-theless be had, thanks to the a posteriori process of working back from its effects.[89]

To this overall account, only two qualifications remain to be added. First, it must be admitted that there is a limit to what can be known about the self, in the same way that, as we saw above, there is a limit to what can be known about the world. But once again, where there are things we cannot know, we can at least know *that* we do not know them, indeed we can at least know that we *cannot* know them; and that, we recall, is "where peace enters in." Peace enters in when we can say, of the knowable, just what it is, and grasp, of the unknowable, that it can never be known. As the narrator of *Texts for Nothing* puts it, "I'd like to be sure I left no stone unturned before reporting me missing and giving up":[90] ataraxia requires only that we turn every stone. We do not need a full-blown picture of the nature of the self; a negative anthropology, to borrow a term from Molloy, will do instead.[91] It will be good enough to identify everything we are not—good enough, like explorers on the brink of an abyss, to chart the contours of the forbidden territory. Step nine: trace the limits of possible knowledge.[92]

Second, it should be repeated that the discovery of (parts of) the self is not, as it is in Proust, a cause for celebration, an end in itself; in Beckett, one seeks it so as to be done with it. "Never found anything that I didn't lose . . .": in Beckett, everything is secured only in order to be discarded.[93] Why is Molloy looking for, and writing about, his mother? *He* may believe that it is in order to understand himself, but as we saw above, the narrator of the *Unnamable* knows better. "I'm looking for my mother to kill her," he writes, thinking of his time spent under the guise of Molloy; "I should have thought of that a bit earlier, before being born."[94] All of a sudden a quest for identity turns into a quest for *non*identity, a drive not to find but to *eliminate* the mother, in order never to have been born. In order, so to speak, to be unborn again.

Lying in a ditch or sinking into a lawn can only be a temporary stop-gap, never enough to quell the voices definitively; in order to overcome once and for all the desire for selfhood, *one must do everything possible to find it.* One must *be*, as the protagonist of *How It Is* puts it, before one can cease being; one must "get into [one's] story," as the narrator of *Texts for Nothing* concurs, "in order to get out of it"; one must be caught, in the words of *The Unnamable*, so as to be thrown away.[95] Step ten: find the self to lose the self.

The Beckettian Spiral

Here's what we know, then, about the ten-stage process of deindividuation. We start out wanting to lose ourselves, in order to attain peace of mind. We seek this directly, simply by ignoring ourselves, so to speak. But the questions are too insistent. So we try to be done with them by *answering* them, whether by exploring the world or, when that proves unavailing, by writing our autobiography. But this doesn't work either: we succeed only in *inventing*, in constructing a persona whose life makes perfect sense but who, perhaps in part for that very reason, is not actually us. But this seems like a version of the solution we were first looking for, namely an escape from ourselves, so maybe we have inadvertently achieved what we set out to do. But no, it's not a real escape, for the very fact that we keep telling more or less the same story—that unbroken series of philosophical tramps with hats and Irish accents in French—means that it is, after all, our story; not our story in the sense of the story *about* us, but our story in the sense of the story *belonging* to us, the one we and we alone are uniquely equipped (or uniquely doomed) to tell. But this, in turn, seems like a version of the solution we were looking for *second*, which is self-knowledge. We do end up, at last, able to say something about ourselves. We try again, telling a second story that captures the essential and eliminates some of the inessential. We fail again, but as Beckett would say, we fail better. We keep spiraling downward, toward the core of being and the boundary of knowledge. Hope is held out of one day going silent, by knowing all that can be known, and—just as important—by knowing that everything else is firmly out of reach.

Though some (to repeat) have seen Beckett's works as revolving in endless circles,[96] the shape of their movement is actually a spiral, neither a linear forward thrust nor an abject return to zero but a process that, over time, yields incremental gains. Only Molloy and Moran aim to find themselves—or lose themselves—in the outside world (Molloy's mother, Molloy's ditch; Moran's quarry, Moran's bees). Only Molloy commits his story to writing in the (largely) naive belief in his power to find himself in the telling. Malone learns to tell stories as diversions. And the final narrator learns to work back from these diversions to knowledge of self, oscillating henceforth between fiction and declaration.

As the trilogy moves forward, so it moves *inward*, narrowing from Molloy's open spaces to the confines of his mother's room, from the cramped quarters of Malone to Mahood's jar; shedding Moran's vocation and Molloy's mobility and Malone's body and Mahood's fullness of mind;[97] leaving behind the various avatars and coming, finally, to speak of the I, in the (hesitant) recognition that this has been the task all along, that it (and it alone) has been there all along.[98] "Faith, that's an idea," says the final narrator, "mutilate, mutilate, and perhaps some day . . . you'll succeed in beginning to look like yourself."[99] By gradually paring away the inessential, the trilogy spirals down toward the core, toward the bedrock of the certain and the inexorable inscrutability of everything else.[100]

An End to Everything?

There may, perhaps, be even more at stake than this. If it turns out that Schopenhauer is right—and Beckett at times suspects that he is[101]—then our individual existence is only part of the picture: at another, deeper level, there is just a single undivided substance (the "Will"), a roiling, seething, undifferentiated mass of energy.[102] Particulars like human beings (or dachshunds, or oak trees) are, at base, only offshoots, projections, "objectifications" of the Will, like the various pseudopodia on an amoeba. "The forms are many," as Malone puts it, "in which the unchanging seeks relief from its formlessness."[103]

Now this means, as a corollary, that existence as a human individual is inherently fraught. We have as it were fallen away from the oneness of being; our very existence is in a sense a sin. "The true meaning of tragedy," writes Schopenhauer, "is the deeper insight that what the hero atones for is not his own particular sins but original sin, in other words, the guilt of existence itself"; "the tragic figure," echoes Beckett in his Proust book, "represents the expiation of original sin, of the original and eternal sin of him and all his 'socii malorum,' the sin of having been born."[104] That, perhaps, is why Malone feels that everyone is a criminal ("so long as it is what is called a living being you can't go wrong, you have the guilty one"), why the narrator of *The Unnamable* suspects that he was given a task at birth "as a punishment for having been born," and why the narrator of *Texts for Nothing* describes life as "that obscure assize where to be is to be guilty."[105] Life in the phenomenal world (here termed "the world as representation") is guilt, before we have even begun to act.

Life in the world as representation is also *pain*. We are doomed as soon as we are born; human existence, as Beckett strongly and hilariously implies in *Murphy*, is a chess game in which pawn to king 4 is "the primary cause of all White's subsequent difficulties."[106] From then on, it can offer us only two things, suffering and tedium. As offshoots of the Will, we are entities that are constantly driven by desire. If a particular desire is unsatisfied, we suffer; if it is satisfied, we lose interest, become bored, languish in ennui—which is to say, we begin to suffer in a new way, suffer from the obstruction of a different desire, a higher-order desire, the desire for desire itself.[107] Either way, then, we will continue indefinitely to be helpless victims of frustration. At best we can hope for a constant stream of new yearnings, the speed of their mutual succession distracting us from the fact that none of them makes us happy. "The nature of man," as Schopenhauer puts it, "consists in the fact that his will strives, is satisfied, strives anew, and so on and on; in fact his happiness and well-being consist only in the transition from desire to satisfaction, and from this to a fresh desire, such transition going forward rapidly. For the non-appearance of satisfaction is suffering; the empty longing for a new desire is languor, boredom." Beckett's Arsène, in *Watt*, agrees: "to hunger, thirst, lust, every day afresh and every day in vain, after the old prog, the old booze, the old whores, that's the nearest we'll ever get to felicity."[108]

Temporary relief is afforded by aesthetic contemplation, in which we encounter phenomenal realities for the first time as they are in themselves, outside of their actual or possible relations to our own purposes, and thus break free of the "wheel of Ixion" to which our desire normally keeps us chained. In front of a landscape or an artwork, "we forget our individuality, our will, and continue to exist only as pure subject, as clear mirror of the object"; the attention "considers things without interest"; "then all at once the peace, always sought but always escaping us on that first path of willing, comes to us of its own accord . . . the painless state, prized by Epicurus as the highest good" (*WWR*, 1:34, p. 178; 1:38, p. 196). Beckett's Watt knows shining moments like these, moments in which what transpires before his eyes "develop[s] a purely plastic content, and gradually los[es] . . . all meaning, even the most literal," becoming an incident "of great formal brilliance and of indeterminable purport" (72–73, 74). Still, such moments never last; desires always return, and hope, torturing hope, springs alas eternal.[109]

What we need is to overcome desire on a permanent basis; what we need are exercises that, like Murphy's rocking in the dark, may slowly free us from the grip of needs and wants, and deliver us, as Malone would say, into "helplessness and will-lessness."[110] Here as before there are connections to ancient skepticism, as well as to Eastern philosophy.[111] Here too there are connections to Geulincx, who enjoins us to cease wishing for things to be one way when they are another, since we have no control over them in any case.[112] *Ubi nihil vales,* says Geulincx, *ibi nihil velis:* where you are worth nothing (i.e., where you have no power), there you should have no desire.[113]

Schopenhauer, however, goes one stage further. At the high point of his dizzyingly beautiful metaphysical system, Schopenhauer posits the possibility for our asceticism not only to quiet our own individual desires but to put an end to the Will once and for all—which is to say, to put an end to *everything* once and for all. "The whole of the visible world is only the objectification, the mirror, of the Will, accompanying it to knowledge of itself, and indeed . . . to the possibility of its salvation," he writes (*WWR,* 1:52, p. 266).[114] Could the undivided substance that underlies everything have willed, so to speak, its own destruction? Could it have objectified itself in human beings with the precise aim of coming at last to see itself in a mirror, a mirror that shows it the full horror of its existence and thus stuns it into silence, just as spectators at a tragedy (*WWR,* 1:51, 252–53), on witnessing the full horror of *their* existence, begin to give up the ghost? "It's thanks to the earth that revolves that the earth revolves no more," says the trilogy's final narrator, "and pain comes to an end" (381); "all dead or none," concurs *How It Is,* "our justice . . . wills that too" (132).[115] If Schopenhauer is right, then the end of the Beckettian spiral is peace not just for me but for *us,* not just now but forever.

Part 3:   Fail Better

> No matter. Try again. Fail again. Fail better.
> —Beckett, *Worstward Ho*

Glimpses of the Ideal

With regard to a world so permeated with failure it is perhaps heretical to talk of success, even where success means being nothing, feeling nothing, bringing everything to an end. Yet just such a possibility is, in fact, held out by Beckett's texts. Their protagonists do achieve some measure of detachment from the philosophical questions that gnaw at them, some measure of indifference, some measure of pragmatism,[116] indeed some measure of amusement; we should not forget just how funny Beckett's texts can be, nor the extent to which the humor resides in lighthearted play with deeply serious philosophical ideas.

We have already seen Murphy calling the mind-body problem one "of little interest" (*Murphy,* 109), and Molloy equally cheerfully dismissing Leibniz as not particularly important ("at a given moment, pre-established if you like, I don't much mind"[117]). But Molloy goes on to do much the same with free will ("can it be that we are not free? It might be worth looking into"[118]) and also with the purpose of his own quest, both at its inception ("and I, what was I doing there, and why come? These are things that we shall try and discover. But these are things that we must not take seriously") and at its end ("whether it was my town or not, whether somewhere under that faint haze my mother panted on or whether she poisoned the air a hundred miles away, were ludicrously idle questions for a man in my position, though of undeniable interest on the plane of pure knowledge").[119] Later in the trilogy, we find the Heideggerians, "with all their balls about being and existing," coming in for their own share of derision.[120] And in *Texts for Nothing*, the narrator goes so far as to loosen the grip of what he considers the most important question, the question of the way out, "the old crux, on which at first all depends, then much, then little, then nothing."[121] That, in Beckett's world, is the very definition of progress. Even if the characters themselves do not complete the journey, nothing says that the *reader* cannot, whether by continuing the process or by filling in the missing components of the enthymeme that, according to Beckett, every artwork is.[122]

It is tempting to assume that the last words of the trilogy—"you must go on, I can't go on, I'll go on"[123]—leave the speaker much as we found him, still fumbling aloud for a glimmer of understanding, whether we consider his continuation heroic or enforced, and whether we imagine his speech as an endless loop wrapping back to the start of *Molloy* or as a spool that spins ever-longer sentences, outstripping the 1,672-word leviathan on which the novel closes. But what if this is not the case? What if, as the speaker has just sensed ("quick now and try again, *with the words that remain*"[124]), the finale is at hand? (The ending of *The Unnamable* certainly *feels* like an ending, unlike that of *Malone Dies*; the least one can say is that *Beckett* calls a halt, whether or not his character succeeds in doing so.)[125] What if, paradoxically, the words "you must go on, I can't go on, I'll go on" are the very words that "they" have been waiting for? What if the giving up *of giving up itself* is, in Schopenhauerian fashion, the only possible ticket to ataraxia?

It is not inconceivable. After all, the speaker has, in a sense, been spiraling toward the concluding triad over the course of the previous twenty pages:

> I can't go on in any case. But I must go on. So I'll go on. (393)
> I can't go on, you must go on, I'll go on . . . (414)
> . . . you must go on, I can't go on, I'll go on. (414)[126]

And after all, one possibility he has explicitly entertained is that the magic formula may simply be a permutation of words he has already said, simply "the same words, arranged differently."[127] What, then, if the Beckettian spiral has permitted the consciousness at work in the trilogy to find its self and thus to lose it, to be done with philosophy, to overcome desire, to overcome desire for desire, and to overcome even desire for a lack of desire?[128] What if "you must go on, I can't go on, I'll go on" are "the words it behoved to say," which turn out to be "the same words, arranged differently"? What if, ironically, to say "I'll go on" is to earn the right to cease?

Two Caveats

Such, I feel, are the ideas that underlie Beckett's trilogy. It would be a mistake, however, to imagine that the trilogy's purpose is simply to *inform* us of them. After all, one of the crucial premises behind the three novels is precisely that we cannot be argued into—or, more importantly, out of—certain lines of thought. Merely being told it is pointless to seek answers to certain questions is not enough to stop us asking them; just like the entry into philosophy (to recall what we saw in the previous chapter), so too the exit from philosophy depends crucially on a *method*. Finding a self (to lose it) is an undertaking, not a belief system; it requires a technique, not a body of knowledge.

What Beckett is offering us, then, is not a reservoir of information but a spiritual exercise, one that has powerful affinities with those offered by the ancient skeptics, and as therapy for precisely the same disease.[129] We are not supposed to be edified by the "claims" presented in the texts, or to treat their protagonists as positive or negative models; instead we are to look to the *structure* of the text, and to look to it as a formal model for the dissolution of philosophical questions in circumstances of our own. What we stand to learn is not facts or arguments but a method, one by which philosophy can bring itself to an end.

Should we believe this Beckettian view of philosophy and life? Not necessarily. Many would deny that the best thing we can do with existence at large is to bring it to an end. Even when it comes to our individual existence, not everyone would agree that the best thing we can do with it is to rid it of desire. And of those who do, it is not clear that the great majority lay the blame at the feet of philosophy. Does philosophy really have to be a source of mental anguish? Do its core problems really admit of no progress?

Beckett's texts are, to repeat, only for sufferers, which is to say only for those in whom philosophy has become a disease. For such people, however, these texts are an absolute godsend, the only real source, in a world without schools of skepticism, of practice in bringing philosophical desire to an end. And for the rest of us they are still resplendent, gleaming with a strange, ice-cold beauty. Perhaps this is enough: if we are good Beckettians, then we will remain interested in the shape of ideas, even if we do not believe in them.[130]

Coda

And once again I am	Et je suis à nouveau
I will not say alone,	je ne dirais pas seul
no,	non,
that's not like me,	ce n'est pas mon genre,
but,	mais,
how shall I say,	comment dire,
I don't know,	je ne sais pas,
restored to myself,	rendu à moi,
no,	non,
I never left myself,	je ne me suis jamais quitté,
free,	libre,
yes,	voilà,
I don't know what that means	je ne sais pas ce que ça veut dire
but it's the word I mean to use,	mais c'est le mot que j'entends employer,
free to do what,	libre de quoi faire,
to do nothing,	de ne rien faire,
to know,	de savoir,
but what,	mais quoi,
the laws of the mind perhaps,	les lois de la conscience peut-être,
of my mind,	de ma conscience,
that for example water rises	que par exemple l'eau monte
in proportion as it drowns you	à mesure qu'on s'y enfonce
and that you would do better,	et qu'on ferait mieux,
at least no worse,	enfin aussi bien,
to obliterate texts	d'effacer les textes
than to blacken margins,	que de noircir les marges,
to fill in the holes of words	de les boucher
till all is blank and flat	jusqu'à ce que tout soit blanc et lisse
and the whole ghastly business	et que la connerie
looks like what it is,	prenne son vrai visage,
senseless, speechless,	un non-sens cul
issueless misery.	et sans issue.
(*Molloy*, 13)	(*M*, 15–16)

This stunning sentence from *Molloy* speaks of hopelessness but betrays, as it were in spite of itself, a peculiarly Beckettian optimism. At first glance, things look extremely bleak: all we can know, in Kantian fashion, are "the laws of the mind"; all we can see, in Schopenhauerian fashion, is "senseless, speechless, issueless misery"; and all we can do, in Geulincxian fashion, is to take up mental attitudes toward the misery, there being no room for us to affect it. Still, we should not discount the power of those very mental operations, including that of making the misery visible. For the act of filling in the holes of words, or packing margins with commentary—two different but analogous mechanisms of cancellation, two ways of starting from something in order to make a more durable nothing—are both means of catalyzing despair, despair a vehicle for inducing resignation, and resignation, in the end, a road to redemptive silence.

In a way that is typical of the trilogy, the speaker's initial instinct is to deny, to reject, to doubt. "How shall I say? I don't know." "Free to do what? To do nothing." In a way that is equally typical, however, this initial instinct is quickly superseded. It turns out, first, that he *does* feel free to do something, since knowing is a kind of doing. In fact, he is freer even than he himself realizes, since (to all appearances at least) he is at liberty to choose the words he desires: "I don't know what that means but it's the word I *mean* to use," he says, the vocabulary heavily intentional. And it turns out, second, that he *does* know how to say what he is, namely free; just as in the case of the recess/alcove/chapel that we saw above, so here the fumbling for words reaches a resting-place, a *mot juste*, an island of certainty, one that allows the sentence thenceforth to blossom almost unchecked. Involution is followed by convolution, scrupulous retrogression by forward motion.

The spade of doubt, then, ultimately reveals the bedrock of the undoubtable, whether this be the concept one is currently thinking of (freedom), the phenomenological laws of the human mind (from our point of view, the crucial thing is that we are being drowned, not that the water is rising), or the entirely subjective laws of one's own individual consciousness (obliterating texts, to Molloy, is no worse than blackening margins). And at a higher level, where certainty is not possible, doubt establishes certainty at least about this—"*I don't know what that means* but it's the word I mean to use"—at which point, as the cheery tone suggests, the question simply ceases to matter. Already here, so early in the trilogy, and against such a gloomy backdrop, there are faint glimmers of detachment, tiny flickers of amusement ("that for example water rises in proportion as it drowns you"), and, paradoxically, a strange beauty at the moment of deepest desolation. In the perfectly balanced rhyming couplet "un non-sens cul/et sans issue" (reinforced by the internal repetition of [sã]), or in English the perfectly balanced pair of iambs ("senseless, speechless") and dactyls ("issueless misery"), rich with assonance, Beckett bodies forth the serenity of the ataractic life.

NOTES

Introduction

1. Although I wish here to pay a compliment to my student, I do not in any way seek to detract from the accomplishment of students at other institutions. My figures—which are admittedly frivolous, and to be taken with the appropriate grain of salt—are loosely based on *U.S. News & World Report*, which (at time of writing) ranks 191 national universities across the United States, and lists several dozen more to which it just refers as "Tier 2." (Regional and liberal arts colleges are classified separately.) Stanford currently comes in at number five. The 30 percent figure, which is slightly rounded up, is drawn from the 2009 census. See http://www.census.gov/hhes/socdemo/education/data/cps/2009/tables. html. The Wittgenstein line in the epigraph comes from Rhees, 43 (italics removed); I am grateful to Richard Moran for bringing it to my attention.

2. Morrison (in McKay, 420): "I don't want to give my readers something to swallow. I want to give them something to feel and think about." In the same interview, Morrison notes that "if I examine those layers [of character], I don't come up with simple statements about fathers and husbands, such as some people want to see in the books" (ibid.); elsewhere, she insists that a novel is "not . . . a recipe" (Morrison, 341) and that "I just cannot pass out these little pieces of paper with these messages on them telling people who I respect 'this is the way it is'" (in Davis, 232–33). With her deglutitive metaphor Morrison is echoing Henry James, who lamented (427) the "comfortable, good-humoured feeling" some nineteenth-century readers of English novels had "that a novel is a novel as a pudding is a pudding, and that our only business with it could be to swallow it." I explain below how *Song of Solomon* could be seen as, in part, a "formative fiction." That said, the novel works more as a *formal model* than as a *training-ground*; hence the lack of a full chapter dedicated to it in this book. My views on Morrison will become clear, I hope, in future work.

3. When I say "we," I do not of course mean everyone who speaks or writes about literature: there are plenty of wonderful Aristotelians, Bakhtinians, and Nietzscheans out there, not to mention all the Proustians, Shklovskians, Wordsworthians, and so on, many of whom will be mentioned in what follows. It is just that their (our) views have not really caught on in the wider cultural world.

4. This is how Philip Sidney, in the sixteenth century, famously distinguished between fiction and lies: "Now for the poet, he nothing affirms, and therefore never lieth . . . though he recount things not true, yet . . . he telleth them not for true" (103). On the same grounds, fiction should also be distinguished from "bullshit," the eponymous subject of a famous essay by Harry Frankfurt. Liars, writes Frankfurt (130–31), know that what they are saying is false; bullshitters, by contrast, do not know and do not care. Their aim is not so much to convince us of something untrue (ironically, bullshit may accidentally happen to

correspond with reality!) as simply to sound impressive. Still, both liars and bullshitters "represent themselves falsely as endeavoring to communicate the truth" (Frankfurt, 130), and in this they differ from the maker of fictions.

5. Lest there be any misunderstanding, I am not claiming that Mark's Gospel is itself a work of fiction. Since it seeks to persuade readers of its historical accuracy, it can only be (1) the *truth*, (2) a *lie*, or (3) a *mistake*. It *contains*, however, miniature works of fiction, in the form of the parables. When we read, for example, that there was once a man who sent a series of servants (and finally his son) to collect his rent, with disastrous consequences (Mark 12:1–12), we do not assume that Mark's Jesus has in mind an actual individual to whom this actually happened. All readers of the Gospels, believers and skeptics alike, are more or less obliged to take such tales as fictional.

6. Of course, many of the characters and incidents depicted and alluded to in Plato have real-life counterparts; this, however, does not prevent the dialogues from being works of fiction, any more than Napoleon's presence in *War and Peace* prevents that book from being a novel. Plato's use of anachronism—in the *Gorgias*, for example, Archelaus is already ruling Macedonia [470d], even though Pericles has died very recently [503c]—must have been a clear signal to his contemporaries, for whom such events were fresh in the memory, that the conversations could not have taken place as described, and the imputation to "Socrates" of some strikingly un-Socratic things to say can only have strengthened that impression. (Whatever the historical Socrates believed, he cannot have thought both that genuine knowledge is possible and that it is impossible; at least one of the Socrates-types we find in Plato thus departs dramatically from his flesh-and-blood model.) For further discussion, see chapter 4, note 1.

7. Silent reading was already a possibility for some in Chaucer's time, but not the norm. See Joyce Coleman, *Public Reading*.

8. Thus Chaucer, as we will see in chapter 1, was already mocking the urge to point or draw a moral. Edgar Allan Poe, who saw the aim of literary writing as the production of an *effect* ("Philosophy of Composition," 453), contrasted this aim with "the heresy of *The Didactic*" ("Poetic Principle," 468). Charles Baudelaire, backing up Poe's claims, rebuked the "crowd of people" who "imagine that the aim of poetry is some sort of lesson, that its duty is to fortify conscience, or to perfect social behaviour, or even, finally, to demonstrate something or other that is useful. . . . The modes of demonstration of truth are other, and elsewhere. Truth has nothing to do with song" (203–4). Gustave Flaubert agreed: "However much genius you may put into some fable taken as an example, another fable can serve as proof of the opposite; for a denouement is not a conclusion" ("Préface aux *Dernières chansons*," 48; translation mine). And more recently, French author Charles Dantzig has complained that "it is an American vice to think that an artwork has to *teach* something. Likewise, Americans began drinking red wine when they were told it was good for their health; no amount of talk about pleasure would have done the trick. Their thirst for knowledge is naive and honorable" (131, my translation). There are of course plenty of additional names one could mention here; several, indeed, will make an appearance in what follows.

9. In his famous preface to *Phèdre*, Racine claimed that "the smallest faults are severely punished in it. The mere thought of crime is regarded with as much horror as the crime itself. The weaknesses of love are treated in it as real weaknesses; passions are presented to view only to show all the confusion they cause; and vice is everywhere painted in such colours as to make its ugliness known and hated" (76–77). For Philip Sidney, a good work of literature is a sugared pill (151); it presents examples of goodness and wickedness (148–49), both of which meet their appropriate ends (150). (It is worth noting that Sidney even considers *tragedies* to be cases of poetic justice.) On Thomas Rymer, coiner of the term "poetic justice," and his borrowings from French critic René Rapin, see Quinlan, 139–45; on Scaliger, see ibid., 22.

The exemplarity view shows up again in Samuel Johnson's *Rambler*, 4 (esp. 23, 26) and in Percy Shelley's "Defence of Poetry" (960–61)—Shelley's enthusiasm for the verbal arts caused him, as we will see, to embrace just about every positive position imaginable—and is still not dead, as evidenced by the twenty-first-century endorsement of Mark William Roche (225, 246). For a more sophisticated presentation of the view, see Thomas Pavel, *La pensée du roman*, 134 *et passim* (I reviewed this volume in Landy 2005); on the notion of exemplarity, see Stierle and O'Neill.

10. See Alexander Nehamas, *Nietzsche: Life as Literature*, esp. chapters 5 and 6. In the years since the publication of Nehamas's book there have been several additional contributions, including Paul Ricoeur's "Life in Quest of Narrative," J. David Velleman's "Narrative Explanation," and (if I may include myself in such august company) my own work on Proust in *Philosophy as Fiction*, chapter 3.

11. The imaginary reconciliation view has had a number of proponents, including I. A. Richards (1926:20), Cleanth Brooks (2007:801), and more recently the sculptor Martin Puryear, for whom the most interesting art "retains a flickering quality, where opposed ideas can be held in tense coexistence" (77). This view, which dovetails in important ways with Claude Lévi-Strauss's theory of myth (105), may ultimately owe something to Coleridge's theory of imagination (a faculty that, he says, "reveals itself in the balance or reconciliation of opposite or discordant qualities" [150]). It may also, of course, owe something to Hegel—art, as Hegel sees it, gives sensuous expression to the possibility for oppositions to be reconciled—though Hegel, of course, believes that the oppositions are eventually reconciled in *reality*, not just in imagination. For Hegel, cf. Eldridge 2003:77; for the application to states of the soul, see Anderson and Landy, 31–35.

12. Nietzsche: "How can we make things beautiful, attractive, and desirable for us when they are not? . . . Moving away from things until there is a good deal that one no longer sees and there is much that our eye has to add if we are still to see them at all; or seeing things around a corner and as cut out and framed; or to place them so that they partially conceal each other and grant us only glimpses of architectural perspectives; or looking at them through tinted glass or in the light of the sunset; or giving them a surface and skin that is not fully transparent—all this we should learn from artists while being wiser than they are in other matters. For with them this subtle power usually comes to an end where art ends and life begins; but we want to be the poets of our life—first of all in the smallest, most everyday matters" (*Gay Science*, sec. 299). Nietzsche's *Birth of Tragedy*, with its idea of the beautiful Apollonian veneer spread over unbearable Dionysian truth, is also relevant here.

13. In Percy Shelley's canonical statement, "a man, to be greatly good, must imagine intensely and comprehensively; he must put himself in the place . . . of many others" (961). Shelley's view is echoed by Martha Nussbaum: "the literary imagination," she says, "seems to me an essential ingredient of an ethical stance that asks us to concern ourselves with the good of other people whose lives are distant from our own" (1995:xvi; cf. 1999:265). See also Lynn Hunt, 32, 40, and chap. 1 *passim*; Richard Rorty 2001:132–33 and 1998:185; Roche, 26.

14. See Kant, *Critique of Judgment*, sec. 2–5, and Schopenhauer, *WWR*, 1:34, 1:38. In aesthetic contemplation, writes Schopenhauer, the attention "considers things without interest" (*WWR*, 1:34, p. 178); "we forget our individuality, our will, and continue to exist only as pure subject, as clear mirror of the object" (ibid.); "then all at once the peace, always sought but always escaping us on that first path of willing, comes to us of its own accord . . . the painless state, prized by Epicurus as the highest good" (ibid., 1:38, p. 196). (We will return to Schopenhauer, and to the "painless state," in chapter 5.) Admittedly, fictions are on this theory only one of a number of phenomena capable of generating aesthetic contemplation, including all the arts and indeed natural scenery besides (Kant, in fact, focuses almost exclusively on the beauty of the world and has next to nothing to say about art). In typically saccharine fashion, Iris Murdoch turns the Kantian-Schopenhauerian idea to moralizing purposes: since "perfection of form . . . invites unpossessive contemplation" (83), she claims, engagement with great works of art is a way to "clear our minds of selfish care" (82).

15. Schopenhauer is not the only theorist to describe the experience of reading as a model for utopia. For Adorno, it is a space free from the tyranny of consumption, commodification, and utility ("total purposelessness gives the lie to the totality of purposefulness in the world of domination, and only by virtue of this negation . . . has existing society up to now

become aware of another that is possible" [*Minima Moralia*, sec. 144; cf. *Aesthetic Theory*, 343, and "Commitment," 314]); for Eldridge, it is a space of maximal autonomy, in which we witness writers bound by no laws but their own (2003:54); and for Gadamer, it is a space of ideal community, in which local differences are overcome by a shared love for and/ or understanding of an object. ("In the festive," writes Gadamer, "the communal spirit that supports us all and transcends each of us individually represents . . . the real power of the art work" [1986:63].) In similar fashion, Ralph Ellison rightly saw his novels as bringing together readers of different races: "when [the novel is] successful in communicating its vision of experience, that magic thing occurs between the world of the novel and the reader—*indeed, between reader and reader* in their mutual solitude—which we know as communion" (696, my emphasis). On micro-communities forged out of shared affection, see Tamen (3 *et passim*) and Nehamas (2007:81–82).

16. There is considerable debate as to what Aristotle actually meant by catharsis: perhaps he meant that various emotions—including, but not limited to, fear and pity (see *Poetics* 1449b)—are cleaned away thanks to tragedy (this is the view of Jacob Bernays); but perhaps he meant that they were cleaned *up*, which is to say trained to aim reliably at their proper objects (this is the view of Stephen Halliwell and Martha Nussbaum [1986]). What is more, as Jonathan Lear has shown, neither account squares with what Aristotle says in the *Politics* (8:5–7), where cathartic "music" has no improving effect on character at all. See Lear 1988:300–303. For a full history of catharsis theories, see Ford 1995:111–13; see also Nehamas 1992:301, and Landy 2010:222–23.

17. Horace, *Ars poetica* 102–3: "si vis me flere, dolendum est primum ipsi tibi" ("if you wish to move me, you must first grieve yourself"). Compare Wallace Stevens, who writes that poetry "communicates the emotion that generates it," and that "its effect is to arouse the same emotion in others" (111). Stevens, of course, is primarily talking about lyric poetry, but the view can easily be applied more broadly.

18. I am thinking here of Eliot's "objective correlative." As Eliot sees it—rightly, I suspect— there is no need for writers to feel a certain way in order to elicit a comparable reaction in the soul of their readers. What they require instead is the "formula of that particular emotion," which is to say the sequence of elements most likely to generate the desired effect. (See Eliot 1975:48, and cf. to some extent Diderot 1981:132 *et passim*.) Hitchcock, for example, was presumably not the least bit anxious when he engineered all those scenes that so reliably cause anxiety in spectators.

19. See Wordsworth, 83, and compare de Quincey, for whom "human sensibilities are ventilated and continually called out into exercise by . . . literature" (56); hence, for de Quincey, "the pre-eminence over all authors that merely *teach* of the meanest that *moves*" (57). On "Blasiertheit," see Simmel 1903:325–30, and cf. Adorno: "to be still able to perceive anything at all, regardless of its quality, replaces happiness, since omnipotent quantification has taken away the possibility of perception itself" (*Minima Moralia*, sec. 150).

20. Letter to Oskar Pollak, January 27, 1904, in *Letters*, 16. Compare Kendall Walton's view (in "Thoughtwriting") that literary texts are like speechwriters for the soul, offering us the perfect form of words to use to ourselves when we wish to deepen an emotional experience.

21. For literature revealing us to ourselves, see Carroll, 126–60, 142; Bloom 2000:29–30; Vogler, 18–19; Beardsley, 574; Felski, 25; Iser 1980:194, 216, 224, 230; Eldridge 1989:20– 21; and Eldridge 2003:4, 11, 100, 216–17, 223, 226. Hans-Georg Gadamer's hermeneutic theory can also be taken to promise increased self-knowledge at the end of the reading experience (see Iser 2006:34–37), in part because the latter brings to light our tacit presuppositions.

22. See Currie 1995, *passim*, and Walton 1993:12.

23. Bakhtin sees the novel as a device for bringing together a number of "verbal-ideological belief systems" (1981:311) in the form of individual characters, as well as for mingling them in hybrid constructions such as free indirect discourse. And since as he sees it "the ideological becoming of a human being . . . is the process of selectively assimilating the words of others" (1981:341), "an intense struggle within us for hegemony among various

available verbal and ideological points of view" (345–46), the space of reading is (one might infer) the ideal venue for such becoming.

24. Barthes: "To write is to jeopardize the meaning of the world, to put an indirect question that the writer, by an ultimate abstention, refrains from answering. It is each of us who gives the answer . . .; there is no end to answering what has been written beyond hope of an answer: asserted, disputed, superseded—the meanings pass, the question remains" (1964:ix). For Kundera, likewise, "novelistic thinking . . . does not judge; it does not proclaim truths; it questions, it marvels, it plumbs" (2008:70–71). "I have always, deeply, violently, detested those who look for a *position* (political, philosophical, religious, whatever) in a work of art," adds Kundera, "rather than searching it in an *effort to know*" (1996:91; cf. 1988:7).

25. I borrow the term "gap" from Wolfgang Iser. For our present purposes the most relevant passage is in *The Act of Reading*, 189; the notion of the gap is, however, ubiquitous in Iser. The view I am defending in this volume has, as will be seen, much in common with that of Iser and of his fellow "reader response" theorists. It departs from them by focusing on a particular activity uniquely elicited by formative fictions and also, more broadly, by placing a greater emphasis on normativity. Rather than describing what readers (whether single individuals or "interpretive communities") *happen* to do with Plato and Beckett and Mallarmé, I suggest that there is something readers *ought* to do with them, something that—unlike the filling of gaps, in many contexts—they can easily *fail* to do. Over and above the moral "ought" of our responsibility to the author, such cases involve what we might call the eudaimonistic "ought" of our responsibility to ourselves.

26. Richards 1959: 1. Cf. Schiller, who writes that "thanks to aesthetic culture, the freedom to be what [we] ought to be is completely restored to [us]" (letter 21, p. 147).

27. Schiller points to two opposed dangers besetting every individual: "in the first case he will never be *himself*; in the second he will never be *anything else*" (letter 13, p. 123). The aesthetic—again, Schiller is speaking of aesthetic experience in general, but fictions are of course included—helps us to steer clear of both dangers, by doing justice not only to our desire for cohesion (what Schiller calls the formal drive) but also to our desire for change, growth, multiplicity (what Schiller calls the sensuous drive; see letter 12, pp. 118–21). It should be added that Schiller has no time for didactic theories of art; it is only a bad reader, he says, who "will enjoy a serious and moving poem as though it were a sermon" (letter 22, p. 152).

   It may appear that the desire for unity and the desire for growth are simply incompatible. Consider, however, that the achievement of a certain level of success often leads to a wish to go further, to move beyond, to "transcend oneself," in Georg Simmel's phrase (1918). We now see a fresh goal for which to strive, one that was not only unattainable but also inconceivable from the point at which we first started: the desire for growth is, in a sense, nothing but a desire for a new (and superior) form of unity. Life, then, is like the ascent of a peak that conceals behind it, unbeknownst to us, another, taller summit, and so ad infinitum.

28. Thus Proust, in the preface to his translation of Ruskin's *Bible of Amiens* (1987:60): "There is no better way of becoming aware of one's feelings than to try to recreate in oneself what a master has felt. In this profound effort it is our thought, together with his, that we bring to light."

29. As Croce sees it, emotions (the interesting ones at least) generate intuitions, and intuitions rise to the level of consciousness only thanks to their expression in art. See Croce 1965:24–25; Croce 1995:18–19; and Kemp, 172 *et passim*. One might compare A. C. Bradley, for whom the creative writer has in mind merely a "vague imaginative mass pressing for development and definition" (23); without the literary text, then, no development and no definition. And one might also compare Georges Poulet (1980:42–45; 1971:278), who gives powerful, lyrical expression to the idea that literature permits a miraculous entry into the thoughts and feelings of another.

30. Thus Putnam: "if I read Céline's *Journey to the End of the Night* I do not *learn* that love does not exist, that all human beings are hateful and hating. . . . What I learn is to see the world

as it looks to someone who is sure that hypothesis is correct" (488). "That," writes Simone de Beauvoir, "is the miracle of literature, the thing that distinguishes it from information: an *other* truth becomes mine" (82, my translation). Cf. Jacobson 1996:333–34; 1997:167.

31. For Proust, style "is the revelation, which by direct and conscious methods would be impossible, of the qualitative difference, the uniqueness of the fashion in which the world appears to each one of us, a difference which, if there were no art, would remain for ever the secret of every individual." (Although this statement is made by Proust's narrator, at *Time Regained*, 299, we know that Proust feels similarly: see *Essais et articles*, 288, 311.) On metaphor and perspective, see Landy 2004, chap. 1; on the general claim about style, see Wallace Stevens, 120–23; Arthur Danto 1981:198–207; Frank Farrell, 187–89 *et passim*; and M. H. Abrams, 226–31. The title of Abrams's book, *The Mirror and the Lamp*, is an allusion to W. B. Yeats's line that "[the] soul must become its own betrayer, . . . the mirror turn lamp," which Abrams takes to mark a shift, in the Romantic period, from mimetic to expressive (theories of) poetry.

32. That, after all, is how connoisseurs sometimes distinguish authentic artworks from forgeries: the assumption is that we reveal ourselves—or rather betray ourselves—in our manner, our unintentional or semi-intentional style, far more than we do in any deliberate gestures we may make. Cf. Ginzburg, *passim*.

33. Hegel: "In works of art the nations have deposited their richest inner intuitions and ideas" (*Aesthetics*, 1:7; see also the helpful discussion at Eldridge 2003:74–76). In his early phase, Lukács follows suit (*Theory of the Novel*, 32, 40), and the irrepressible Shelley is as happy to sign up to the "spirit of the age" idea (969) as he is to more or less everything else. Robert Pippin, mind you, is a Hegelian of a totally different stripe; his brilliant reading of Henry James (2000:54–88 *et passim*) combines a keen interest in *mentalités* with a compelling account of capacities under training.

34. Frankfurt School theorists could be said to specialize in this approach. Theodor Adorno, for example, calls abstract artworks realistic, since they so perfectly capture, according to him, the abstractness of human relations under advanced capitalism. (See Adorno 1978:306–7; cf. also 1984:45 and 1977:160.) Ernst Bloch, likewise, finds in Expressionist discontinuity a perfect representation of "authentic reality" (22). And Siegfried Kracauer reads the choreography of contemporary dance troupes as reflecting the processes of mechanized production: "the hands in the factory," he writes, "correspond to the legs of the Tiller Girls" (79).

35. Heidegger's essay "On the Origin of the Work of Art" is exceedingly complicated, not to say contradictory; while it appears to be offering a single theory of art, it in fact offers three, with uncertain connections among them. In one (164–65), what an artwork does is to reveal the "Being" of specific objects (a Van Gogh painting, for example, reveals the "Being" of peasant shoes). In a second (169–72), what an artwork does is to reveal a lifeworld: a Greek temple, for example, discloses the "world" of the Greeks. In a third (177–78), what an artwork does is to reveal Being itself, which may mean something like the set of all data of experience prior to conceptualization (cf. Gumbrecht 2004:69–70). Officially, this last outcome is a logical consequence of the first. "In the revelation of the equipmental being of the shoes," writes Heidegger, "beings as a whole . . . attain to unconcealedness" (178); "the working of the work . . . lies in a change . . . of the unconcealedness of beings, and this means, of Being" (184). It is not, however, entirely clear (to say the least) how the one is supposed to lead to the other.

36. One exponent of the knowledge-by-acquaintance view is Susan Feagin. See esp. 110.

37. See for example Harries, *passim*; Ricoeur 1978:151–52 and 1975:57, 69; and Sartre, for whom the writer's job is to "[let] Being sparkle as Being" (106), and thus to "restore the strangeness and opacity of the world" (108). This view is of Heideggerian inspiration; it connects to the third of the theories proposed in the Artwork essay (as described above).

38. Shklovsky: "the purpose of art is to impart the sensation of things as they are perceived and not as they are known. The technique of art is to make objects 'unfamiliar'" (12). See also Tomashevsky, 85, and Eichenbaum, 113–14. Jean Paulhan follows the Shklovsky line,

writing that "poetry is always showing us, in strange ways [*étrangement*], the dog, the stone, or the ray of sun which habit concealed from us . . . poetry [is] seeing with fresh eyes what everyone always sees" (16, 47). So too does Susan Sontag, who bemoans "a steady loss of sharpness in our sensory experience." "All the conditions of modern life," she explains, "conjoin to dull our sensory faculties. . . . What is important now is to recover our senses. We must learn to *see* more, to *hear* more, to *feel* more" (13–14). In recent years Susan Stewart (*passim*) has produced a powerful expansion, application, and rearticulation of the view, beautiful in its own right. And faint traces of the idea may perhaps already be found in Shelley, for whom poetry removes the "film of familiarity which obscures from us the wonder of our being" (967).

39. On *Madame Bovary* as emotion-modulator, see my "Passion, Counter-Passion, Catharsis," esp. 228–29.

40. This position has had a large number of proponents. Balzac famously described the role of the novel as that of competing with the civil register ("faire concurrence à l'État-Civil," 6). Jean-Paul Sartre insisted that its task is to depict reality—indeed the reality of today (70, 75)—and thus, ostensibly, to inflict responsibility upon its readers (37–38). Georg Lukács, who came to feel very much the same way (1977:32, 38), ended up extolling a type of writing that Adorno delightfully dubbed "boy-meets-tractor literature" (1977:173). And Ian Watt not only praised Defoe and Richardson for adopting "the proper purpose of language, 'to convey the knowledge of things,'" but also castigated Laclos and Lafayette for failing to do so (30).

41. To take one example among many, René Girard presents fictions as revealing a truth to set against the lies found everywhere else; that is the force of the French title of his first book, *Mensonge romantique et vérité romanesque*. (The "truth" in question, an immensely dubious one, is that no desire is ever spontaneous.) Just as oddly, Iris Murdoch believes that literature "teaches that nothing in life is of any value except the attempt to be virtuous" (85). For his part, Mark William Roche even sees artworks as making *arguments* (57; see also 84, 208, 211).

42. David Shields, *Reality Hunger*, sec. 379.

43. At the 2006 Academy Awards ceremony, the writers gave Jennifer Lopez some lines to read about Paul Haggis's *Crash*. "In the opening scene," she intoned, "we are told that people feel so isolated these days that they are not above literally crashing into each other as a way of making human contact." What is the force of the "telling" here?

44. Thus Arthur Danto, whom we saw above making an eloquent defense of the expression view, elsewhere insists that artworks are "embodied meanings" (2003:139; see also 13, 25). Umberto Eco periodically speaks of "messages" (1979:22, 120). Wolfgang Iser, who mostly sees fiction as a route to self-knowledge, periodically lapses into deeming it a vehicle for communication (2006:67); *Tom Jones*, for example, ostensibly delivers the "insight that the rigidity of normative principles of eighteenth century thought systems hinders the acquisition of experience" (1980:201n30). Richard Eldridge, who shares Iser's clarificationist impulses, insists that art is communication (2003:97) and yields truth (2003:42). And Stanley Fish, who pays lip service to the idea of literature as a set of effects, seems only to be interested in the "effect of meaning" (1980:74, 83; cf. Tompkins's critique, esp. 206 and 223).

45. Barthes 1975:14 *et passim*. While Barthes' distinction between "lisible" and "scriptible" overlaps to some extent with the distinction I will be drawing between formative fictions (the parables, the *Gorgias*, etc.) and other kinds of fiction, important differences remain, both at the level of process and at the level of outcome. For one thing, the upshot is something more than mere "jouissance," that pleasure which Barthes celebrates for its self-indulgent sterility; for another, the formative approach does not accord infinite latitude to the reader, but understands certain types of move to have been anticipated, indeed programmed in, by the author. That is not to say that such moves are *required*—unlike (say) the effort of comprehending individual words and sentences, the effort of "rewriting" is always optional—but if we do choose to take up the offer of active engagement, we will all do so in markedly similar ways.

46. I am thinking, for example, of J. M. Coetzee's "At the Gate," that Kafkaesque depiction of a world in which fiction-writers are stringently required to declare their beliefs.

47. Francine Prose puts the point particularly well: "only rarely do [high school] teachers propose that writing might be worth reading closely. Instead, students are informed that literature is principally a vehicle for the soporific moral blather they suffer daily from their parents" (78). Philip Pullman makes the same claim in relation to poetry, lamenting that "in an atmosphere of suspicion, resentment, and hostility, many poems are interrogated until they confess, and what they confess is usually worthless, as the results of torture always are: broken little scraps of information, platitudes, banalities" (2008:4). "And this," adds Pullman, "is the process we call education." (On the banality of almost all "messages" embedded in literary works, see Stolnitz 1991 and 1992.) Dickens himself, notes Alexander Nehamas, recognized the need to make a different kind of appeal. "In *Oliver Twist*, when Oliver is overwhelmed by the great number of books in Mr. Brownlow's house, that good man tells him: 'You shall read them, if you behave well.' Even Dickens, the most edifying of novelists, could see that aesthetic values aren't justified by their moral significance and couldn't bring himself to write, 'If you read them, you shall behave well'" (2007:138).

48. I have argued for this in my "Corruption by Literature." So too, in perhaps stronger terms, has Francine Prose: "the new model English-class graduate," she writes (83–84), "values empathy and imagination less than the ability to make quick and irreversible judgments, to entertain and maintain simplistic immovable opinions about guilt and innocence. . . . What results from these educational methods is a mode of thinking (or, more accurately, of *not* thinking) that equips our kids for the future: Future McDonald's employees. Future corporate board members."

49. I speak here of *benefit* rather than *utility*, since I believe the first term captures better the nature of our (ideal) feelings. As a number of critics have suggested (see esp. Booth 1988:172–82 *et passim*), works of fiction are like friends, and while we rightly think of friendship as conferring immense benefits upon our lives, we equally rightly shudder to call it "useful": to do so would be to take up an instrumentalizing attitude toward the people we are closest to. (Cf. Nehamas 2007:55–57.) We do not *exploit* great works of fiction, but we may nevertheless allow them to help us, and may be tremendously grateful— just as we are to our friends—when they enrich our lives.

50. On the semantic/pragmatic distinction, cf. Richards: "a statement may be used for the sake of the reference, true or false, which it causes. This is the scientific use of language. But it may also be used for the sake of the effects in emotion and attitude produced by the reference it occasions. This is the emotive use of language" (1959:267).

51. For "locutionary," "illocutionary," and "perlocutionary" dimensions of sentences, see Austin, esp. 94–101; for an application to longer utterances, including books, see Skinner 45–46. Since the term "performative" (Austin, 5, 25) has become such a buzzword in my discipline, perhaps it is worth pointing out that there is nothing performative about the texts I will be discussing. The term has a technical sense: a given sentence is a performative if and only if it both declares you to be doing something and itself constitutes the doing. (For example, saying "I promise" both declares you to be promising and is itself the act of promising.) There is no connection between this and what Plato is up to, for example, in leaving holes in the logic and inviting the reader to mend them.

52. In works that actually advance arguments, it may be appropriate to speak of the articulation and reception of a view; such works, however, are rare. I return to this point in chapter 1.

53. See Dewey, *Art as Experience*; Sartre, 56; Richards 1959:22; Rosenblatt 1978:12, 20–21; Bradley, 4; Cleanth Brooks 1956:213; Iser 1978:281. According to Gary Kemp (173, 189), Croce and Collingwood also insist on the experiential aspect of the aesthetic.

54. See *Gadamer in Conversation*, 71.

55. I appeal here to a distinction made by Bernard Williams, who sees morality (which asks what my duty is) as a subset of ethics (which asks simply how I should live). See Williams 1985:1–6 *et passim*.

56. The idea that minds have a variety of capacities has been around for a very long time; the Greek δύναμις became the Latin *facultas*, which in turn became the English "faculty" (but also, among other things, the German *Vermögen*). I do not wish here to enter into any debates about the nature—let alone, heaven help me, the location—of such mental powers, which is why I am studiously using the word "capacity" instead of the word "faculty." I hope my reader will concede to me, on the basis of empirical observation, that individuals have the capacity to think logically, to use figurative language, to step back from their representations, and so on, and that these capacities can be strengthened through exercise.

57. It turns out that enjoying a good novel is an extraordinarily complex process, involving all kinds of mental activity on the part of the reader. Let us distinguish between two categories of activity, one of which involves efforts that are relatively required (and of which we are barely conscious), the other of which involves efforts that are relatively optional (and of which we are at least somewhat aware). In the first category we find (1) the basic understanding of sentences; (2) the visualization of characters and events; (3) the reconstruction of a character's personality on the basis of scattered pieces of fragmentary and perspectival information; (4) the reconstruction of the chronology of events (extracting *fabula*, as the Formalists would say, from *sjuzhet*); (5) the inferring of events that, though unpresented, must have taken place; (6) the anticipation of future events (suspense and surprise prove that we do this, even if we are not aware of it); (7) the formation of an emotional (or in Walton's terms "quasi-emotional") response; (8) the formulation of laws governing the particular fictional universe; (9) the differentiation between figure and ground; (10) the filling-in of gaps; (11) the deciphering of an underlying system of ideas and values; and (12) the taking up of an attitude toward that system. (In almost all of these cases, incidentally, we are dealing with hypotheses that are steadily revised.) The second category includes (13) the monitoring of information sources; (14) a selection among emotional responses, including the rejection of those determined to be unwarranted; (15) the adoption of an attitude toward oneself (what I have been calling "clarification"); (16) the attempt to play the role of ideal reader in order to appreciate the work to the fullest; (17) the construction of counterfactual scenarios ("what if Emma Bovary hadn't married Charles?"); and (18) the rereading of a work (in whole or in part). It also includes (19) those activities we have seen to be necessary for a full-blooded encounter with formative fictions. For most of the above, see the introduction to Eco 1979; Iser 1978:281–84; Iser 1980:111–17, 166; Todorov 1980:70–75; Bordwell and Thompson, 57, 76, 87–88; Rosenblatt 1978:10–11, 42–43. For quasi-emotions, see Walton 1978; for the laws of a fictional world, see Pavel 1986; for keeping track of sources, see Zunshine 47–65; for counterfactual scenarios, see Morson 1998 and Prince, ii–iii; for rereading, see Călinescu.

58. Again, it may be asked why I am placing Mallarmé, a lyric poet, alongside writers of fiction. After all, lyric poems do not need to present imaginary situations; they can be aphoristic (Philip Larkin's "This Be the Verse"), descriptive (Rilke's "Herbst"), confessional (William Carlos Williams's "This Is Just to Say"), and so on. Some lyric poems, however, *do* present imaginary situations, and many of Mallarmé's verses—including "Ses purs ongles," the primary focus of chapter 3—fall into that category. Indeed, Mallarmé himself uses the term "fiction" in relation to "Un coup de dés": "la fiction affleurera et dissipera," he predicts, "autour des arrêts fragmentaires d'une phrase capitale" ("the fiction will surface and dissipate. . . around fragmentary breaks in a primary sentence" [*OC* 1:392, my translation]). That said, I would have no objection to readers wishing to extend the theory defended in this book to lyric poetry at large. The key distinction I wish to draw here is not between fiction and nonfiction but between literary and non-literary, since the training I am talking about takes place thanks to formal devices like Romantic irony, extended metaphor, or multilayered hypotaxis, and since such devices are more often found (and more often foregrounded) in literary works, whether narrative, lyric, or dramatic.

59. As Ricoeur points out (1975:49–52), one of the main problems with Structuralism is that it tends to overlook the temporal dimension of literary works.

60. As I mentioned above, I take to heart Alexander Nehamas's warning that we do artworks an injustice by treating them as mere means to our pre-established ends. I might, however, qualify this position slightly. While it is true that some artworks have effects on us that no one can predict (and indeed that no one *should* predict), there are cases in which we are free to form substantial prior expectations, with no loss of reverence for the object. When something is labeled a tragedy, for example, we can reasonably expect to be moved (the same, incidentally, is true of Hollywood "weepies," like *Love Story*); or again, when something is clearly designed as it were for export to other cultures (*Raise the Red Lantern*, say), we can reasonably expect to learn something about what it feels like, or at least what the author thinks it feels like, to belong to a particular national or ethnic or religious group at a given place and time. Formative fictions, finally, constitute an intermediate case. Before we begin reading, we do not know what we want from them or what they want from us (this distinguishes formative fictions from weepies and cultural-immersion pieces). At a certain point, however, we must understand what the offer is and choose, or decline, to take the work up on it (this distinguishes formative fictions from those full-blown Nehamasian catalyst works with their utterly unpredictable effects).

61. I allude here to Nehamas's "Postulated Author" article, the definitive theory of intention and interpretation.

62. Thus Matei Călinescu: "each book, we might say, comes with its own user's manual" (116–17). "A text," agrees Todorov, "always contains within itself directions for its own consumption" (1980:77); see also Eco 1979:8, and Peter Brooks, xii. As Iser notes, the manual—what he calls the set of "codes" governing reader-text interaction—is scattered throughout the text, and must be reassembled before we can understand what to do with it (1980:166).

63. The term is Dilthey's, the idea Schleiermacher's (though Ramberg and Gjesdal find it already in Spinoza). Heidegger picked up the idea in *Being and Time*, as did Gadamer in *Truth and Method*. I am grateful to Stanley Corngold for helping me to see its relevance for the formative approach.

64. In line with Rudolf Bultmann's *Vorverständnis*, what I am proposing is perhaps a *Vorvermögen*. I return to "pre-understanding" and "pre-capacity" in chapter 2.

65. Notice that even the ability to *read* is, in some cases, not a requirement: the parables, after all, were originally delivered in oral form.

66. For the literary text as gift, cf. Sartre 60, 67; as we have seen, however, Sartre also considers it a mirror in which the reader should look and be ashamed. The kind of gift you receive from your unfavorite uncle.

67. This, incidentally, is another reason to keep the term "performative" at bay in the present context. Performative utterances do not require very much work on the hearer's part in order to "go through": when someone says "I promise to walk your dog," for example, all we really need to do is listen. (See Austin, 22.) Formative fictions, by contrast, only function if the reader actively manipulates them, whether (say) by playing with their metaphors, mending their arguments, or unearthing their secret structures.

68. Again compare Barthes, for whom "the goal of literary work . . . is to make the reader no longer a consumer, but a producer of the text" (1975:4; cf. 1988:162). This emphasis on readerly responsibility, and on the possibility of failure, distinguishes my position not only from that of Nussbaum et al. (to be discussed in chapter 1) but also from that of Stanley Fish, who considers us to be almost entirely constrained by the "interpretive community" we have the (mis)fortune of belonging to. A sentence, he says, is "an action made upon a reader" (1980:23); "what happens to one informed reader of a work will happen, within a range of nonessential variation, to another" (1980:52); in the end, "the brakes are on everywhere" (1989:83). As Gerald Graff rather colorfully puts it, Fish's reader is "a kind of moron" (37).

69. I am departing very slightly here from Kendall Walton (1978:25–27), who defends subsequent readings of a work as offering experiences similar to the first. On rereading generally, see Călinescu and Maar.

70. Michael Saler has referred to this as the "public sphere of the imagination" (2005:63). For additional thoughts on the value of readerly communities, see Stow 417–20 and Nehamas 2007:81–82.

71. "How wonderful it would be, dear Agathon, if the foolish were filled with wisdom simply by touching the wise. If only wisdom were like water, which always flows from a full cup into an empty one when we connect them with a piece of yarn" (*Symposium* 175d–e).

72. My view thus differs from that of Hans Ulrich Gumbrecht, who opposes meaning-mongering not just in the context of fiction but in that of life at large. (See *Production of Presence*, 51–90 *et passim*.) Like Susan Sontag (7), Gumbrecht invites us to focus on the surface of things—to experience their "presence"—rather than seeking to look beneath or beyond them. While I sympathize tremendously with Gumbrecht's diagnosis of the problem in literary studies, I cannot quite share either his proposed solution or his broader vision. When it comes to literature, first of all, the meaning/presence dichotomy seems a little stark: as I have attempted to show, there are other important options, including clarification, formal modeling, and training. When it comes to the natural world, second, it is not clear that explanations automatically remove enchantment, given the fact that scientific understanding, as Douglas Hofstadter reminds us (434), "doesn't 'explain away'; rather, it adds mystery." And in the human realm, finally, a refusal to look behind behavior to reasons and significance (couldn't my friend have had a good excuse for showing up late? what will the real consequences be of that new law with the positive-sounding name?) might, in the end, prove both personally and politically damaging.

73. "Whenever the people are well-informed, they can be trusted with their own government" (letter to Richard Price, January 8, 1789, *Letters*, 102).

74. As we saw above, moralizing theories often start from the idea that sentiment is the route to right behavior, sometimes coupled with the idea that reason is in the way. I must confess to not being quite so sanguine about sentiment, which can (notoriously) lead us in all kinds of undesirable directions, including by means of misplaced and excessive empathy. (It would be a terrible result, for example, if a reader of *Lolita* ended up empathizing with pedophiles.) Nor would I diagnose our contemporary condition as one involving a surfeit of rationality. A little more concern for grounding—a little more willingness and competence to offer reasons for our moral intuitions—could, in fact, go a long way.

75. The same is true, of course, for works that aim at clarification (see chapter 1): here, too, a genuine interest in the issues at stake is a clear prerequisite for their full effect.

76. On this point, cf. Iser 1978:275 and 1980:108. It seems to me that aleatory writings, which place such high demands on their consumers—or, to put it another way, which reward them so little—will rarely if ever function as formative fictions. In the face of *Zang Tumb Tuuum*, for example, we are more likely to savor the sentences at a safe distance than to attempt to make them cohere. Formative fictions, by contrast, make it clear that something important is at stake, that some of the pieces have already been put in place, and that some progress is possible, even if that progress should only take the form of charting the contours of the mystery. Amid oceans of ambiguity, their continents of clarity always stand firm.

77. Another reason to concern oneself with the semantic dimension in Mallarmé is that the poetry, as we will see, systematically *refines away the real*, turning it into pure form. Unlike abstract art, which could be said to give us a foretaste of utopia, Mallarmé's poetry represents the route one has to travel in order to arrive there. For certain purposes, therefore, it is of greater assistance.

78. Eliot 1975:93. One might compare here a beautiful paragraph in Proust (*A l'ombre des jeunes filles en fleurs*, 258) in which the narrator notes that nature has a way of bringing about physical and spiritual fecundity thanks to a series of benevolent deceptions. When bees think they are merely drinking nectar, he points out, they are also spreading pollen; when lovers think they are achieving their goal of sensual pleasure, they are also perpetuating the species; and when we visit a place we have not seen before in order to understand the captivating person who lives there, our real gain is exposure to a new landscape. Pollination, reproduction, and the expansion of the imagination are, for Proust's narrator, vastly

more important than nectar, sex, and understanding. Without the latter, however, the former would never happen.

79. Adorno on *Endgame*: "after the Second War, everything is destroyed" (1982:122); "Beckett's trashcans are the emblem of a culture restored after Auschwitz" (143); and most absurdly, "insecticide . . . all along pointed to the genocidal camps" (145). Similarly, Anthony Uhlmann reads the featureless landscape of *The Unnamable* as an allegory of "wartorn France" (1999:137–86; cf. Calder, 110), while for his part, Gary Adelman believes (why not?) that *The Unnamable* is about a Jew in the Holocaust (67–84).

80. "Then it will all be over with the Murphys, Merciers, Molloys, Morans and Malones" (*Three Novels*, 236); "when I think of the time I've wasted with these bran-dips, beginning with Murphy, who wasn't even the first" (390–91); "I am neither . . . Murphy, nor Watt, nor Mercier . . . nor any of the others whose very names I forget, who told me I was they, who I must have tried to be" (326).

81. Even here, note that *Eleuthéria*, which Beckett wrote after the war, is formally similar to *Murphy* (allowances made of course for the difference in genre).

82. As Steven J. Rosen rightly remarks, "his skepticism is classical; there is no reason to regard it as a product of a particular historical situation" (53). Reviewing a volume of Beckett's letters, J. M. Coetzee is struck by what he calls a "serene indifference to politics"; "in the age of Stalin and Mussolini and Hitler, of the Great Depression and the Spanish civil war, references to world affairs in Beckett's letters can be counted on the fingers of one hand" (2009:13).

83. *Fin de partie*, 56.

84. As Sartre and others have recognized, certain features of the human condition—our mortality, for example, or our limited knowledge—are indifferent to history. Even romantic love turns out to be somewhat less culturally specific than many have imagined: see Gottschall and Nordland, *passim*.

85. Still less is this an *evolutionary* theory of all fiction. For various reasons, well documented by Jonathan Kramnick in "Against Literary Darwinism," it makes no sense to speak of an aptitude for fiction being an *adaptation*, a trait that could be "selected for." (If something is not in the DNA, it cannot count as an adaptation.) It is also by no means clear that fiction has been around for very long, in evolutionary terms. Did early humans really exchange acknowledgedly made-up tales around the "Pleistocene campfire," as Denis Dutton likes to imagine (457)? Impossible to know for sure of course, but the least one can say is that the idea is massively speculative.

86. Contrast, again, many evolutionary approaches that, more or less by necessity, are committed to the posit that all fictions serve an identical set of purposes.

87. At the beginning of *Die Ausnahme und die Regel*—one of Brecht's *Lehrstücke*—the chorus says, speaking of the play to come: "Findet es befremdend, wenn auch nicht fremd . . . damit nichts unveränderlich gelte" ("find it alienating, albeit not alien . . . so that nothing should appear immutable") (Brecht 1969:94, my translation). Brecht is of course highly eloquent on the subject of his own work; see Brecht 1964.

88. This is Lanier Anderson's view, as presented viva voce in lectures for our "Philosophy and Literature" class.

89. See my "Passion, Counter-Passion, Catharsis."

90. This is Lisa Zunshine's compelling theory (see esp. 27–36, but also 159–62). Unlike Nussbaum, Zunshine recognizes that increased social skills need not lead to increased altruism; great manipulators require the ability to "read minds" just as much as great benefactors do. There is, accordingly, no reason to see fiction as making us more moral. In fact, Zunshine is not even sure fiction makes us slicker social operators (35, 125); to that extent (and also to the extent that I see her view as applying only to certain character-heavy, closed-world fictions, rather than to fiction *tout court*) I am reading her a little against the grain.

91. The ideal response may in the end be a Sartrean one: select an interpretation and commit to it, in full awareness of its partiality. It is worth noting that the opportunity for training is, here as elsewhere, only an offer and not a requirement; large numbers of critics have in

fact read Kafka in the light of a single allegorical schema that they themselves have taken to be exhaustive. In the case of *The Trial*, for example, many have ignored all evidence that Josef K. is partly responsible for his situation, preferring to lay the blame squarely at the feet of the Court (and to construe the latter, typically, as a tyrannical state apparatus). For Josef K.'s guilt, see Marson *passim*.

92. As Daniel Kahneman and Amos Tversky have shown, the vast majority of our actions are driven by automated psychological mechanisms (what they call "System 1"); it is only rarely that System 1 breaks down, causing us to shift to conscious deliberation ("System 2"). (See summary in Kahneman 2003.) I would add, first, that System 2 has the capacity not just to override local decisions but also to make adjustments to System 1; and second, that reading complicated works of fiction, like *Song of Solomon*, may well give us practice at making such adjustments. I have written about Proustian training in *Philosophy as Fiction* (141–45), and about *Adaptation* in "Still Life in a Narrative Age." On mental agility generally, cf. Boyd, 33.

93. Aristotle: "those who make the best decisions do not seem to be the same as those with the best beliefs; on the contrary, some seem to have better beliefs, but to make the wrong choice" (*EN* 1112a8–10); "it is our decisions, . . . not our beliefs, that make the characters we have" (*EN* 1112a3–4). (Here and in what follows, I abbreviate *Nichomachean Ethics* to *EN*.)

94. "Virtue of character results from habit" (*EN* 1103a15–16); "arguments and teaching surely do not influence everyone, but the soul of the student needs to have been prepared by habits, . . . like ground that is to nourish seed" (*EN* 1179b24–26); "we need to have been brought up in fine habits if we are to be adequate students of what is fine and just" (*EN* 1095b4–6).

Chapter 1

1. Line 177. Hereafter, line numbers will be given in parentheses in the text.

2. Cf. Lamarque and Olsen, 385; Livingston, 82. Compare also Carroll, 130: "where artworks . . . express general moral precepts, or are underwritten by them, those principles or precepts are typically so obvious and thin that it strains credulity to think that we learn them from artworks. Instead, very often, it seems more likely that a thoughtful preteenager will have mastered them already. Yes, there is an argument against murder in *Crime and Punishment*, but surely it is implausible to think that it requires a novel as elaborate as Dostoyevsky's to teach it, and even if Dostoyevsky designed the novel as a teaching aid, did anyone really learn that murder is wrong from it? . . . In fact, it is probably a precondition of actually comprehending *Crime and Punishment* that the readers already grasp the moral precepts that motivate the narrative."

3. Cf. Lamarque and Olsen, 384.

4. Cf. Stolnitz 1992:196.

5. Erica speaks in accordance with the view of any number of Chaucer scholars. For one example, see Holbrook, 119, cited as the epigraph to this section.

6. See Manning, 414. Here is what Paul actually says: "For whatever was written *in former days* was written for our instruction, that by steadfastness and by the encouragement of the scriptures we might have hope" (Romans 15:4, my emphasis). It is true that Chaucer cites the same line in his own voice in the "Retraction." Since, however, the point of the Retraction is to denounce a subset of *The Canterbury Tales* (along with several other works) precisely for *failing* to edify, the situation remains at least as complicated as before. If Chaucer is serious in saying that some of the tales "tend toward sin," then he surely cannot also believe that the stories in question "were written for our instruction"; and if he recognizes that some stories are not written for our instruction, then he is forced to relinquish the universal claim.

7. Scheps (5) counts ten morals in all. There could be more: intriguingly, the Nun's Priest refuses to reuse the *original* moral tag for the fable—"the wicked shall fall by his own wickedness" (Proverbs 11:5)—from John Bromyard's *Summa praedicantum*. See Myers, 212.

8. Cf. "Lo, how Fortune turneth sodeinly/The hope and pryde eek [also] of hir [her] enemy!" (637–38).

9. Cf. Stolnitz 1992:196; Posner 1998:405; Lamarque and Olsen, 368 and 380; Jacobson 1996:330. Jacobson goes on to conclude (331) that fictions merely confirm the opinions we had going in. For some reason, however, he also holds that fictions may be used to effect a change in our attitudes (335; 1997:186–87). Nor can David Lewis quite seem to make up his mind: fictions, he writes, can prove "modal truths," such as whether there could be such a thing as a dignified beggar; but fictions can also persuade us to believe in impossibilities (278). If the second statement is true, then surely the "proof" of the first statement is no proof at all.

10. Cf. Posner 1997:14, Carroll 160n28. There are, of course, many who see their lives as having been changed by Austen or Tolstoy or Morrison or Proust. As I will shortly explain, however, such change is not actually the result of a fictional narrative working single-handedly on a level-headed reader. Whereas incremental and deliberate self-refinement is indeed a genuine possibility, as is a newfound awareness of one's deepest commitments, an actual shift in Weltanschauung requires something else, whether (1) a set of bona fide arguments contained within the text (and/or in supplementary material), (2) a failure on the reader's part to mark the boundary between fiction and nonfiction, or (3) implicit or explicit prompting from institutions of reading. People will indeed try to "learn" things from fictions if we tell them to. It's just that this is not, all things considered, a particularly desirable outcome.

11. Contrast the case of Martin Luther King, who heard Gandhi's life story and concluded—rightly—that nonviolent resistance can be effective. It is fully rational to adjust our beliefs and behavior on the basis of *true* stories. That, incidentally, is why Harriet Beecher Stowe, who is so often mentioned in these contexts, published not one but *two* books about slavery, both *Uncle Tom's Cabin* (1852) and, a year later, *A Key to Uncle Tom's Cabin*. The nonfiction account was of vital importance in securing conviction, but today's proponents of moral improvement through fiction tend not to mention it.

12. As Carroll (146) points out, we do not need *fictional* examples to persuade us (say) that power corrupts, or that no one should be called happy until he or she is dead: the real world offers us quite enough case studies.

13. "Wommenes counseils been ful ofte colde [fatal];/Wommenes counseil broghte us first to wo,/And made Adam fro Paradys to go" (490–92). Admittedly, the Nun's Priest goes on to disclaim the allegation, hiding behind his character: "Thise been the cokkes wordes, and nat mine;/I can noon [no] harm of no womman divyne" (499–500). But this is presumably only for the benefit of his patron, the Prioress. Nothing in the context suggests that it was in fact Chauntecleer speaking.

14. Cf. Wheatley, 112–13.

15. "But al for noght; I sette noght an hawe [I don't give a fig]

> Of his proverbes n'of his olde sawe,
> Ne I wolde nat of him corrected be.
> I hate him that my vices telleth me,
> And so do mo, God woot, of us than I."
> ("Wife of Bath," 659–63)

16. As Gallick claims (244).

17. See Holbrook, 122–23, and Shallers, 327, for two variants.

18. Myers describes (but does not endorse) this reading. See Myers, 210–11.

19. Travis (170–73) lays out and also critiques this interpretation.

20. For the rooster as negative exemplum, see (among others) Holbrook and Lenaghan. Some critics (Lenaghan again, and Myers, 219–20) view the Nun's Priest himself as the key negative example; such critics are, however, still arguing for the moral effectiveness of fictions, having merely moved up a level from the story spun by the Nun's Priest to the story spun by Chaucer. Chaucer appears to head off even this higher-level exemplarity when he has the host, Harry Bailly, respond in the basest physical terms to the Nun's Priest's fable

(see the epigraph to the current section, taken from lines 683–88). Those most in need of improvement, Chaucer seems to feel, are also those most indifferent to moral tales.

21. Rorty describes his brand of Pragmatism as "urging that we try to extend our sense of 'we' to people whom we have previously thought of as 'they'" (1989:192). "That is why," he continues, "detailed descriptions of particular varieties of pain and humiliation (in, e.g., novels or ethnographies), rather than philosophical or religious treatises, [are] the modern intellectual's principal contributions to moral progress." (See also 1989:94–95.) He clearly believes that empathy (imaginative entry into another person's world) will automatically lead to compassion (concern for that individual and for others of his or her ilk); this is striking given his insistence elsewhere that "there can be sensitive killers, cruel aesthetes, pitiless poets" (1989:157). As for Nussbaum, though she sometimes qualifies under pressure ("empathy is likely to be hooked up to compassion only in someone who has had a good early education in childhood, one that teaches concern for others" [1998:352]), she generally feels, as we are about to see, that "the [novelistic] genre itself, on account of some general features of its structure, constructs empathy *and compassion*" (1995:10, my emphasis). Contrast, again, the approach of Lisa Zunshine, who views the capacity to "read minds" as something we typically use to improve our own situation, not to remedy that of others (Zunshine 27–33 *et passim*). One does not have to be particularly cynical to see examples everywhere one turns, starting from one's own life.

22. See Currie 1998:163, 166, 173; 1995b:251 and 257. Kendall Walton has also been tempted by this approach: see 1994:34 (and 1997 for the general simulation view). On Socratism in Nussbaum, cf. Posner 1997:10.

23. Nussbaum's view is in agreement with that of Iris Murdoch, who takes virtue to consist in seeing clearly and responding justly (84, 85). For Murdoch, art assists us in both of these tasks; it also encourages us, thanks to the famous "disinterestedness" of aesthetic contemplation, to move beyond the confines of the self (83); it reveals, in Platonic fashion, the existence of the Good (86, 91); and, we recall, it even "teaches that nothing in life is of any value except the attempt to be virtuous" (85). A number of art lovers may find themselves wondering why, after all the beautiful works they have appreciated throughout the years, they still find other things valuable in life beyond morality, still do not believe in the Platonic Form of the Good, and still consider the self a worthwhile object of concern.

It should be noted that Nussbaum sometimes takes a more Rortyan tack, writing that "works of art can cut through our tendencies to deny humanity to our fellow human beings" (1999:265; cf. 1998:350 and 356, and 1995:39); her reading of Ralph Ellison's *Invisible Man* is along these lines. It is an open question to what extent the two outlooks are compatible, given that, as Eileen John points out (1995:314, 318), there is no need for subtlety—subtlety can, indeed, be a positive *obstacle*—when it comes to addressing problems like racism. (For another critique of Nussbaum, see Lamarque and Olsen 386–97.)

24. It is true that Booth's definition of "ethics" is so broad as to encompass, apparently, all of human activity ("*Vision? Powerful?* Again ethical language" [1998:392]); under such a description, ethics does indeed appear "inescapable." On the other hand, the examples Booth gives of ethical improvement through fiction—such as recognizing the humanity of other racial groups (1998:377)—tend to be standardly (and narrowly) moral. For similar equivocation in Nussbaum, see 1987:169; 1983b:202; 1998:365n21.

25. Cf. "the novel . . . is a morally controversial form, expressing in its very shape and style, in its modes of interaction with its readers, a normative sense of life" (1995:2). Mind you, Nussbaum elsewhere claims that "[her] argument is confined to a narrow group of preselected works" (1998:346), by which she presumably means Anglo-American realist novels dealing with "social and political themes" (1995:10). Here too, then, there is a certain degree of equivocation.

26. Thus Nussbaum believes that novels will only affect us when their influence is beneficial: "Reading can lead us to alter some of our standing judgments, but it is also the case that these judgments can cause us to reject some experiences of reading as deforming or pernicious" (1995:10). If, however, our standing judgments are sufficiently well formed as to be

up to the task of rejecting pernicious reading material, why do they need to be altered? And if they need altering, how do they manage to ward off Sade and Riefenstahl?

Related concerns might be raised with regard to Gregory Currie's simulation theory. "Projecting myself into the life of another," writes Currie, "has, potentially, the double function of telling me about his mental life and about my own possible future course of action; whatever I do, I had better make sure that things don't turn out *that* way for me... Both of [these functions] have a moral significance. In empathizing with others I come to share their mental states, which powerfully reinforces my tendency to take their interests into account.... And the same process makes the actions and outcomes of others guides to my own planning" (1998:169). Again, there is an asymmetry. If the empathy and aversion are to serve *moral* purposes, then surely our empathy must be directed toward deserving individuals, our aversion toward suspect characters. But how, if we are not already properly disposed, do we make the distinction? What is to stop us empathizing with villains, and thus reinforcing our tendency to take the interests of mafiosi (*Goodfellas*) and child abusers (*Lolita*) into account? Conversely, what if I watch a dramatization of the life of Christ and decide that I had better make sure things don't turn out *that* way for me?

Currie's optimism here is all the more surprising when one considers the delightful assessment of empathy he delivered three years earlier (1995b:257): "In order to defeat my enemy I may need to simulate his mental operations, so as to know what he will do. That need not make me like him any better." There are clearly two Curries, one who believes that simulation evolved because it helped us become "better social creatures" (1997:72), and another—red in tooth and claw—who knows that simulation also makes us more effective *fighters*.

27. "If the work's obnoxious message does not destroy its aesthetic value, it nevertheless renders it morally inaccessible. That must count as an aesthetic as well as a moral defect" (Walton 1994:30). Notice that only the beauty of "obnoxious" works is inaccessible, not that of (say) sanctimonious works.

Gendler's version of imaginative resistance is, to be fair, the most convincing, precisely because she rules such cases out of court; as long as it does not look like we are being invited to "export" the deviant value system to the real world, she writes, we do not feel it necessary to resist (73–74). An asymmetry still remains, however: we resist any *immoral* schemata we are invited to export, but allow the moral ones to course unchecked through our welcoming souls. As I will argue below, it is just as easy for us to resist excessively *pious* fictions—even those with whose values our real-world selves agree.

28. Gendler, 58. In this chapter, I will be using the second half of this sentence (the claim that moral divergence causes imaginative resistance). I also wonder, however, about the first half (the claim that factual divergence does not). James Bond films usually include a scene in which a dozen machine guns are all firing continuously upon the hero from different angles, and he escapes death because somehow every single bullet misses its target. The result, for many viewers, is a temporary loss of absorption. A curious result: we who are quite willing to entertain the possibility of gunfights on skis, cars that turn into submarines, and characters named Goldfinger or Pussy Galore, find our fun disrupted by a single hail of bullets! The reason is that a good part of our pleasure derives from the spectacle of *ingenuity*, of cunning solutions to complex predicaments within the constraints co-established by the fictional world and the laws of physics. The examples to which philosophers standardly refer ("imagine a world in which six times two is not twelve") are perhaps not as revealing as cases like these, where concerns for verisimilitude—partial as they may be—intersect directly with our motivation for make-believe.

29. Perhaps we do not always imaginatively endorse murder while watching, say, *Goodfellas*. But I believe we do imaginatively endorse theft, larceny, bank robbery, fraud, and so on while watching *The Sting*, *Butch Cassidy and the Sundance Kid*, or any number of outlaw films. And the conclusion of *Silence of the Lambs* leaves us, quite curiously, feeling glad for Hannibal Lecter that he has secured himself a meal (of human flesh).

30. Gendler (77) contends that cowboy films reduce our moral outrage by making the victims appear to deserve their fate. The mummy-denying rationalist, however, only deserves his

fate by the standards of the topsy-turvy worldview internal to the fiction. Objectively speaking, the rationalist is an innocent, and we should, on the Humean account, be resisting with all our might. I would suggest that much of what goes on in outlaw films (think, for example, of the Mexican police massacred, to our great satisfaction, by Butch Cassidy and the Sundance Kid) follows a similar pattern.

Compare Currie (1997:74): "the lovers in *The Postman Always Rings Twice* are not very appealing examples of humankind, but most of us manage some sort of identification with their murderous project." Nor is our misplaced empathy limited to such extreme cases, according to Currie. "We frequently take the part of people in fiction whom we could not like or take the part of in real life," he writes, citing the example of a novel about Oxbridge dons competing for the position of master. "The way I care," he continues, "seems at odds with the kind of person I am" (1997:65).

31. Alfred Hitchcock, for one, seems to think so. "When a burglar goes into a room," he notes, "all the time he's going through the drawers, the public is generally anxious for him." And in *Psycho*, "when [Anthony] Perkins is looking at the car sinking in the pond, even though he's burying a body, when the car stops sinking for a moment, the public is thinking, 'I hope it goes all the way down!' It's a natural instinct" (Truffaut, 207).

32. Cf. Pavel 1986:85, 90, 92.

33. Cf. Posner 1998:404, 407 and Eileen John: "Works of fiction do not provide 'normal' perceptual fields, and readers do not approach them with 'normal' perceptual habits" (1995:309).

34. Daniel Jacobson (1997:186) points out that a tearjerker may (inadvertently) *preclude* the kind of empathy I might very well feel in a real-life situation. Richard Moran also acknowledges that moralizing fictions are a prime source of imaginative resistance (99; cf. Mothersill, 94). Still, Moran sees such fictions as inspiring resistance by foreclosing autonomous judgment on the part of their consumers, not by proposing standards to which the latter do not aspire. When it comes to this second type of resistance (105)—resistance, that is, to specific implied norms, rather than to a general sense of coercion—Moran clearly thinks in terms of norms that are deficiently rather than excessively moral. Thus the prime example he gives is the difficulty we would experience if faced with a variant of *Macbeth* in which Duncan's murder "was unfortunate only for having interfered with Macbeth's sleep" (95). He thus rejoins Walton, it seems to me, on this point.

35. I am thinking of Dostoyevsky's "underground man," who imagines himself sticking his tongue out at a perfect crystal edifice (*Notes from Underground*, 31–32) and who reacts to "the sublime and the beautiful" by doing "hideous things" (7).

36. Of course, there are plenty who believe that *Clarissa* is improving and *Goodfellas* harmful. This, too, leaves me skeptical. If my mental capacities are so ill-formed as to leave me at the mercy of *Goodfellas*, easily led to conclude that it is excellent to kill and dreadful to report crimes, then why should I be trusted to draw the appropriate lessons from *Clarissa*?

37. Diderot, "Éloge de Richardson," 128. The hypothesis of lurking irony may gain some support from Diderot's remark, in the *Paradoxe sur le comédien*, about the citizen who leaves his vices at the door only to "take them up again on the way out. There he is just, impartial, a good father, a good friend, a friend of virtue; and I have often seen wicked men next to me taking deep umbrage at actions that they would not have failed to commit if they had found themselves in the same circumstances" (167, my translation; although the speaker is officially "the first interlocutor," he is clearly identified as Diderot at 147).

Diderot is echoing here a purportedly true story told by Plutarch in *The Life of Pelopidas*. Alexander of Pherae, a tyrant who "buried men alive, and sometimes dressed them in the skins of wild boars or bears, and then set his hunting dogs upon them and either tore them in pieces or shot them down" (29.4), once burst into tears during a performance of *The Trojan Women*, "weeping over the sorrows of Hecuba and Andromache" (29.5). His interest in casual murder, notes Plutarch, remained unaffected.

38. Compare an odd, possibly inadvertent admission from Booth: "thus in our moments of actual reading we are led to become quite different from who we are *when we put down the book*" (1998:378, my emphasis). And Posner, more deliberately: "one of the pleasures that

literature does engender in its readers . . . is the pleasure of imagining utopian resolutions of the conflicts that beset the human condition. I just don't think this pleasure translates into action" (1998:411n14).

39. "When a man has admired fine actions in fables, and wept over imaginary sufferings, what more can be demanded of him? Is he not pleased with himself? Does he not congratulate himself on his noble soul? Has he not acquitted himself of all he owes virtue by the homage he has just rendered it?" asks Rousseau rather sardonically in his *Lettre à d'Alembert*, as though mocking Diderot (or Diderot's persona) a few years in advance. "Thus," Rousseau concludes, "the most useful effect of the best tragedies is to reduce all the duties of man to some passing, sterile, and fruitless emotions, to make us applaud our courage in praising that of others, our humanity in pitying the ills we could have healed" (78–79, my translation; cf. Jacobson 1997:156). James Harold agrees that "many serious moral situations in life do not call out for a reflective response; *action* is called for; reflection may be morally out of place" (267); Jonathan Lear makes related remarks in a different context (1988:306); and "Tom Stoppard once said that if you see an injustice taking place outside your window, the least useful thing you can do is to write a play about it. I would go further, suggesting that there is something wrong in writing plays about that sort of injustice in which we have an obligation to intervene, since it puts the audience at just the sort of distance the concept of psychic distance means to describe" (Danto 1981:22).

40. It is, in general, a curious fact that those who spend their time reading great literature do not always turn into paragons of virtue (Posner 1997:5). (As K. K. Ruthven puts it, "despite their familiarity with the classics, professors of literature do not appear to lead better lives than other people, and frequently display unbecoming virulence on the subject of one another's shortcomings" [184].) Nussbaum's response—that "professors of literature are often jaded and detached," and "don't read with the freshness and responsiveness of ordinary readers" (1998:353)—presumably does not apply to Nussbaum herself, whose passion for James remains palpably undiminished.

41. Cf. Posner 1997:18. Nussbaum is not alone in her strategy: Roche too has decided to blame the reader if he or she has the temerity not to be improved (47, 220).

42. As Noël Carroll puts it, "we still understand virtually *nothing* about the behavioral consequences of consuming art" (133). Suzanne Keen's recent work confirms Carroll's skepticism: after performing an exhaustive survey of empirical studies on the subject, Keen concludes that "the link between narrative empathy and altruism is . . . tenuous" (2006:212; see also Keen 2007). Conversely, a government-appointed Committee on Obscenity and Film Censorship, headed by Bernard Williams, reported in 1979 that it could find no definitive connection between filmed and real violence. Wayne Booth concedes this point in his article on television (Booth 1987:387).

43. "The artist can assist us by cutting through the blur of habit and the self-deceptions habit abets. . . . When we follow him as attentive readers, and our readings themselves are accessible ethical acts" (1998:344); "our own attention to his characters will itself, if we read well, be a high case of moral attention" (1987:186); indeed "the *highest* task is to be people 'on whom nothing is lost'" (1987:169, my emphasis).

44. Nussbaum 1998:355. Candace Vogler has a delightful response to this: "one sometimes rereads novels on airplanes," she writes (33), "in order to avoid conversation with the occupant of the next seat."

45. Bob and Fanny Assingham, writes Nussbaum, "perform the function, more or less, of a Greek tragic chorus. 'Participants by fond attention' just as we are . . ., they perform, together, an activity of attending and judging and interpreting that is parallel to ours, if even more deeply immersed and implicated" (1987:181). One has to wonder: if Fanny Assingham is "even more deeply immersed and implicated" than we are, and yet she still takes an "aestheticizing" attitude (ibid.) toward Maggie and company, then what chance do we readers have?

      To be fair, Nussbaum does acknowledge that Fanny "takes fine-tuned perception to a dangerously rootless extreme" and "delights in the complexity of these particulars for its own sake, without sufficiently feeling the pull of a moral obligation to any" (1987:181–82). Yet this moral obligation is precisely what Nussbaum claims, over and over again, is "constructed" (1995:10), "awakened" (1999:278), and "shaped" (1998:353) by novels like *The Golden Bowl*—novels that, to repeat, make Fanny Assinghams of us all.

46. On this point, see John 1997:236–38.

47. Some might argue that Derek Parfit's examples constitute an exception. Others (myself included) would counter that many of his science-fiction cases are so far-fetched as to be unreliable even as a guide to our own intuitions.

48. On this point, see Jacobson 1996:331. And on the more general divergence of literary texts from philosophical test cases, see O'Neill (esp. 9 and 18).

49. Robert Louis Stevenson put the same point very eloquently in his "Humble Remonstrance" to Henry James. "Our art is occupied," he wrote, "not so much in capturing the lineaments of each fact, as in marshalling all of them towards a common end. For the welter of impressions . . . which life presents, it substitutes a certain artificial series of impressions, . . . all aiming at the same effect, all eloquent of the same idea, all chiming together like consonant notes in music. . . . Life is monstrous, infinite, illogical, abrupt, and poignant; a work of art, in comparison, is neat, finite, self-contained, rational, flowing, and emasculate" (918–19).

50. This, I think, is the one lacuna in Jerome Stolnitz's argument: he overlooks the fact that philosophical ideas can come packaged in literary forms (Parmenides, Berkeley, Nietzsche). Ironically, he cites Plato as having complained that creative writers do not have firsthand knowledge of their topic (1992:198)—forgetting that this complaint is uttered, in the *Ion*, by a *fictional character* ("Socrates").

51. Nussbaum considers *The Golden Bowl* a "persuasive argument that these features hold of human life in general" (1983a:41). It is an argument a fortiori: if even the virtuous Maggie sees that the bowl is broken, then it must be broken for everyone. But its force depends on viewing a literary character's journey from birth to death as a "human life" (ibid.), and fiction as a straightforward extension of reality (1987:180).

52. For the ostensibly unpleasant consequences of sucking one's thumb, see *Slovenly Peter* (*Struwwelpeter*). I refer here to children in possession of "theory of mind" (i.e., the awareness of others as autonomous agents, with thoughts and desires of their own), a capacity that develops in normal individuals between the ages of three and four. I am grateful to Stacie Friend for this qualification.

53. In Rousseau's words (1979:115), "they are taught less not to let [the cheese] fall from their beaks than to make it fall from the beak of another." Rousseau also cites *La cigale et la fourmi*, in which an industrious ant refuses to help out an indolent cricket. Children, says Rousseau, take it to be recommending that they decline to lend a hand (like the ant), not that they avoid being feckless (like the cricket). Nor does this situation always come to an end with childhood: consider the fact that the film *All Quiet on the Western Front* was actually used as propaganda *by the military* in the 1940s (Broyles); consider also the strange situation in 1944 Paris, when Anouilh staged *Antigone* as a protest against occupation, and the Germans allowed it because they read it as a paean to Creon (Knox, 22). In this last case, *both* sides were wrong, guilty of a deep misunderstanding about Sophocles' play (on which more below).

54. Achilles in the *Iliad* (18.115–21): "I will accept my own death, at whatever time Zeus wishes to bring it about. . . . Now I must win excellent glory." Achilles in the *Odyssey* (11.488–91): "O shining Odysseus, never try to console me for dying. I would rather follow the plow as thrall to another man, one with no land allotted him and not much to live on, than be a king over all the perished dead."

55. See Thucydides 3.37–48.

56. Cf. Tanner, 62.

57. It is often (and correctly) noted of Emma Bovary that she makes the mistake of deriving her opinions on love from novels. What is less often seen is that her interests, during her convent years, keep *changing*. She, too, is easily swayed from one value to another, from adventure to history to mysticism: "Couriers were killed at every relay, horses ridden to

death on every page; there were gloomy forests, broken hearts, vows, sobs, tears and kisses, skiffs in the moonlight, nightingales in thickets; the noblemen were all brave as lions, gentle as lambs, incredibly virtuous, always beautifully dressed, and wept copiously on every occasion. *For six months,* when she was fifteen, Emma begrimed her hands with this dust from old lending libraries. *Later,* reading Walter Scott, she became infatuated with everything historical and dreamed about oaken chests and guardrooms and troubadours. . . . *When her mother died . . .* she let herself meander along Lamartinian paths, listening to the throbbing of harps on lakes, to all the songs of the dying swans, to the falling of every leaf, to the flight of pure virgins ascending to heaven, and to the voice of the Eternal speaking in the valleys. *Gradually these things began to bore her . . .* " (43, 45; my emphasis).

    I am, of course, aware of the irony involved in citing *Madame Bovary* in the context of the present argument, and hope I will not be taken as implying that Flaubert's novel has the power to change the minds of its readers, neatly converting them from bovarysts to anti-bovarysts. The fact that today's advocates of a fiction-rich diet are themselves almost certain to have read *Madame Bovary* at some point in their lives speaks, in my opinion, for itself.

58. Thus Nussbaum claims not only that Ralph Ellison helps us understand "how a history of racial stereotyping can affect self-esteem, achievement, and love" but also that "Ellison's work conveys this understanding through and in the pleasure that it imparts" (1999:267). Any dangerous pleasure we risk deriving from the narrative is thus mercifully redeemed by being put to an honorable end.

59. "In a genre such as the novel, a turning away from traditional political concerns to private concerns and formal experimentation is awfully likely to express a wish to avoid some unpleasant social reality," Nussbaum writes (1999:280), echoing her earlier claim that Posner selects his reading material so as to shelter himself from "the claim of a painful reality" (1998:361). As always, a healthy moral concern—indeed, an obsessive and exclusive moral concern, governing all aspects of our life—is presumed to be where we *start*; amoral spaces are carved out *later,* by willed acts of irresponsibility. The novel is, by default, about "traditional political concerns," and only subsequently perverted to private matters. Not everyone would agree with that assessment.

60. More recently, Mark William Roche has advanced the same pair of positions: (1) literature is either morally improving or emptily entertaining ("if literature had no ethical value, it would be a mere diversion that we needn't take seriously"); (2) emptily entertaining art is positively pernicious ("bad art, seeking to substitute beauty for morality,. . . exerts a corrupting influence on society"). See Roche, 21, 64–65. Intriguingly, both Roche and Nussbaum turn out to be echoing—one assumes inadvertently—the Hollywood Production Code, that infamous 1930 statute which forbade revenge plots, the cancan, and scenes of interracial affection. In their rationale, the framers of the Code explicitly rejected the idea that any aesthetic product can be morally neutral, alleging instead that there are only two kinds of art, "entertainment which tends to improve the race" and "entertainment which tends to degrade human beings." Moralism makes some strange bedfellows.

61. Cf. Bakhtin 1988.

62. There is also, to repeat, an affective variant of this cognitive clarificationism. While some literary texts may help me to know what I know, that is, others may help me to feel what I feel. Holocaust fictions are instructive in this regard: we do not read or watch them for moral edification—we do not need to *learn* that Nazism is evil—but instead, it seems to me, for an opportunity to grieve.

63. On this point, see also Bloom 2000:22; Eldridge 2003:216–17; Mullin *passim*; Danto 1986:156; and Carroll: "the successful narrative becomes the occasion for exercising knowledge, concepts, and emotions that we have already, in one sense, learned"; "in mobilizing what we already know and what we can already feel, the narrative artwork can become an occasion for us to deepen our understanding of what we know and what we feel" (141, 142). Carroll, however, believes that clarification can easily lead to "re-gestalting," and thus to profound "moral reform" (143, 149). In my view this is a little too

optimistic. Even if re-gestalting does result from engagement with literary texts, there is no guarantee that it will operate in the direction of increased altruism; even if I become aware of a conflict in my value system and desire to overcome it, there is no guarantee that I will retain the noble commitment and shed the ignoble. As Alexander Nehamas so powerfully puts it, spending time with things of beauty "will have an effect on me which I cannot predict in advance. Once that effect is in place, I may have changed into someone I would not have wanted to be before I began. But I may now no longer be able to see that what I am, perhaps, is perverted. How can I tell if I have followed the right course? Which standards should I apply to myself?" (Nehamas 2000:6; cf. Nehamas 2007:57, 127).

64. In droves, philosophers have followed Aristotle in suggesting that the ideal friend is one who helps us to be a better person; Cocking and Kennett, who argue (286) that the primary service a friend can perform is to help us to be who we are, form a rare exception.

65. Cf. Currie 1998:163, 174. Whatever the genre of the work that contains them, writes Walton, we judge characters by our everyday moral standards (1994:37); this claim seems unwarranted to me, for reasons I have already articulated.

66. "Of all the masterpieces of the classical and the modern world," Hegel famously writes, "the *Antigone* seems to me to be the most magnificent and satisfying work of art of this kind" (1218); "the heroes of Greek classical tragedy are confronted by circumstances in which, after firmly identifying themselves with the one ethical 'pathos' which alone corresponds to their own already established nature, they necessarily come into conflict with the opposite but equally justified ethical power" (1226).

It would be hard to see the *Antigone* as seeking to equip us with "fine awareness": surely we already understand the duties we have to our family and to the larger community, and even the fact that they cannot all be satisfied at once. What the play does, instead, is to make us think hard about the relative *strength* of their claims on us, and about how we wish to adjudicate between them in cases of conflict. In the end, a *hierarchy of values* may well be of more use to us than the most finely tuned intuitions.

67. Thus Robert Pippin: "in some general sense, it might be true that prejudice rests on stereotypes and a certain distance from the reality of particular lives, and that gripping literary accounts of such individuals might begin to make one uneasy about one's prejudices, but if the novel is not very good (like, in my view at least, Dickens's saccharine *Hard Times*, and like other novels out to make such a point) it is just as likely that 'the individual' presented will instantiate just another Christian cliché, the good-hearted worker uncorrupted by power and money, or that the villains will be stereotypes, and one's moral reaction . . . itself will be stereotypical, will amount to a self-satisfied feeling that because one has rejected Grandgrind, one has a good heart, that one's sympathies are all in the right place" (2002:83).

68. Misguided readers, writes Milan Kundera, "seek at the novel's core not an inquiry but a moral position" (1988:7), for in reality, "the novel's spirit is the spirit of complexity. Every novel says to the reader: 'Things are not as simple as you think.' That is the novel's eternal truth, but it grows steadily harder to hear amid the din of easy, quick answers" (ibid., 18). Compare Mikhail Bakhtin, who privileges "heteroglot" novels (1981:278); Hilary Putnam, in whose view literature serves not to "depict solutions" but rather to "aid us in the imaginative re-creation of moral perplexities" (485); and Eileen John, who suggests that "works of fiction, rather than providing new ways of thinking, sometimes lead us to places of obscurity . . . provid[ing] a context in which we can think fruitfully about the conceptual issues raised" (1998:340).

69. Booth admits that "no story will produce changes in readers unless they are already in some respect susceptible to a given kind of influence" (1998:368); Currie acknowledges that fictions, like electron microscopes, are best used by "those well able to benefit from them" (1998:178); and Nussbaum recognizes the objection that "a person who is obtuse in life will also be an obtuse reader of James's text. How can literature show us or train us in anything, when . . . the very moral qualities that make for good reading are the ones that are allegedly in need of development?" (1987:187). Still, this does not stop Nussbaum from insisting—as we saw above—that "it is impossible to care about the characters and

their fate in the way the text invites, without having some very definite political and moral interests awakened in oneself" (1999:278).

Chapter 2

1. Here and throughout the chapter, I use "Mark" as shorthand for "the Gospel of Mark." I take no position on the identity of its author, which has been the subject of some debate.
2. "He did not speak to them without a parable" (Mark 4:34). Cf. Matt. 13:34: "All this Jesus said to the crowds in parables; indeed he said nothing to them without a parable." Here and throughout I cite the Revised Standard Version of the Bible. Greek originals are from the Interlinear NIV.
3. This is a hotly contested topic, but there does appear to be precedent in the Old Testament *mashal*—e.g., 2 Sam. 12:1–10—and in the Tannaitic sayings of the Talmud, which even include parables of sowing and harvesting (Oesterley, 8). (Some of the Tannaitic sayings, while *transcribed* considerably later, originate in the period preceding Jesus's ministry.) They are often as obscure as those of Jesus (see Cranfield, 160 and Daube, 142; contrast Jones, 78 and Crossan, 19). The difference may be that Jesus's parables have more surprising endings—or, as I suspect, just that they are more central to his pedagogical practice. For a brief overview of the use of parables within biblical and rabbinic Judaism, see Porton.
4. It is important to repeat that when I speak of fictions in the book of Mark, I am referring only to the parables and not to the Gospel as a whole. While fictions are works of imagination designed to be taken as such, the book of Mark is designed to be understood as a true history, an accurate depiction of the life of Christ; accordingly, even those who doubt its accuracy must use another term to characterize it. The parables, by contrast, overtly present events that never happened, characters that never existed, and conversations that did not take place, with no intention of deceiving anyone into thinking otherwise (Jesus does not, for example, expect his audience to believe that there was an *actual* landlord who sent his *actual* son to deal with some violent tenants).

    A parable, then, is a fictional narrative. To be precise, it is a brief fictional narrative, extremely short on detail, and pointing beyond its literal surface to a figured meaning hovering somewhere above or behind it. (That it is immediately understood as pointing beyond itself has in part to do with contextual factors—there would be no reason for a teacher to tell such a story if it were merely an anecdote from life—and also in part with cultural-historical factors: certain motifs, like seeds and sowers, already have a history of figurative use before Jesus borrows them.) It features human actors and occupies itself with moral or spiritual concerns (unlike the *fable*, whose animal stories typically remain within the realm of the pragmatic); it recounts a single occurrence in the past tense (unlike the *similitude*, which favors the present tense and typical situations); and although it tends to end with some kind of unexpected twist, it seeks a modicum of verisimilitude, of correspondence between narrated events and recognizable everyday scenarios (unlike the *allegory*, whose various incidents need only correspond to an extratextual story—say, that of mankind's fall and redemption—and may therefore make little sense without knowledge of that story). Examples of twists include all of the laborers receiving the same amount of pay, regardless of how long they have worked (Matt. 20:1–16); the vineyard owner sending his son into the hands of the wicked husbandmen (Mark 12:1–9, Matt. 21:33–46, Luke 20:9–19, Thomas 65); the farmer telling his servants not to weed his field (Matt. 13:24–30); and the man trading everything he has for a single pearl (Matt. 13:45–46). (Cf. Ricoeur 1975:115–18.) For all of this, see B. T. D. Smith, 17; Dodd, 5–6; Via 1967:5–6, 11–12; Donahue, 7; Manson, 64–65; New Interpreter's Bible 299, 568.
5. Very few would claim that the purpose was self-protection—that Jesus, knowing his message to be controversial, sought to conceal it from the authorities. Given that Jesus was willing to upset the tables of the money-changers, argue with the Pharisees, and ultimately go to the cross for his beliefs, this view seems a little hard to sustain.

6. Quoted in Kissinger, 50. This is also the view of Luther and, some centuries later, that of Richard C. Trench (see Kissinger, 44, 63).

7. This was the central claim of Adolf Jülicher, who transformed parable interpretation in the late nineteenth century. (For discussion, see Ricoeur 1975:91.) Other examples include Wilder—"he said the same things in what we call layman's language in his parables of the Kingdom . . . he brought theology down into daily life" (86)—and B. T. D. Smith: "by means of simile and similitude the unfamiliar and difficult can be explained in terms of the known" (20). See also to some extent Donahue, 11, and the New Jerome (Brown et al., 605). Jülicher's view may appear to concord with Matt. 13:13, in which Jesus says that he uses parables *"because* seeing they do not see," as opposed to using parables *"so that* they may indeed see but not perceive" (Mark 4:12). As I will show, however, the contrast between Mark and Matthew is less stark than it may seem.

8. The "impress" idea belongs to Joachim Jeremias (9), the vividness idea to John Chrysostom (see Kissinger, 28).

9. For the argument-by-analogy idea, see Ricoeur, who cites Aristotle's claim in *Rhetoric* 2.20 that the simile is an instrument of proof (1975:90); see also Via 1967:19.

10. B. T. D. Smith combines all of these claims into a single theory: parables, he writes, make ideas more vivid; grab attention; illustrate a truth by means of an example; explain the unfamiliar in terms of the familiar; and, just for good measure, also constitute an argument by analogy. See B. T. D. Smith, 19, 20, 126.

11. This parable is also found at Matt. 13:1–23, Luke 8:4–17, and Thomas 9. (The Gospel of Thomas is a non-canonical "Sayings Gospel" rediscovered at Nag Hammadi in 1945.)

12. Here the Revised Standard Version is clearly superior to the King James, which has "And when he was alone, they that were about him with the twelve asked of him the parable." Given the Greek—"ἠρώτων αὐτὸν . . . τὰς παραβολάς"—it should read "they that were about him with the twelve asked of him the parable*s*," plural, which is to say, "they that were about him with the twelve asked him about the parables."

13. That, in fact, is how the Gospel of Thomas reports it: "Jesus said, 'Now the sower went out, took a handful [of seeds], and scattered them. Some fell on the road; the birds came and gathered them up. Others fell on the rock, did not take root in the soil, and did not produce ears. And others fell on thorns; they choked the seed[s] and worms ate them. And others fell on the good soil and produced good fruit: it bore sixty per measure and a hundred and twenty per measure'" (Thomas 9). The Gospel of Thomas simply leaves it there and moves on.

14. B. T. D. Smith, 61–73. For God as sower, cf. Isa. 55:10, Jer. 31:27, Ezek. 36:9, Hosea 2:23, Zech. 10:9 (Hunter 1971:35); for the injunction not to sow among thorns, cf. Jer. 4:3 (Drury 1973:369; Jeremias, 9).

15. In Frank Kermode's words, "the opinion [that the parables serve the goal of clarity] is maintained with an expense of learning I can't begin to emulate, against what seems obvious" (25).

16. As Via points out, if you don't already know what the parable is saying, then you will not understand it; accordingly, parables are incapable of creating disciples (at least by means of their content). See Via 1965:430, 432.

    The parable of the Laborers in the Vineyard (Matt. 20:1–16), in which an employer pays everyone the same wage regardless of how many hours they have put in, is a particularly strange tale. No real-life employer would do that (notice that this puts the idea of argument by analogy in serious trouble), and it does not feel intuitively like a good thing. Furthermore, the apparent moral—that divine justice consists in paying no attention to merit—conflicts with the apparent moral of the Talents (Matt. 25:14–30, Luke 19:11–27), in which the master rewards his servants in proportion to how well they have used the money deposited with them.

17. As Manson so beautifully puts it (57), "whole volumes have been written in exposition of compositions whose meaning is supposed [according to contemporary scholars] to be obvious." The parable, continues Manson, "is emphatically not a mere sermon illustration for

the purpose of stating some abstract proposition of ethics or theology in a simple pictorial form for the benefit of the unlearned" (65; cf. 72–73). See also NIB 299.

18. The key figure here is Albert Schweitzer (see Kissinger, 92), but the NIB also flirts with the idea (8:303, 570).

19. This is the view of C. H. Dodd (148–50, 154–56).

20. This is a widely held view. Thus Jeremias: "in spite of every failure the Kingdom of God comes at last" (92). Hunter: "in spite of all frustrations and failures, God's rule advances" (1971:36; cf. 1960:100). The New Jerome: "the message is that, despite some failures, the sower's work ultimately succeeds for the most part. . . . The story gives hope and encouragement" (655). And the New Interpreter's Bible: "the victory of the kingdom of God is sure. . . . Believers should not be . . . discouraged" (309). See also M. Grant (92–93). Wilder's position is more nuanced. Jesus, he points out, can hardly be making a convincing argument by analogy, since in real life many a harvest *fails*. Wilder's own view (84-85) is that the parable of the Sower indicates not the confidence that an ordinary farmer should have, based on his experience, but the confidence that *Jesus* has, based on his foreknowledge of what is to come. Our confidence comes as a result of his.

21. On this debate, see Cadoux, 23; Cranfield, 160; Dodd, 3, 145; Jülicher 2:514–38; New Interpreter's Bible 305; Scott, 355. Jeremias points out (62) that the now apocryphal text Esdras uses sowing metaphors in both senses. In one chapter (4 Esdras 9:31) the seed is something implanted by God in a human soul; in another, we human beings are ourselves the seeds, scattered across the world. "For just as the farmer sows many seeds upon the ground and plants a multitude of seedlings, and yet not all that have been sown will come up in due season, and not all that were planted will take root; so also those who have been sown in the world will not all be saved" (4 Esdras 8:41, cited in Bultmann 1963:202, Scott, 360).

22. This is Scott's point—though Scott also sees the parable as showing that "in failure and everydayness lies the miracle of God's activity" (361).

23. See Donahue (46), and to some extent Oesterley (40).

24. This is more or less the view of John Maldonatus (see Kissinger, 57).

25. Cadoux, 155.

26. M. Grant, 94; Cadoux, 15; New Jerome 1368.

27. "And he [God] said, 'Go, and say to this people: "Hear and hear, but do not understand; see and see, but do not perceive." Make the heart of this people fat, and their ears heavy, and shut their eyes; lest they see with their eyes, and hear with their ears, and understand with their hearts, and turn and be healed'" (Isa. 6:9–10).

28. New Jerusalem Bible 98. A final option: "for those outside everything is in parables—*for those, that is, who* see but do not perceive, and hear but do not understand." According to Jeremias (14–15n25), *ἵνα* may be a mistranslation of the Aramaic particle *d'*, which *can* mean "so that," but can also function as a relative pronoun, meaning simply "which" or "who."

29. "The last words," writes Manson, "would seem to mean: 'For if they did [understand], they would repent and receive forgiveness'" (78). This is particularly strange given that Manson in general favors the esoteric approach.

30. Jeremias believes (15) that "we must translate Mk iv, 11 f.: '. . . unless they turn and God will forgive them.'" His evidence is that Mark would probably have been working from the Aramaic translation of Isaiah, which renders *pen* (lest) as *dilma* (lest or unless). This is all rather hopeful.

31. See, e.g., Matt. 13:35.

32. Manson bites the bullet and says that Mark gets Isaiah wrong (78). This is of course possible, but it does not seem entirely likely to me, the Isaiah passage being so clear (and the implied author of Mark so astute).

33. It could perhaps be argued that the ones asking for an explanation are "they that were about him *with* the twelve," and that the apostles themselves do understand. But no such distinction is made twenty-four lines later, where Mark tells us that "privately to his own disciples he [Jesus] explained everything." Consider also that it is once again "the

disciples" in general who are involved in the delightful "leaven of the Pharisees" exchange: "And he cautioned them, saying, 'Take heed, beware of the leaven of the Pharisees and the leaven of Herod.' And they discussed it with one another, saying, 'We have no bread'" (Mark 8:15–16).

34. As B. T. D. Smith points out (29), "Mark's theory of the purpose of Christ's parabolic teaching is only part of a larger theory." On Mark's "messianic secret," see Wrede and Tuckett.

35. "And he strictly charged them that no one should know this" (Mark 5:43); "and he charged them to tell no one" (7:36); "see that you say nothing to any one" (1:44).

36. See Via 1967:9; F. Grant, 699; and the New Jerome Bible 605–6. Amusingly, the New Interpreter's Bible adopts *both* lines of defense, even though they are mutually exclusive. On the one hand, "Matthew does not share Mark's understanding of the secret messiah-ship and its corollary, the misunderstanding of the disciples" (304); on the other, Mark does not believe in it himself: "the overall tenor of [Mark] 4:11 does not suggest secrecy. . . Jesus would not endorse the policy of cutting off access to forgiveness, since he came to offer forgiveness and to call sinners" (572).

37. And from Luke, who also uses ἵνα (8:10).

38. Cf. Donohue, 41. Strangely, the New Jerome sees Matthew as quoting Isaiah 6 at greater length "so that the reader can see its positive intent to save" (656); surely the "lest" puts this in serious doubt.

39. Michael Petrin, pers. comm.

40. "And his disciples came to him, saying, 'Explain to us the parable of the weeds of the field'" (Matt. 13:36). On the unintelligibility of parables even in Matthew, see Cadoux, 18; Jones, 64; and Via 1965:430–31. As Via sees it, Matthew's Jesus is actually *more* insistent than Mark's Jesus on the need to keep outsiders out; if he says "because" rather than "so that," he merely means "because people are obtuse, they are more easily deceived." (See Via 1967:9; the invented quotation is mine.)

41. The standard view is that Mark was written shortly after the destruction of the Temple (70 CE), to which it alludes in chapter 13. See, e.g., Eisenman, 56; Helms, 8.

42. See, e.g., Jeremias, 11–12.

43. The idea that the parables were originally crystal clear but gradually started to *appear* obscure, once their initial context had been forgotten, is by now an extremely widely held one. Having originated with Jülicher (see Kissinger 74–76), it was adopted by Bultmann ("the original meaning of many similitudes has become irrecoverable in the course of the tradition" [1963:199]), by B. T. D. Smith ("the Marcan theory registers the fact that some of the parables had become obscure with the loss of their context" [28]), and by Cadoux, who writes "we cannot think that Jesus spoke except to be understood . . . the speaker who needs to interpret his parables is not master of his method" (16, 19). Cadoux's version of the theory was picked up by Hunter (1960:50n1) and by the NIB: "a parable that must be explained is not from a master teacher" (305). See also Perrin (87); Drury (1985:54–55); Montefiore (1:123); and M. Grant (92).

44. See, again, Jeremias, 11–12.

45. Jesus's parables must have been clear at the time, claims Dodd (4), because the idea of stories with hidden meanings is a Hellenistic one; in the Jewish world, by contrast, parables are just a mode of illustration. But in Ezekiel, *mashal* (parable) is synonymous with *ḥidah* (riddle) (Ezek. 17:2); Ezekiel complains that the people accuse him of speaking in parables (Ezek. 20:49), an accusation that would not make sense if parables were merely aids to comprehension; and plenty of Old Testament and rabbinic parables meet with befuddlement and/or require elucidation (Kermode, 29; Daube, 142; Oesterley, 4–5). Cranfield sums it up very succinctly: "Jesus' parables, it is said, were all at the time clear enough, but later, partly because, when the original context was forgotten, the parables would seem difficult, partly because of the tendency to allegorize, and partly through the influence of Hellenistic religious ideas, there grew up the idea that they were 'mysteries' needing interpretation and that the interpretation was a matter of esoteric teaching. But . . . [*mashal*] can mean a dark, perplexing saying that is meant to stimulate hard thinking . . . There is nothing

improbable in the suggestion that sometimes the disciples asked for, and Jesus gave, an explanation" (159–60).

46. For a brief introduction to the field of historical Jesus research, see Charlesworth.

47. The best-known publication of the Jesus Seminar is *The Five Gospels*, edited by Funk and Hoover. This book claims to demonstrate—based on votes cast by the seventy-four members of the Jesus Seminar—that "eighty-two percent of the words ascribed to Jesus in the gospels were not actually spoken by him" (5). For critical assessments of the Jesus Seminar's methodology and conclusions, see Witherington, 42–57, and Wright; for responses to such critiques, see Funk 1996 and Miller; and for a different approach to the sayings of Jesus, see Chilton and Evans.

48. Harvey, 441.

49. Contrast the book of Genesis, in which—notoriously—God creates mankind not once but twice, the first time together ("man and woman he created them"), the second separately ("I will make him a helper fit for him"). There are of course many other indications of multiple sources in the Pentateuch.

50. Cf. New Interpreter's Bible: "readers are forced to wonder whether the disciples truly are 'insiders'" (569). For S. H. Smith, "there are no true insiders" (366): not the enemies, of course, and not the crowds, but also not family and not even disciples. Compare Drury 1973:371, 375; Kelber, 125; Ricoeur 1982:354.

51. On Marcan determinism, see Via 1967:8; Donahue, 41; New Jerome 65; Kermode, 45. One could easily think of the parables along the lines of Calvin's claim that "there is the general call, by which God invites all equally to himself through the outward preaching of the word—even those to whom he holds it out as a savor of death, and as the occasion for severer condemnation" (*Institutes* 3.24.8): while the parables are an offer of help to everyone, that is, they also seal the fate of the reprobate by driving them away (and, arguably, *increase* their stock of sins by adding that of failing to listen). "For those who do not become disciples," agrees the NIB, "the parables . . . function not as teaching but as judgment" (305).

52. Some claim that since there was no persecution to speak of in Jesus's day, the warning at Mark 4:17 is an anachronism, further proof of the early church (and/or "Mark") putting words in the master's mouth. Luke's version, by contrast, speaks only of temptation: "And the ones on the rock are those who, when they hear the word, receive it with joy; but these have no root, they believe for a while and *in time of temptation* fall away" (Luke 8:13, my emphasis). See Oesterley, 44; New Interpreter's Bible 305; Dodd, 145. Still, it is uncontroversial that Jesus himself suffered persecution during his lifetime (cf. Cranfield, 160–61). I myself am not taking a stand on this question, for reasons stated above.

53. Mark's vision resembles that of Thomas, who places his version of the Sower right after the "Dragnet": "And He said, 'The Kingdom is like a wise fisherman who cast his net into the sea and drew it up from the sea full of small fish. Among them the wise fisherman found a fine large fish. He threw all the small fish back into the sea and chose the large fish without difficulty. Whoever has ears to hear, let him hear.' Jesus said, 'Now the sower went out, took a handful [of seeds], and scattered them . . .'" (Thomas 8–9). As Elaine Pagels has demonstrated (140, 147), one part of the early church chose to be maximally inclusive—maximally "catholic"—with the result that it became enormously successful; the "Gnostic" sects, by contrast, kept the bar high and, unsurprisingly perhaps, died out. To be sure, these sects depart drastically from Mark in positing a new *principle* of selectivity, having to do with secret knowledge of a hidden God (Pagels 14–15, 22, 36–37, 40), but they share nonetheless the ethos of exclusion. (For the influence of Mark on second-century Gnostic theologian Valentinus, see Pagels, 14.)

54. Cf. Dodd's famous definition: "At its simplest the parable is a metaphor or simile drawn from nature or common life, arresting the hearer by its vividness or strangeness, and leaving the mind in sufficient doubt about its precise application to tease it into active thought" (Dodd, 5). See also Via 1967:10; Oesterley, 5; Jones, 60; Cranfield, 159. Michael Grant agrees that the parables prompt reflection—but for Grant, it turns out, this is only in the service of finding the "message" (90–94).

55. Cf. Bultmann 1963:192; Jeremias, 159; and Jones, for whom parables are "less answers to questions than challenges to pronounce judgments on a situation or attitude" (78).

56. Cf. Manson: "the parable is in practice a test: and the response of a man to it is what determines whether he shall ever get beyond it to the secret of the Kingdom" (76).

57. I am referring to the seed growing of itself (Mark 4:26–29), the fig tree (13:28–29), the absent householder (13:34–37), the light under a bushel (4:21), and the divided kingdom (3:24–26), respectively. A major proponent of the life-lessons approach is Adolf Jülicher; his writings decisively shifted parable interpretation away from the allegorical method.

58. Crossan proposes a Heideggerian approach in which the parables catalyze "the revelation of something 'wholly other'" (2). As Donahue explains (15–16), the idea is that when their verisimilitude breaks down, the listener's vision of reality is shattered, and he or she becomes ready for the gift of God's kingdom. My sense, however, is that the parables' twists leave many simply mystified and resistant (the equal treatment of the laborers, for example, feels like an injustice); it is the imagery that reliably attracts.

59. See Dodd, 1–2; Kissinger, 18–19, 38–39, 65.

60. Aquinas, "Whether in Holy Scripture a word may have several senses?" (*Summa* 1.1.10, Reply to Objection 1). After Luther, who rejected "free allegory," allegorical interpretations became more restrained (Kermode, 37). As I see it, however, even the relatively subdued allegorical approaches were still missing the point.

61. This is also an objection to those who, like Via (1965:432), read the "more" that will be given as referring to a literal explanation (the seed is the word, the thorns are temptations, and so on) and to those who, like Funk (1966:214), read it along clarificationist lines: from our individual reaction to a given parable, Funk suggests, we learn something about who we are. Funk's approach has much in common with the one I defended, in chapter 1, for *Antigone*-style works; it does not, however, seem quite adequate for the Sower.

62. For Cadoux (150), it is the *content* of the Syrophoenician woman's words that does the trick: what warms Jesus's heart is her reassurance that he can be of help to the wider world even if Israel should reject him. This, however, presupposes a Jesus uncertain of the future, concerned about his impact, gratified by reassurance—human, all too human.

63. The book of Matthew is of course a separate work, and can offer no evidence for claims about the book of Mark. Still, one could read Matthew 15:28 as a gloss on Mark 7:29, an *explanation* for Jesus's change of heart, one that the author of Mark might himself have endorsed. In any case, the Marcan view functions perfectly well on its own, without the reference to faith.

64. Every parable calls out for interpretation yet also resists complete comprehension. On the hermeneutic inexhaustibility of the parables, see Ricoeur 1975:80; Crossan, 13; Funk 1966:134–35; Oesterley, 13; Via 1967:32–33.

65. Valéry: "L'essence de la prose est de périr,—c'est-à-dire d'être 'comprise,'—c'est-à-dire, d'être dissoute, détruite sans retour, entièrement remplacée par l'image ou par l'impulsion qu'elle signifie selon la convention du langage" (1501). "Mais au contraire, le poème ne meurt pas pour avoir servi; il est fait expressément pour renaître de ses cendres et redevenir indéfiniment ce qu'il vient d'être" (1373).

66. "Interpretation of parables should take place," says Funk, "in parables" (1966:196). Cf. Ricoeur, who writes that the aim of the parables is to "instill in [the reader] a capacity to continue the movement of metaphorization beyond the time of reading" (1982:355, my translation).

67. See, e.g., Bultmann 1960:294; Via 1967:45.

68. I am leaving open here the question of what such capacities look like at the level of brain states. Some very interesting work has been done in this domain, and it appears that the processing of metaphors tends to feature greater activity in the right hemisphere and—intriguingly—in the medial frontal cortex, an area thought to be involved in our sense of self. (Abstract metaphors may also draw on the precuneus.) Experimental psychologists, meanwhile, have noted important differences between the comprehension of dead metaphors and that of live metaphors, with the latter often requiring "theory of mind" for their decoding: when a speaker brings together two objects in a novel way, it turns out, we

typically use our beliefs about her attitudes and intentions to guide our conjectures as to
the basis of her comparison. (For a good example of experimental-psychological research,
see Gardner and Winner.) Experimental psychologists have also separated out what it
takes to *understand* live metaphors from what it takes to *produce* them; this second distinction will be central to my argument.

69. Cf. Manson: "those in whom religious insight and faith are awakened by the hearing of
parables press into the inner circle for more. Once more the saying applies: 'To him that
hath shall be given'" (76). See also to some extent Oesterley, 41.

70. Cf. NIB 8:573.

71. Here I depart from Wilder, who insists that "there is no great leap out of the world here"
(74), and from Donahue, who follows him on this point (14).

72. "And a crowd was sitting about him; and they said to him, 'Your mother and your brothers
are outside, asking for you.' And he replied, 'Who are my mother and my brothers?' And
looking around on those who sat about him, he said, 'Here are my mother and my brothers!
Whoever does the will of God is my brother, and sister, and mother'" (Mark 3:32–35).

73. "And Jesus looking upon him loved him, and said to him, 'You lack one thing; go, sell what
you have, and give to the poor, and you will have treasure in heaven; and come, follow me'"
(Mark 10:21). Cf. Matt. 6:19–20: "Do not lay up for yourselves treasures on earth, where
moth and rust consume and where thieves break in and steal, but lay up for yourselves
treasures in heaven." Compare also "the true circumcision in spirit" (Thomas 53).

74. Cf. Manson, who writes that the parables' "object is . . . to turn the affections from things
that change and pass to things that have the quality of eternity" (81), and to some extent
Fuchs: "this is after all the meaning of Jesus' addresses which use images. . . . Everyone
who is called to the Basileia . . . is drawn over on to God's side and learns to see everything
with God's eyes" (155). Ricoeur, too, views the parable form as redescribing human reality from the standpoint of the kingdom idea (1975:34, 84, 104); for him, however, what
does the work is not the metaphor itself but the striking twist at the end of each parable,
the "extravagance," as he puts it, which shows that Jesus's kingdom "is not of this world"
(1982:359). As for Donahue and McFague, both briefly gesture in this direction ("in effect, the message of the kingdom is that the world points beyond itself," declares Donahue; "the use of parable with the native power of metaphor to point beyond itself means
that in effect the medium is the message" [10]) but in the end both come down on the
side of parable as intimation of Jesus's subjective outlook. Thus Donahue claims that
each parable "brings to expression his [Jesus's] self-understanding of his mission" (2),
and McFague says that the parables "are, as Perrin points out, 'highly personal texts'
which express 'the vision of reality of their author.'. . . In a parable we are, as Perrin says,
confronted by Jesus' vision of reality and challenged to decide what we will do about it"
(61, 67).

75. This, as we just saw, is Donahue's position. Crossan believes, similarly, that "they [the
parables] express and they contain the temporality of Jesus' experience of God . . . [and]
Jesus' response to the Kingdom" (32). It is significant, I think, that Crossan's own readings
end up surprisingly articulable, even conventional—the Good Samaritan tells us that even
Samaritans can be good (62); the Sower reassures us of "the advent of bountiful harvest
despite the losses of sowing" (50)—given that the parables are supposed to convey a profound, expansive, and inexpressible vision.

76. As Ricoeur so beautifully puts it, though without drawing the same conclusion, parabolic
discourse is "le passage du récit au paradigme" (Ricoeur 1982:341). (Or, more prosaically,
"The parable . . . is the conjunction of a *narrative form* with a *metaphorical process*" [Ricoeur
1975:30].)

77. Harvey, 432.

78. Cf. to some extent Donahue, 16.

79. Representatives of the "consequent eschatology" position include Schweitzer (New
Jerome 1365) and Weiss (69).

80. The "inaugurated eschatology" position is usually associated with Jeremias. See New
Jerome 1366.

81. Representatives of the "realized eschatology" position include Dodd, Ritschl, Hermann, Harnack, and Rauschenbusch. See Kissinger, 84, 86, 88, 99; New Jerome 1365–66. For all three positions, see Crossan, 23–24.

82. Cf. Manson: "the 'Sower' is a parable about parabolic teaching" (76).

83. My complaint here is similar to that of Kierkegaard, who worried that Christianity, a religion centered (as he saw it) on faith, had devolved into a "Christendom" for which faith had become an optional extra. Today's preachers, he argued, make the mistake of offering their congregation *certainties*—thus inadvertently removing the need for faith—and of making the path to Christianity *easy*. "Although it may be beautiful and well intentioned," he wrote, "to want to help people to become Christians by making it easy," in reality "the merit of the religious discourse is in making the way difficult, because the way is the decisive thing" (*Concluding Unscientific Postscript*, 381, 428; cf. *Fear and Trembling*, 136).

84. There are so many theories of metaphor that it is perhaps rather foolhardy to summarize them in a footnote. But for the sake of concision, let us say very generally that a first group of people sees metaphors as *saying* something, a second group sees them as *showing* something, and a third group sees them as *doing* something. In the "saying" camp, headed by I. A. Richards, are those who think metaphor clarifies, by reducing the unknown to the known, the abstract to the concrete; those who think metaphors insinuate, by operating on multiple levels and thus hinting at more than they appear to convey; those who think metaphors persuade, perhaps by recruiting the hearer to fill in the missing term (Danto); and those who think metaphors shed light on the target concept, allowing us to see things we hadn't seen before. (Paul de Man clearly assumes that all metaphors have light-shedding as their aim, and that they therefore fail; needless to say, his starting point is a vast oversimplification.) In the "showing" camp, headed by Proust, are those who think metaphors transmit not an idea but an *experience* (this is close to Eliot's "objective correlative") and those who think metaphors reveal the subjective world of the speaker, the idiosyncratic way in which he or she organizes the world (Proust). And in the "doing" camp (headed by Davidson) are those who think metaphors create order, by forging connections among disparate objects; those who think metaphors *remove* order, softening the edges of excessively rigid concepts (Harries, Wallace Stevens, Beistegui); and those who think metaphors prompt an open-ended investigation (Cavell, and perhaps Breton). Each of these theories accounts for certain uses of metaphor. But none, I think, is universally applicable (in this, I agree with Hills). And none quite captures the joy with which we so often receive and create original images. See Richards 1965:94; Danto, 169–71; de Man, 71; Eliot, 48; Davidson *passim*; Harries, 78; Beistegui, 149; Cavell, 78–79; Breton, 30–36; Hills, 42; for Proust, see Landy 2004:59–60.

85. I am paraphrasing; the Dickinson poem in question begins "I dwell in Possibility—/A fairer House than Prose," implying that the speaker dwells in *poetry* (the obvious contrast term to "prose") rather than in metaphor more specifically. Taking the poem as a whole, however, we can reasonably imagine that metaphor is what Dickinson most centrally has in mind.

86. Here I am influenced by Schopenhauer (*WWR*, 1:51, pp. 248–51) and by an unpublished paper by Shafiq Shamel.

87. For some of the poem's exiles, life falls into two parts, a before and an after: from Troy to Epirus (Andromache), from Africa to France (the "*négresse*"), from family to solitude (the orphans), from Paris to the Channel Islands (Hugo). The speaker, however, has seen the "old Paris" (line 7) give way to a transitional Paris of "scaffolding" and "blocks" (30), only for this, in turn, to be replaced by the Paris of "new palaces" (30) and the "new Carrousel [court]" (6). The verbs in the poem's first section, moving through present ("*je pense*," 1), perfect ("*a fécondé*," 5), imperfect ("*s'étalait*," 13), simple past ("*je vis*," 14), and pluperfect ("*s'était évadé*," 17), beautifully reinforce the sense of relentless transformation. When substantial change happens once, we adjust to it. When it happens all the time—such, notes Gumbrecht (2004:97), is the very condition of modernity—we are lost, cast adrift on an ocean of mutability. "The form of a city," as Baudelaire's speaker puts it, "changes faster, alas! than the heart of a mortal."

88. "Tout l'univers visible n'est qu'un magasin d'images et de signes auxquels l'imagination donnera une place et une valeur relatives" ("Salon de 1859," in *OC*, 755). In Baudelaire's theory, notice, what gives value to the images we produce is not some connection to a transcendent realm but, instead, the imagination; the value granted is, as a result, not absolute but relative. Thus it would be a mistake to think of Baudelaire as appealing here to the famous Swedenborgian notion of "correspondences," a notion Baudelaire entertained but to which he could not bring himself to give his full and enduring assent.

Chapter 3

1. *Gay Science*, sec. 7 (1882). The German term *Wissenschaft* can of course also denote "scholarship" more generally, but the narrower definition seems appropriate here. I have, however, replaced Kaufmann's "most insidious" with "thorniest" (for *heikeligste*). As for the two epigraphs, they come from Weber, 139, and Clarke 1972:139.
2. "There was an awful rainbow once in heaven:/We know her woof, her texture; she is given/ In the dull catalogue of common things./Philosophy will clip an Angel's wings . . ." (Keats, *Lamia* [1820], part 2, lines 231–34). On the disenchantment of the rainbow, see Fisher, 118–19, and Abrams, 303–12.
3. Some key dates in nineteenth-century disenchantment: D. F. Strauss's *Life of Jesus*, 1835; Ludwig Feuerbach's *Essence of Christianity*, 1841; Charles Darwin's *On the Origin of Species*, 1859; Ernest Renan's *Life of Jesus*, 1863.
4. On Nietzsche's account, what brought about the demise of Christianity as belief system is—paradoxically enough—Christianity's own morality (of ruthlessly honest self-examination): "it is the awe-inspiring *catastrophe* of two thousand years of training in truthfulness that finally forbids itself the *lie involved in belief in God*" (*Genealogy of Morals*, 3:27; cf. *Gay Science*, sec. 357). In his own way, Marcel Gauchet (4 *et passim*) also traces the disenchantment of the world to Christianity.
5. "Have you not heard of that madman who lit a lantern in the bright morning hours, ran to the market place and cried incessantly: 'I seek God! I seek God!'—As many of *those who did not believe in God* were standing around just then, he provoked much laughter" (*Gay Science*, sec. 125, my emphasis).
6. On Robert-Houdin in Algeria, see Severn, 32–35.
7. Cook, 200. Thus, for example, Alexander Herrmann and Harry Kellar exposed the tricks of the spiritualists (Severn, 50; Cook, 199). Robert-Houdin was of course not the first magician to downplay his own powers (Cook, 185). Some seventeenth-century magicians were already speaking in terms of *legerdemain* (Cook, 171), a tradition that continued in the eighteenth century with Comus and the soberly dressed Isaac Fawkes (During, 81–89). In the early nineteenth century, Robertson and Rubens Peale were presenting their "phantasmagorias" as the very antidote to belief (Cook, 172–73, 177), and Antonio Blitz, one of Robert-Houdin's immediate precursors, claimed the same thing for his conjuring (Cook, 180). Still, Robert-Houdin consolidated the practice, making it henceforth nonoptional.
8. Thus Robert-Houdin: "these fanatics took him for a real sorcerer, and attacked him with sticks; and they were even going to throw him into a lime-kiln, had not Comte escaped by causing a terrible voice to issue from the kiln, which routed them" (1859:98). Jules Garinet reports other events from this period, such as the 1818 murder by one Julien Desbourdes of a man who, he thought, had cursed him (Garinet, 289–90). For Oehler and Pinetti, see During, 93–94; Cook, 179.
9. The same held true at least into the 1860s. "Many declared I was the devil in disguise; others exclaimed, 'That man is Satan's agent,'" writes Blitz of his experiences as entertainer for Civil War wounded in Philadelphia hospitals. Still other patients, he continues, "thought I was the person to go to the front, and extract the bullets from the enemy's guns. Not a few considered me anti-religious, because I performed, apparently, such wicked things" (Blitz, 420).
10. Mackay, 2:176. See Julia de Fontenelle (esp. 3, 13) for Christian arguments against magic in the seventeenth century. In England, by contrast, witchcraft as crime was alive and well,

thanks to the *Demonology* of King James, a work that established precise criteria for determining the guilt of an accused party.

11. Mackay, 1:220; Mariel 1973:164. Even Cagliostro's death notice presented him as having possessed special powers (Mariel 1973:168). For Boissier and company, see *Dictionnaire européen des lumières*, s.v. "Sorcellerie"; Fiard, *passim*; and Garinet, 279–81, 345.

12. Mallarmé, "Magie," in *OC* 2:307 ("des pratiques que le maintien, à la cour papale, d'une charge en vue de les confondre, désigne comme vivaces"). For the Code of Pasquelone, see Mariel 1973:153.

13. Garinet, 289 ("finit par prendre position dans le *pudendum* de la demoiselle").

14. Around 1770, after all, a certain Father Apollinaire had been "caught in bed, chasing the Devil from the lower parts of the maidservant of Henriet, vicar of Saint-Humiers" (surpris au lit, chassant le diable des parties inférieures de la servante d'Henriet, curé de Saint-Humiers [Garinet, 344]).

15. "There shall not be found among you . . . any one who practices divination, a soothsayer, or an augur, or a sorcerer, or a charmer, or a medium, or a wizard, or a necromancer. For whoever does these things is an abomination to the Lord; and because of these abominable practices the Lord your God is driving them out before you" (Deut. 18:10–12). The New Testament tale of porcine possession is also told at Matt. 8:28–34, Luke 8:26–39.

16. The spiritualist movement, of course, claimed many high-born victims. In 1857, Napoléon III was taken in by the performance of medium Daniel Dunglas Home. And Robert-Houdin himself claimed to have regarded his first street magician as a "superhuman being" (11).

17. In general, Robert-Houdin attracted a more well-heeled audience—and charged more for admission—than contemporaries such as John Henry Anderson (see During, 117, 119, 128). Magic's move into the theater only solidified its new status as middle-class (and upper-class) entertainment (Cook, 167).

18. "'Messieurs,' disais-je avec le sérieux d'un professeur de la Sorbonne, 'je viens de découvrir dans l'éther une nouvelle propriété vraiment merveilleuse. Lorsque cette liqueur est à son plus haut degré de concentration, si on la fait respirer à un être vivant, le corps du patient devient en peu d'instants aussi léger qu'un ballon.' Cette exposition terminée, je procédais à l'expérience. Je plaçais trois tabourets sur un banc de bois. Mon fils montait sur celui du milieu, et je lui faisais étendre les bras, que je soutenais en l'air au moyen de deux cannes qui reposaient chacune sur un tabouret. Je mettais alors simplement sous le nez de l'enfant un flacon vide que je débouchais avec soin, mais dans la coulisse on jetait de l'éther sur une pelle de fer très chaude, afin que la vapeur s'en répandît dans la salle. Mon fils s'endormait aussitôt, et ses pieds devenus plus légers commençaient à quitter le tabouret. Jugeant alors l'opération réussie, je retirais le tabouret de manière que l'enfant ne se trouvait plus soutenu que par les deux cannes. Cet étrange équilibre excitait déjà dans le public une grande surprise. Elle augmentait encore lorsqu'on me voyait retirer l'une des deux cannes et le tabouret qui la soutenait; et enfin elle arrivait à son comble, lorsqu'après avoir élevé avec le petit doigt mon fils jusqu'à la position horizontale, je le laissais ainsi endormi dans l'espace, et que pour narguer les lois de la gravitation, j'ôtais encore les pieds du banc qui se trouvait sous cet édifice impossible" (2:303–4). The English translation (312) is not faithful here, and gives only a fragment of the text I have cited.

19. Cf. Francesco: "the mythology they drove out and expelled was not gone from the world; it hid itself and became entrenched where the Enlightened least expected it and where it therefore remained most invisibly concealed: behind modern science itself, behind technology. Science and technology became magical" (235).

20. Cf. Fisher: "every stage of explanation . . . has consistently dispelled the extraordinary only to produce, in the very act of explanation, newer forms of wonder" (89). And see Cook (173), During (20–21, 83–89), and Nightingale (16–17, 33–37).

21. This rather militates against During's claim (62–64)—perhaps the only one from which I would depart—that magic shows are not a replacement for faith. Cf. to some extent Cook, 179–80.

22. *Catechism*, 100. For Comte's new faith, see 51; God (now in the form of humanity), 45; Providence, 1; explanation of the world, 41; immortality, 55; morality, 51; rituals, 90. In

Littré's opinion, Comte was not compos mentis when he wrote all this; Lévy-Bruhl, however, felt that Comte's "religion" followed logically from his other doctrines. And Comte and Renan were not alone in considering positivism a new religion. Thus, for example, Charles Jeannolle concurred that "le positivisme est une Eglise, une religion. Si nous ne sommes pas religieux, nous n'avons pas de raison d'être." See Gérard, 160, for Littré, Lévy-Bruhl, and Jeannolle.

23. Homais: "What fanaticism promised in times past to the elect, science is now achieving for all men!" (*Madame Bovary*, 209). Renan: "Science is thus a religion; science alone will make symbols henceforth; science alone can resolve for humanity the eternal problems whose solution its nature imperiously demands" (1890:108, my translation). *L'avenir de la science* was not published in its entirety until 1890, but an excerpt that appeared in 1849 already presents science as something otherworldly (1849:148) that will single-handedly reveal to us the meaning of life (1849:146).

24. P. T. Barnum felt similarly: "the public appears to be disposed to be amused even when they are conscious of being deceived" (171).

25. Quoted in Burlingame, 42. The writer is an anonymous theater critic of the 1860s.

26. This idea has something in common with Freud's suggestion, in "The Uncanny" (241–42, 247), that certain forms of literature provide their readers or spectators with an opportunity for re-immersion in atavistic beliefs, beliefs that have ostensibly (rationally) long been superseded. There are, however, two differences: in terms of the content, Robert-Houdin shows science itself (counterintuitively enough) to be joining the ranks of superseded beliefs; in terms of the process, Robert-Houdin's viewers, unlike the readers of E. T. A. Hoffmann, are being invited to indulge *consciously* in the fantasy—perhaps even to spin lucid fantasies of their own, on return to everyday life.

27. R. Irwin, vi.

28. The Church of Carmel was founded by self-proclaimed prophet Eugène Vintras in 1839 and deemed sacrilegious by Pope Pius IX in 1848. On the death of Vintras in 1875, Boullan—an excommunicated priest—took over, and moved to Lyon with some of Vintras's adherents. By all accounts, these Carmelites celebrated black masses (or, at the very least, scandalously sexualized ceremonies) under the guise of conventional religious observance. See ibid., iv; Mariel 1971:84–85.

29. See J. Webb, 97, 258n8; Bricaud, 40; R. Irwin, iv. De Guaïta had learned of the Church of Carmel's practices in 1887; his informant, Oswald Wirth, had posed as a prospective convert in order to extract information from Boullan (J. Webb, 97; Wirth, 101–2). The following year, de Guaïta established the French Rosicrucian order, in conjunction with Joséphin Péladan. The pair parted company in 1890, in what came to be known as the "War of the Two Roses"; Péladan started the *Ordre de la Rose-Croix du Temple et du Graal* (Order of the Rose Cross of the Temple and the Grail), and the two orders immediately excommunicated one another. See Mariel 1971:374; J. Webb, 108–14.

30. Bois: "C'est maintenant un fait incontestable . . . l'abbé Boullan, qui vient de mourir subitement à Lyon, a été frappé par des colères invisibles et par des mains criminelles armées de foudres occultes, de forces redoutables et inconnues." Huysmans (speaking to Horace Bianchon): "À moi qui vous parle, ils ont tout fait pour me nuire! Chaque soir, à la minute précise où je vais m'endormir, je reçois sur le crâne et sur la face . . . comment dirais-je? . . . des coups de poing fluidiques. Je voudrais croire que je suis tout bonnement en proie à de fausses sensations . . . dues à l'extrême sensibilité de mon système nerveux; mais j'incline à penser que c'est bel et bien affaire de magie. La preuve, c'est que mon chat, qui ne risque pas, lui, d'être un halluciné, a des secousses à la même heure et de la même sorte que moi" (*Le Figaro*, January 10, 1893). For Huysmans' exorcism paste, see R. Irwin, vi.

31. Jules Bois also fought a duel with occultist Gérard Encausse, a.k.a. "Papus," whom he had classed along with de Guaïta as a sorcerer. No real damage was done in either duel. (See R. Irwin, vi; Descaves, 256; J. Webb 98–99.)

32. "Je dis qu'existe entre les vieux procédés et le Sortilège, que demeure la poésie, une parité secrète. . . . Évoquer, dans une ombre exprès, l'objet tu, par des mots allusifs, jamais directs, se réduisant à du silence égal, présente la tentative proche de créer: qui tire sa

vraisemblance de ceci, que l'opération tient entière dans la limite de l'idée. Or l'idée d'un objet uniquement est mise en jeu par l'Enchanteur de Lettres, avec une justesse telle que, certes, cela scintille, à l'illusion du regard. Le vers, trait incantatoire! et, qui suivant me déniera au cercle que perpétuellement ferme, ouvre la rime une similitude avec les ronds, parmi l'herbe, de la fée ou du magicien" (*National Observer*, January 28, 1893, 263–64; reprinted in *OC*, 2:309.). Mallarmé is here echoing (among others) Charles Baudelaire, who felt that "manier savamment une langue, c'est pratiquer une espèce de sorcellerie évocatoire" ("Théophile Gautier," in *OC*, 501) and who saw speech and writing as "opérations magiques, sorcellerie évocatoire" (*Fusées*, in *OC*, 395). When translating Mallarmé's impenetrable prose, throughout this chapter, I have aimed for relative clarity, and can only apologize for the many oversimplifications this has required.

33. "Une fenêtre nocturne ouverte, . . . sans meubles, sinon l'ébauche plausible de vagues consoles, un cadre, belliqueux et agonisant, de miroir appendu au fond, avec sa réflexion, stellaire et incompréhensible, de la Grande Ourse, qui relie au ciel seul ce logis abandonné du monde" (letter to Cazalis, July 18, 1868, *Correspondance*, 1:278–79). Mallarmé appended this note on sending the original version of "Ses purs ongles" (then titled "Sonnet allégorique de lui-même") for publication in a collection of poems. Oddly, Mallarmé's piece ended up not being included in the collection.

34. For the identity of the two apparitions, cf. Jean-Pierre Richard, 221. On my (and Richard's) reading, the stars that appear in the window are reflected in the mirror—just as they are in the sonnet's 1868 precursor, *Sonnet allégorique de lui-même*, which ends "sur la glace encor/De scintillations le septuor se fixe" (13–14). Yet in the 1887 version, the mirror is said to be *near* the window ("proche la croisée," line 9). If the mirror is next to the window, how can the stars be reflected in it? At the risk of pedantry, let me suggest an answer. The window is at the right edge of the northern wall, and the mirror is on the left edge of the eastern wall; starlight, traversing the window at an angle, is reflected in the mirror that stands "close to" it.

35. It might be objected that the poem's two parts cannot be analogous, since they are separated, at the *volta*, by the word *mais*. It might further be objected, more specifically, that the sestet is more optimistic than the octave (see, e.g., Pearson, 158–59). While this would, to be sure, bring "Ses purs ongles" into line with sonnets like "Une dentelle," I am not quite convinced that it is an accurate assessment. Mallarmé was content, in the earlier version, to join the two halves with an "*et*," and with good reason. For an equal quantity of suffering and transcendence is surely to be found on both sides of the conjunction. In the octave, there is not only anguish but also the resplendent elevation that emerges from it; in the sestet, there is not only a septet of scintillations but also a nymph in her death throes. Indeed, the nymph's "agony" neatly reproduces the "anguish" of the opening: just as *L'Angoisse* opens the second line of the quatrains, *Agonise*, its near-anagram, kicks off the second line of the tercets. Thus the conjunction *mais* does not, in fact, lead us from darkness to light. Instead, it leads directly into suffering ("But near the vacant window to the north, something gold/Twists in agony") and only indirectly into transcendence. What, then, *is* the force of the *mais*? I tentatively suggest that the contrast is a *spatial* one. On the tables, no ptyx (a happy absence); by the window, however, a mirror (an agonized presence).

36. Of the four poems collected together under the rubric *Plusieurs sonnets*, no fewer than three make reference to constellations: not just *le septuor* in "Ses purs ongles" (line 14) but also the *guirlandes célèbres* in "Quand l'ombre" (6) and *le Cygne* (presumably Cycnus) at the end of "Le vierge" (14). Ursa Major also plays a prominent, and famous, role in "Un coup de dés," where capital letters loudly proclaim "RIEN . . . N'AURA EU LIEU . . . QUE LE LIEU . . . EXCEPTÉ PEUT-ÊTRE UNE CONSTELLATION."

37. Ovid tells the Callisto story at *Metamorphoses* 2:401–507, and Mallarmé mentions it in *Les dieux antiques* (*OC*, 2:1528–29). The allusion is perhaps clearer in Mallarmé's earlier version of the sonnet, where the nymph is accompanied by "un dieu" (a god) rather than by hostile unicorns. According to Davies (136n19), the first critic to spot the Callisto allusion was Christopher Brennan.

38. Ursa Major is close to the celestial North Pole, and two of its stars famously point to Polaris. If Mallarmé does indeed have Callisto in mind, then presumably the *septuor* is that part of the constellation commonly known as the "Plough," "Big Dipper," or "Septentrion." It is to this constellation-within-a-constellation (or "asterism") that Mallarmé returns, once again specifying its position, in "Un coup de dés": "ce doit être/le Septentrion aussi Nord . . ."

39. The religious connotations of the *croisée* are perhaps most evident in Mallarmé's "Les fenêtres": "Je fuis et je m'accroche à toutes les croisées/D'où l'on tourne l'épaule à la vie, et,/béni,/Dans leur verre, lavé d'éternelles rosées,/Que dore le matin chaste de l'Infini/Je me mire et me vois ange!" (25–29). [I flee and I cling to all the windows/From which one turns one's back on life, and blessed,/In their glass, washed by eternal dews,/Gilded by the chaste morning of the Infinite,/I am reflected and see myself an Angel!] It might be added that *croisée* may also denote "transept crossing"—the site at which, in a cathedral, the transept intersects with the nave—and *crédence* a "credence table," likewise to be found in churches (Marchal, 172n4).

40. "Ce vieux et méchant plumage, terrassé, heureusement, Dieu" (Mallarmé to Cazalis, May 14, 1867, *Correspondance*, 1:241). Compare Mallarmé's wonderful and untranslatable injunction in "La musique et les lettres" (*OC*, 2:73): "Là-bas, où que ce soit, nier l'indicible, qui ment." (An English approximation might run "over there, wherever that may be, deny the unsayable, which lies.")

41. Cf. to some extent Nelson, 55.

42. The three-part drama is reflected in the structure of the verbs. Each panel of the diptych opens with a pair of active verbs (*dédiant, soutient*; *agonise, ruant*), briefly surrenders to passives (*brûlé, aboli*; *défunte, fermé*), and at last resolves in reflexives (*s'honore*; *se fixe*). This is a double repetition of "Le vierge," in which we first encounter a frozen swan attempting, actively, to shake himself loose from the ice ("tout son col *secouera* cette blanche agonie," 9), then learn that this "agony" is inflicted—the swan now inert—by the universe ("par l'espace *infligé*," 10), and finally see the swan accepting his fate, choosing it, making active what was passive, in a culminating moment of middle-voice *amor fati*: "Il *s'immobilise* au songe froid de mépris/Que vêt parmi l'exil inutile le Cygne" (13–14).

43. To some extent, Mallarmé is using what Gardner Davies (108–14, 137, *et passim*) would call the "solar drama"—the daily death of the sun—as the armature on which to prop the rest of his poem.

44. *Will to Power* 585A, 1887–88 (emphasis removed).

45. Without too much argument, Charles Chadwick suggests (104) that the idea of something being allegorical of itself is a patent absurdity; the sonnet, Chadwick concludes, must be allegorical of *him*self (Mallarmé) rather than of *it*self (the poem). (This, incidentally, was already a common view in the 1950s: see, e.g., Michaud, 75.) Chadwick also dismisses the "*sensation . . . cabalistique*" Mallarmé attributes to his poem (108). In the present chapter I hope to show that these Mallarméan claims of incantation and self-allegorizing are at least not trivially false.

46. Some scholars—like Barbara Johnson (265)—have pushed the idea of a Mallarmé driven to write, paradoxically, by a fear of not being able to. Mallarmé's "Symphonie littéraire," where he refers to the "muse moderne de l'Impuissance" (*OC*, 2:281), provides a degree of support for such an approach; still, it is far from clear that this early essay should be taken as providing the key to the entirety of his poetic production.

47. This sets "Ses purs ongles" apart from the other three members of the *Plusieurs sonnets*, where we find "*mon* absent tombeau" ("Victorieusement fui," 4); "Il a ployé son aile indubitable en *moi*" ("Quand l'ombre," 4); and, in admittedly more muted fashion, "Va-t-il *nous* déchirer avec un coup d'aile ivre . . ." ("Le vierge," 2). My emphasis throughout.

48. "Je suis maintenant impersonnel, et non plus Stéphane que tu as connu,—mais une aptitude qu'a l'univers Spirituel à se voir et à se développer, à travers ce qui fut moi" (Mallarmé to Cazalis, May 14, 1867, *Correspondance*, 1:241–42); cf. "j'aime à me refugier dans l'impersonnalité—qui me semble une consécration" (Mallarmé to Lefébure, May 17, 1867, ibid., 1:246). On the shift from imitation to expression—from "mirror" to "lamp"—see Abrams, 57 *et passim*; on impersonality, see Friedrich, 21.

49. Thus E. S. Burt: "this representation of the scene depends on a spectator (the poet), and insofar as there is a point of view, this eye must be located. But, as the poem tells us, there is no I: 'Car le Maître est allé puiser des pleurs au Styx'" (101).

50. "L'oeuvre pure implique la disparition élocutoire du poëte, qui cède l'initiative aux mots" ("Crise de vers," in *OC*, 2:211).

51. So too in "Un coup de dés," the "Maître" is shipwrecked, but a consciousness remains to imagine that "rien . . . n'aura eu lieu . . . que le lieu . . . excepté *peut-être* une constellation" (my emphasis).

52. Needless to say, those critics are legion who have wished to present Mallarmé as a poet ceding all control to the entirely random play of language. Roger Pearson, for example, claims that after the existential crisis of 1867, "a Post-structuralist Mallarmé is conceived: the willing, passive instrument of words which have more to say than he can ever foresee or adequately control" (41); "he no longer sought to express himself through language but now sought to let language express itself through him" (142); "his own writing had shown him how little the poet writes the poem; how it is rather the poem . . . which 'writes' the poet" (297); and of course "the signifier is allowed free play" (172). "Du fait que l'homme parle," Blanchot agrees, "l'homme est déjà mort . . . ce langage ne suppose personne qui l'exprime, personne qui l'entende: il *se* parle et il *s'écrit*" (1949:48). "Lire reviendrait alors," Vincent Kaufmann adds, "à ne pas imposer au poème un sens qui lui serait comme extérieur, relevant de l'imaginaire du seul lecteur, mais à entendre . . . toutes les virtualités d'une langue" (51). Leo Bersani, too, speaks of "Mallarmé's extraordinary surrender to the contingent" (1981:57). Yet Mallarmé expressly states, in more than one place, that his work is *not* aleatory in the slightest. In good literature, he insists, there is room only for the *illusion* of chance: "tout hasard doit être banni de l'oeuvre moderne et n'y peut être que feint" ("Le corbeau," *OC*, 2:772); "[le] hasard . . . ne doit . . . jamais qu'être simulé" ("Planches et feuillets," *OC*, 2:195).

53. In the 1868 letter to Cazalis, Mallarmé strongly implies that the poem's content—an empty room, with stars reflected in a mirror—is supposed to stand for its action: "une fenêtre nocturne ouverte, . . . sans meubles, sinon l'ébauche plausible de vagues consoles, un cadre, belliqueux et agonisant, de miroir appendu au fond, avec sa réflexion, stellaire et incompréhensible, de la Grande Ourse, qui relie au ciel seul ce logis abandonné du monde. *J'ai pris ce sujet d'un sonnet nul et se réfléchissant de toutes les façons*" (*Correspondance*, 1:279, my emphasis; translation for the first part of this statement is given in an earlier note). For emptiness and mirroring, cf. Mallarmé's remark to François Coppée: "ce à quoi nous devons viser surtout est que, dans le poème, les mots . . . se reflètent les uns sur les autres jusqu'à paraître ne plus avoir leur couleur propre, mais n'être que les transitions d'une gamme" (December 5, 1866, *Correspondance*, 1:234).

54. It is extremely unusual for a sonnet to use only two rhymes. Further, "Ses purs ongles" is unique among Mallarmé's mature sonnets in having three sets of alternating rhymes (abab) interrupted by a couplet (bb). The rhyme scheme here is abab abab bb abab; Mallarmé's other mature sonnets either begin with two sets of enclosed rhymes (abba abba cc dede: this holds for the remainder of the *Plusieurs sonnets*, and for all three poems in the triptych) or leave the couplet till last (abab cdcd efef gg: "Toute l'âme résumée," the "Petits airs," "La chevelure vol," etc.). The unpublished "Sonnet allégorique de lui-même," with its abab abab baa bba rhyme scheme, is again unique in Mallarmé's oeuvre.

    For the reversal of masculine and feminine rhymes, cf. Garnier, 28; Pearson, 146; Noulet, 177. A "feminine" rhyme-word is one that ends in a silent e (*amphore*, for example).

55. The earlier version, "Sonnet allégorique de lui-même," has seven rhymes in [ix] and seven rhymes in [ɔR]: a perfect counterpart, at the level of form, to the reflected constellation. (For the general idea of fourteen lines and seven reflected stars, see Noulet, 191; Noulet claims here that this is what makes the sonnet "allegorical of itself.")

56. Dragonetti: "l'oreille qui entend *-or, -ix* se souvient de l'*oryx*. On raconte que la corne de la licorne était en réalité la corne d'une antilope appelée *oryx*" (69). Cf. Citron, 306, and Robb: "the unicorn of the *sonnet en yx* may have been conjured up by the unused rhyme, 'oryx'" (12).

57. For Mallarmé, it would not be enough merely to rhyme on [ix]. Following Banville and others (Banville: "sans consonne d'appui, pas de Rime et, par conséquent, pas de poésie"), Mallarmé insists on including the preceding consonant in the rhyme (Wieckowski, 139). The "pyx" idea is Chisholm's (quoted in G. Davies, 117).

58. Cf. Dällenbach, 180.

59. R. G. Cohn, 244. Could there perhaps be an analogous effect at the alphabetic level, with **ab**oli (6), **c**ar (7), and **déf**unte (11)? Such a reading would be impermissibly far-fetched were it not for Mallarmé's "Une dentelle," whose first stanza includes the words **abs**ence and s'**ab**olit, and whose second stanza spells out C-D-E-F in acrostic ("**C**et unanime blanc conflit/**D**'une guirlande avec la même,/**E**nfui contre la vitre blême/**F**lotte plus qu'il n'ensevelit"). It may *still* be impermissibly far-fetched.

60. There are, in fact, exactly seven seven-letter words in the poem: *bibelot* (6), *inanité* (6), *croisée* (9), *vacante* (9), *agonise* (10), *défunte* (12), and *septuor* (14). For the connection between *Ses purs* and *septuor*, see Ricardou, 209–13. While *ses purs*, he notes, comprises 3 + 4 letters, *sept-uor* comprises 4 + 3: the "handle" and "bowl" of the Plough, he suggests, reflected in a mirror.

61. In a "straight" crossword, each clue is a synonym for the target word (thus, for example, "cease" could be a straight clue for "stop"). In a "cryptic" crossword, each clue still contains a synonym, but adds a second way of arriving at the solution. This second path no longer deals exclusively in meanings, but has to do instead with the letters or sounds contained in the target word. Thus, for example, "cease upending pots" could be a cryptic clue for "stop": "cease" is again the synonym, while the remainder of the clue invites us to reverse the order of letters *p-o-t-s*. Or again "conceal Jekyll's double, by the sound of it" might yield "hide" (a pun on "Hyde"); and so too might "conceal in the March ides" (here, the letters *h-i-d-e* are literally *in* the letters *m-a-r-c-h-i-d-e-s*).

   Is it too much of a stretch to read certain Mallarméan devices along similar lines? In "À la nue," for instance, a siren (*sirène*) is *heard*, and not just seen, "*dans* le **si** blanc cheveu qui t**raîne**" (my emphasis). Or again, in "Le pitre châtié," *nacre* (at the end of one line) morphs anagrammatically into *rance* (at the start of the next) just as the clown's makeup begins to run. And so here at the heart of "Ses purs ongles," it is as though we were set the challenge of finding a word that accurately characterizes line 6 while also punning on s'*honore*; *sonore* becomes the only possible solution.

62. In the manner, say, of T. S. Eliot's "objective correlative." See Eliot, 48.

63. Proust's narrator speaks, in *The Guermantes Way*, of "those finished works of art . . . in which every part in turn receives from the rest a justification which it confers on them in turn" [ces oeuvres d'art achevées . . . où chaque partie . . . reçoit des autres sa raison d'être] (*Guermantes Way*, 737; *Le côté de Guermantes*, 520). For this idea, cf. Nehamas 1985:229.

64. Mallarmé to Lefébure (May 3, 1868, *Correspondance*, 1:274): "concertez-vous pour m'envoyer le sens réel du mot ptyx, on m'assure qu'il n'existe dans aucune langue, ce que je préférerais de beaucoup afin de me donner le charme de le créer par la magie de la rime" ("put your heads together to send me the real meaning of the word ptyx, they tell me it does not exist in any language, which I would greatly prefer, so that I might charm myself with the thought of creating it by the magic of rhyme"). As Noulet points out (184), a ptyx had already cropped up in Victor Hugo's poem "Satyre"; whether or not Mallarmé had "Satyre" in mind, it is most unlikely he believed the Greek word to be entirely nonexistent.

65. "À côté d'*ombre*, opaque, *ténèbres* se fonce peu; quelle déception, devant la perversité conférant à *jour* comme à *nuit*, contradictoirement, des timbres obscur ici, là clair" ("Crise de vers," *OC*, 2:208). Astonishingly perhaps, Mallarmé seems to go out of his way to use these precise terms, and in prominent positions at that. In "Toast funèbre," for instance, *nuit* and *jour* are each deployed at the end of a line, *nuit* in fact twice, since it is used both as noun ("night") and as verb ("harms"). In *Hérodiade*, *ténèbres* also finds itself at the rhyme twice (once in the "Ouverture ancienne," once in the "Cantique de Saint Jean"). And "Quand l'ombre," as if wishing to make palpable the claim that "à côté d'*ombre* . . . *ténèbres* se fonce peu," actually sets the two words "next to" one another in the same poem (they are

separated only by six lines). It is, presumably, the recalcitrant terms that stand most in need of relegitimation. Perhaps this is also why Mallarmé so often places proper nouns at the rhyme: "tutélaire/Baudelaire," "haleine/Verlaine," "altier/Gautier," "tu vis/Puvis," "jusqu'au/Vasco," and the rather daring "que puisse l'air/Whistler," to cite a few examples. (See "Le tombeau de Charles Baudelaire," "Tombeau," "Toast funèbre," "Toute aurore," "Au seul souci de voyager," and "Billet à Whistler," respectively.) It is as though Mallarméan poetry gradually extends the perimeter of its magic circle in order to draw more and more of the obstinately unruly world within its scope.

66. "Le vers qui de plusieurs vocables refait un mot total, neuf, étranger à la langue et comme incantatoire . . . niant, d'un trait souverain, le hasard demeuré aux termes" ("Crise de vers," *OC*, 2:213).

67. "Le hasard vaincu mot par mot, indéfectiblement le blanc revient, tout à l'heure gratuit, certain maintenant, pour conclure que rien au delà et authentiquer le silence" ("Le mystère dans les lettres," *OC*, 2:234). (I take "rien au delà" to mean "nothing further remains to be said.") Compare also "Crise de vers" (*OC*, 2:208): "Qu'une moyenne étendue de mots, sous la compréhension du regard, se range en traits définitifs, avec quoi le silence." ("Let an average expanse of words, under the understanding of the gaze, organize themselves into definitive lines, with which—silence.") "Mimique," similarly, begins "Le silence, seul luxe après les rimes . . ." (*OC*, 2:178).

68. Cf. Bénichou—"il faut du réel . . . pour figurer le néant" (146)—and also, to some extent, Bergson (278–79).

69. Compare Clov's dream in Beckett's *Endgame* (57): "A world where all would be silent and still and each thing in its last place, under the last dust."

70. "Les choses existent, nous n'avons pas à les créer; nous n'avons qu'à en saisir les rapports; et ce sont les fils de ces rapports qui forment les vers et les orchestres" ("Sur l'évolution littéraire," *OC*, 2:702). In "Crise de vers," Mallarmé similarly defines the ideal poetic "Music" as "the set of connections existing in everything" ("l'ensemble des rapports existant dans tout," *OC*, 2:212). And Mallarmé instructs Edmund Gosse to "use 'Music' in the Greek sense, at bottom signifying Idea, or rhythm among the connections" ("Employez Musique dans le sens grec, au fond signifiant l'Idée ou rythme entre les rapports" [January 10, 1893, *Correspondance*, 6:26]). For *rapports*, cf. Edelstein, 55–57.

71. In his eulogy for Villiers de l'Isle-Adam (*OC*, 2:23), Mallarmé defines the act of writing, rather paradoxically, as a "duty to re-create everything . . . in order to affirm that one is indeed where one should be" ("quelque devoir de tout recréer, . . . pour avérer qu'on est bien là où l'on doit être"). We do not need to be transported to another world; we just need to "re-create" this one, by imagining connections between everything and everything else. In a sense, perhaps, this is akin to Nietzsche's *amor fati*.

72. "En se laissant aller à le murmurer plusieurs fois on éprouve une sensation assez cabalistique" (the 1868 letter to Cazalis, *Correspondance*, 1:278).

73. For the literary reading experience as itself sublime, see Kirk Pillow, esp. chap. 3.

74. Compare also the famous line from "Crise de vers" (*OC*, 2:213): "Je dis: une fleur! et, hors de l'oubli où ma voix relègue aucun contour, en tant que quelque chose d'autre que les calices sus, musicalement se lève, idée même et suave, l'absente de tous bouquets." [I say: a flower! and, from the oblivion to which my voice banishes all contours, as something other than the known calyxes, there musically arises—the idea itself, delicate—the one [flower] missing from all bouquets.]

75. Further remarks on lucid self-delusion in Mallarmé may be found in Landy 1994 and, with less rigor, in Landy 1997.

76. Some, like Noulet (184), have wanted to see the *ptyx* as a seashell, perhaps on the questionable assumption that its *inanité sonore* means "emptiness that produces noise." Many, like Nelson (52), now prefer the idea that *ptyx* means "fold." The "fold" reading seems to me to be vitiated by the fact that the 1868 version characterizes the *ptyx* as a "vessel" (*vaisseau*, 6).

77. "Quel pivot . . . à l'intelligibilité? Il faut une garantie—La Syntaxe" (*OC*, 2:232–33).

78. Robb, 63 (citing Ross G. Arthur). Gardner Davies (117) already rules out this reading, on the same grounds.

79. Cf. Davies, 118. It might be objected that *nul ptyx* explains *salon vide*, rather than "pas de cinéraire amphore." My reading is, however, given some support by the 1868 version, which speaks of a "*noir salon*," not a "salon *vide*" ("Sur des consoles, en le noir Salon: nul ptyx"). Here in the 1868 version, the absence of a ptyx cannot possibly account for the room being dark; it must, therefore, account for the absence of funereal urns mentioned slightly earlier.

80. Reportedly, Mallarmé explained to Leconte de Lisle that "le ptyx est insolite, puisqu'il n'y en a pas; il résonne bien, puisqu'il rime; et ce n'en est pas moins un vaisseau d'inanité, puisqu'il n'a jamais existé!" [The ptyx is unusual, since there aren't any; it is resonant, since it rhymes; and it is nevertheless a vessel of inanity, since it never existed!] (Adolphe Racot, "Les Parnassiens," *Le Gaulois*, March 26, 1875; quoted in Robb, 63.) If true, this would suggest that Mallarmé understood the sonority as attaching to the *word*, not to the *object*. No need, then, for seashells.

81. Throughout this chapter I simply assume the possibility of intentional self-deception without arguing for it, such argument being beyond the scope of my discussion. Interested readers might wish to consult Mele (133), Baghramian (93), King-Farlow (132–33), Radden (115), and Svece (*passim*). At the very least, it is clear that many individuals are quite happy to report being able to trick themselves into higher performance, whether by means of actions like setting their watch fast or by means of thoughts like "just one more lap and then I'll stop." Could it be that the (weak) modularity of the brain is what underlies such intriguing mental feats?

82. In "L'Azur," the poet seeks to escape from the lure of transcendence (figured as the blue of the sky) only to conclude, famously, "Où fuir dans la révolte inutile et perverse?/*Je suis hanté. L'Azur! l'Azur! l'Azur! l'Azur!*" The "certes, n'est que ce qui est" line comes from "La musique et les lettres," *OC*, 2:67.

83. "Oui, *je le sais*, nous ne sommes que de vaines formes de la matière, mais bien sublimes pour avoir inventé Dieu et notre âme. Si sublimes, mon ami! que je veux me donner ce spectacle de la matière, ayant conscience d'être et, cependant, s'élançant forcenément dans le Rêve qu'elle sait n'être pas, chantant l'Âme et toutes ces divines impressions pareilles qui se sont amassées en nous depuis les premiers âges et proclamant, devant le Rien qui est la vérité, ces glorieux mensonges!" (letter to Cazalis, April 1866, *Correspondance*, 1:207–8; my emphasis in the English). On glorious lies, cf. Olds *passim*.

84. For this, one should compare Mallarmé's *L'après-midi d'un faune*. On waking up in the heat of the afternoon, Mallarmé's faun finds that the nymphs he has apparently embraced were in fact figments of his imagination. Yet the faun is as much thrilled as disappointed at the idea that he is responsible for their existence. "Réfléchissons . . . ou si les femmes dont tu gloses/Figurent un souhait de tes sens fabuleux!" (8–9; note the excited exclamation mark). The faun takes a fierce and defensive pride (14–22) in the purely internal nature of his creation, in the fact that the scene is generated not by inspiration from above but by the exhalation of an artificial breath, "Le visible et serein souffle *artificiel*/De l'inspiration" (21–22, my emphasis). For a more extensive treatment, see Landy 1994.

85. This restriction of the definition is important, since it is entirely possible for a text to point to itself *without* undermining the referential illusion. Indeed in some cases, self-conscious interludes are positively supposed to *strengthen* the audience's suspension of disbelief (consider, for example, the prologue to Shakespeare's *Henry V*). Mentions of fictional characters from works by other authors can have a similar effect. See Alter, 109; Dällenbach, 115.

86. See *Ulysses*, 769; *Time Regained*, 225 (translation modified); *Paludes*, 12; *Endgame*, 78; *Le roi se meurt*, 22 ("tu vas mourir à la fin du spectacle"); Brecht 1964:136–40; *If on a Winter's Night a Traveler*, 3.

87. See Alter, chap. 4, and Muecke, 183–85 (esp. 185, where Muecke points out that even Friedrich Schlegel's own *Lucinde* does not really fit the bill, and neither, in spite of Schlegel's claims, does Goethe's *Wilhelm Meister*). There are of course some legitimately reflexive premodernist fictions, such as Henry Fielding's *Tom Jones* (1749), Lawrence Sterne's *Tristram Shandy* (1760–67), and Denis Diderot's *Jacques le fataliste* (1765–83); other

examples could no doubt be adduced too. But the definition of genuine reflexivity (or "Romantic irony") should not be overstretched. I do not think it should be applied, for instance, to pure parodies, since here the oscillation between credulity and skepticism is lacking (cf. Fowler, 126). The criterion of fundamental seriousness (cf. Bishop, 1) might pose problems for works like Byron's *Don Juan* (1821) and for some of the works cited by Nicholas Paige (*passim*). Further, it is not clear that Stendhal and Thackeray, with their gentle mockery, poke major holes in the referential fabric (see Alter, 116, 126; Bourgeois, 106). Finally, one should I think rule out (*pace* Bourgeois, 102–4) those texts that merely start or end with a bursting of the fictional bubble. As Alter argues, a properly reflexive text is one that "*systematically* flaunts its own condition of artifice" (x, my emphasis); it must be, in Schlegel's terms, a "permanente Parekbase" (permanent parabasis), an "incessant self-parody," filled with irony "durchgängig im Ganzen und überall" (thoroughly, entirely, and ubiquitously), "a wonderfully perennial alternation of enthusiasm and irony, which lives even in the smallest part of the whole." (See "Philosophische Lehrjahre," frag. 668 (*KA* 18:85); Lyceum frag. 108; Lyceum frag. 42; Bishop, 8.) On these grounds, Aristophanes himself is to be excluded from the reflexive canon, and so perhaps is Cervantes, given that the oft-mentioned *Don Quixote* (1605–15) is only briefly self-undermining.

88. For the idea of the "shifting dominant" in literary history, see Jakobson, 85. By 1925, it was possible for Ortega y Gasset to "doubt that any young person of our time can be impressed by a poem, a painting, or a piece of music that is not flavored with a dash of irony" (48). Fredric Jameson, in 1984, went even further. For him, it is "a commonplace that the very thrust of literary modernism . . . has had as one significant structuralist consequence the transformation of the cultural text into an *auto-referential* discourse, whose content is a perpetual interrogation of its own conditions of possibility" (250). According to Michael Saler (2003:621), reflexivity became a staple of *mass* cultural productions too, starting at the turn of the twentieth century. Saler 2005 is also invaluable on the subject of what he calls the "ironic imagination." His position and mine differ only, it seems to me, on the role of literary reflexivity (see 2005:65).

89. For this position, see, e.g., Muecke, 189; Furst 1988:308; Gumbrecht 2000:209–10. Gumbrecht draws on Niklas Luhmann's concept of a "second-order observer."

90. Cf. Barthes 1986:287. "The poet wishes to indicate that his vision has been earned," agrees Robert Penn Warren, "that it can survive reference to the complexities and contradictions of experience" (26). In a delightful postscript to *The Name of the Rose* (530–31), Umberto Eco describes this as the general "postmodern attitude": "I think of the postmodern attitude as that of a man who loves a very cultivated woman and knows he cannot say to her, 'I love you madly,' because he knows that she knows (and that she knows that he knows) that these words have already been written by Barbara Cartland. Still, there is a solution. He can say, 'As Barbara Cartland would put it, I love you madly.' At this point, having avoided false innocence, having said clearly that it is no longer possible to speak innocently, he will nevertheless have said what he wanted to say to the woman: that he loves her."

91. "J'enrage d'être empêtré d'une diable de philosophie que mon esprit ne peut s'empêcher d'approuver et mon coeur de démentir" (letter to Sophie Volland, quoted in Bishop, 35).

92. For the general point about Romantic irony, cf. Bishop, 2; for Diderot's distance from his characters in *Jacques*, see Loy, 151.

93. The first quotation is from "Über Goethes Meister" (*KA*, 2:131), the second from "Philosophische Lehrjahre" (*KA*, 18:628); translations are those of Bishop (4) and Furst (1984:28). Elsewhere, Schlegel extols "the mood that surveys everything and rises infinitely above all limitations, even above its own art, virtue, or genius" (Lyceum frag. 42). For Romantic irony as a route to freedom, see Bishop, 1; Furst 1988:301; Muecke, 198; Lukács 1971:93.

94. Schlegel's position is actually a little more complicated than this. In his view, self-irony allows us not only to step back from ourselves but also to go *beyond* ourselves, so to speak, since it enables us to approach—albeit without ever reaching—absolute knowledge, moving closer and closer with each new negation. (See Furst 1984:43–44; Muecke, 200; Bishop, 9.) For Mallarmé, by contrast, the truth is both readily attainable and undesirable:

we recall him "proclamant, *devant le Rien qui est la vérité*, ces glorieux mensonges" (my emphasis). For him, accordingly, Romantic irony is not a means for inching nearer to that truth but, quite the reverse, a way to escape from its clutches.

95. Eysteinsson, 113–14. "Self-consciousness," according to Eysteinsson, "relates to the very possibility of becoming aware of the social process of operating communication and generating meaning" (113), which is to say, "becoming aware that conventionalized relations between reality and received modes of communication are by no means 'natural' and inevitable" (115).

96. Eugene Lunn is more nuanced: "The modernist work often willfully reveals its own reality as a construction or artifice, which may take the form of an hermetic and aristocratic mystique of creativity (as in much early symbolism); visual or linguistic distortion to convey intense states of mind (strongest in expressionism); or suggestions that the wider social world is built and rebuilt by human beings and not 'given' and unalterable (as in Bauhaus architecture or constructivist theatre)" (35). The addition of the adjective "social" is particularly important.

Compare also Charles Russell, in whose view the postmodernist text or artwork "points to itself as a particular expression of a specific meaning system, as a construct that explicitly *says something* about the process of creating meaning" (183, my emphasis); Michael Bell, who writes that "the pervasive concern with the construction of meaning helps explain the emphasis in all the modernist arts on the nature of their own medium" (16); and Christian Quendler, who suggests that in postmodernist metafiction, "the critical self-exposure of fiction correlates on to a critique of established conceptions of reality" (160).

97. This is Jorge Luis Borges's explanation of the *mise en abyme* effects in Shakespeare and Cervantes. "Why does it disturb us that Don Quixote be a reader of the *Quixote* and Hamlet a spectator of *Hamlet*? I believe I have found the reason: these inversions suggest that if the characters of a fictional work can be readers or spectators, we, its readers or spectators, can be fictitious" (196). The same Borges, however, elsewhere admits (233–34) that skepticism is just a convenient fantasy, that denying the world and doubting the self are "apparent desperations and secret consolations." Our destiny, he writes, "is not frightful by being unreal; it is frightful because it is irreversible and iron-clad. . . . The world, unfortunately, is real; I, unfortunately, am Borges."

Chapter 4

1. Fourth-century Athenians did not, of course, employ the terms "literature" or "fiction." It is, however, sufficient for my purposes to establish that they were used to engaging with, and indeed enjoying, written or spoken dialogues that were universally recognized as being imaginary. And we know that they were, since fifth-century comedies (still in circulation during the fourth century) routinely revolved around far-fetched (and non-mythical) plots: no one could possibly assume that contemporary audiences took the *Lysistrata*, for instance, to be a representation of something that had happened in their own homes. Even tragedies—like Agathon's *Antheus*, the example Aristotle gives at *Poetics* 1451b22–24—were sometimes invented in their entirety. Thus Aristotle can hardly have been alone in understanding that there were truth-tellers (such as historians), there were liars, and then there were poets. (For the contrast between poets and historians, see *Poetics* 1451b1–6.) It seems to me that Plato's audience may already have suspected, and been invited to suspect, that at least some of what they were reading was neither an attempt to report Socrates accurately (history) nor an attempt to put forward a false view of Socrates (deceit), but instead something else, something to be evaluated on other terms—just as Socrates, in the *Phaedrus* (264c), suggests evaluating fabricated speeches on the basis of their construction, not merely on their effectiveness, and certainly not on their correspondence to speeches that were actually made.

Whether the (implicit) understanding of fictionality dawned in the fifth century, as Margalit Finkelberg claims (26–27), or in the fourth, as Andrew Ford has it (2002:230–31), we may reasonably speculate that Plato's dialogues postdated it. Ford goes so far as to suggest that "something like the eighteenth-century notion of literature was formulated in the fourth century B.C.E." (2002:4). Arthur Danto feels similarly: "It has often been noted that the Greeks . . . did not have a word for art in their vocabulary. But they certainly had a concept of art" (2003:xiii).

2. Unless otherwise specified, translations of Plato are from the Hackett *Complete Works*. I will be using the following system of abbreviations: *Apol.* (*Apology*), *Chrm.* (*Charmides*), *Euthyd.* (*Euthydemus*), *Gorg.* (*Gorgias*), *HMin.* (*Hippias Minor*), *Lach.* (*Laches*), *Phd.* (*Phaedo*), *Phdr.* (*Phaedrus*), *Pol.* (*Politicus* [*Statesman*]), *Prot.* (*Protagoras*), *Rep.* (*Republic*), *Soph.* (*Sophist*), *Symp.* (*Symposium*), *Tht.* (*Theaetetus*).

3. I refer to the translation by one Floyer Sydenham. It should be noted that Sydenham may, in part, have been acting out of moral scruples. According to Thomas Taylor, who restored the Alcibiades speech in 1804, Sydenham suppressed it on the grounds "that some part of it is so grossly indecent that it may offend the virtuous and encourage the vicious." See Plato 1996, 11:487.

4. In Léon Robin's study of the *Symposium* (23), the "analyse du banquet" stops at Stephanus page 212a. Similarly, John F. Miller omits all mention of Alcibiades, presenting Socrates as "mouthpiece for Plato's sublimest vision" (25) and his speech as "culmination" of the dialogue (19). I have also seen a syllabus for a 1999 introduction-to-philosophy class on which students are warned, "We will skip the drunken speech of Alcibiades. Suffice it to say that drunks are most witty to themselves."

5. Friedländer is unwittingly echoing the sentiments of a young Friedrich Nietzsche: "the reader of the dialogue must remain uncertain as to the extent to which this insight . . . can be realized in life at all. This is why Alcibiades then appears. . . . Socrates' impact on such an estranged man . . . is the most wonderful vehicle Plato could possibly have introduced as proof of the reciprocal effect of love for beauty. Alcibiades . . . shows the practical side of the man devoted to beauty, while Socrates shows the theoretical side" (4).

6. Cf. Clay (190, 196–97) and Warner (161). Barker, too, defends the Alcibiades speech, arguing—yet again—that "its role is . . . to reinforce those conclusions," namely "the conclusions for which Diotima had so eloquently spoken" (184). And Cobb, for all his understanding of Platonic irony (8) and for all his incisive criticisms of the Agathon elenchus (to which we will return), ends up with the standard view about Alcibiades: "Alcibiades is still operating on the lowest level of Diotima's staircase, while Socrates is at the highest level" (83).

7. Cf. L. Strauss 2001:168. Arieti (110), who also buys the defense-against-corruption-charges line, is at least willing to accept the corollary: having done nothing to "give birth in the beauty of" Alcibiades, Socrates must come off as something of a failure by his own lights.

8. "Despite the provenance of this composition from a dialogue of Plato's middle period, its Socrates is unmistakably the philosopher of the earlier one: he is portrayed as voicing that total disavowal of knowledge which is so striking a feature of the Socrates of the earlier period who . . . is Plato's re-creation of the historical figure. The discourse of Diotima which Socrates professes to report . . . is as strong an affirmation of Plato's *un*Socratic doctrine of transcendent Forms as is anything he ever wrote. But Alcibiades has not heard what Socrates says he learned from Diotima. In the speech about Socrates Alcibiades now proceeds to deliver . . ., Plato brings back to life the earlier *un*Platonic Socrates" (Vlastos 1991:33).

9. "I'd like to tell the truth. . . . You will hear the truth about Love" (199b); "This, Phaedrus and the rest of you, was what Diotima told me. I was persuaded" (212b).

10. I preserve the masculine here, in keeping with the male-to-male focus of the *Symposium*. It is, however, quite possible that Plato considered biological sex irrelevant to the question.

11. Diotima: "there if anywhere should a person live his life, beholding [θεωμένῳ] that Beauty. If you once see that, it won't occur to you to measure beauty by gold or clothing or beautiful boys and youths—who, if you see them now, strike you out of your senses, and make you, you and many others, eager to be with [συνόντες] the boys you love and look

at them forever, if there were any way to do that, forgetting food and drink, everything but looking at [θεᾶσθαι] them and being with [συνεῖναι] them. But how would it be, in our view, . . . if someone got to see the Beautiful itself, absolute, pure, unmixed, not polluted by human flesh or colors or any other great nonsense of mortality, but if he could see the divine Beauty itself in its one form? Do you think it would be a poor life for a human being to look there and to behold it [θεωμένου] . . . and to be with [συνόντος] it?" (211d–212a).

It is noteworthy that Plato scholars tend to take seriously the claim (by Diotima) that philosophers lack wisdom as it were by definition—"no one . . . who is wise already loves wisdom. . . . Those who love wisdom [οἱ φιλοσοφοῦντες] fall in between those two extremes [of wisdom and ignorance]" (204a)—even though it stands in some tension with this later claim (also by Diotima) that philosophers can obtain direct and enduring contact with the Forms. Thus Patterson writes *both* that Plato believes philosophers are those who know their own ignorance (212) *and* that Plato believes beautiful souls embody true Knowledge, learnable and teachable (206). He does not seem to see any need to adjudicate between these two beliefs, or to bring them into alignment. Similarly, O'Brien writes, within the space of three pages (123–25), (1) that Socrates possessed "the awareness of the limits of his own knowledge"; (2) that "knowledge of good and evil . . . alone assures good, noble, and beneficial action"; and (3) that "Socrates exemplifies all the many aspects of the good and the noble." But if Socrates' knowledge is limited, and if knowledge is necessary for virtue, how can Socrates be a paragon of excellence? (Cf. Nehamas 1998:67, 1999:69.)

12. Irwin (1977:169), Patterson (205), and Price (44–48, 53–54) are united in the belief that the ideal lover can hold on to previous desires even while moving up to the next level. But Diotima's words clearly speak against such a reading: "he must become a lover of all beautiful bodies, and he must think that this wild gaping after just one body is a small thing and despise it" (210b); "[he must] see the Beautiful itself, absolute, pure, unmixed, *not polluted by human flesh* or colors or any other great nonsense of mortality" (211e, my emphasis). (Vlastos bites this bullet at 1973:31.)

Compare also D. Frede (412–13 and 416–17), who wishes to align the ascetic *Symposium* with the eros-friendly *Phaedrus*. "Alcibiades is rejected," she writes, merely "because he is not willing to mend his ways" (413)—otherwise, no doubt, Socrates would have accepted his offer. But this cannot work: Socrates rejects Alcibiades *before* he knows whether the latter is a way-mender or a recidivist.

13. Cf. Nehamas 1999:348–49: "lovers desire the higher objects of love as soon as they become aware of their existence." It is true that at 210e5–6, Diotima refers to the πόνοι (efforts, travails) undergone by the staircase-climber, suggesting that the Ascent is not in fact quite so automatic after all. Could it be, then, that Diotima is hinting at an extensive, elaborate process of education, perhaps indeed the very process articulated in the *Republic*? Could each stair take not seconds or minutes but *years* to climb? This is how Patricia Slatin, who presented her thoughts to me in a set of exceedingly persuasive personal communications, reads the relevant passages.

In my view, however, that approach would leave the core problem intact. Even if any number of training mechanisms were involved along the way, their purpose would presumably be to instill the correct belief in the mind of the initiate, since it is this belief—*and nothing else*—that does the work of propelling him up to the next level. Take, for example, step three on the ladder of love: "he must think that the beauty of people's souls is more valuable than the beauty of their bodies, so that [ὥστε] if someone is decent in his soul, even though he is scarcely blooming in his body, our lover must be content to love and care for him" (210b–c). If the initiate is ready to love an unattractive person, it is *purely because he believes that the beauty of soul is more important*, and for no other reason. (That is the force of the ὥστε.) The claim is a striking one, since it is hard to imagine many being eager to engage in erotic encounters with partners they consider unattractive; surely the famous "Socratic intellectualism" is on full display here. All in all, the situation in Plato's *Symposium* seems very different from that of Plato's *Phaedrus*, where the "charioteer" (reason) can be absolutely certain about the right course of action, having recollected the Form of Temperance (254b), and yet still have to contend, at length, with the unruly "horse" of desire. More on that below.

14. For care of the self, cf. *Phd.* 82d, 107c, 115b.

15. Socrates may "prove" in the *Protagoras* that an out-and-out hedonist cannot consistently believe in the possibility of being overcome by desire, but Alcibiades, as presented here, is not an out-and-out hedonist (he is, after all, tempted by the Socratic way of life).

16. It has been objected to me (by Christopher Bobonich, Charles Griswold, Alexander Nehamas, and Maurice P. Rehm, in separate personal communications; I am grateful to all four) that Alcibiades does not really *know* what is good for him. If he deserts philosophy, therefore, his errancy—which should not, strictly speaking, be counted as *akrasia*—remains entirely compatible with Socrates' position that correct action requires nothing more than knowledge of what is right. My own feeling, as stated above, is that Alcibiades understands the situation surprisingly well, certainly well enough to persist in the care of the soul, were it actually the case that our rational assessment of a situation is always un-assailable by desire. But even if we were to see Alcibiades as lacking knowledge in the rele-vant sense, he would *still* be a counterexample to Socratic intellectualism. For in fact, Socrates' view is not just that knowledge is sufficient for action; it is, instead, the far stron-ger thesis that *belief* is sufficient for action. That, presumably, is why it is enough for the initiate to *think* [ἡγήσασθαι] that the beauty of souls is more valuable than the beauty of bodies (*Symp.* 210b) in order for his desire to be redirected accordingly. (At this stage of the Ascent, we should recall, the initiate has not yet encountered the Forms; full-scale knowledge is, then, a clear-cut impossibility.) While the sufficiency-of-belief view is admit-tedly only implicit in the *Symposium*, it is explicit in the *Protagoras*. "No one who knows *or believes* [οὔτε εἰδὼς οὔτε οἰόμενος] there is something else better than what he is doing, something possible, will go on doing what he had been doing, when he could be doing what is better," Socrates says here; "no one goes willingly toward the bad *or what he believes to be bad* [ἐπί γε τὰ κακὰ οὐδεὶς ἑκὼν ἔρχεται οὐδὲ ἐπὶ ἃ οἴεται κακὰ εἶναι]" (*Prot.* 358b-c, my emphasis; cf. M. Frede 1992a:xxix).

One could phrase the matter as a choice of incongruities. Either knowledge is required for us to be ruled by reason, in which case it is very hard to explain the lover's preternatu-rally smooth Ascent; or else belief is sufficient, in which case Alcibiades, who clearly believed the examined life to be good for him, should not have strayed from the straight path.

17. I agree with Martha Nussbaum that it is over-hasty "to treat as Plato's only the view expressed in the speech of Diotima as repeated by Socrates," since Plato "describes a cer-tain theory of love and then follows that description with a counterexample to the theory" (1986:167). Nussbaum is not, however, referring to Alcibiades' motivational conflict. What interests her is what Alcibiades *says*, rather than what he *is*; what needs qualifying, on her view, is the Socratic tendency to abstract away from particulars, rather than the virtue-knowledge biconditional. In my view, the Platonic irony in the *Symposium* is there to put in question how easy, rather than (or at most in addition to) how desirable, it would be to put Diotima's Ascent into practice.

For an earlier statement (1968) of the Nussbaum view, see Stanley Rosen, who writes that "the love of Socrates for Alcibiades is deficient" (280) and that "the *Symposium* . . . is a criticism as well as an encomium of Socrates" (xxxv); swimming very much against the tide of Plato scholarship, Rosen considers that, far from implying Socrates' innocence with regard to Alcibiades (283), "the main purpose of the second part of Alcibiades' speech is to charge Socrates with hybris" (301). Compare also Lear (1999:163) and Vlastos (1973:31). For a diametrically opposed reading, see Warner: "Alcibiades' . . . insistence on down to earth particularity serves," on his account, "to reinforce Diotima's otherwise inordinately high-flown conclusions" (161).

18. I am not, of course, claiming that the fictional character Alcibiades proves the existence of motivational conflict (if so, then Circe in Homer might prove the existence of witches). I am merely arguing that Alcibiades' characterization proves something about *Plato's*

attitude toward such conflict. It does so all the more, perhaps, for being the sole instance of an interlocutor informing Socrates that he endorses his recommendations but that he cannot bring himself to implement them. I am grateful to Alexander Nehamas for bringing this fact to my attention.

19. "This is what Diotima's ascent lacks: the resistance which needs to be overcome," writes Jonathan Lear. "This, I believe, is a possibility Plato saw; and he saw that it was a possibility which Socrates ignored. It is Socrates' failure to grasp this possibility which is dramatized in the *Symposium*" (1999:166). On Lear's compelling view, "Alcibiades would be seen as *acting out* a refutation of Socrates' theory of love" (ibid., 149).

20. This might explain the reference to "cowardice and unmanliness" in the passage I am about to cite.

21. Thus R. E. Allen writes that "Eros, whose object is the beautiful [as in the *Symposium*] may [nevertheless] seek, as the *Phaedrus* claims it does, bad things" (1966:463), and Dorothea Frede states that the *Phaedrus* "explains . . . the temptations and containment of carnal desire" (417)—as though these "temptations" were there to be explained, and the idea of seeking bad things so much as conceivable, in the Diotima speech! On a side note, Frede also wishes to align the two dialogues over the issue of immortality. In the Great Speech of the *Phaedrus*, Socrates describes in some detail what happens to souls after death and before (re)birth; in the *Symposium*, by contrast, Socrates-Diotima explicitly denies such immortality, and proposes instead an ersatz pseudo-immortality of (spiritual) progeny. Like Price (29–34), Frede plays down the discrepancy, claiming that it is simply a matter of focus, the *Phaedrus* dealing with one aspect of human existence, the *Symposium* with another. But if that had been Plato's desire, he could easily have satisfied it by leaving the question of actual immortality *open* in the *Symposium*. Rejecting such attempts at conciliation, Hackforth suggests that "the *Symposium* was written when Plato had come to feel doubts about the validity of that . . . argument for the soul's immortality" (1950:45). What Hackforth says about immortality I would (also) say about motivational conflict.

22. For a summary of differences between the views of the "early" Socrates (sometimes taken to be the views of the *historical* Socrates, at least on Plato's reconstruction) and those of the "middle-period" Socrates, see Vlastos 1991:48–49; the claim that Plato gradually abandoned the Socratic paradoxes was already made by Zeller in 1889 (2:1, 746–48) and Raeder in 1920 (96–97, 99, 210–11, 215, 402). (Compare, to some extent, Gomperz, 353.) The alternative position, which was held by most readers up until the late nineteenth century and has been revived, more recently, by L. Strauss (1964:61–62), Klein (10), O'Brien, Stanley Rosen (xxxiii), Kahn (1996), Griswold (1999a), and others, suggests that Plato's beliefs did *not* substantially develop over the course of his writing career, but that the dialogues together form a reasonably unified system. I will return to the unitarian approach toward the end of this chapter.

23. For conflicting sources of motivation in the *Republic*, see esp. *Rep.* 435b–444b. The language of *Rep.* 440a–b—"don't we often notice in other cases that when appetite forces someone contrary to rational calculation, he reproaches himself and gets angry with that in him that's doing the forcing, so that of the two factions that are fighting a civil war, so to speak, spirit allies itself with reason?"—is particularly close to that of our *Phaedrus* passage. For the possibility of backsliding even on the part of the best-intentioned and most informed individuals, consider what Socrates says here about the need to forswear poetry: "we'll behave like people who have fallen in love with someone but who force themselves to stay away from him, because they realize that their passion isn't beneficial . . . whenever we listen to it, we'll repeat the argument we have just now put forward like an incantation so as to preserve ourselves from slipping back into that childish passion for poetry which the majority of people have" (*Rep.* 607e–608a).

24. "No . . . tool makes anyone who picks it up a craftsman or champion unless he has acquired the requisite *knowledge* and has had sufficient *practice.* . . . And doesn't it also require a person whose *nature* is suited to that way of life?" (*Rep.* 374d–e, my emphasis). Compare also *Meno* 70a, *Phdr.* 269d, and O'Brien *passim* (esp. 95–96, 107, 146n27, 151).

25. "The *Phaedrus* . . . depends crucially on the notion of the divided soul, which Plato first introduced in the *Republic* and which accounts for the difficulty that lovers have in controlling their sexual appetites even after they have begun to realize that love is primarily directed not toward sex but toward philosophy. By contrast, the *Symposium* does not appeal to such a divided soul. An undivided soul, all of it always desiring what it considers best, is subject to no such conflicts. It cannot possibly be tempted by desires for the body once it has determined that the soul is more beautiful and therefore worthier of love. And according to the *Symposium*, lovers desire the higher objects of love as soon as they become aware of their existence" (Nehamas 1999:348).

    Cf. Vlastos: "whereas Socrates had thought reason all-powerful this new tripartite model endows each of the three parts with independent dynamism: each is in principle autonomously motivating and may, therefore, successfully resist each of the other two" (1991:86); "if Socrates' assumptions are correct, what is necessary *and sufficient* for moral reformation is intellectual enlightenment. The reformer's job is then to make us see that to indulge bad appetites or passion would be damaging to our own happiness. If he can bring us to understand our good we shall be bound to pursue it: our own desire for the good will drive us to it; incontinence (ἀκρασία)—doing the worse while knowing the better—will then be a psychic impossibility. Not so if the reformer were proceeding on Plato's tripartite analysis" (ibid., 88).

    And Michael Frede on the *Protagoras*: "if we find this highly intellectualistic account of the passions as judgments of some kind implausible, we should keep in mind that it is only Plato, in the *Republic*, who, precisely to explain how one can act against the interests of one's reason, for the first time introduces different parts of the soul, each with its own desires, allowing us to understand how irrational desire may overcome the dictates of desire and reason. Here in the *Protagoras*, Socrates seems to argue as if the soul were just reason" (1992a:xxx).

26. Vlastos has the *Symposium* immediately followed by the *Republic*, which, in turn, is immediately followed by the *Phaedrus* (1991:47); the Plato entry in the *Oxford Companion to Philosophy* claims that "the usual chronology for the middle period includes *Phaedo*, *Symposium*, *Republic*, *Phaedrus*, in that order" (Bostock, 683); Nehamas has *Symposium* and *Republic* separated only by *Phaedo* (1998:196n33); and other scholars (e.g., Brandwood, xvii) do likewise.

27. This is all the more salient given the fact that one of the main proponents of the developmental hypothesis, Gregory Vlastos, sees no difficulty in attributing *akrasia* (overcoming of reason by desire) to Alcibiades: "we know that the speaker is a highly acratic character" (1991:35). Vlastos writes this in an unrelated context, and no doubt fails to see the conflict it sets up with his general picture of the Platonic corpus.

    Some scholars, like Dover (165) and D. Frede (403), do in fact concede that Plato has, by the time of the *Symposium*, already adopted the tripartite psychology of the *Republic*. They do not, however, conclude from this that Alcibiades' speech and Socrates' speech stand in tension with one another: on the contrary, Frede's view is that "Alcibiades unwittingly echoes Diotima's claims" (410n230).

28. At least two explanations have been offered for the remarkable ease with which the lover scales his ladder. According to Irwin (1977:170–71), the Ascent is a type of elenchus: in search of beauty, the lover tries out one hypothesis (as it were) after another, rejecting each until he hits on the right one. As Price correctly counters, however, the Ascent is driven by *attraction*, not dissatisfaction (42; cf. Lawrence, 218). On Patterson's account (196), the lover never acquires a *new* desire but instead merely discovers what his old desire has, deep down, been all along; it was always in fact love of the Form of Beauty, but it somehow disguised itself as erotic passion, interest in laws, and so on. While Patterson's theory is ingenious, it is hard to reconcile with the heavily intellectualist language of the Ascent ("when he grasps this . . . he must think . . . he must think . . . he will think" [210b–c]) and with the existence of intermediate steps (why should my love for souls replace my love for bodies, even before I have seen the Form of Beauty?).

29. As we saw above, several Plato scholars take Alcibiades to be an uncommonly obtuse individual; if Alcibiades flees Socrates, they suggest, it is only because he does not understand what the latter has to offer him. This is also the view of Dilman (41), as well as of Barker, who writes that "a person who sees Socrates as a piper has misunderstood the nature of his activity, and cannot benefit from it" (188). Mark Lutz at least recognizes the problem—"perhaps Alcibiades bears most of the blame for being unwilling or unable to absorb what Socrates tries to teach him. But even if this were the case, Alcibiades' inability to learn from Socrates would cast doubt on his claims that human beings by nature are moved by [a desire] to be noble and good" (130)—yet he still ends up speculating that "Alcibiades represents a human type that is unusually resistant to education" (148–49).

   Alcibiades, however, is no Thrasymachus. He is eager to learn from Socrates, ready to attend to his soul, and (to repeat) clearly aware of the gulf in importance between politics and philosophy. To be sure, he probably does not understand *everything* there is to know about the philosophical life; but what more can one expect of a neophyte? It would be a strange result indeed if Socratic education required its novices to have, almost from the get-go, a complete comprehension of what they are letting themselves in for.

30. Jonathan Lear does recognize this as a serious problem: "Only those who *already* have a divine-erotic principle within them will be able to learn from Socrates' example, but they are the ones who don't really need him. . . . The others Socrates leaves to their own devices" (1999:161). See also Dover (164), Arieti (110), and Stanley Rosen (290, 301, 306). Similar remarks may be made about the *Gorgias*, where Socrates claims that it is pleasurable to be corrected, including by means of corporal punishment. Why, then, is Callicles not enjoying his medicine? Irwin's answer is that Callicles is weird: "for him pleasure and benefit do not go together, since his pleasures and inclinations are misguided" (1979:123). But Socrates has not been saying that *perfect* humans enjoy having their errors beaten out of them (surely perfect humans do not require such treatment!); rather, he has been saying that *all* humans enjoy it. I might as well say that all humans enjoy being whipped as much as the Baron de Charlus . . . except those poor fools whose pleasures and inclinations are misguided.

31. Thus Dilman writes that "when Socrates says 'we will what is good' he does not purport to convey information about human beings. . . . His remark is a grammatical one in the sense that it tells us something about his use of the word 'will'" (39). Dilman adds (36) that Socrates "must know in himself the temptation to take the easy way out, to put oneself first, not to stick up for what is right in the face of adversity." Nothing (in the early dialogues at least) suggests anything of the sort, and plenty (even in the middle-period *Symposium*, both in the Ascent speech and in Alcibiades' encomium) suggests the reverse.

32. Socrates also converses, of course, with Diotima. But this interaction is merely reported (perhaps indeed fabricated) by Socrates, whereas the exchange with Agathon is presented as taking place in real time.

33. There may also be problems with claim (5), that all good things are beautiful. As Benardete notes, "on the basis of the presumed identity of the beautiful and the good, Socrates had gotten Agathon to agree that eros is not the good; but among the traits Eros has . . . are several that are good without being attractive. He is tough, shoeless, and homeless" (193). Socrates himself, it might be added, combines unparalleled virtue with a physical appearance that leaves something to be desired: at *Theaetetus* 143e, for example, Theodorus rather tactlessly informs Socrates that he has met a young man who "is not handsome, but [instead] looks like you" (οὐκ ἔστι καλός, προσέοικε δὲ σοί; my translation). Still, the Greek word καλός is notoriously ambiguous, and one could easily imagine a defense of (5) along the lines of a particular definition. The defense might end up being circular—good things are beautiful because whatever is beautiful (καλός) is *ipso facto* good—but I am going to resist pursuing it, since there are so many other, less equivocal difficulties besetting the Agathon elenchus.

34. "Pauline predication": as in "love is always patient and kind; love is never jealous; love is not boastful or conceited, it is never rude . . ." (1 Cor. 4–5). This at least is the way Vlastos uses the term, which he borrowed from Sandra Peterson (cf. Nehamas 1999:190n13).

35. Cf. Nussbaum 1986:178. R. E. Allen is surprisingly pointed in his response to Nussbaum: "the White Queen, as a result of practice, sometimes believed six impossible things before breakfast. Perhaps you can too" (1984, 2:101). Like most Plato scholars, Allen cannot countenance Socrates making a mistake—since Socrates is, on his assumption, the mouthpiece for Plato. Hence Allen's rhetorical question: "if Plato were as slipshod in argument as this, why bother to read him?" (100). As soon as we understand that Plato may at times be deliberately making Socrates fail, I would answer, we may have all the *more* reason to "bother to read him."

36. Cf. Dover, 135; Cobb, 70–71.

37. Compare the exchange between Socrates and the eponymous sophist in the *Protagoras*. As in the *Symposium*, Socrates assumes that if something is not *f*, then it is the opposite of *f*; Protagoras, however, pulls him up short.

   SOCRATES: What are we going to say if he asks next, "Isn't piety the sort of thing that is just, and isn't justice the sort of thing that is pious? . . . Is piety the sort of thing to be not just, and therefore unjust [μὴ δίκαιον, ἀλλ' ἄδικον], and justice impious?" What are we going to say to him? Personally, I would answer . . . that justice is the same kind of thing as piety, and piety as justice. . . .

   PROTAGORAS: It's not so absolutely clear a case to me, Socrates, as to make me grant that justice is pious, and piety just. It seems a distinction is in order here. . . . Justice does have some resemblance to piety. Anything at all resembles any other thing in some way. . . . But it's not right to call things [the same] because they resemble each other in some way, however slight, or to call them [different] because there is some slight point of dissimilarity. (*Prot.* 331a–e)

   Vlastos calls Socrates' argument here—which he continues to make, in spite of Protagoras's rebuke—a "miserably lame duck, . . . deduced by the shadiest of logic" (1956:xxix). Klosko agrees, adding that "there seems to be some sort of plan at work in all this, though it is difficult to say what it is" (1979:141). For my own hypothesis as to Plato's "plan," see below.

38. Plato knows better about the existence of intermediary states (the μέσον or μεταξύ), as we can tell not only from the Diotima speech but also from *Gorg.* 467e, *Phd.* 89e–90a, *Rep.* 583c, *Soph.* 257b, *Lysis* 216c–218a, and elsewhere. Cf. O'Brien, 132.

39. We have to remember that Socrates is engaged in a conversation here, not writing a treatise. Accordingly, it is hard to imagine that he can mean anything very technical by "love lacks good things." Is he, for example, trying to say that since love lacks all beautiful things, and since some of those beautiful things are also good, it therefore lacks *those things that happen to be both beautiful and good*? (See Stokes, 144.) I find that very doubtful, especially given that in this part of the argument, Socrates is establishing his inference on the basis of the weaker claim that love lacks beautiful things, not on the basis of the stronger claim that love lacks *all* beautiful things without exception. (If love only lacks *some* beautiful things, then it could conceivably lack those beautiful things that are not good, and no others: it is not true, therefore, that "love lacks good things" follows logically from "love lacks beautiful things" and "all good things are beautiful.") What is more, Socrates is simply not entitled to the stronger claim. As we saw above, love does *not*, in fact, lack all beautiful things, and Socrates knows it. Either way, then, claim (6)—"love lacks good things"—has been reached on the basis of invalid reasoning.

40. M. A. Stewart claims (21 *et passim*) that Plato did not understand fallacy; Sprague (1962 *passim*; 1977:50), M. Frede (1992b:203), and Waterfield (302) think differently. Nehamas (1989:xvi) goes so far as to consider the Agathon elenchus a *parody* of Socratic dialectic. His reasons, mind you, differ from mine, and he views the Ascent speech as unironized Platonic doctrine (ibid., xiii).

41. Amazingly, some have sought to extricate Socrates even from this crashing error. Thus we find O'Brien writing that Protagoras did not agree merely that courageous people are confident, but that courageous people are *the* confident [τοὺς θαρραλέους]; "this slip," he adds, "allows us to acquit Socrates of the fallacy charged to him" (134). (Strangely enough, one doesn't find volunteers willing to embark on a similar rescue mission for Euthyphro.)

Taking a different tack, Vlastos proposes a retranslation: instead of "the wisest are the most confident and the most confident are the most courageous," he offers "[the wisest are the most confident] and being most confident are also bravest" (1956:xxxiii, n34). That meaning is not entirely excluded by the Greek, but it requires us to believe that Socrates has suddenly abandoned a rather careful, copula-rich style for something uttered "hastily and not as lucidly as he should have" (ibid.). Plato is not recording an actual conversation, and he has full liberty to make Socrates speak with as little haste as he pleases. Why does he allow Socrates to give even the *impression* of having failed to distribute the middle? And why, when Protagoras has pulled Socrates up on his mistake, does he not have the latter protest his innocence?

42. "Strictly speaking, the conclusion does not follow; love might possess present beauty and desire future beauty," writes Warner (169), but this "would be grotesque" (170).

43. According to Price (18), Socrates' view is not that love lacks *all* beauty but only that it lacks *some* beauty, namely the *eternal* variety. This reading has the unfortunate disadvantage of conflicting with what Socrates actually says. Allen is the one who tells us that "the *lover* is lacking, ugly in as much as he's a lover" (1984, 2:44). And Warner's is the view about the oneness of beauty (170).

44. R. E. Allen: "Socrates further assumes that Eros is always love of the beautiful, or the good—the two terms are here used interchangeably . . . he is entitled to this assumption: Agathon had said that ' . . . there is no love of the ugly.' It follows that, since Eros is love of what it lacks, it cannot be beautiful or good. . . . Agathon is refuted" (1984, 2:43). Actually, it does not follow, since (i) Eros could desire continued possession of something it already has, and (ii) nothing Agathon says entitles Socrates to assume that the beautiful and the good may be used interchangeably. (Indeed, if they *were* being used interchangeably, why would Socrates need a separate step [201c] to establish that love lacks good things?) M. C. Stokes gives a fuller account of how Socrates could be seen to derive all necessary premises from Agathon's speech, adding that Agathon clearly considers Eros to be eternally beautiful (127–28). On Stokes's view, that disqualifies the continued-possession counter. If, however, one really wished to pursue that increasingly fantastical line of argument, one could object that Agathon says nothing about the relevant *mental states* of Eros. Perhaps Eros could desire his future beauty, unaware that it is assured.

45. Thus Benardete, whom we saw above raising challenges against the identification of beauty and goodness, nonetheless feels that Agathon has been "brought to see his error" (180). And Arieti, who takes a rather deflationary attitude toward Socrates' actual speech, classing it alongside those of Pausanias, Eryximachus, and company as a reflection on its author rather than on the truth (105–7), considers dialectic—as instantiated, here, by the exchange between Socrates and Agathon—to be the antidote to all this egotism (111).

46. "What did this thing was the truth," writes Mitchell (109). Cf. D. Frede, 399n5; Hadot, 161. Contrast, however, D. Anderson (67): "'I see no means of contradicting you' . . . The means were there, but he [Agathon] missed them."

47. Price, for one, blames Diotima for some of the shortcomings in the speech: "living one's life and transmitting it are processes similar in kind. Plato could better her in making that out" (35). Others have even speculated that Diotima's biological sex is designed, in a Greek context, to cast doubt on her claims (see Halperin, chap. 6). However this may be, the fact remains that Socrates officially endorses them.

48.

SOCRATES: Tell me whether you still think that Pericles, Cimon, Miltiades, and Themistocles have proved to be good citizens [ἀγαθοὶ πολῖται].
CALLICLES: Yes, I do.
SOCRATES: So if they were good ones, each of them was obviously making the citizens better than they were before. . . . So when Pericles first began giving speeches among the people, the Athenians were worse than when he gave his last ones?
CALLICLES: Presumably.

SOCRATES: Not "presumably," my good man. It necessarily follows from what we've agreed, if he really was a good citizen [ἀνάγκη ἐκ τῶν ὡμολογημένων, εἴπερ ἀγαθός γ᾽ ἦν ἐκεῖνος πολίτης]. (515c–d)

Notice that on Socrates' view, it is not sufficient for public figures to make *efforts* toward the improvement of their fellow Athenians; they must *succeed* in making them better people. If they turn against you, this means you have not improved them; if you have not improved them, you are not a good citizen. As Socrates explicitly states, actual improvement of one's constituents "necessarily follows" from one's being a good citizen under his definition. As I am about to show, this way of thinking has the unfortunate disadvantage of making Socrates a bad citizen.

49. Irwin observes (1979:237) that the Athenians did not come as close to inflicting the death penalty as Socrates suggests; nor did Pericles build ships and walls in order to please the people—on the contrary, the people had to be *forced* to accept these measures (Thucydides 1.90.3; Herodotus 7.144.1–2). Socrates' story, Irwin concludes, "is a perversion of the historical conditions" (235). It is of course impossible to know what Plato's own view of Pericles was, but we can at least note that his Socrates is not always quite so critical. In the *Meno* (99b–c), Socrates appears to accept that Pericles had talent, claiming merely that he lacked *wisdom* (cf. Merlan, 413); in the *Protagoras* (319e–320a), Socrates goes so far as to grant Pericles wisdom, claiming merely that he lacked the ability to transmit it to his children. But then Socrates himself was, in real life, equally incapable of passing his wisdom on to *his* children (Nehamas 1999:12–13). There appear to be no end of Pericles ironies in Plato.

50. Elsewhere, Socrates refers to himself—strikingly, given his frequent diffidence—as someone who is good: if he were ever to be killed, he tells Callicles, "it would be a wicked man doing this to a good man [ἀγαθὸν]" (521b).

51. We are in fact reminded of Socrates' execution much earlier in the dialogue, when Socrates says that it is better to be executed unjustly than to execute someone else unjustly (469b), and then again when Callicles first brings up the possibility that Socrates will be unable to defend himself if he is wrongly accused (486a–b; 511a–b, 521b). Readers of the dialogue tend to note (a) that it contains numerous allusions to the death of Socrates (Friedländer, 2:261; Allen 1984, 2:189; Irwin 1979:240); (b) that Socrates "proves" Pericles a bad politician (Friedländer, 2:270; Irwin 1979:233–35); and (c) that Socrates claims to be the one true politician in Athens (Friedländer, 2:271; Allen 1984, 2:189; Irwin 1979:241). They do not draw the conclusion that Socrates must be just as bad a politician (and citizen) as Pericles, or Pericles just as good as Socrates.

Nehamas forms a rare exception. "Does this argument not apply even more directly to Socrates himself," he asks, given that Socrates "was not nearly but actually and horribly executed by his own countrymen?" (1999:48). Still, even Nehamas does not see Platonic irony at work: "in the *Gorgias*, more radically *and perhaps more as Plato's own spokesman*, Socrates is made to deny that the great statesmen even possessed *areté* themselves since, he argues, they seem to have left the citizens actually worse than they found them when they came to power" (1999:38, my emphasis).

52. There may perhaps be some Socratic irony here, as well as Platonic irony. For Socrates is, and must surely know himself to be, a master rhetorician. He claims here that if taken to court on charges of corrupting the youth, "I won't be able to say . . . 'Yes, I say and do all these things in the interest of justice, my "honored judges"' —to use that expression you people use—nor anything else" (522b–c). The *Apology*, of course, shows Socrates using just such language in his defense. (As the *Apology* portrays it, the trial's outcome has nothing to do with his abilities as a speaker, even if it may have something to do with what he chooses to say.)

53. In the *Gorgias*, Socrates claims that he has the capacity, like a moral weatherproofer, to endow people with protection against doing wrong: "if someone were to . . . prove that I am unable to provide this protection for myself or for anyone else, I would feel shame at being refuted" (*Gorg.* 522d). On that basis, surely Socrates stands "refuted." Could we not

bring forward Alcibiades (or Callicles for that matter) as an example of someone for whom Socrates has failed to provide the advertised protection? How about Charmides, who (in the fiction at least) asks to be taught by Socrates "every day until you say I have had enough" (*Chrm.* 176b), but who (in reality) goes on to become one of the Thirty Tyrants? Or how about Nicias, whose superstition is famously about to lose the Syracusan expedition for Athens but who—like Alcibiades—seems to share many of Socrates' views, as well as to endorse and understand his methods? (Not only does Nicias define courage as wisdom with respect to what is to be feared [*Lach.* 194d–195a] but he embraces the elenchus, explaining "I . . . don't regard it as at all a bad thing to have it brought to our attention that we have done or are doing wrong. Rather I think that a man who does not run away from such treatment . . . will necessarily pay more attention to the rest of his life" [*Lach.* 188a]). Indeed, as Nehamas has noted (1999:70–71, and 102), Socrates never improves *anyone* in the elenctic dialogues. Could we not, then, turn Socrates' question to Callicles around and ask, "Well now, has Socrates ever improved any of the citizens? Is there anyone who because of Socrates has turned out admirable and good?" (*Gorg.* 515a, paraphrased).

54. The conventional wisdom about Plato thus manifests a strange asymmetry. Just as long as we have the *Symposium* in our hands, we are supposed to regard Alcibiades as exonerating Socrates, who cannot be held accountable for the behavior of those who associate with him. As soon as we pick up the *Gorgias*, however, we are told to look with scorn upon the sophists, who disclaim responsibility for their disciples.

55. Socrates: "the whole of Greece has not noticed for forty years that Protagoras corrupts those who frequent him . . . to this very day his reputation has stood high; and not only Protagoras but a great many others" (*Meno* 91d–e).

56. Thus Socrates to Callicles: "you should now be making yourself as much like the Athenian people as possible if you expect to endear yourself to them and have great power in the city. . . . You mustn't be their imitator but be naturally like them in your own person if you expect to produce any genuine result toward winning the friendship of the Athenian people. . . . For each group of people takes delight in speeches that are given in its own character, and resents those given in an alien manner" (513a–c).

57. R. E. Allen offers a sober, this-worldly, non-question-begging explanation for the view that justice is good for the just. "To satisfy our own needs we must rely on our fellows," he writes, "and if we are to rely on our fellows, we must aim at their good as well as, and as part of, our own" (1984, 2:227). That may very well be true of real life, but it is probably not what Plato's Socrates has in mind. In the *Republic*, after all, Socrates states that "a decent person is most self-sufficient in living well and, above all others, has the least need of anyone else" (*Rep.* 387d).

58. "The more able and expert a mind is, the better it is, and more capable, whatever the activity, of acting both well and badly" (*HMin.* 375e–376a); "whenever someone is a clever guardian, then, he is also a clever thief. . . . If a just person is clever at guarding money, therefore, he must also be clever at stealing it" (*Rep.* 334a). Elsewhere, Plato's Socrates claims that "moderation, and justice, courage, intelligence . . . at times harm us, at other times benefit us" (*Meno* 88a–b; cf. *Rep.* 491a–b, *Rep.* 518e–519a, *Euthyd.* 281d–e).

59. Rhetoric, as Gorgias presents it, is "concerned with those matters that are just *and unjust*" (454b, my emphasis). If, therefore, orators teach their charges the meaning of justice, they presumably also teach them the meaning of *injustice*.

60. One could of course also ask whether it is really legitimate to infer from the case of carpentry to the case of oratory. When Gorgias says he teaches his pupils what is just and what is unjust, it is quite possible that he is referring to a body of *knowledge* (for example, "it is legitimate to kill in self-defense"; "it is not legitimate to commit treason") rather than to a set of *skills*. In other words, Gorgias may very well be claiming to teach his pupils not *how to be just* but merely *what justice is* (and in the legal sense, at that). Since Socrates' arguments here are sufficiently problematic on an internal basis, however, I shall leave this aside.

61. "A person trained in oratory (ῥητορικός) *knows* what is just. Thus, he is just, must act justly, and cannot do wrong. Here Socrates shows that Gorgias is caught in

a contradiction" (Friedländer, 2:250). R. E. Allen, who recognizes that there are serious issues with Socrates' argument (1984, 2:195), nonetheless feels that it would be sufficient for Socrates to say that rhetoric is not *reliably* good; since Gorgias has "tripped over the joint claims that rhetoric is an art dealing with issues of right and wrong and yet morally neutral" (195–96), Socrates has, for Allen, effectively won the debate. This weaker criticism of rhetoric would, however, *not* be sufficient to place Gorgias in a contradiction. For there is no conflict between (1) rhetoric failing to make all students good and (2) some students not being good; nor, more generally, is it impossible for a craft (1) to deal with issues of right and wrong and (2) to remain itself morally neutral. That is what the legal profession is for.

62. Irwin is under no illusions about the "refutation" of Gorgias. "The 'disharmony' is between Gorgias' views and Socrates' views, not internal to Gorgias' views," he writes (1979:128); after all, "a shepherd does not make his sheep into shepherds" (214). But then, since he has no room for Platonic irony—if Socrates believes *p*, he clearly feels, then Plato must believe *p* too—Irwin is left in something of a quandary. He can only conclude that "the G[orgias] makes claims inconsistent with the Socratic Paradox [that virtue is knowledge and vice ignorance]. . . . But we have seen that the *G[orgias]* does not explicitly reject the Socratic Paradox" (222). (When he says "the *Gorgias* does not explicitly reject the Socratic Paradox," he presumably means that *Socrates* does not explicitly reject the Socratic Paradox; this, of course, is not the same thing at all.) Indeed, in a later work Irwin goes so far as to claim that "Plato shows [in the *Gorgias*] why the Socratic view is more difficult to reject than we might at first have thought" (1995:99).

63. "I would see the charge of inconsistency at 457e as an example of Socratic irony" (Kahn 1983:84). While Kahn admits that Socrates' *argument* for the Socratic Paradox is "surprisingly weak" (82), he clearly believes that we are supposed to accept the Paradox itself (110). As I have been attempting to show, however, the Pericles section seems to me to constitute decisive evidence that Plato rejects it.

64. Again, see Cooper, who straightforwardly acknowledges that Socrates "appeals to considerations he has given Gorgias no reason at all to accept" (1999:44n20).

65. Lanier Anderson has dubbed this phenomenon "inverse akrasia." See Anderson and Landy 2001:44n26. "Alcibiades is divided against himself," agrees Stanley Rosen (290); "despite the magnitude of his ambition he is never completely and genuinely possessed by it." Still, Rosen ultimately appears to feel (like so many others) that Alcibiades lacks *knowledge*, rather than the strength to do what he wants (300).

66. Critical responses to the two dialogues also bear striking similarities. Each dialogue is usually taken to constitute "Plato's defence of Socrates, his life, his methods and his doctrines, against various challenges" (Irwin 1979:4); and in either case, scholars tend to assume *both* (1) that it is the interlocutor's fault (that is, the fault of Alcibiades or Callicles) if, succumbing to the temptation of politics, he fails to heed Socrates *and* (2) that there is no such thing as temptation—even though (1) and (2) are mutually exclusive. Friedländer makes both claims on the same page (2:266): "if pleasures may be both good and bad, it is clear that we must desire those that are good. Once we know the difference between good and pleasure, there can be no doubt as to which should rule"; "he [Callicles] concedes that there is something in what Socrates is saying when the latter demonstrates the superiority of the just life. . . . But Kallikles cannot appropriate this conclusion for his own life, and Socrates knows why: love of the demos (ὁ δήμου ἔρως) lures him, counteracting the influence of Socrates."

67. At times in the *Gorgias*, Socrates does appear to allow for the existence of non-rational, good-independent desires (Irwin 1979:7, 190–91, 195, 221; Cooper 1999:59)—but somehow without noticing that he is doing so, or at least without noticing the insuperable conflict this sets up within his belief system. As Irwin puts it (1995:218), "Socrates' previous argument against the value of rhetoric assumed the truth of the Socratic Paradox. The defence of temperance and continence assumes the falsity of the Paradox. The conclusions of these two main lines of argument in the dialogue are never satisfactorily reconciled." Should we say, as Plato scholars have a way of doing in other circumstances, that

Socrates is expressing his own view when he denies the existence of good-independent desires, and merely rehearsing the view of his interlocutor (Callicles) when he does not? Would it be more charitable to assume this or to acknowledge that, in a dialogue that witnesses Socrates proudly proclaiming "what philosophy says always stays the same" (482a), he starts out in position A, moves to not-A, and returns again without any warning (at 509d; see Irwin 1995:229) to A?

Gerasimos Santas, who takes the Socratic paradoxes as expressions of Plato's own beliefs in the "earlier dialogues" (1964:147)—including the *Protagoras*, the *Gorgias*, and the *Meno*—believes he can help out with a slight qualification. "I suggest," he writes, "that Plato meant that if a man has knowledge of what is virtuous and *also* knowledge that it is better for one to do what is virtuous, then he will always . . . behave virtuously" (159). This qualification ostensibly rescues Plato from absurdity, since the revised paradox allows for cases in which people commit evil acts while knowing they are wrong. Yet even if I know both that an action is bad and that bad things harm me, I may still choose to do it. As Santas himself admits, without seeing the extent of the damage to his argument, it may be a mistake for "Plato" to speak "as if there is no stronger desire or passion than this central desire for things that are good for one" (163).

68. Once again, compare Cooper (1999:32): "Callicles conspicuously employs ideas . . . which depart from those Socrates himself relies on in other Socratic dialogues and indeed earlier in this one. Furthermore, these ideas line up very closely with the quite different ideas on these matters espoused by the Socrates of the *Republic*. . . . I believe that we should see Plato in the *Gorgias* as recognizing and drawing attention to weaknesses—doubtful points—in the Socratic moral psychology. . . . So Socrates is not speaking simply and straightforwardly as Plato's mouthpiece in this dialogue."

69. According to Nicholas White (140, 148, et passim; cf. to some extent Irwin 1979:205–6), Callicles' mistake is that he does not always or fully appreciate the need for "rational prudence." If he genuinely wishes to maximize the amount of pleasure he experiences over the course of his life, then he will have to *plan*, sacrificing present delights for the sake of larger future satisfactions; it will not do to indulge in "whatever he may have an appetite for at the time" (492a). There is thus a conflict in his belief system, and it is this conflict that Socrates sets out to expose. But even if rational planning really is what Socrates has in mind—and Cooper, for one, thinks it is not (1999:55n41, 57n44)—it is surely noteworthy that Pericles stands as an exemplar of the skill. Pericles, an orator, knows very well which short-term interests should be subordinated to which long-term gains, and also advocates the power required to implement such decisions. What need, then, for philosopher-kings?

70. Recall again *Meno* 91d–e: "to this very day his [Protagoras's] reputation has stood high; and not only Protagoras but a great many others [enjoy such esteem]."

71. That is, it already assumes that rhetoric is impotent. For the view that a politician has to resemble the majority in order to receive its vote depends on the unsubstantiated premise that successful *deception* of the majority (what Socrates here calls "imitation") is impossible. Callicles has absolutely no reason to accept such a premise ("I'm not really convinced by you," he retorts at 513c), and neither have we. It is notoriously feasible to rule a population by means of trickery; indeed the Socrates of Plato's *Republic*, who is quite comfortable with the "noble lie," proposes nothing different (414b–c, 459c–d). All of this does not, however, prevent Irwin from awarding victory to Socrates. "Callicles is embarrassed," he writes, "when he has to face the consequences of his own position, which contradict his own ideals" (1979:240); "Plato suggests that Callicles cannot maintain his self-respect; his chosen way of achieving his goals makes him depend on the public opinion of the masses he despises" (1979:179).

72. In the *Gorgias*, Socrates appears to take it for granted that all pleasure derives from the mere removal of pain (hence his strange argument at 496d–e). In the *Republic*, by contrast, Socrates enjoins Glaucon to bear in mind "the pleasures that don't come out of pains, so that you won't suppose in their case also that it is the nature of pleasure to be the cessation of pain or of pain to be the cessation of pleasure" (*Rep.* 584b). Should we really

blame Callicles for characterizing Socrates' picture as "nonsense" (494d)? (On this point, cf. Irwin 1979:192, 196.)

73. Polus is careful, at 474c–d, to distinguish between the admirable (τὸ καλόν, with its opposite τὸ αἰσχρόν) and the beneficial (τὸ ἀγαθόν, with its opposite τὸ κακόν). Socrates will effectively run the two together, arguing that the admirable thing to do just so happens also to be what is most beneficial for the agent.

74. Aristotle allows not just for akrasia but even for positive perversity: "one person," he says, "pursues excesses of things because they are excesses and because he decides on it, for themselves and not for some further result" (*EN* 1150a18–22).

   In assuming we always desire things that are actually good for us, Socrates may be falling victim to a case of "opaque context" (Kahn 1983:115; 1996:140): from (1) I want what is good for me and (2) what is good for me turns out to be X, it does *not* follow that (3) I want X. To take an analogous example, (1) Oedipus deliberately killed a man at a crossroads, and (2) that man turned out to be his father, but we are surely not going to conclude that (3) Oedipus deliberately killed his father. (Unless, of course, we are incorrigible Freudians.)

75. Some scholars, like Allen (1984, 2:205), are entirely satisfied with Socrates' argument here: "if *a* is more ugly or shameful than *b*, *a* surpasses *b* either in pain or in evil. Refutation follows from this lemma as of course." Others, however, have seen the problem. "When Polus said that doing wrong was less admirable, he clearly meant that it was less ὠφέλιμον [useful] *for the community*, and from this it does not immediately follow that it is less ὠφέλιμον *for the agent*" (Dodds, 249); "useful *to whom*? Why precisely to the person punished, and not rather to society, the protection of which, after all, is one of the uncontested ends of punishment?" (Gomperz, 347; see also Vlastos 1991:144; Mackenzie, 180, 241, 244; and even Kahn 1983:117).

   Gomperz is probably the only one who takes Plato to be deliberately placing specious arguments in Socrates' mouth. Dodds provides Socrates with two incompatible alibis: (1) neither he nor Plato could have known this was a fallacy, given that "when the *Gorgias* was written the study of logic was still in its earliest infancy" (249); (2) Socrates is "repay[ing] the Sophists in their own coin" (ibid.). Similarly, Vlastos believes (1) that Plato—and a fortiori Socrates—"is himself unaware of the fallacy" (1991:148) and (2) that "Socrates giv[es] Polus not less than he deserves." (1991:156)

76. I leave aside here the rather important caveat that in an imperfect society—and which society is not?—punishment cannot be relied on to benefit the criminal. "If . . . the system in the present society is not just," notes Irwin (1979:163), "then Polus has no good reason to accept punishment in present society if he can help it." (See also Dodds, 254; Mackenzie, 181–82.) Once again, the context surely forces us to consider Socrates' own case, and wonder whether his execution did him, personally, any good.

77. R. E. Allen attempts to extricate Socrates from the contradiction: "punishment, if it is imposed justly, is imposed . . . for the sake of the soul of the wrongdoer—or if he is beyond cure, *for his own sake and that of his fellows*" (1984, 2:208, my emphasis). But Socrates says only that incurables are punished for the sake of others, not that they are also punished for their own sake. Cf. Dodds, 254.

78. Socrates himself appears to recognize that punishment may be good for the *community*, not (or at least not just) for the offender: "don't we also put a person to death," he asks, "because we suppose that doing that is better *for us* [ἄμεινον . . . ἡμῖν] than not doing it?" (468b, my emphasis).

79. Vlastos notes that Socrates' argument here depends on the "Socratic fallacy" and is therefore ineffectual against Polus (1991:146, cf. 278, 304); Kahn agrees that it is "a weak and tricky argument" (1983:111); and Irwin, who notes that Isocrates dismissed the "miserable Archelaus" line as a mere philosopher's paradox, sums up as follows: "he [Socrates] has not proved that the tyrant or rhetor does not know what is good for him, or that I would not become a tyrant or rhetor if I knew what was good for me" (1979:150, 146). Friedländer, mind you, is quite happy to speak of "the defeat of Polus" (2:256), and O'Brien is just as happy to praise the "inexorable logic" (90) which proves that "wickedness involves

the greatest injury to the wicked" and that "to suffer punishment for injustice is actually a benefit" (89). Some are barely able to contain their excitement at "the brilliant 466a–468e" (Penner, 301), "Socrates' most effective argument" (ibid., 313); "if ever man was laid by the heels in argument, it was Polus," adds an exuberant Allen (1984, 2:199).

80. Here Socrates has mysteriously metamorphosed into Euthyphro. Cf. Friedländer: "how far we are moving in a paradoxical world is shown by the conclusion (480c) that we should accuse ourselves and relatives or friends, to uncover their offenses—yet we know how the author of the *Euthyphro* condemned the charge brought by a son against his father when this actually happened before a court in Athens" (2:258). No paradoxicality, however, for Allen, who is quite taken with the idea that "the usefulness of rhetoric must consist in obtaining punishment for ourselves, our family, or our country" (1984, 2:206). "Fallacy," he insists, "is often in the eye of the beholder."

81. Socrates specifies that the enemy has not done anything unjust to the person in question (480e). And even if he had, Socrates might very well consider it impermissible to retaliate. In the *Republic*, his counterpart is adamant that "it isn't the function of a just person to harm a friend *or anyone else*," enemies included (335d, my emphasis); the *Crito* Socrates, similarly, insists that one must not, "when wronged, inflict wrong in return, as the majority believe, since one must never do wrong" (49b).

82. In the *Gorgias*, Socrates insists repeatedly that there be no long speeches (448d, 449b, 461d). Yet he himself makes two of them, not just the myth at the end but also the classification of crafts and knacks at 464b–466a. In both cases, he blames his interlocutor: "I deserve to be forgiven, though, for when I made my statements short you didn't understand" (465e, to Polus); "you've made me deliver a real popular harangue, Callicles, because you aren't willing to answer" (519d). Friedländer sees no problem here, finding it merely "amusing" that Socrates gives a lecture right after criticizing Polus for so doing (2:252). (Oddly, Friedländer also believes that "Socrates is incapable of delivering speeches" [1:155]!) Cooper, however, notes the conflict (1999:42n17). And Nehamas (1999:96) points out that a similar thing happens in the *Protagoras*. After hearing a few remarks totaling less than a Stephanus page (334a–c), Socrates complains to Protagoras that "if someone speaks to me at length I tend to forget the subject of the speech," adding "I don't have the ability to make those long speeches: I only wish I did" (334c–d, 335c). He then goes on, at 342a–347a, to deliver a five-page peroration—ironically enough, about "laconic brevity" (343a).

83. George Klosko sees the irony: "Socrates, who asserts that he is speaking not for himself but for philosophy, in this confrontation with three rhetoricians, concludes the encounter with a rhetorical plea" (1983:593). Klosko, however, takes Plato to be critiquing the aims and methods of the historical Socrates; that explanation seems somewhat unlikely, given the rather un-Socratic content of the speech in question.

84. Henry Teloh and Jyl Gentzler are unusual in acknowledging the strong component of rhetoric in Socrates' performance; both, however, seek to offer a defense for it. For Teloh (35), the ends justify the means: "Callicles must be made susceptible to dialectic, and only the force of rhetorical persuasion can achieve this." For Gentzler (42), Socrates is deliberately revealing the bankruptcy of rhetoric (as well as proving that he could have been an orator himself, had he so desired). Teloh's argument strikes me as special pleading, and Gentzler's—while ingenious—as not entirely convincing (for one thing, it would be open to Callicles to reject *this* rhetorical performance as inept, while continuing to believe in the power of rhetoric more generally). And in any case, both Gentzler and Teloh miss, I think, the clear *ressentiment* in the specific words chosen by Socrates.

85. This in contrast to Xenophon's Socrates, who "is so innocuous that Kierkegaard wondered why the Athenians would have ever been tempted to put such a man to death" (Nehamas 1998:107; cf. 209n68, and Kierkegaard 1992:15–16). Irwin acknowledges the animus against Callicles—"Plato takes a rather unattractively malicious pleasure in depicting the incompetence of the unjust and unphilosophical man . . . facing the life after death" (1979:248)—but attributes it, for some reason, to Plato. Vlastos, who finds similar animus in the *Protagoras*, makes no such misattribution. Socrates "is not a wholly attractive

figure in this dialogue," he writes (1956:xxiv); "his handling of Protagoras is merciless, if not cruel" (ibid.).

86. Irwin does notice many a problem in Socrates' reasoning, but sees these as Plato's own mistakes, later to be corrected. He concludes his analysis by saying that "the argument of the *G[orgias]* should be studied both for its own sake and as a first attempt at the task attempted again in the *R[epublic]*" (1979:250). Nowhere does he countenance the possibility that Plato might *already* know, say, that an individual talented at guarding will also be talented at stealing, and that Plato deliberately withholds such knowledge from his literary character. Similar remarks could be made about Beversluis, who recognizes that Socrates fails to defeat Gorgias (312–13), Polus (331), or Callicles (357), who notes that Socrates' arguments are "singularly unconvincing; indeed, most of them are demonstrably fallacious or unsound" (367–68), but who hesitates to attribute such reservations to Plato (371).

87. See Cooper 1999:52n32. The dialogue ends with Socrates saying "let's not follow the [way of life] that you *believe in* and *call on* me to follow. For that one is worthless, Callicles" (527e, my emphasis). Even before this, Socrates' failure to bludgeon his opponent into submission has been clear. At a certain point, Callicles begins humoring Socrates, just giving him the answers he wants (497a–c, 505c, 509e–510a, 514a, 516b); then Callicles stops responding altogether, and Socrates starts questioning *himself*, in what appears to be almost a parody of the elenchus; finally, Socrates delivers his immense speech about the afterlife, without any help even from his alter ego. A similar thing happens in the *Protagoras* (360e), when the title character decides merely to placate Socrates, rather than offering a serious response.

88. The most powerful objection comes from McKim (1988 *passim*) and Kahn (1996:138), who brilliantly hypothesize that the very shame felt by each of the three interlocutors betrays an unacknowledged adherence to virtue. Still, their conclusion only follows if the interlocutors are feeling what we would now call *guilt*, as against shame proper. A fifth- or fourth-century Athenian male might well feel ashamed if he spent all of his life philosophizing, turned his friends in to the authorities, or resisted taking revenge when harmed; such shame would presumably not constitute evidence of his fitness for Socratic excellence. (Callicles, we should note, considers it "ridiculous and unmanly" to continue doing philosophy into one's adult years and "shameful" to leave oneself an easy target for one's enemies: see 484c–486d, 508c–d, 522c.) And however things may stand with Gorgias and Polus, Callicles succumbs not to embarrassment but to a pair of arguments that are probably the weakest in the entire dialogue.

The first of the two is particularly egregious: "do you observe the result, that when you say that a thirsty person drinks, you're saying that a person who's in pain [because thirsty] simultaneously feels enjoyment [because drinking]? . . . But you say that it's impossible for a person who's doing well to be doing badly at the same time. . . . So, feeling enjoyment isn't the same as doing well, and being in pain isn't the same as doing badly" (496e–497a). This is hardly a cast-iron proof, since all Callicles needs is a simple distinction. As Irwin notes, "if I am healthy and sick, I am healthy in one part . . . and sick in another. Why might we not also say that I enjoy in one part and feel pain in another?" (1979:202). And after all, why should it be any more possible to feel pain and pleasure simultaneously than to be doing well and doing badly simultaneously?

It will not do to explain away the situation (à la M. A. Stewart) as a lacuna in ancient Greek logic. For when it suits him, Plato is perfectly happy to have Socrates make all the necessary distinctions: "if someone said that a person who is standing still but moving his hands and head is moving and standing still at the same time, we wouldn't consider, I think, that he ought to put it like that. What he ought to say is that one part of the person is standing still and another part is moving" (*Rep.* 436c; cf. *Tht.* 165c–d). And in the *Euthydemus*, Plato is clearly satirizing the sophists who refuse to do so (see e.g. 296a–b, and Waterfield, who notes [302] that "throughout the dialogues, Socrates is made to commit fallacies, often ones which are scarcely less blatant than some of Euthydemus' and Dionysodorus', and often the same ones that these two sophists commit"). It will also not do to appeal (à la White [151]) to Socratic irony. Instead we have to recognize that Socrates is here deploying a sophist's trick in order to browbeat his opponent into making an unforced concession.

89. For "incommensurability," see MacIntyre 1990. Dilman admits that Socrates cannot convince Polus without begging the question; an interlocutor will not accept Socrates' premises, in other words, unless he already believes that goodness is good for the agent (35). Compare Griswold on the *Protagoras*: "Socrates cannot, through force of argument alone, justify to someone his own stance about what fundamentally matters unless his interlocutor is already disposed to Socrates' base line view of what matters" (1999b:305). For his part, Irwin concedes that any argument against the existence of akrasia is circular—unless, that is, it is directed to a hedonist like Callicles (1977:105). Accordingly, Irwin considers Callicles to be "beaten" (1979:206).

90. Cf. Irwin: "Socrates replies that even the toughest interlocutor, Callicles, must find himself admitting . . . the truth of Socrates' views. Agreement between Socrates and Callicles will show that Socrates' beliefs are inescapable for any rational person" (1979:4). And for all his reservations on specific points, Irwin does not hesitate to conclude that overall Socrates is right, and that (to repeat) "Callicles . . . has been beaten" (206). But of course, as Klosko notes, "having explicitly made the point that his opponent must be convinced if he is to be accounted successful, Socrates is unable to convince Callicles of anything" (1983:593). Callicles does not admit "the truth of Socrates' views"; he merely pretends to, in order to be done with the exchange.

   On Cooper's view, it is not just that Callicles refuses to accept Socrates' claims; it is that he is *right* to refuse. For "Socrates has not in fact refuted Callicles" (1999:73–74). Socrates, explains Cooper, "evidently thinks that these arguments are sufficient to show that the life to which Callicles urges him is no good at all. . . . But, from what Plato writes in preparing and presenting both sides of the dispute, the reader should infer that Plato himself does not agree" (ibid. 68). Cooper shows (73) that Callicles could maintain his hedonism even while accepting a distinction between good and bad pleasures; he goes so far as to claim— a far cry from Irwin and Allen!—that "Callicles' ideal is quite an attractive one" (56n41). (Compare Klosko 1984:131.)

91. Note also that the quest for elenctic certainty requires good faith on the part of all discussants: "you'd no longer be adequately inquiring into the truth of the matter with me," Socrates chides Callicles, "if you speak contrary to what you think" (*Gorg.* 495a). Such a quest is incompatible, therefore, with Socratic irony. Cf. Saunders: "Socrates insists that the interlocutor must himself believe in his answer. . . . Hence if Socrates himself commits a fallacy, it is presumably not deliberate" (31, 31n2). And Vlastos: "could we be expected to think of Socrates as 'examining' Polus . . . and 'examining' himself thereby . . . by fooling his opponent? Resorting to deception in that procedure would be . . . ruining whatever hope Socrates might have had of giving to him or getting from him this kind of help" (1991:147; cf. 1991:43, 134). And Nehamas: "if the results of the elenchus . . . are to be true, then they must be reached on the basis of beliefs that are not only sincerely held but that are also themselves true" (1999:66).

92. Cf. Vlastos 1956:xxviii–xxx, and also xxxix ("anyone who could excogitate by pure deduction a fact of human nature would have to be more than a master of argument—he would have to be a wizard"). Vlastos assumes, however, that the mistake must be *Plato's*; it is, after all, the "grand methodological hypothesis" of Vlastos's work that "in any given dialogue Plato allows the persona of Socrates only what he (Plato), at the time, considers true" (1991:117, 117n50). On Vlastos's account (ibid., 113–14), and also on Nehamas's (1999:65–66), the *Gorgias*-period Plato holds (1) that everyone possesses a stock of true moral beliefs somewhere within his or her soul, (2) that only this set is internally coherent, and (3) that refutation will accordingly leave none but the true beliefs standing. It is only around the time of the *Meno*, where Socrates is able to argue an untutored slave into retracting hypotheses but not into offering better ones, that Plato changes his mind (Vlastos 1991:119). One cannot help thinking that if these were actually Plato's opinions, the *Gorgias*—where Gorgias and Polus both pick the

wrong view to reject, and Callicles refuses to be convinced—would be a strange way of putting them on display.

93. On the same basis, the *Cambridge* informs us that in the *Meno*, "Plato demonstrates that even a slave ignorant of geometry can begin to learn the subject through questioning" (710): no mention here of the flagrant problems with the "demonstration," as pointed out by D. Anderson (135) and others.

   Another recent claim that the voice of the middle and late period Socrates "has always been considered to be unmistakably Plato's own" is made by Alexander Nehamas (1998:101; though contrast 1999:xix).

94. "This is why Plato in the *Timaeus* identifies matter and space: he identifies 'what participates' with 'space,' although in his so-called 'unwritten teachings' [ἐν τοῖς λεγομένοις ἀγράφοις δόγμασιν] he gives a different account of 'what participates'" (*Physics* 4.2, 209b). As for what Plato *did* put in writing, we have reason to think that the dialogues began their lives on wax tablets (see Diogenes Laertius [3.37] for the case of the *Laws*); papyrus transcription came later. When I speak of Plato committing his thoughts to papyrus, therefore, I have in mind the process as a whole.

95. See, e.g., Stanley Rosen (xv). The esoteric-doctrine view may take some comfort from the fact that Plato clearly understands the *possibility*, at least, of using inconclusive written works in conjunction with an oral instruction reserved for initiates: evidence may be found at *Tht.* 152c, 180b, 184a.

96. In the *Protagoras*, Socrates continues to assume that there is no such thing as motivational conflict, insisting that "knowledge . . . always prevails, whenever it is present, over pleasure and everything else" (357c) and, as we saw earlier, that "no one who knows or believes there is something else better than what he is doing, something possible, will go on doing what he had been doing, when he could be doing what is better . . . no one goes willingly toward the bad or [even] what he believes to be bad" (358b–d; cf. 345e, 352c, 357c). Knowledge, on his view, is thus both necessary and sufficient for virtuous action (Vlastos 1956:xxxviii n47), with the corollary that all vice has its origin in ignorance. Protagoras, by contrast, realizes that excellence in any domain requires (a) natural talent and (b) training as well as (c) knowledge (327a–d, 351a). Protagoras's triad of necessary conditions makes a reappearance in the *Republic*—this time in the mouth of Socrates. Horneffer (6–7, 10, 19) and Tejera (136) have made similar claims for the *Hippias Minor*. On the triad of necessary conditions, cf. O'Brien, 107.

   For additional statements of the "Socratic Paradox," see *Lach.* 199d and *Meno* 77b–78b. An intriguingly different formulation is found at *Crito* 49a, where Socrates asks, "Do we say that one *must* never in any way do wrong willingly, or *must* one do wrong in one way and not in another?" [οὐδενὶ τρόπῳ φαμὲν ἑκόντας ἀδικητέον εἶναι, ἢ τινὶ μὲν ἀδικητέον τρόπῳ τινὶ δὲ οὔ;] (my emphasis; the normative force is carried by the gerundive suffix -τέον). It is as though Socrates, who is here discussing the merits of a potential jailbreak, for once acknowledges the possibility that he *could*, though he will not, choose the bad course of action. (Compare, perhaps, the *Hippias Minor*: "it is not those who unintentionally cause injury, commit crimes, tell lies, deceive and make mistakes who are better; no, those who intentionally do all this are better" [372d]; here, however, Socrates may be deploying the claim as part of a reductio.)

97. My view is potentially compatible with that of those, like Kahn, who consider Plato's philosophical position to have remained constant from start to finish. But I should note that on the whole I find the developmental hypothesis (once modified) more compelling. Any development-denier is obliged to do two things: first, square the "Socratic paradoxes" with the existence of motivational conflict; second, find hints of Plato's overall solution in the "earliest" dialogues. Thus O'Brien, who considers it simply "intolerable" to posit that "Plato uses Socrates to attack Socratic doctrine" (100), and who concludes that "Plato taught that no man did wrong intentionally" throughout his career (108–9), attempts to defend the firmly-held "ethical paradoxes" (92) by arguing (a) that they represent an ideal state of affairs and (b) that they work in reality, as long as we complete them by adding in a good nature and an effective training (19 and 107 respectively). O'Brien also claims to

detect this solution between the lines not just in the *Protagoras* but in the *Laches* and the *Charmides* too (109–10, 122, 143). Still, O'Brien's two defenses (ideal and real) contradict one another; further, the fact that not all humans are endowed with virtuous natures would seem to vitiate the strong claim that "no man does wrong intentionally." (Archelaus, as we saw above, probably does exactly what he wants to do.) My point, however, is not that it is *impossible* to produce a development-denying reconstruction, merely that it is difficult.

98. Cf. Griswold: "Socrates objected that the written word cannot ask or answer questions, does not know when to speak and when not, and cannot defend itself. Plato's dialogues do, however, overcome these objections at least in part. . . . For they announce their deeper message only to those readers able enough to find it" (1986:221). And Stanley Rosen: "Just as Socrates tests the nature of his interlocutors, so Plato tests the nature of his readers. Just as Socrates is protected from unsatisfactory companions by his daimonion, so Plato is protected from unsatisfactory readers by his irony" (xx–xxi). See also Schleiermacher, 14; L. Strauss 1964:52–54; D. Anderson, 63.

99. Griswold notes that there can be—as Plato knows—no way to argue someone into philosophy, since willingness to engage in rational debate presupposes an acceptance of its fundamental commitments. Accordingly, Plato's objective in deploying irony is to "draw the reader into philosophizing" (1988:160): as soon as she begins to protest about the logical leaps, Plato has her (minimally) on his side. This is an account with which I have much sympathy. I would only add that the strategy will fail in most cases, leaving some readers cold (the Callicles types) and filling others with misplaced warmth (the Apollodorus types). Wholesale conversion is, in my view, far less likely than the bringing "on line" of a disposition that already exists in the reader.

100. On this point, see esp. Griswold (1986:10–14, and 2002:88, 95, 99–100), Cooper (1999:50–51), Scott (74–75), Nails 16 (and indeed to some extent the entire *Who Speaks for Plato?* volume), and Krentz (39, 43). Cf. also Cobb (8), M. Frede (1992b:219), Goldschmidt (3), Stanley Rosen (xviii, xxv), Saunders (36), Schaerer (87, 216), and Williams (1990:ix). Note that it is Platonic irony, and not the dialogue form per se, that makes such training possible; Berkeley's dialogues, for example, do not function this way. (See Cooper 1997:xxii n21, M. Frede 1992b:203–4; for a history of attention and inattention to the dialogue form, see Krentz, 44–45n3.) Since, however, a separation between author and protagonist is indispensable, the writing must at least be *literary* in nature.

101. If the pleasant were the good, says Socrates at 494c–e, then incessant itch-scratchers and even catamites would be living enviable lives. This is of course an absurd result.

102. Thus in *Politicus* the Visitor notes that when a child is tested on spelling, "the inquiry takes place [less] for the sake of the single question set before him [than] for the sake of his becoming more able to answer all questions relating to letters"; so too the inquiry he himself is conducting with Young Socrates into the nature of a statesman—which is to say, the entire content of the dialogue—is "set before us [less] for the sake of that very thing [than] for the sake of our becoming better dialecticians in relation to all subjects" (*Pol.* 285d). Hence Hadot: "the subject-matter of the dialogue counts less than the method applied in it" (93).

103. Cf. Nehamas (1999:22): "what cannot be transmitted . . . is the ability to follow the methods and to apply the rules." The elenctic dialogues put the method on display; the ironic dialogues go one step further, requiring us to come up with our own objections, rather than passively following Socrates' lead. They are therefore, I would argue, more effective as training devices.

104. Plato *could*, of course, have designed his dialogues so as to yield knowledge in spite of (or even by means of) authorial irony. Some—like Schleiermacher (17–18), Jaeger (2:91), Brandis (2:159–60), and O'Brien (109–10)—have contended that the truth is always there to be read between the lines, making each dialogue a riddle with a ready answer. Others have suggested that the solution, an "esoteric doctrine," needs to be provided separately and privately by Plato. And then there are those (including Friedländer, 1:169–70; Lawrence, 222; and D. Anderson, 93–94) who see the dialogues as yielding knowledge by

revelation, since absolute truth (they say) does not take conceptual form; all the training in dialectic is, according to them, just preparation, just a way to make the soul apt to receive that life-transforming vision. As I have tried to show, however, there is on many occasions simply no knowledge to be had, whether epiphanic or otherwise; knowledge, at such junctures, is simply not the *point*. (The line from *Politicus* cited above seems to confirm this admirably.) I do not even quite share the view of those who, like Christopher Rowe for example, present the function of Platonic irony as that of allowing the author to distance himself from his own beliefs. (See Rowe, 88–89; M. Frede 1992b:214–15; Merlan, 423–24; Stanley Rosen, xxi; Kahn 1996:388; Griswold 1986:248n27; and Griswold 1999a:394.) While I have a great deal of sympathy for that approach, I take Platonic irony to be largely *reader-directed*, an invitation to the fine-tuning of a vital cognitive capacity.

105. I am running together here a number of claims made in different dialogues; they would not, of course, all be endorsed by every Socrates. Dialogues like the *Protagoras*, for example, feature a character Socrates who, as we saw above, refuses to recognize the existence of genuine motivational conflict.

106. Cf. Cobb, 71. Consider also the way in which Plato, via Agathon, Socrates, and "Diotima," presents us in the *Symposium* with a series of positions, each of which is no sooner adopted than it is (overtly or quietly) discarded. Eros is first beautiful (195a), then ugly because seeking to possess what it lacks (201c), then only *part* ugly (202d), and then (potentially) beautiful and simply seeking to *remain* that way—"love is wanting to possess the good forever" (205e)—before finally turning into a desire neither to obtain nor yet to retain but instead to *create* beauty, "whether in body or in soul" (206b). Perhaps there is an implication that the refinement could continue even beyond what we are given in the dialogue; perhaps, in other words, there is an instigation to go further on our own. Similar remarks could possibly be made about retractions in the *Phaedrus* (see *Phdr.* 242b–243b, 265b–d, and Nehamas 1999:349–53) and in the *Theaetetus* (191b, 195c, 199c, 200a).

107. I depart here from Martin Warner's view that Apollodorus, "unlike Alcibiades, has . . . opened his eyes towards the light" (162). The same Apollodorus is, incidentally, also making a bit of a spectacle of himself in the *Phaedo* (59a, 117d), rather to Socrates' disapproval (117d–e).

108. Note that Socrates' arguments about immortality in the *Phaedo* are not mere intellectual games but designed, instead, to help us overcome the fear of death: "You should, said Socrates, sing a charm over him [ἐπᾴδειν] every day until you have charmed away [ἐξεπᾴσητε] his fears" (77e); "a man should repeat this to himself as if it were an incantation [ὥσπερ ἐπᾴδειν]" (114d). For the use of argument (λόγος) as incantatory charm (ἐπῳδή), compare also *Rep.* 608a.

109. Those who have taken Plato to consider philosophy a way of life include Stanley Rosen, xix; Charles Griswold 1986:231; and of course Pierre Hadot, 91–93, 107, 154, 157. For the most part, mind you, Hadot focuses on Socratic (not Platonic) irony, as though Plato and Socrates always went hand in hand; he frequently assumes Socrates is speaking for Plato (see, e.g., 149 and 91, respectively).

110. I am grateful to Anthony Long for pressing me on this point, and to Charles Griswold and Lanier Anderson for their very helpful input. Patricia Slatin and Vanessa de Harven were each generous enough to engage in extended, copious, and immensely enlightening exchanges with me on the subject, and I am deeply appreciative in both cases.

111. Some, following Irwin (1979:240), might point to the fact that Socrates merely claims to "*attempt* the true political craft." (The Greek verb is ἐπιχειρεῖν, "to turn one's hand to.") The problem here is that Socrates immediately goes on, without qualification, to say that he is the only one who *does* politics. "I believe that I'm one of a few Athenians, so as not to say the only one, to attempt the true political craft [οἶμαι μετ' ὀλίγων Ἀθηναίων, ἵνα μὴ εἴπω μόνος, ἐπιχειρεῖν τῇ ὡς ἀληθῶς πολιτικῇ τέχνῃ] and the only one among our contemporaries to practice [the true] politics [καὶ πράττειν τὰ πολιτικὰ μόνος τῶν νῦν]" (*Gorg.* 521d, translation modified, italics mine). That the two verbs are being used quasi-synonymously may find some support in the *Apology* where—intriguingly enough— Socrates uses both terms in order to *deny* being a politician. His daimonion, he says here,

"has prevented me from taking part in politics [τὰ πολιτικὰ πράττειν]. . . . If I had long ago attempted to take part in politics [εἰ ἐγὼ πάλαι ἐπεχείρησα πράττειν τὰ πολιτικὰ πράγματα], I should have died long ago" (*Apol.* 31d; translation modified). I am grateful to Patricia Slatin for drawing my attention to this passage.

112. What Socrates actually says is very close to this, but not identical. Instead of admitting that he may well fail in his "political" mission, he says only that he may end up executed. He gives no sign of believing that execution will count as evidence of failure in his case, as near-execution ostensibly does in the case of Pericles.

113. To put it another way, if the problem were simply that Pericles set himself the wrong target, *the events of his life would be utterly irrelevant*. Even if he had gone throughout his career without the slightest hint of controversy and had been universally lionized by all Athenians, he would still, on this account, have been a bad citizen. So why bother bringing up his near-execution? Clearly what counts for Socrates are *results*, not just intentions.

114. Anytus, the most powerful of Socrates' three accusers, is a character in the *Meno*.

115. Again, I am borrowing this important observation from Nehamas 1999:70–71, 102. Plato himself, of course, could be cited as an example of someone whom Socrates converted to philosophy. But at the time of the (imagined) debate about Pericles, Plato was at most four years old.

116. Socrates to Callicles: "Now, please describe for me precisely the type of care for the city to which you are calling me. Is it that of striving valiantly with the Athenians to make them as good as possible, *like a doctor*, or is it like one ready to serve them . . . for their gratification?" (521a, my emphasis).

117. In 430 and 429 BC a plague struck Athens, wiping out up to a third of its inhabitants. The plague may have been caused by overcrowding, with the rural population having taken shelter behind the city walls. Perhaps this is what Socrates has in mind when he says that "the city is swollen and festering" as a result of the construction of walls and "such trash as that" (519a). That said, the dramatic date of the *Gorgias* is 427 BC—three years after the plague first broke out—and Gorgias and company remain sufficiently impressed to cite the long walls as one of Pericles' (and Themistocles') great achievements (455d-e). And as for dockyards, it is hard to see anyone doubting their importance to the Athenian cause.

118. Again, see Thucydides 1.90.3, Herodotus 7.144.1–2, and Irwin 1979:237. Thucydides (2.65.8–9) makes a special point of noting that Pericles, unlike his successors, never flattered the multitude and never pandered to its whims. When Socrates accuses Themistocles, Cimon, Miltiades, and Pericles of merely gratifying the Athenians (502e) and "filling up [their] appetites" (503c–d), it is hard to see on what he is basing his belief.

119. Pericles built or rebuilt a series of temples, including the Parthenon and the Propylaea. Socrates *does* refer to temples in the *Gorgias*, but only in the context of a hypothetical discussion about what kind of person should be entrusted with major building projects. He does *not* mention them, by contrast, when he comes to list the accomplishments of Pericles and company. Instead he says (we recall) that they "filled the city with harbors and dockyards, walls, and tribute payments and such trash as that [καὶ τοιούτων φλυαριῶν]" (519a).

120. At 464b–e, Socrates proposes a complicated set of distinctions. There are, he tells Polus, two genuinely skilled ways (τέχναι) of tending to bodies and two genuinely skilled ways of tending to souls. Gymnastics and medicine improve the body; legislation and justice, the twin branches of political craft, improve the soul. Corresponding to each τέχνη, meanwhile, is a counterfeit practice, a spurious non-craft that trades on appearances. Whereas gymnastics make the body actually *be* healthy, cosmetics make the body merely *seem* healthy; whereas medicine gives the body something that is actually good, cookery gives it something that is dressed up to appear good; so, too, sophistry is the deceptive double of legislation, rhetoric the deceptive double of justice. Later in the dialogue, Socrates twice rehearses similar arguments for Callicles' benefit. Neither Polus nor Callicles endorses the taxonomy, however. Polus simply ignores most of it and zeroes in on a single claim—oratory is flattery—that he takes to be unacceptable (466a). Callicles lends his assent, but only because he has decided to humor Socrates: "I'm going along with you, both

to expedite your argument and to gratify Gorgias" (501c); "Certainly, if that pleases you more" (514a); "You love to win, Socrates" (515b); "Oh yes, so I may gratify you" (516b).

121. Gorgias is the first to bring up the subject of the long walls (455e); he clearly considers them a major accomplishment. So too Callicles who, in response to Socrates' challenge to name great individuals from former times "through whom the Athenians are reputed to have become better" (503b), immediately cites Themistocles, Cimon, Miltiades, and Pericles.

122. Translation may not be our friend here, since these days "making souls better" commonly implies increasing their moral or religious standing. Gorgias, however, presumably considers himself to be making souls better by augmenting their rhetorical abilities and sense of power. "Soul" (ψυχή) needs to be understood more neutrally as something close to "inward part," "mind," or the like.

123. Another strange argument: one who takes care of animals is expected to make them gentler; human beings are animals; ergo, one who takes care of human beings is expected to make them gentler (516a–c). Using this logic one could also say that one who takes care of animals is expected to keep them locked in a barn; human beings are animals; ergo, one who takes care of human beings is expected to keep them locked in a barn.

124. Again, this is more or less the position of Socrates in the *Meno* (99b–c) and in the *Protagoras* (319e–320a).

125. Socrates: "whenever the city lays its hands on one of its politicians . . ., [the politicians say] they're being unjustly brought to ruin by it . . . . But that's completely false. Not a single city leader could ever be brought to ruin by the very city he's the leader of" (*Gorg.* 519b–c).

126. Notice (to repeat) that Gorgias does not claim to "teach justice" in the sense of teaching people to be just. He admits only to teaching them what justice *is*. Socrates: "Does he [the orator] lack knowledge . . . of what is good or what is bad, of what is admirable or what is shameful, or just and unjust [οὐκ εἰδώς, τί ἀγαθὸν ἢ τί κακόν ἐστιν ἢ τί καλὸν ἢ τί αἰσχρὸν ἢ δίκαιον ἢ ἄδικον]? . . . [And] must the prospective student of oratory already be knowledgeable in these things before coming to you? And if he doesn't, will you, the oratory teacher, not teach him?" (459d–e). Gorgias: "Well, Socrates, I suppose that if he really doesn't have this knowledge, he'll learn these things from me as well" (460a). If Gorgias had presented rhetoricians as ἀρετῆς διδάσκαλοι ("teachers of excellence," 519c), he might perhaps be in a different situation, forced to explain that his concept of excellence differs from that of Socrates. But as it is, he has no case to answer.

Chapter 5

1. *Three Novels*, 388–89; *L'innommable*, 169–71. In what follows, I will be using the following system of abbreviations for Beckett's corpus. *M* will stand for *Molloy* (the original French version); *MM* for *Malone meurt*; *I* for *L'innommable*; *NTR* for *Nouvelles et textes pour rien*; *CC* for *Comment c'est*. Where I cite from the English version of the trilogy (Beckett's own translation, for the most part), I will generally just give a page number.

2. The paradigmatic case is John Calder's *The Philosophy of Samuel Beckett*, a book which more or less opens with the claim that "what future generations can expect to find in his [Beckett's] work is above all an ethical and philosophical message; the novels and plays will increasingly be seen as the wrapping for that message" (1). So too the Hamiltons invoke "Beckett's message about man" (11); in Martha Nussbaum, Beckett's works are "an expression of a religious view of life" (1990b:309); in John Fletcher (1970:176), they point a moral; in David Hayman (156), they shed light on existence; in Hugh Kenner (10), they affirm some general truth; in Thomas Cousineau (120), they seek to convince; in Maurice Blanchot (1986:147–48), they make evident something that is merely implicit in other literary works; and in Georges Bataille (131), they are "telling us" about reality. (See also Iser 1978:260–61.)

   More promising readings have been put forward by Martin Esslin (10), who sees Beckett as attempting to re-create in the reader, in the manner of Eliot's "objective correlative," something *analogous* to his experience (instead of *expressing* it per se); by Brian Fitch, for whom the function of Beckett's works is that of allowing each reader to establish a relationship to him- or herself (1977:104); and by Anthony Uhlmann (2001:358) and Andrew Gibson (102), who, with a Heideggerian gesture that has become quite fashionable, present Beckett's works as making possible the advent of Being/truth (cf. perhaps Cousineau, 134–35). As chapter 1 indicates, I am sympathetic in general to the Clarification hypothesis. I am also sympathetic to the Revelation view with regard to certain fictions, though I am not convinced it applies particularly well to Beckett. In good measure this is because the telos here appears to be a Buddhist nothingness rather than a Heideggerian plenitude, a full absence (so to speak) rather than a full presence.

3. Thus Lawrence Miller: "the dilemmas Beckett explores . . . , while they have the form of failures of expressive ambition, are still expressive" (xi; cf. 134). Such readings often draw on the *Three Dialogues*, in which Beckett writes of the "expression that there is nothing to express, nothing with which to express, nothing from which to express, no power to express, no desire to express, together with the obligation to express" (103). To be sure, Molloy does suggest something of the sort—"not to want to say, not to know what you want to say, not to be able to say what you think you want to say, and never to stop saying . . . , that is the thing to keep in mind, even in the heat of composition" (28) [ne pas vouloir dire, ne pas savoir ce qu'on veut dire, ne pas pouvoir [dire] ce qu'on croit qu'on veut dire, et toujours dire . . . , voilà ce qu'il importe de ne pas perdre de vue, dans la chaleur de la rédaction (*M*, 36)]—but already here the ontological problem ("nothing to express") has dropped out, leaving only the epistemological ("not to know what you want to say"), the conative ("not to want to say"), and the expressive ("not to be able to say"); and later, as we shall see, these problems will find solutions of their own.

4. Thus the narrator of *The Unnamable* speculates as to why "they" have told him a particular story: "there's a story for you, that was to teach me the nature of emotion, that's called emotion, what emotion can do, given favourable conditions, what love can do, well well, so that's emotion, that's love, and trains, the nature of trains, . . . it was to teach me how to reason, it was to tempt me to go, to the place where you can come to an end" (407) [en voilà une histoire, c'était pour que je sache ce que c'est que l'émotion, ça s'appelle l'émotion, ce que peut l'émotion, données des conditions favorables, ce que peut l'amour, alors c'est ça l'émotion, ce que c'est que les trains, . . . c'était pour m'apprendre à raisonner, c'était pour m'induire à y aller, là où on peut finir (*I*, 200)]. Notice that there are three separate hypotheses here—instruction, training, manipulation—and that the instruction theory is bathetically undermined by the rather hilarious "trains."

Similar parody is to be found in *Molloy*, where the main character finds a "moral" in his vicious assault on a stranger: "So I smartly freed a crutch and dealt him a good dint on the skull. That calmed him. . . . People imagine, because you are old, poor, crippled, terrified, that you can't stand up for yourself, and generally speaking that is so. But given favourable conditions, a feeble and awkward assailant, in your own class what, and a lonely place, and you have a good chance of showing what stuff you are made of. And it is doubtless in order to revive interest in this possibility, too often forgotten, that I have delayed over an incident of no interest in itself, *like all that has a moral*" (84–85, my emphasis). [Je dégageai donc prestement une béquille et lui en assénai un bon coup sur le crâne. Cela le calma. . . . Les gens s'imaginent, parce qu'on est vieux, pauvre, infirme et craintif, qu'on est incapable de se défendre, et d'une manière générale, cela est vrai. Mais étant donné des conditions favorables, un agresseur débile et maladroit, à votre taille quoi, et un lieu écarté, il est quelquefois permis de montrer de quel bois on se chauffe. Et c'est sans doute aux fins de rappeler cette possibilité, trop souvent oubliée, que je me suis attardé sur un incident en lui-même sans intérêt, *comme tout ce qui instruit, ou avertit* (*M*, 113–14, my emphasis).]

5. *Molloy*, 64; "ne rien savoir, ce n'est rien, ne rien vouloir savoir non plus, mais ne rien pouvoir savoir, savoir ne rien pouvoir savoir, voilà par où passe la paix" (*M*, 85).

6. *Molloy*: "I grew calm again and was restored . . . to my old ataraxy" (42). [Je parvins à me calmer et à retrouver . . . cette ataraxie (*M*, 55).] *Watt*: "Watt suffered neither from the

presence of Mr Knott, nor from his absence. . . . This ataraxy covered the entire house-room, the pleasure-garden, the vegetable-garden and of course Arthur. So that when the time came for Watt to depart, he walked to the gate with the utmost serenity" (207–8).

7. He is, to be precise, a Pyrrhonian: unlike Academic skeptics, Pyrrhonian skeptics did not permit themselves to judge certain propositions more probable than others. For the connection between Beckett and ancient skepticism, see Steven J. Rosen, 52–54 (compare also Hesla, 121). Other interpreters, like Calder (1), have cast Beckett as an ancient *Stoic*; this, I think, is to miss the force of the carefully opposed claims. The vast majority, however, have not made the link to Hellenistic philosophy in any way. The *Beckett and Philosophy* collection (in which, predictably enough, twentieth-century skeptic Jacques Derrida is ubiquitous) makes no mention of Sextus Empiricus. Nor, incidentally, is there anything to speak of here on Malebranche, Leibniz, and Geulincx. Even Schopenhauer receives only sporadic mention—quite shocking, I think, given the title of the volume and given Beckett's deep engagement with *The World as Will and Representation*.

8. Needless to say, post-structuralist approaches to Beckett are legion. Many believe that language is the core issue in Beckett (see, e.g., Federman, 112) and/or that Beckett is keen to undermine its referential power (see, e.g., Fitch 1977:95–98). Beckett does indeed come close to such positions (the "German Letter" of 1937 articulates views on the subject), and they do make much more sense applied to *The Unnamable* than they do to, say, *In Search of Lost Time*. Still, Beckett ultimately departs from them in decisive if subtle ways. First of all, Beckett does *not* undermine the referential function of language in his works. Granted, his characters often fail to find adequate terminology for their condition and, in addition, sometimes lie (Moran, famously: "It was not midnight. It was not raining." [Il n'était pas minuit. Il ne pleuvait pas.]), but this is against a background of reasonable success (Moran must at least be telling the truth *now*, even if he wasn't earlier) without which, indeed, such predicaments would be meaningless. If there were absolutely no certainty, no doubt would be possible—what would it be doubt *about*?—and if there were no referentiality, no doubt could be transmitted. "No, he could never have spoken at all of these things, if all [of them] had continued to mean nothing, as some continued to mean nothing, that is to say, right up to the end" (*Watt*, 77).

Second, language is only one issue among many in Beckett. "There is no use indicting words," remarks Malone (195), "they are no shoddier than what they peddle." [Plus la peine de faire le procès aux mots. Ils ne sont pas plus creux que ce qu'ils charrient. (*MM*, 34)] The narrator in *The Unnamable* may keep repeating that the words he speaks are not his, but as we will see, the very act of saying this suggests the existence of a self standing back from the language it has inherited. Indeed at one point he switches from the mantra that "I'm all these words . . . and nothing else" to the striking admission that "yes, [I'm] something else, . . . I'm something quite different, a quite different thing, a wordless thing" (386) [je suis tous ces mots . . . et pas autre chose, si, tout autre chose, . . . je suis tout autre chose, une chose muette (*I*, 166)]. There *is* a preverbal self at work in Beckett's texts; there exists—and arguably, this character himself is—that purportedly impossible bête noire of the linguistically turned: a nonlinguistic mental entity.

And finally, the post-structuralist attitude would surely be a little too confident for Beckett's liking. Mercier (175) reports Beckett as dismissing a completely negative picture of existence: "that would be to judge, and we are not in a position to judge." The post-structuralists, Beckett might say, have it too easy; they neglect the possibility of uncertainty; they fail to recognize that thoroughgoing doubt is not a starting point but something that must be worked for.

On the non-centrality of language, cf. Badiou (in Gibson, 103); on the fundamental distinction between truth and falsehood, see Champigny, 123; on the retention of the referent, see P. J. Murphy, 236; on the success of communication, see Richardson, 137; on the ultimate positivity of Beckett, see Miller, xii; and on the foolishness of believing that skeptical theories will lead to revolution, see Bersani, who notes that in fact these ideas "are particularly congenial to political conservatism" (1970:331).

9. This is a crucial qualification. Unlike Richard Rorty, Beckett does not dismiss the history of philosophy as an uninterrupted series of groundless answers to pointless questions. He considers the questions urgent, and is entirely happy to endorse partial solutions (*ubi nihil vales, ibi nihil velis* being a powerful example) along the way. We should therefore not accept Adorno's verdict that in Beckett "philosophy ... proclaims its bankruptcy" (1982:121), Uhlmann's claim that all philosophy in Beckett is parody (Uhlmann 1999:158), or Hill's hypothesis that chapter 6 of *Murphy* is mock metaphysics (18). The separation between mind and body is something that Beckett takes very seriously; so too the question of how to find the self in order to lose it. As Mercier rightly suggests (169), philosophy in the trilogy is not just a matter of structural convenience but the very heart of the matter. (Cf. Wicker, 42.)

10. "I even feel a strange desire come over me," proclaims Malone at one point, "the desire to know what I am doing, and why. So I near the goal I set myself in my young days," he adds, *"and which prevented me from living"* (194, emphasis mine). [Je sens même une étrange envie me gagner, celle de savoir ce que je fais, et pourquoi, et de le dire. Ainsi je touche au but que je m'étais proposé dans mon jeune âge et qui m'a empêché de vivre (*MM*, 32).]

11. "La maladie principale de l'homme est la curiosité inquiète des choses qu'il ne peut savoir." In the Trotter translation, which I have modified slightly, this is fragment 18, p. 13.

12. εἰ μὲν φιλοσοφητέον φιλοσοφητέον καὶ εἰ μὴ φιλοσοφητέον φιλοσοφητέον· πάντως ἄρα φιλοσοφητέον (*Protrepticus* 7.27–28, in *Aristotelis fragmenta selecta*; translation modified).

13. The term is from Proust: "if intellect does not deserve the crown of crowns, only intellect is able to award it. And if intellect ranks only second in the hierarchy of virtues, intellect alone is able to proclaim that the first place must be given to instinct" (*By Way of Sainte-Beuve*, 21). Or again, "it is life that, little by little, case by case, enables us to observe that what is most important to our hearts or to our minds is taught us not by reasoning but by other powers. And then it is the intelligence itself which, acknowledging their superiority, abdicates to them through reasoning and consents to become their collaborator and their servant" (*The Fugitive*, 569).

14. Toward the end of *Texts for Nothing*, the narrator announces—with palpable relief—that "the wish to know ... is gone" (154) [le désir de savoir ... n'y est pas (*NTR*, 205)].

15. "What am I to do, what shall I do, what should I do, in my situation, how proceed? By aporia pure and simple? Or by affirmations and negations invalidated as uttered, or sooner or later? ... I say aporia without knowing what it means. Can one be ephectic otherwise than unawares? I don't know" (291). [Comment faire, comment vais-je faire, que dois-je faire, dans la situation où je suis, comment procéder? Par pure aporie ou bien par affirmations et négations infirmées au fur et à mesure, ou tôt ou tard. ... [J]e dis aporie sans savoir ce que ça veut dire. Peut-on être éphectique autrement qu'à son insu? Je ne sais pas (*I*, 7–8).] *Ephexis* is another word for suspension of judgment.

16. 406; "on annonce, puis on renonce, c'est ainsi, ça fait continuer, ça fait venir la fin" (*I*, 199). This continues into the *Texts for Nothing*: "And it's still the same road I'm trudging, *up yes and down no*, towards one yet to be named, *so that he may leave me in peace*"; "believing *this, then that, then nothing more*" (144–45, my emphasis). [Et je suis encore en route, par oui et par non, vers un encore à nommer, pour qu'il me laisse la paix (*NTR*, 189–90); j'ai ... une tête qui croit ceci, qui croit cela, qui ne croit plus (*NTR*, 190–91).]

17. "Car en moi il y a toujours eu deux pitres, entre autres, celui qui ne demande qu'à rester là où il se trouve et celui qui s'imagine qu'il serait un peu moins mal plus loin. ... Et je leur cédais à tour de rôle, à ces tristes compères, pour leur permettre de comprendre leur erreur" (*M*, 64). (For the English, see the epigraph to the present chapter.) Note, again, that it is not just a matter of deciding to give up and stay put; the speaker of that thought is every bit as much a "fool" as the voice of optimism. We may find a welcoming ditch from time to time, but it is not permitted us to linger there. (Even Murphy has to *rock* himself into stillness.) Resignation is not waiting to be found but must be *made*, at the cost of painstaking labor—the labor, precisely, of indulging antithetical foolishnesses turn and turn about. I am grateful to Phil Galligan for pressing me on this point.

18. Something of the Pyrrhonian tradition resurfaced during the twentieth century in the form of Ludwig Wittgenstein's later work. "Thoughts that are at peace. That is what someone who philosophizes yearns for," Wittgenstein famously announced (*Culture and Value*, 43); and again, equally famously, "the real discovery is the one that makes me capable of stopping doing philosophy when I want to.—The one that gives philosophy peace, so that it is no longer tormented by questions which bring *itself* in question" (*Philosophical Investigations*, sec. 133). Following Wittgenstein, Richard Rorty strenuously advocated a dissolution of those "pseudo-problems" that, on his account, stand in the way of real-world progress: "the vocabulary which centers around these traditional distinctions [appearance-reality, matter-mind, made-found, sensible-intellectual, etc.] has become an obstacle to our social hopes" (1999:xii). (On Beckett and Wittgenstein, see Miller, esp. 16–17; on Wittgensteinian echoes of Sextus, see Plant; on the "therapeutic" approach to Wittgenstein's philosophy, see Hagberg; for a different way of linking Beckett and Wittgenstein, see Perloff.)

   It is more helpful, however, to align Beckett with Sextus than with Wittgenstein or Rorty. There is, to start with, some debate over Wittgenstein's own position on the role of philosophy. And as for Rorty, he differs from Beckett over the issues (Beckett would not entirely agree with his list of "pseudo-problems"), the goal (Beckett has little interest in "social hope"), and above all the method. Rorty, who brooks no distinction between language and thought, proposes the "gradual inculcation of new ways of speaking" (Rorty in Niznik and Sanders, 34), while famously continuing to speak just like everyone else. Beckett, by contrast, joins Sextus in offering a *spiritual exercise*, one that uses language to affect something that is *not* language, and one that also depends on individual effort.

19. Sextus Empiricus 1.8 (p. 7). See also 1.31 (pp. 20–23) and 1.232 (pp. 142–43).

20. Richard Rorty's view is that if we just read enough different approaches to a given question from the history of philosophy, this alone will suffice to make us despair of ever making any progress. Pragmatists, he writes, "follow Hegel in saying that 'philosophy is its time grasped in thought.' Anti-pragmatists follow Plato in striving for an escape from conversation to something atemporal which lies in the background of all possible conversations. I do not think one can decide between Hegel and Plato *save by meditating on the past efforts of the philosophical tradition* to escape from time and history. One can see these efforts as worthwhile, getting better, worth continuing. Or one can see them as doomed and perverse. I do not know what would count as a noncircular metaphysical or epistemological or semantical argument for seeing them in either way. So I think that *the decision has to be made simply by reading the history of philosophy and drawing a moral*" (1982:174, my emphasis). Beckett would disagree.

21. Cf. *The Calmative* (in *Complete Short Prose*, 62): "All I say cancels out, I'll have said nothing." [Tout ce que je dis s'annule, je n'aurai rien dit. (*NTR*, 41)] Compare also Hesla, 114.

22. *Murphy*, 245–46. One of the most delightful instances of cancellation in all of Beckett is the chess game Murphy plays with Endon in the asylum (*Murphy*, 243–45). If one follows the moves listed in the text in standard chess notation, one realizes that Endon's initial "strategy" has been gradually to return every possible piece to its starting position, and Murphy's has been to mirror Endon. In the end, Murphy resigns: once again we see the familiar pattern of *assertion*, *retraction*, and *resignation*.

23. *Murphy*, 148–49. Cf. "the deeper silence succeeding Pim's song" (*How It Is*, 58). Compare also Deleuze: "un vrai silence, pas une simple fatigue de parler" (66–67).

24. 369; "quand tout se taira, quand tout s'arrêtera, c'est que les mots auront été dits, ceux qu'il importait de dire" (*I*, 138). Cf. *Malone*: "if I ever stop talking it will be because there is nothing more to be said" (236) [si jamais je me tais c'est qu'il n'y aura plus rien à dire (*MM*, 103)].

25. 291; "peut-on être éphectique autrement qu'à son insu?" (*I*, 8).

26. Cf. "I'll be silence, I'll know I'm silence, no, in the silence you can't know" (*Texts for Nothing*, 132, lacking in the original [*NTR*, 169]); the last six words here echo the famous "in the silence you don't know" (414) [dans le silence on ne sait pas (*I*, 213)] from the trilogy's final sentence. In *The Unnamable*, it might be argued that the character Worm is a thought

experiment designed to test whether it is possible to start from ignorance and move to awareness of that ignorance—without anything further—just as the character Mahood could be seen, conversely, as a thought experiment designed to test whether it is possible to start from knowledge and reach ignorance while still retaining just that much awareness.

27. "Être vraiment enfin dans l'impossibilité de bouger, ça doit être quelque chose! ... Et avec ça ... la perte de la mémoire! Et juste assez de cerveau resté intact pour pouvoir jubiler!" (*M*, 191).

28. I am speaking figuratively here: there are, of course, plenty of additional disparities between Beckett and the ancient skeptics. Unlike Beckett, for example, the skeptics were perfectly happy to let philosophical investigation (*zetesis*) continue, just so long as it remained undogmatic; nor did they consider the overcoming of individuation a necessary stepping-stone on the way to ataraxia. This latter idea, as we are about to see in part 2, is more the legacy of Schopenhauer. That said, the core of the Beckettian position—that tranquility is the goal, and that self-cancelling mental operations are the central means— remains heavily ancient-skeptical.

29. Cf. Badiou, Scarry, and Miller. Badiou: "we should also refrain from the belief that Beckett sinks into an interrogation that is sufficient unto itself, solving none of the problems that it has posed. On the contrary, the work of the prose is intended to isolate and allow to emerge the few points with respect to which thinking can become affirmative" (41). Scarry: "given complexity and uncertainty, Beckett, in effect, clears the boards and begins again with those things about which we can be certain" (92). Miller: "as the novel [*The Unnamable*] progresses, a surplus of uncancelled affirmations and meaning accumulates" (168).

30. I am drawing on the comprehensive study of Beckettian rhetoric by Bruno Clément. See esp. 41, 36.

31. In *The Unnamable*, likewise, the narrator frequently claims to know just one thing, only to retract or betray this self-restriction: "I don't know who it's all about, that's all I know, *no, I must know something else*" (404) [je ne sais pas de qui il s'agit, c'est tout ce que je sais, non, je dois savoir autre chose (*I*, 196)]; "I haven't stirred, that's all I know, *no, I know something else*, it's not I, I always forget that" (412) [je n'ai pas bougé, c'est tout ce que je sais, non, je sais autre chose, ce n'est pas moi, je l'oublie toujours (*I*, 210)]; "it's not worth having, that's all I know, it's not I, that's all I know, ... you must go on, that's all I know" (414) [il ne vaut rien, c'est tout ce que je sais, ce n'est pas moi, c'est tout ce que je sais ... il faut continuer, c'est tout ce que je sais (*I*, 212)]. (Cf., in *Texts for Nothing*, "I'm here, that's all I know, *and that it's still not me*" [113]; "je suis ici, c'est tout ce que je sais, *et que ce n'est toujours pas moi*" [*NTR*, 136].) My emphasis throughout. In cases like these, we should be distrustful of the speaker's distrust.

32. "Au bout il y avait deux renfoncements, non, ce n'est pas le mot. ... J'entrai dans l'un des recoins, non plus ... je traversai l'impasse pour aller dans l'autre chapelle, voilà" (*M*, 81). This is Clément's "metabole" (Clément 46–47); on the search for the *mot juste*, see also Fitch 1961:17. An example in *The Unnamable*—"the earth would have to quake, it isn't earth, one doesn't know what it is, it's like sargasso, no, it's like molasses, no, no matter ... it's like potter's clay ... it's like shit, there we have it at last, there it is at last, the right word, one has only to seek, seek in vain, to be sure of finding in the end, it's a question of elimination" (364–65) [il faudrait que la terre tremble, ce n'est pas de la terre, on ne sait pas ce que c'est, c'est comme de la sargasse, non, c'est comme de la mélasse, non plus, n'importe ... c'est comme de la fange ... c'est comme de la glaise ... c'est comme de la merde, voilà enfin, le voilà enfin, le mot juste, il suffit de chercher, il suffit de se tromper, on finit par trouver, c'est une question d'élimination (*I*, 129–31)]—is oddly misread by Sherzer, who sees it as proving that "words are inadequate" (95). It "proves," if anything, just the opposite.

33. Here is one more, with emphasis added: "Respite then, once in a way, if one can call that respite, when one waits to know one's fate, saying, Perhaps it's not that at all, and saying, Where do these words come from that pour out of my mouth, and what do they mean, no, saying nothing, for the words don't carry any more, if one can call that waiting, when

there's no reason for it, and one listens, *that stet*, without reason, as one has always listened, because one day listening began, because it cannot stop, that's not a reason, if one can call that respite." (370) [Donc repos tous les, si on peut appeler ça un repos, où l'on attend, de connaître son sort, en disant, D'où viennent ces mots qui me sortent par la bouche et que signifient-ils, non, en ne disant rien, car les mots n'arrivent plus, si on peut appeler ça une attente, où il n'y a pas de raison, où l'on écoute, *ça stet*, sans raison, comme depuis le début, parce qu'on s'est mis un jour à écouter, parce qu'on ne peut plus s'arrêter, ce n'est pas une raison, si on peut appeler ça un repos. (*I*, 139)]

34. By *refinement* I mean a narrowing of the circle around the object, a tightening of the net, an increase in conceptual clarity (example: not a recess, not an alcove, but a chapel). By *qualification* I mean the addition of restrictions, limiting a claim's application to *some* of the relevant class of phenomena at *some* times from *some* angles. Here is a beautiful specimen, doubly qualifying, from the "we would seem to know for certain" sentence in *The Unnamable*: "there is no great difference here between one expression and the next, when you've grasped one you've grasped them all . . . all, how you exaggerate, always out for the whole hog, the all of all and the all of nothing, never in the happy golden, never, always, it's too much, too little, [*it would be better to say*] often, seldom" (388); [ça ne change guère, ici, d'une expression à l'autre, qui en saisit une les saisit toutes . . . toutes, comme vous y allez, toujours pour le tout, le tout qu'est tout, le tout qu'est rien, jamais dans le milieu, jamais, toujours, c'est trop, c'est trop peu, souvent, rarement (*I*, 169)]. Are *all* expressions functionally identical? No; *many* may be, but some are not. The narrator has exaggerated here, just as he always does—but no, this too is an exaggeration: sometimes he exaggerates and sometimes he doesn't.

35. Cf. Solomon, 144; Tesanovic, 181. I am grateful to Phoebe Prioleau for these references.

36. Cf. Hesla, 115–16.

37. *Watt*, 117, my emphasis. Cf. *Watt*, 78: "to explain had always been to exorcize, for Watt."

38. Will, for example, a particular character reappear? "I'll never see him again, yes I will . . . he'll come back, to keep me company, only the wicked are solitary, I'll see him again . . . or he'll never come back, *it's one or the other*" (398) [je ne le verrai plus, si . . . il reviendra, me tenir compagnie, seuls les méchants sont seuls, je le reverrai . . . ou il ne reviendra pas, *de deux choses l'une* (*I*, 186)]. (Emphasis mine.) Hypothesis one: the character will reappear. Hypothesis two: the character will not reappear. Hypothesis three: we are not in a position to know; such "evidence" as we have for one side or another is never going to be sufficient.

39. *Pace* Ruby Cohn, who sees Beckett's work as "a comedy or irony *dissolving without resolving* the classical questions about the quiddity of the world and that of man, about the center of the self . . ." (1962:167, my emphasis).

40. One fascinating example is the story "they" tell the narrator in *The Unnamable*, the story of an ill-fated love affair. It ends with the husband committing suicide and his body being cut down from its noose by his mother or mother-in-law while the wife remains locked out of the house. The tale raises two questions of interest to the narrator: (1) who locked the door that the wife finds shut; (2) whose mother cuts the body down. Now whereas the first question cannot be answered, the second *can*, as it turns out. "[S]he takes down her son, or her son-in-law, I don't know, *it must be her son, since she cries* . . . it isn't the son-in-law and the daughter, it's the daughter-in-law and the son, how I reason to be sure this evening, it was to teach me how to reason, it was to tempt me to go, to the place where you can come to an end" (406–7) [elle pousse des cris déchirants, tout en dépendant son fils, ou son gendre, je ne sais pas, *ça doit être son fils, puisqu'elle crie* . . . ce n'est pas le gendre et la fille, c'est le fils et la bru, comme je raisonne bien ce soir, c'était pour m'apprendre à raisonner, c'était pour m'induire à y aller, là où on peut finir (*I*, 200)]. (Emphasis mine.) Reason, then, by allowing us both to make reliable deductions and to draw a line around what can be known in any given circumstance, both to solve and to dissolve, is what allows us, eventually, to "come to an end."

41. *The Unnamable*, 377. ("Mais voyons, mon cher, voilà, voilà qui vous êtes, regardez cette photo, et voici la fiche . . ., faites un effort, à votre âge, être sans identité, c'est une honte"

[*I*, 150].) Could the identity crisis be prompted by the need for authentic action—the need, that is, to know what would count as doing that which one really wants? Perhaps Moran, who initially accepts without murmur the task imposed on him from without, slowly begins to ask himself what is motivating him to continue; perhaps this in turn leads to a probing of the self; and perhaps, as Edith Kern and others have suggested, the action of the Moran segment is in fact the earliest action depicted in the trilogy. See Kern, 41; Janvier 58; Hesla, 96.

42. Beckett did note the importance of diachronic concerns in Proust's novel—here, as he put it, "life is a succession of habits, since the individual is a succession of individuals" (*Proust*, 19)—and made room for them, too, in his own work. In the first volume of the trilogy, Moran is rendered speechless (154; *M*, 209–10) by the fact that he feels the same while having clearly altered: "Question. How did I feel?/Answer. Much as usual./Question. And yet I had changed and was still changing?/Answer. Yes./Question. And in spite of this I felt much as usual?/Answer. Yes./Question. How was this to be explained?/Answer." [*Question*. Comment me sentais-je?/*Réponse*. A peu près comme d'habitude./*Question*./Pourtant j'avais changé et je changerais toujours?/*Réponse*. Oui./*Question*. Et malgré cela je me sentais à peu près comme d'habitude?/*Réponse*. Oui./*Question*. Comment cela se faisait-il?/*Réponse*.] And for the narrator of *The Unnamable*, the problem appears even starker, his life appearing to vary by the second ("you talk of time, seconds of time, there are some people [who] add them together to make a life, I can't, each one is the first" (395) [on parle du temps, des secondes, il y en a qui les ajoutent les unes aux autres pour en faire une vie, moi je ne peux pas, chacune est la première (*I*, 181)]). Under such circumstances, how is one to think of one's life as a totality? "All my life long," says Malone, "I have dreamt of the moment when . . . I might draw the line and make the tot" (181) [toute ma vie j'ai rêvé du moment où . . . je pourrais tirer le trait et faire la somme (*MM*, 11)]. "Moment upon moment, pattering down," agrees Hamm in *Endgame*, "and all life long you wait for that to mount up to a life" (70). [Instants sur instants, plouff, plouff, . . . et toute la vie on attend que ça vous fasse une vie (*Fin de partie*, 93).] All this said, synchronic issues, to which I now turn, are vastly more important in Beckett.

43. Some have sought to add supplementary, spurious problems, as though matters were not sufficiently complicated. Astro, for example, decides that "insofar as a hat can change wearers," this "shows how questionable [the] sense of self is" (58). That is certainly a new approach. In an effort to extend suspicion beyond the human realm, Hill claims that "objects do not conform to the rules of clear and distinct identity" (71), his main evidence being the strange item that may or may not be a knife-rest. As Steven J. Rosen points out, however (10), this item is still *something*—it has, in Molloy's words, "a most specific function" (64)—and so the problem here is merely an epistemological one. Further, there are plenty of objects, like bicycles, that cause no such trouble. "What a rest to speak of bicycles and horns," sighs Molloy, quite understandably (16); "I would gladly write four thousand words on it alone," echoes Moran (155). [Parler de bicyclettes et de cornes, quel repos (*M*, 20); j'écrirais volontiers quatre mille mots dessus (*M*, 211).] As for the sucking-stones, it is surely not the case that because they all taste the same, it follows that they "have no essential identity" (Hill, 72). Again, a difficulty we may have in telling particulars apart (by means of a single sensory faculty, at that!) should not be mistaken for a lack of individuating properties inherent in each.

44. Astro, 67–74; Fletcher 1970:158–62. Molloy is not a native speaker of French: "je dirais brandissais," he says, "si j'ignorais encore mieux le génie de *votre* langue" (*M*, 46, my emphasis).

45. In Gaelic, *baile* means "town"; rather delightfully, then, Molloy comes from a town called Town.

46. "Two shapes . . . entered into collision before me. They fell and I saw them no more. I naturally thought of the pseudocouple Mercier-Camier" (*The Unnamable*, 296–97). [Deux formes . . . sont entrées en collision devant moi. Elles sont tombées et je ne les ai plus vues. J'ai naturellement pensé au pseudocouple Mercier-Camier (*I*, 16).]

47. The jar metaphor (or jar symbol, by the end) crops up in all three parts of the trilogy—"I stayed in my jar" (*Molloy*, 49); "perhaps after all I am in a kind of vault" (*Malone*, 219); "my

jar" (*The Unnamable*, 340)—as well as in *Murphy*: "Murphy's mind pictured itself as a large hollow sphere, hermetically closed to the universe without" (107). [French: "je restais dans ma boîte" (*M*, 65); "Peut-être après tout que je suis dans une sorte de caveau" (*MM*, 74); "ma jarre" (*I*, 89).] For the elastic, see *Molloy*, 11: "in spite of my soul's leap out to him, at the end of its elastic, I saw him only darkly" [malgré cet élan vers lui de mon âme, au bout de son élastique, je le voyais mal (*M*, 13)].

48. Beckett to Cissie Sinclair, August 14, 1937, *Letters* 536. Alain Badiou has recently suggested that Beckett shifts, in the course of his career, toward a greater attention to (and belief in) interaction with others. This chronology seems hard to sustain, given (1) late single-character works like *Ping*; (2) early multiple-character works like *Murphy* (or indeed *Mercier et Camier*, which brings the "pseudocouple" on stage for the first time); and (3) the continued failure of meaningful communication (think of the "language lesson" in *How It Is*, Hamm and Clov in *Endgame*, Winnie and Willie in *Happy Days*, and so on).

49. 19; "si je dois chercher un jour un sens à ma vie, on ne sait jamais, c'est de ce côté-là que je gratterai d'abord" (*M*, 23).

50. 391; "je cherche ma mère, pour la tuer" (*I*, 175).

51. Not everyone would agree with this assumption—Maurice Merleau-Ponty, for example, would presumably differ—and not everyone would attribute it to Beckett. Paul Davies believes that Molloy is *wrong* to take the attitude he does; he and Beckett's other characters are, he says, "casualties of Cartesianism" (45).

52. 330; "l'âme étant notoirement à l'abri des ablations et délabrements" (*I*, 73).

53. "And when I see my hands . . . they are not mine" (66); "My feet, you see, never took me to my mother unless they received a definite order to do so" (30). Cf. Malone: "my feet . . . are so much further from me than all the rest, from my head I mean, for that is where I am fled" (234). [Et quand je regarde mes mains . . . elles ne sont pas à moi (*M*, 88); Mes pieds, voyez-vous, ne me conduisaient jamais chez ma mère sans une injonction de plus haut, à cet effet (*M*, 38); mes pieds . . . tellement plus loin de moi que tout le reste, de ma tête je veux dire, car c'est là où je me suis réfugié (*MM*, 99).] For all this, cf. Fletcher 1970:140–42.

54. This is not to discount John Locke's claim that "as far as any intelligent being can repeat the idea of any past action with the same consciousness it had of it at first, and with the same consciousness it has of any present action; so far it is the same personal self" (*Essay*, 2.17.10). Personal identity, for Locke, does not require that we recall everything that has happened in our life; on the contrary, a single incident will do—"*any* past action"—or indeed a rotation of different single incidents. It is not the events themselves that define us, then, or the fact that we remember them, but the *way* in which we remember them, the specific "consciousness" we have of them.

55. *Krapp's Last Tape*, 58.

56. Cf. Hesla, 118. This point is similar to the problem noted by Hume—"when I enter most intimately into what I call *myself*, I always stumble on some particular perception or other . . . I can never catch *myself*" (*Treatise*, 252)—and to Kant's observation, in the *Critique of Pure Reason*, that "in the representation 'I am,' nothing manifold is given" (Ak. B 138; p. 157 in the Kemp Smith translation). The French version of the *Malone* line runs as follows: "c'est sur moi que mes sens sont braqués . . . Je ne suis pas pour eux" (*MM*, 19).

57. The narrator of *The Unnamable* appears at one point to wonder if he himself might be the pineal gland: "perhaps that's what I am, the thing that divides the world in two, on the one side the outside, on the other the inside . . . I'm neither one side nor the other, I'm in the middle . . . on the one hand the mind, on the other the world, I don't belong to either" (383). [C'est peut-être ça que je suis, la chose qui divise le monde en deux, d'une part le dehors, de l'autre le dedans . . . je ne suis ni d'un côté ni de l'autre, je suis au milieu . . . d'un côté c'est le crâne, de l'autre le monde, je ne suis ni de l'un ni de l'autre (*I*, 160).] Descartes' earliest readers raised questions about the interaction problem, and he responded, tellingly enough, by placing it entirely outside of his philosophical system. Although his methodological principles commit him to endorsing only those ideas that can be perceived clearly and distinctly, to distrusting the evidence of the senses, and to meditating his way

into the truth, he nonetheless informs Princess Elizabeth of Bohemia that "it is . . . by *abstaining* from meditating . . . that one learns to conceive the union of soul and body" (my emphasis). "What belongs to the union of soul and body can be understood only in an obscure way," he adds, "even when the intellect is aided by imagination, but is understood very clearly by means of the senses" (letter of June 28, 1643, in *Philosophical Writings,* 279–80).

58. 297–98. "Je les vois encore, mes délégués. Il m'en ont raconté sur les hommes, sur la lumière. Je n'ai pas voulu les croire. N'empêche qu'il m'en est resté. Mais où, quand, par quelle voie, me suis-je entretenu avec ces messieurs? Sont-ils venus me déranger ici? Non, ici personne ne m'a jamais dérangé. Ailleurs alors. Mais je n'ai jamais été ailleurs. . . . Ce qui me laisse perplexe, c'est de devoir ces connaissances à des gens avec qui je n'ai jamais pu entrer en communication. Enfin le fait est là. A moins que ce ne soient des connaissances innées, comme celles ayant trait au bien et au mal. Cela me semble peu vraisemblable. Une connaissance innée de ma mère, par exemple, est-ce concevable? Pas pour moi" (*I*, 17–18).

59. Kant: "We have, then, to explicate the concept of a will that is to be esteemed in itself and that is good apart from any further purpose, *as it already dwells in natural sound understanding and needs not so much to be taught as only to be clarified*—this concept that always takes first place in estimating the total worth of our actions and constitutes the condition of all the rest" (*Groundwork*, 397, my emphasis). Kant departed from the empiricists in considering the mind pre-equipped with enough material to reach nontrivial conclusions on its own (in technical language, to make synthetic a priori judgments). Prior to the passage from *The Unnamable* mentioned above, the debate between Kant and the empiricists already surfaces in Molloy's speculation as to what he is free to know—"to know, but what, the laws of the mind perhaps" (13) [de savoir, mais quoi, les lois de la conscience peut-être (*Molloy*, 16)]—and in Malone's hilarious invention of a character, Jackson, who attempts to teach his parrot the scholastic dictum "nihil in intellectu quod non prius in sensu" (nothing is in the intellect that was not first in the senses). "All he had to offer in the way of dumb companions was a pink and grey parrot. He used to try and teach it to say, Nihil in intellectu, etc. These first three words the bird managed well enough, but the celebrated restriction was too much for it, all you heard was a series of squawks" (218). [En fait de compagnons muets il ne disposait que d'un perroquet, gris et rouge, auquel il apprenait à dire, Nihil in intellectu, etc. Ces trois premiers mots, l'oiseau les prononçait bien, mais la célèbre restriction ne passait pas, on n'entendait que couah couah couah couah couah (*MM*, 72).]

60. In Descartes, God's goodness guarantees that any "clear and distinct" ideas we have must correspond to the way things are in reality; God is not a deceiver. Molloy, by contrast, rather hilariously reverses this: "I think that all that is false may more readily be reduced," he says, "to notions clear and distinct" (82). [Je crois que tout ce qui est faux se laisse davantage réduire, en notions claires et distinctes (*M*, 110).] Cf. Kenner, 120; Pilling 1976:113–14.

61. Cf. *How It Is*: "suddenly yip left right off we go . . . the dog follows . . . no reference to us | it had the same notion at the same instant | Malebranche less the rosy hue" (30) [soudain hop gauche droite nous voilà partis . . . le chien suit . . . rien à voir avec nous | il a eu la même idée au même instant | du Malebranche en moins rose (*CC*, 45)]. On Malebranche and company, see Pilling 1976:116; Ruby Cohn 1965:170; Bersani 1970:313. Here and throughout I insert vertical bars into quotations from *How It Is*, for the sake of clarity.

62. 12, my emphasis. "À un moment donné, préétabli si vous voulez, moi je veux bien, le monsieur revint sur ses pas" (*M*, 14). Cf. "I am . . . out in the heart again of the pre-established harmony, . . . which makes so sweet a music" (*Molloy*, 62); "[je suis] à nouveau en plein dans l'harmonie préétablie, qui fait une si douce musique" (*M*, 83).

63. 1.12, pp. 5–6; 1.29, p. 11. Translation slightly modified.

64. *Molloy*, 27, 49. French: "ce fossé. J'y disparaîtrais volontiers, m'enfonçant de plus en plus sous l'influence des pluies" (*M*, 35); "ma vie que faisait sienne ce jardin chevauchant la terre des abîmes et des déserts. Oui, il m'arrivait d'oublier non seulement qui j'étais, mais que j'étais, d'oublier d'être" (*M*, 64–65).

65. 149; "il me devenait indifférent de me posséder" (*M*, 202).

66. In *Not I*, too, the protagonist believes she has been called upon to "tell how it had been": "something she had to tell . . . could that be it? . . . something that would tell . . . how it was . . . something that would tell how it had been . . . how she had lived . . . lived on and on. . ." (221). In *Texts for Nothing*, intriguingly, the narrator feels a similar desire but attributes it directly to himself rather than to any outside entity: "a story is not compulsory, just a life, that's the mistake I made, . . . to have wanted a story for myself, whereas life alone is enough" (116) [une histoire n'est pas de rigueur, rien qu'une vie, voilà le tort que j'ai eu, . . . m'être voulu une histoire, alors que la vie seule suffit (*NTR*, 142)].

67. 396; "j'ai inventé mes souvenirs . . . pas un seul n'est sur moi" (*I*, 182).

68. At the close of their narrations, Molloy and Moran both end up referring to themselves in the third person: "Molloy could stay, where he happened to be" (91); "it [the voice] did not use the words that Moran had been taught when he was little" (176). [Molloy pouvait rester, là où il était (*M*, 124); elle ne se servait pas des mots qu'on avait appris au petit Moran (*M*, 238).] The feeling is one of serenity—the ultimate goal is still that of over-coming selfhood—but since only the *me* is involved and not the *I*, since Molloy and Moran are becoming mere characters in the process of being sloughed off, this serenity is neces-sarily short-lived.

69. 236; "à ce moment-là c'en sera fait des Murphy, Mercier, Molloy, Moran et autres Malone" (*MM* 103).

70. "While waiting I shall tell myself stories, if I can" (180); "all is pretext, Sapo and the birds, Moll, the peasants . . . , pretext for not coming to the point" (276). Compare *Molloy*—"what I need now is stories" (13)—and *The Unnamable*: "perhaps I shall be obliged, in order not to peter out, to invent another fairy-tale" (307). [D'ici là je vais me raconter des histoires, si je peux (*MM* 8); tout est prétexte, Sapo et les oiseaux, Moll, les paysans . . . , prétexte pour ne pas en venir au fait (*MM*, 171); ce dont j'ai besoin c'est des histoires (*M*, 15); je vais peut-être être obligé, afin de ne pas tarir, d'inventer encore une féerie (*I*, 35).]

71. 195; "je recommençais. Mais peu à peu dans une autre intention. Non plus celle de réussir, mais celle d'échouer" (*MM*, 34).

72. 189; "je me demande si ce n'est pas encore de moi qu'il s'agit, malgré mes précautions. Vais-je être incapable, jusqu'à la fin, de mentir sur autre chose?" (*MM*, 23).

73. 32; "on croit inventer, s'échapper, on ne fait que balbutier sa leçon, des bribes d'un pensum appris et oublié" (*M*, 41). This "pensum" recurs in *The Unnamable*—"yes, I have a pensum to discharge, before I can be free. . . . I was given a pensum, at birth perhaps, as a punish-ment for having been born perhaps, . . . and I've forgotten what it is" (310) [oui, j'ai un pensum à faire, avant d'être libre. . . . On m'a donné un pensum, à ma naissance peut-être, pour me punir d'être né peut-être, . . . et j'ai oublié en quoi il consiste (*I*, 39)]—and then again in the English version of *Texts for Nothing* (129; cf. *NTR*, 165). Compare also *Watt*: "Watt spoke as one speaking to dictation, or reciting, parrot-like, a text, by long repetition become familiar" (156).

74. 412; "toutes ces histoires de voyageurs, ces histoires de coincés, elles sont de moi" (*I*, 210). In *How It Is*, again, "you invent | but real or imaginary | no knowing" (72) [on invente | mais comment savoir | imaginaire | réel | on ne peut pas (*CC*, 113)].

75. Cf. Abbott, who notes that in the trilogy "creation becomes reportage" just as much as "reportage becomes creation" (114–15).

76. 394; "je raconterai une vieille histoire de Mahood, n'importe laquelle, elles sont toutes pareilles" (*I*, 179).

77. This may be what Bersani has in mind when he writes that Malone "gives the lie to the impossibility of expression" (1970:319).

78. 52, 34; my emphasis. In the original, "je préférais le jardin à la maison, à en juger par les longues heures que j'y passais" (*M*, 69); "je devais avoir besoin de ma mère, sinon pourquoi m'acharner à aller chez elle?" (*M*, 44).

79. Beckett's clearest acknowledgment of a true self which assures the consistency of an indi-vidual's beliefs, desires, and actions across time, which cannot be put into propositional language, and to which artists strive to give expression, is to be found in his essay "Les

deux besoins." "Il n'y a sans doute que l'artiste qui puisse finir par voir . . . la monotone centralité de ce qu'un chacun veut, pense, fait et souffre, de ce qu'un chacun est," he writes here. "Ce foyer, autour duquel l'artiste peut prendre conscience de tourner, comme la monade . . . autour d'elle-même, on ne peut évidemment [pas] en parler . . . sans en falsifier l'idée" (*Disjecta*, 55). The entity that, in *The Unnamable*, "seems the truest possession, because the most unchanging" (346) [ce qu'ayant de moins changeant on croit avoir de plus réel (*I*, 100)] may well be that same *foyer*.

80. "There is no one, I've looked, no one but me, no, not me either, I've looked everywhere, [yes,] there must be someone, the voice must belong to someone . . ., I am it" (408) [il n'y a personne, . . . j'ai cherché, il n'y a que moi, non plus, moi non plus, j'ai cherché partout, il doit y avoir quelqu'un, cette voix doit appartenir à quelqu'un . . . je suis elle (*I*, 203)]. Cf. *Texts for Nothing*, 146: "a voice speaks that can be none but mine, since there is none but me" [une voix parle qui ne peut être que la mienne, puisqu'il n'y a que moi (*NTR*, 193)].

81. That, of course, is Descartes' *cogito*. Beckett quoted an antecedent thereof—Augustine's *fallor ergo sum*—in his early poem *Whoroscope*. For another instance of a quasi-cogito, cf. *How It Is*: "my voice otherwise nothing | therefore nothing otherwise my voice | therefore my voice" (95) [ma voix sinon rien | donc rien sinon ma voix | donc ma voix (*CC*, 149)]; on the unreliability of the claim "it's not I," cf. P. Davies, 53.

82. Cf. Fitch 1977:65 (and to some extent Bersani 1970:314, 327).

83. "And another question, what am I doing in Mahood's story, and in Worm's, or rather what are they doing in mine, there are some irons in the fire to be going on with, let them melt" (377) [et, autre question, que viens-je faire dans ces histoires de Mahood et de Worm, ou plutôt que viennent-ils faire dans la mienne, en voilà du pain sur la planche, qu'il y moisisse (*I*, 149)]. Other examples (with emphasis added): "I would sweep, with the *clipped wings of necessity*, to my mother" (27); "I can't believe it. *No, I will not lie, I can easily conceive it*" (14); "I looked at the plain rolling away as far as the eye could see. *No, not quite so far as that*" (91) [pour que j'y vole, chez ma mère, sur les ailes *de poule* de la nécessité (*M*, 35); Je ne peux le croire. *Non, je ne mentirai pas, je le conçois facilement* (*M*, 17); Je regardai la plaine qui se déferlait devant moi à perte de vue. *Non, pas tout à fait à perte de vue* (*M*, 122)]. On Beckett's use of clichés, see Barry, *passim*.

84. 390–91; "quand j'y pense, au temps que j'ai perdu avec ces paquets de sciure, à commencer par Murphy, qui n'était pas le premier, alors que je m'avais moi, à domicile, sous la main, croulant sous mes propres peau et os, des vrais, crevant de solitude et d'oubli, au point que je venais à douter de mon existence, et encore, aujourd'hui, je n'y crois pas une seconde, de sorte que je dois dire, quand je parle, Qui parle" (*I*, 173).

85. 388; "il y a moi, je le sens, oui, je l'avoue, je m'incline, il y a moi" (*I*, 169).

86. So too in *How It Is*, the narrator finally comes to an acknowledgment that the voice has all along been his own: "that wasn't how it was | no | not at all | no . . . there was something | yes | but nothing of all that | no | all balls from start to finish | yes | this voice quaqua all balls | yes | only one voice here | yes | mine | yes . . . I have a voice | yes | in me | yes . . . I murmur | yes . . . | I | yes" (144–45); "never any procession | no | nor any journey | no | never any Pim | no | nor any Bom | no | never anyone | no | only me . . . yes | so that was true | yes | it was true about me | yes . . . only me in any case | yes | alone | yes | in the mud | yes | the dark | yes . . . my voice | yes | mine | yes | not another's | no | mine alone | yes | sure | yes" (146). Compare *Not I*: "a voice she did not recognize . . . at first . . . so long since it had sounded . . . then finally had to admit . . . could be none other . . . than her own" (219). (French originals in *Comment c'est*: "ça s'est passé autrement | oui | tout à fait | oui . . . il s'est passé quelque chose | oui | mais rien de tout ça | non | de la foutaise d'un bout à l'autre | cette voix quaqua | oui | de la foutaise | oui | qu'une voix ici | oui | la mienne | oui . . . j'a[i] une voix moi | oui | en moi | oui . . . je murmure moi | oui . . . | moi | oui" [224–25]; "jamais eu de procession | non | ni de voyage | non | jamais eu de Pim | non | ni de Bom | non | jamais eu personne | non | que moi . . . oui | ça alors c'était vrai | oui | moi c'était vrai | oui . . . que moi en tout cas | oui | seul | oui | dans la boue | oui | le noir | oui . . . moi | oui | ma voix à moi | oui | pas à un autre | non | à moi tout seul | oui | sûr | oui" [226–27].)

87. See Nehamas 1998:2–5, and Anderson and Landy, 26.

88. Many, needless to say, are those who claim that in Beckett the self is straightforwardly nonexistent. Thus Northrop Frye: "in *The Unnamable* we come as near to the core of the onion as it is possible to come, and discover of course [*"of course"!*] that there is no core, no undividable unit of continuous personality" (32). Solomon too refers to "the empty core of being"; Fitch concurs that the self is a void (1977:99, 104); and if we are to follow Webb's logic, "since the Unnamable cannot even find his own voice among the voices of the characters speaking through him, the whole issue of personal identity dissolves into meaninglessness" (E. Webb, 82). Other critics seem to take up a rather uncertain stance on the subject. Thus Bersani reads the trilogy and *How It Is* as "Beckett's efforts to approach that *reality* of consciousness about which language lies" (1970:315, my emphasis)—but then goes on to declare that the notion of a self prior to expression is an illusion (330). Reversing the order, Thiher begins by saying that it is "farcical" to think that there is something beyond language (87)—and then, two pages later, presents Beckett's texts as "allow[ing] for the view that there might be . . . a self to be translated by what is other than the self of language" (89). Cousineau somehow manages to articulate both positions (the self is inexpressible, the self is pure nothingness) on a single page (116). There is, however, a third group of readers who feel, as O'Hara does, that "if a specific succession of local phenomena deserves to be named Molloy or Moran or Malone or Mahood, it is because something—the identity, the self—has remained constant despite or within this flux" (14). Wolfgang Iser, who writes that "what cannot be integrated is shown to be the true reality, which defies the effort of the conscious mind to grasp it" (1978:171), should be included in that bracket.

89. Following Deleuze and Guattari, Cousineau claims (18–20) that the destruction of the self in Beckett is designed to reawaken primal desire, the desire one had in an original state of fragmentation prior to the advent of the "I." There really is not much evidence for this. Quite the contrary, there are strong suggestions that desire is precisely what is to be overcome, and that the telos is the Schopenhauerian-Skeptical one of freedom from yearning and freedom from care.

90. 127; "j'aimerais savoir si j'ai tout fait, avant de me porter manquant, et d'abandonner" (*NTR*, 161).

91. To be precise, Molloy does not quite use the term "anthropologie négative"—a phrase that appears in Beckett's posthumously published *Eleuthéria* (146)—but it is nonetheless clearly implicit in the connection he draws between anthropology and negative theology. "What I liked in anthropology," he says, "was . . . its relentless definition of man, as if he were no better than God, in terms of what he is not" (39) [ce que j'aimais dans l'anthropologie, c'était sa puissance de négation, son acharnement à définir l'homme, à l'instar de Dieu, en termes de ce qu'il n'est pas (*M*, 51–52)]. On negative theology, cf. Schwab, 115 (though Schwab believes that the self is a pure nothingness); on the *via negativa*, cf. Hesla, 115, and Champigny, 122.

92. "First I'll say what I'm not, that's how they taught me to proceed, then what I am" (326) [je dirai d'abord ce que je ne suis pas, c'est comme ça qu'ils m'ont appris à procéder, puis ce que je suis (*I*, 65)]. Sure enough, in a single sentence the narrator dismisses three successive hypotheses: *not* a corpse, *not* a fetus, *not* a spermatozoon (379–80). On this point, cf. Prioleau, 65.

93. As in Proust, so in Beckett each protagonist is in search of self; as in Proust, so in Beckett each has to surmount Humean challenges to personal identity; as in Proust, so in Beckett each resorts to telling his life in the form of a somewhat fictionalized story. Yet unlike in Proust, the characters never reach a very clear understanding of who they are; unlike in Proust, their stories fail to unify a life across time; and unlike in Proust, above all, the aim is not, in the end, to have or find or fashion a self. Here, quite the contrary, the aim is to lose, or dismantle, or stop having one. Beckett, I think, accepts what Proust believes about what it would take to be a self; he accepts the nature of the difficulties standing in the way; he accepts that human beings experience an urge to overcome these difficulties, and to discover or create a coherent identity for themselves; *but he does not agree that this is a good*

thing. Selfhood, for Beckett, is something to be escaped, not embraced. The real aim is tranquility, and tranquility means returning to a (literal or metaphorical) oneness of being.

On Beckett's somewhat ambivalent relationship to Proust, see Zurbrugg, 263. The playful mockery is at its most delicious, it seems to me, in the first volume of the trilogy: "And *if I had not lost my sense of smell* the smell of lavender would always make me think of Lousse," writes Molloy, "in accordance with the well-known mechanism of association" (48, my emphasis). [Et j'aurais conservé le sens de l'odorat que l'odeur du spic me ferait toujours penser à Lousse, selon le mécanisme bien connu de l'association (*M*, 63).]

94. 391; "je cherche ma mère, pour la tuer, il fallait y penser plus tôt, avant de naître" (*I*, 175). Perhaps there is a connection here with Mahood's fond hope that he ended up in the innards of his mother: "I like to fancy, even if it is not true, that it was in mother's entrails I spent the last days of my long voyage" (323–24) [j'aime à penser, quoique je n'en aie pas la certitude, que c'est dans le bas-ventre de maman que j'ai terminé, pendant des journées entières, mon long voyage (*I*, 61–62)]. And cf. also, in *Texts for Nothing*, "he's looking for me to kill me" (114) [il me cherche pour me tuer (*NTR*, 140)].

95. *How It Is*: "We'll end | if we ever end | by having been" (108; this is a departure from the original French, which reads simply "nous finirons bien par avoir été" [*CC*, 168]). *Texts for Nothing*: "get into my story in order to get out of it" (112; "aller dans mon histoire, pour pouvoir en sortir" [*NTR*, 135–36]). *The Unnamable*: "I don't say they won't catch me in the end. I wish they would, to be thrown away" (346) [je ne dis pas qu'ils ne finiront pas par m'avoir. Je le voudrais bien, pour être jeté (*I*, 98–99)].

Elsewhere in *The Unnamable*, the narrator presents himself as striving "to know what I am . . . *and what I should do to stop being it*" (412) and "to say what has to be said, about me, . . . *so as to have nothing more to say*" (394); for their part, his putative tormentors may well be "waiting for me to say I'm someone, to say I'm somewhere, *to put me out, into the silence*" (410) [savoir qui je suis . . . *et comment faire pour ne plus l'être* (*I*, 209); dire ce qu'il faut dire, sur moi . . . *pour n'avoir plus rien à dire* (*I*, 179); c'est peut-être ce qu'ils attendent, . . . que je me dise quelqu'un, que je me dise quelque part, *pour me mettre dehors, dans le silence* (*I*, 206)]. My emphasis throughout.

96. Thus Tesanovic: "Ainsi va la continuation circulaire dans la *Trilogie*, conçue comme un perpetuum mobile textuel. . . . Ce mouvement incessant à l'intérieur d'un cercle . . . fait partie du méta-discours de l'échec, pour lequel la répétition est de règle" (101, 107).

97. These characters are all avatars or projections of a single consciousness: "I am neither . . . Murphy, nor Watt, nor Mercier, nor—no, I can't even bring myself to name them, nor any of the others whose very names I forget, who told me I was they, who I must have tried to be" (326). [Je ne suis . . . ni Murphy, ni Watt, ni Mercier, non, je ne veux pas les nommer, ni aucun des autres dont j'oublie jusqu'aux noms, qui m'ont dit que j'étais eux, que j'ai dû essayer d'être (*I*, 65).] Cf. 303, 395–96, 390, 403 (*I*, 28, 173, 182, 194–95).

98. In spite of all the hesitations, retractions, and confusions, an overall progression is nonetheless discernible. One by one, the narrator of *The Unnamable* disposes of Mahood (375; *I*, 147), Worm (378, 390; *I*, 151, 173), and the nebulous outsiders who have been directing and observing him ("and the voice goes on, it's not theirs, they were never there . . . there was never anyone, anyone but me, anything but me, talking to me of me" [394–95]); he acknowledges that the various characters have been figments of his imagination ("I invented him [Mahood], him and so many others" [395]); he speculates that speaking of them, rather than of himself, has been his big mistake ("when I think of the time I've wasted with these bran-dips, beginning with Murphy, who wasn't even the first, when I had me . . . within easy reach" [390]); and he even grudgingly concedes that he may be the one who has been speaking the entire time ("who is talking, not I . . . it's I am talking" [385–86]; "it was never I, I've never stirred, I've listened, [no,] I must have spoken, why deny it, why not admit it" [412]). [Et la voix continue, ce n'est pas la leur, ils n'ont jamais été là . . . il n'y a jamais eu personne, personne que moi, rien que moi, me parlant de moi (*I*, 179–80); c'est moi qui l'ai inventé, lui et tant d'autres (*I*, 182); quand j'y pense, au temps

que j'ai perdu avec ces paquets de sciure, à commencer par Murphy, qui n'était pas le premier, alors que je m'avais moi, à domicile, sous la main (*I*, 173); qui est-ce qui parle, ce n'est pas moi qui parle . . . c'est moi qui parle (*I*, 165–66); ça n'a jamais été moi, je n'ai pas bougé, j'ai écouté, [non,] j'ai dû parler, pourquoi vouloir que non (*I*, 219–20).] By the end, there is not a single mention of the characters, or of "them"; everything is about the narrator himself; and the possibility opens up of an eventual release from affliction.

99. 315; "tiens, c'est une idée . . . j'arriverai presque peut-être, à coups de mutilations . . . à faire figure de moi" (*I*, 47).

100. Cf. Kern, 42 ("the destruction of the body and the senses is a further stripping away of all that is contingent in order to bare that which is essential"); O'Hara, 14 ("the progress of the trilogy and indeed of Beckett's fiction is in large measure the peeling of the self toward its ideal core"); and Hesla, 115.

101. "When I was ill," Beckett wrote to Tom MacGreevy in 1937, "I found the only thing I could read was Schopenhauer. . . . I always knew he was one of the ones that mattered most to me, and it is a pleasure more real than any pleasure for a long time to begin to understand now why it is so" (September 21, 1937, *Letters* 550). Whether Beckett actually subscribes to the full-blown metaphysics of *The World as Will and Representation* or whether he just uses it strategically, as a story that could yield further impetus to the overcoming of self, Schopenhauer remains a crucial inspiration throughout his career.

102. It is perhaps worth insisting that even under the Schopenhauerian two-world scenario, the self does not just disappear immediately in a puff of metaphysics. Scholars who speak of Beckett putting the self in doubt usually have in mind a contrast between entities that exist and pseudo-entities that do not: while the self is an illusion, they would say, the body (for instance) is real. This, however, is not the kind of appearance/reality distinction Schopenhauer is proposing. From a Schopenhauerian standpoint, bodies are just as much a part of the world as representation as anything else, and therefore just as illusory in a strictly metaphysical sense. Conversely, individual existents remain phenomenological realities (realities, that is, within the world as representation). Everything we see may be illusory, but the self is not *especially* illusory; no more illusory, for example, than bodies or Pomeranians or post-structuralist theorists.

103. 197; "les formes sont variées où l'immuable se soulage d'être sans forme" (*MM*, 38).

104. *WWR* 1:51, p. 254 (translation slightly modified); Beckett, *Proust*, 67. The phrase "socii malorum," which Beckett again borrows from Schopenhauer, means "companions in misery."

105. *Malone*, 259; *Unnamable*, 310; *Texts*, 117. French: "du moment que c'est encore ce qu'on appelle un vivant il n'y a pas à se tromper, c'est le coupable" (*MM*, 142); "pour me punir d'être né" (*I*, 39); "cette instance obscure où être est être coupable" (*NTR*, 145–46).

106. *Murphy*, 244, footnote (b).

107. See Reginster, 122. Compare, in *Watt*, the longing for longing: "then the gnashing ends, or it goes on, and one is in the pit, in the hollow, *the longing for longing gone*, the horror of horror, and one is in the hollow, at the foot of all the hills at last, the ways down, the ways up, and free, free at last, for an instant free at last, nothing at last" (202, my emphasis). Cf. also *Anna Karenina* (529): "he [Vronsky] was soon aware that there was springing up in his heart a desire for desires—*ennui*."

108. *WWR*, 1:52, p. 260; *Watt*, 44. "Prog" is food obtained by begging.

109. Hope in Beckett is always cruel. "Is not a uniform suffering preferable," asks the trilogy's final narrator, "to one which, by its ups and downs, is liable at certain moments to encourage the view that perhaps after all it is not eternal?" (367). Alas, the powers that be are continually prone to "arrange for me to have little attacks of hope from time to time" (397). (Cf. *Molloy*, 83: "From time to time. What tenderness in these little words, what savagery.") [Une souffrance étale n'est-elle pas préférable à celle dont les fluctuations donnent par instants à croire qu'après tout elle ne durera peut-être pas toujours? (*I*, 134); ils s'arrangeraient pour que je puisse avoir des poussées d'espoir . . . ils s'arrangeraient . . . pour que j'imagine des choses, de temps en temps (*I*, 185); De temps en temps. Quelle bonté dans ces petits mots, quelle férocité. (*M*, 112).]

110. Malone describes Macmann as "seeking a way out . . . in helplessness and will-lessness" (278) [cherchant une issue . . . vers la noire joie de passer seul et vide, ne rien pouvant, ne rien voulant (*MM*, 173–74)]. Cf. *Murphy*: "Thus as his body set him free more and more in his mind, he took to spending less and less time in the light, spitting at the breakers of the world; and less in the half light, where the choice of bliss introduced an element of effort; and more and more in the dark, in the will-lessness, a mote in its absolute freedom" (113). It should be noted that suicide is not an acceptable option, since suicide is still an act of will (see Schopenhauer, *WWR*, 1:69, pp. 398–400). Death must, instead—as Molloy says—be a matter of "backsliding": "I took the vegetable knife from my pocket and set about opening my wrist. But pain soon got the better of me . . . life seems made up of backsliding, and death itself must be a kind of backsliding" (61). [Je pris dans ma poche le couteau à légumes et m'appliquai à m'en ouvrir le poignet. Mais la douleur eut vite fait de me vaincre . . . la vie est faite de récidives, on dirait, et la mort aussi doit être une sorte de récidive (*M*, 82).]

111. In Schopenhauer the connection to Eastern philosophy is explicit throughout; in Beckett there are only brief allusions, as when the narrator of *How It Is* mentions an "oriental" who "has renounced." "I too will renounce," he continues, "I will have no more desires" (56) [un oriental | mon rêve | il a renoncé | je renoncerai aussi | je n'aurai plus de désirs (*CC*, 87)].

112. As Geulincx sees it, we have no control over events in the world or even over our *volitions* but only over our *attitude* toward said events and volitions, and we may as well align that attitude with the will of God. Why, asks Geulincx, pray for storm on a sunny day? All we have, to borrow another beautiful image from Geulincx (*Annotata ad ethicam*, 167), is the freedom to roam the deck of a ship that is bearing us off. Adding in some details of his own—the ship is that of Odysseus, travelling west; the passenger is a galley-man, crawling east—Beckett recycles the metaphor on numerous occasions. *Molloy*: "Geulincx . . . left me free, on the black boat of Ulysses, to crawl towards the East, along the deck. That is a great measure of freedom for him who has not the pioneering spirit" (51). *The Unnamable*: "I. Who might that be? The galley-man, bound for the Pillars of Hercules, who drops his sweep under the cover of night and crawls between the thwarts, towards the rising sun, unseen by the guard, praying for storm" (336). *The Unnamable* again: "I am he who will never be caught, never delivered, who crawls between the thwarts, towards the new day that promises to be glorious, festooned with lifebelts, praying for rack and ruin" (339). *How It Is*: "little heap in the stern | it's me . . . I'm looking for an isle | home at last . . . I fall on my knees | crawl forward | clink of chains" (86). [Geulincx . . . m'accordait la liberté, sur le noir navire d'Ulysse, de me couler vers le levant, sur le pont. C'est une grande liberté pour qui n'a pas l'âme des pionniers (*M*, 67); Je. Qui ça? Le galérien, fonçant vers les piliers d'Hercule, qui la nuit, trompant la vigilance du garde-chiourme, lâche sa rame et rampe entre les bancs, vers le levant, en appelant l'orage (*I*, 83); Je suis celui qu'on n'aura pas, qui ne sera pas délivré, qui rampe entre les bancs, vers le nouveau jour qui s'annonce splendide, bardé de ceintures de sauvetage, appelant le naufrage (*I*, 87); Petit tas à l'arrière | moi . . . je cherche une île | home enfin . . . je tombe à genoux | rampe vers l'avant | cliquetis de chaînes (*CC*, 134–35).] On Geulincx, see Ruby Cohn 1965:172.

113. Beckett borrows this line in *Murphy*—"in the beautiful Belgo-Latin of Arnold Geulincx: *Ubi nihil vales, ibi nihil velis*" (178)—and cites it again, as a crucial source of his writing, in a famous letter to Sigle Kennedy of June 14, 1967 (quoted in *Disjecta*, 113). "If I were in the unenviable position of having to study my work," he writes here, "my points of departure would be the 'Naught is more real . . .' and the 'Ubi nihil vales . . .' both already in *Murphy* and neither very rational." As for "naught is more real," it is an allusion to Democritus's (and Leucippus's) belief that "being is no more real than not-being" (οὐθὲν μᾶλλον τὸ ὂν τοῦ μὴ ὄντος εἶναί φασιν [Aristotle, *Met.* 1, 985b8–9])—which is to say, the void exists just as much as atoms do. Beckett deploys it not only in *Murphy* ("his other senses also found themselves at peace . . . not the numb peace of their own suspension, but the positive peace that comes when the somethings give way, or perhaps simply add up, to the Nothing, than which in the guffaw of the Abderite [Democritus] naught is more real" [246]) but also in *Malone Dies* (192; *MM*, 30).

114. In the second volume, Schopenhauer adds that "an individual human being may alter the very ground of being, right up to using a 'different kind of willing' in order to will the Will out of existence" (*WWR*, 2:37); "the accident (the intellect), so to speak, subdues and eliminates the substance (the will)" (*WWR*, 2:30). In both cases, however, it is unclear whether what is "eliminated" is the individual will or the Will in general (there is of course no difference in capitalization in the original German).

115. "C'est la terre qui tourne qui fait ça, qui fait que la terre ne tourne plus . . . que la souffrance cesse" (*I*, 156); "notre justice . . . veut ça aussi | tous morts ou personne" (*CC*, 205). Cf. "then it will be over, thanks to me all will be over, and they'll depart, one by one, or they'll drop . . . and never move again, thanks to me" (376) [alors ce sera fini, grâce à moi ce sera fini, ils s'en iront, un à un, ou ils tomberont . . . ils ne bougeront plus, grâce à moi (*I*, 148)].

116. The final narrator: "by far the better of these hypotheses, *from the point of view of usefulness*, is the former" (296) [au point de vue de l'utilité, c'est la première de ces hypothèses de loin la meilleure (*I*, 16)]. Cf. *Watt*, 37: "of these two explanations Watt thought he preferred the latter, *as being the more beautiful*." Emphasis mine in both cases.

117. 12; "à un moment donné, préétabli si vous voulez, moi je veux bien . . ." (*M*, 14).

118. 36; "ne serait-on pas libre? C'est à examiner" (*M*, 47). Cf. *The Unnamable*: "The problem of liberty too, *as sure as fate*, will come up for my consideration *at the pre-established moment*" (338, my emphasis). [Le problème de la liberté, j'en traiterai aussi, c'est couru, au moment préétabli (*I*, 86).]

119. 14, 91. "Et moi qu'étais-je venu y faire? C'est ce que nous allons essayer de savoir. D'ailleurs ne prenons pas ces choses-là au sérieux" (*M*, 17); "que ce fût ma ville ou non, que sous ces frêles fumées quelque part ma mère respirât ou qu'elle empestât l'atmosphère à cent milles de là, c'étaient là des questions prodigieusement oiseuses, pour un homme dans ma situation, quoique d'un indéniable intérêt sur le plan de la connaissance pure" (*M*, 123). It is worth noting that by the end of the novel, readers care as little as he does whether or not Molloy has reached what he took to be his goal.

120. 348; "ils doivent m'estimer suffisamment abruti, avec leurs histoires d'être et d'existence" (*I*, 103).

121. 137; "au profit du vrai propos, dont d'abord tout dépend, puis beaucoup, puis peu, puis rien" (*NTR*, 177).

122. The enthymeme idea is to be found in "Les deux besoins" (*Disjecta*, 57): "aux enthymèmes de l'art," Beckett writes here, "ce sont les conclusions qui manquent et non pas les prémisses."

123. 414; "il faut continuer, je ne peux pas continuer, je vais continuer" (*I*, 213).

124. 413, my emphasis; cf. Hesla, 120. Original: "il faut vite essayer, avec les mots qui restent" (*I*, 211).

125. In an interview (Shenker, 148), Beckett famously declared *The Unnamable* an absolute terminus: "in the last book—'L'Innommable'—there's complete disintegration. No 'I,' no 'have,' no 'being.' No nominative, no accusative, no verb. There's no way to go on." It is surely not true that, as Ludovic Janvier claims (71), the final page of *Malone Dies* already conveys a sense of completion, with the protagonist having found the core of his being and having thus been able to make an end. Janvier himself appears, ten pages later (81), to retract this idea.

126. "Je ne vais pas pouvoir continuer en tout cas. Mais je dois continuer. Je vais continuer" (*I*, 177); "je ne peux pas continuer, il faut continuer, je vais donc continuer" (*I*, 213); "il faut continuer, je ne peux pas continuer, je vais continuer" (*I*, 213). In the English version this begins earlier, with "I can't go on" already on page 386; the original, however, reads simply "j'en ai assez" (*I*, 165).

127. "When all goes silent, and comes to an end, it will be because the words have been said, those it behoved to say, no need to know which, no means of knowing which, they'll be there somewhere, in the heap, in the torrent, not necessarily the last. . . . Perhaps they are somewhere there, the words that count, in what has just been said, the words it behoved to say, they need not be more than a few. . . . I hear them whispering[,] . . . [']We'll have to go through it all again, in other words, or in the same words, arranged differently[']"

(369–70). [Quand tout se taira, quand tout s'arrêtera, c'est que les mots auront été dits, ceux qu'il importait de dire, on n'aura pas besoin de savoir lesquels, on ne pourra pas savoir lesquels, ils seront là quelque part, dans le tas, dans le flot, pas forcément les derniers.... Ils sont peut-être là-dedans, quelque part, dans ce qu'ils viennent de dire, les mots qu'il fallait dire, ils ne sont pas forcément nombreux.... je les entends murmurer ... Tout est à recommencer, dans d'autres termes, ou dans les mêmes termes, autrement ordonnés (*I*, 138–39).] In *Texts for Nothing*, again, "I say it, patiently, variously, trying to vary, for you never know, it's perhaps all a question of hitting on the right aggregate" (133) [je le dis, patiemment, en variant, en essayant de varier, car on ne sait jamais, il s'agit peut-être seulement de tomber sur le bon agrégat (*NTR*, 172)]. So too in *Not I*: "try something else ... think of something else ... hit on it in the end ... think everything [if you] keep on long enough ... then forgiven" (222).

Many of Beckett's works play with permutation (Molloy's sucking-stones, Murphy's biscuits, the combinatory form of the later dramas). Could it be that permutation is *an algorithm for saying everything* and thus leaving nothing further ever to be said? "Let us go on," says Molloy, "on and on heaping up and up, until there is no room, no light, for any more" (14) [poursuivons ... meublons, meublons, jusqu'au plein noir (*M*, 17)]. Could it be something akin to Arthur C. Clarke's vision of Tibetan monks devising a computer program to find all the names of God and thereby bring the universe to an end? (The last line of Clarke's story [1967:11]: "Overhead, without any fuss, the stars were going out.")

128. This is not the standard view—see, e.g., Solomon, 145—but P. Davies (63) and Hesla (122, 128) share it, more or less.

129. Sextus: "Sceptics are philanthropic and wish to cure ... the Dogmatists" (3.280, p. 216).

130. Beckett: "I am interested in the shape of ideas even if I do not believe in them." (See Hobson, 153.)

WORKS CITED

Abbott, H. Porter. *The Fiction of Samuel Beckett: Form and Effect.* Berkeley: U California P, 1973.

Abrams, M. H. *The Mirror and the Lamp: Romantic Theory and the Critical Tradition.* Oxford: Oxford UP, 1953.

Acheson, James. "Murphy's Metaphysics." *The Beckett Studies Reader.* Ed. S. E. Gontarski. Gainesville: U P of Florida, 1993. 78–93.

Adelman, Gary. *Naming Beckett's Unnamable.* Cranbury, NJ: Associated University Presses, 2004.

Adorno, Theodor. *Aesthetic Theory.* Trans. C. Lenhardt. Ed. Gretel Adorno and Rolf Tiedemann. Oxford: Routledge, 1984 [1970].

———. "Commitment." *The Essential Frankfurt Reader.* Ed. Andrew Arato and Eike Gebhardt. Oxford: Blackwell, 1978. 300–318.

———. *Minima Moralia: Reflections from Damaged Life.* Trans. Samuel Weber and Shierry Weber. London: Verso, 1967.

———. "Reconciliation under Duress." *Aesthetics and Politics.* Ed. Ronald Taylor. London: NLB, 1977. 151–76.

———. "Trying to Understand Endgame." Trans. Michael T. Jones. *New German Critique* 9.2 (1982): 119–50.

Allen, R. E. *The Dialogues of Plato.* 4 vols. New Haven, CT: Yale UP, 1984.

———. "The Elenchus of Agathon: *Symposium* 199c–201c." *Monist* 50 (1966): 460–63.

Alter, Robert. *Partial Magic.* Berkeley: U California P, 1975.

Anderson, Daniel E. *The Masks of Dionysos: A Commentary on Plato's "Symposium."* Albany: SUNY P, 1993.

Anderson, R. Lanier, and Joshua Landy. "Philosophy as Self-Fashioning: Alexander Nehamas's Art of Living." *Diacritics* 31 (2001): 25–54.

Aquinas, Thomas. *Basic Writings of Saint Thomas Aquinas: God and the Order of Creation.* Trans. Anton Charles Pegis. Indianapolis: Hackett, 1997.

Arieti, James. *Interpreting Plato: The Dialogues as Drama.* Savage, MD: Rowman & Littlefield, 1991.

Aristotle. *Aristotelis fragmenta selecta.* Ed. David Ross. Oxford: Oxford UP, 1955.

———. *Metaphysics.* Ed. W. Christ. Leipzig: Teubner, 1906.

———. *Nicomachean Ethics.* Trans. Terence Irwin. Indianapolis: Hackett, 1985.

———. *On Poetics.* Trans. Seth Benardete and Michael Davis. South Bend, IN: St. Augustine's P, 2002.

———. *Physics.* Trans. Robin Waterfield. Oxford: Oxford UP, 1996.

———. *Poetics.* Trans. W. H. Fyfe. London: William Heinemann, 1932.

———. *Politics.* Trans. C. D. C. Reeve. Indianapolis: Hackett, 1998.

Astro, Alan. *Understanding Samuel Beckett.* Columbia: U South Carolina P, 1990.

Augustine. *Quaestiones evangeliorum.* Turnholt: Brepols, 1980.

Austin, J. L. *How to Do Things with Words.* Ed. J. O. Urmson and Marina Sbisá. Cambridge, MA: Harvard UP, 1975.

Badiou, Alain. *On Beckett.* Trans. Nina Power and Alberto Toscano. Manchester: Clinamen P, 2003.

Baghramian, Maria. "Strategies of Self-Deception." *Irish Philosophical Journal* 3.2 (1986): 83–97.

Baird, J. Arthur. "A Pragmatic Approach to Parable Exegesis: Some New Evidence on Mark 4:11, 33–34." *Journal of Biblical Literature* 76 (1957): 201–7.

Baird, William. "What Is the Kerygma? A Study of I Cor. 15:3–8 and Gal. 1:11–17." *Journal of Biblical Literature* 76 (1957): 181–91.

Bakhtin, M. M. *The Dialogic Imagination.* Trans. Caryl Emerson and Michael Holquist. Austin: U Texas P, 1981.

———. *Rabelais and His World.* Trans. Hélène Iswolsky. Bloomington: Indiana UP, 1988.

Balzac, Honoré de. "Avant-Propos." *La comédie humaine.* Vol. 1. Paris: Gallimard, 1951 [1842]. 3–16.

Barfield, Steven. "Beckett and Heidegger: A Critical Survey." *Beckett and Philosophy.* Ed. Richard Lane. London: Palgrave, 2002. 154–65.

Barker, Andrew. "The Daughters of Memory." *Musica e Storia* 2 (1993): 171–90.

Barnum, P. T. *The Life of P. T. Barnum, Written by Himself.* London: Sampson Low, 1855.

Barry, Elizabeth. *Beckett and Authority: The Uses of Cliché.* Houndmills: Palgrave Macmillan, 2006.

Barthes, Roland. "From Work to Text." Trans. Stephen Heath. *Image, Music, Text.* New York: Noonday P, 1988. 155–64.

———. "Longtemps, je me suis couché de bonne heure." Trans. Richard Howard. *The Rustle of Language.* New York: Hill & Wang, 1986. 277–90.

———. *On Racine.* Trans. Richard Howard. New York: Hill & Wang, 1964.

———. *The Pleasure of the Text.* Trans. Richard Miller. New York: Hill & Wang, 1975.

———. *S/Z.* Trans. Richard Miller. New York: Hill & Wang, 1975.

Bataille, Georges. "Molloy's Silence." Trans. John Pilling. *On Beckett: Essays and Criticism.* Ed. S. E. Gontarski. New York: Grove P, 1986. 131–39.

Baudelaire, Charles. "Further Notes on Edgar Poe." Trans. P. E. Charvet. *Baudelaire: Selected Writings on Art and Artists.* London: Penguin, 1972 [1857]. 188–208.

———. *Oeuvres complètes.* Paris: Robert Laffont, 1980.

Beardsley, Monroe C. *Aesthetics from Classical Greece to the Present.* Tuscaloosa: U Alabama P, 1975.

Beauvoir, Simone de. *Que peut la littérature?* Paris: Union générale d'éditions, 1965.

Beckett, Samuel. *Cap au pire.* Paris: Minuit, 1991.

———. *Comment c'est.* Paris: Minuit, 1961.

———. "Eh Joe." *Samuel Beckett: Collected Shorter Plays.* New York: Grove P, 1984. 199–207.

———. *Eleuthéria.* Paris: Minuit, 1995.

———. *Endgame.* New York: Grove, 1958.

———. *Fin de partie.* Paris: Minuit, 1957.

———. "German Letter of 1937." *Disjecta: Miscellaneous Writings and a Dramatic Fragment.* Ed. Ruby Cohn. London: John Calder, 1983. 51–54, 170–73.

———. *How It Is.* New York: Grove P, 1964.

———. "Krapp's Last Tape." *Samuel Beckett: Collected Shorter Plays.* New York: Grove P, 1984. 53–63.

———. *L'innommable.* Paris: Minuit, 1953.

———. *La dernière bande, suivi de Cendres.* Paris: Minuit, 1959.

———. *The Letters of Samuel Beckett.* Vol. 1, *1929–1940.* Ed. George Craig, Martha Dow Fehsenfeld, Dan Gunn, and Lois More Overbeck. Cambridge: Cambridge UP, 2009.

———. *Malone meurt.* Paris: Minuit, 1951.

———. *Molloy.* Paris: Minuit, 1951.

———. *Murphy.* New York: Grove P, 1957.

———. "Not I." *Samuel Beckett: Collected Shorter Plays.* New York: Grove P, 1984. 213–23.

———. *Nouvelles et textes pour rien.* Paris: Minuit, 1958.

———. "Play." *Samuel Beckett: Collected Shorter Plays.* New York: Grove P, 1984. 145–60.

———. *Proust/Three Dialogues.* London: Calder, 1965.

———. "Texts for Nothing." *The Complete Short Prose, 1929–1989.* Ed. S. E. Gontarski. New York: Grove P, 1995. 100–154.

————. *Three Novels: Molloy, Malone Dies, The Unnamable.* London: Grove, 1994.

————. *Watt.* New York: Grove P, 1953.

————. *Worstward Ho.* London: Calder, 1983.

Beistegui, Miguel de. *Jouissance de Proust: Pour une esthetique de la metaphore.* Paris: Encre marine, 2007.

Bell, Michael. "The Metaphysics of Modernism." *The Cambridge Companion to Modernism.* Ed. Michael Levenson. Cambridge: Cambridge UP, 1999. 9–32.

Benardete, Seth. "On Plato's *Symposium*." *Plato's Symposium.* Chicago: U Chicago P, 2001. 179–99.

Bénichou, Paul. *Selon Mallarmé.* Paris: Gallimard, 1995.

Bergson, Henri. *Creative Evolution.* Trans. Arthur Mitchell. New York: Modern Library, 1944.

Bernays, Jacob. "Aristotle on the Effect of Tragedy." Trans. Jennifer Barnes. *Oxford Readings in Ancient Literary Criticism.* Ed. Andrew Laird. Oxford: Oxford University Press, 2006 [1857]. 158-75.

Bersani, Leo. *Balzac to Beckett: Center and Circumference in French Fiction.* New York: Oxford UP, 1970.

————. *The Death of Stéphane Mallarmé.* Cambridge: Cambridge UP, 1981.

Beversluis, John. *Cross-Examining Socrates.* Cambridge: Cambridge UP, 2000.

Bianchon, Horace. "L'envoûtement." *Le Figaro,* January 10, 1893.

Bishop, Lloyd. *Romantic Irony in French Literature from Diderot to Beckett.* Nashville: Vanderbilt UP, 1989.

Blake, William. "The Everlasting Gospel." *The Complete Poetry and Prose of William Blake.* Ed. David V. Erdman. New York: Anchor, 1997 [c. 1818]. 518–25.

Blanchot, Maurice. *La part du Feu.* Paris: Gallimard, 1949.

————. "Where Now? Who Now?" Trans. Richard Howard. *On Beckett: Essays and Criticism.* Ed. S. E. Gontarski. New York: Grove P, 1986. 141–49.

Blitz, Antonio. *Fifty Years in the Magic Circle.* Hartford: Belknap & Bliss, 1871.

Bloch, Ernst. "Discussing Expressionism." *Aesthetics and Politics.* Ed. Ronald Taylor. London: NLB, 1977. 16–27.

Bloom, Harold. *How to Read and Why.* New York: Scribner, 2000.

————. *The Western Canon.* New York: Riverhead, 1995.

Bois, Jules. "L'envoûtement et la mort du docteur Boullan." *Gil Blas,* January 9, 1893, 2.

Boissier, A. *Recueil de diverses lettres au sujet des maléfices et du sortilège.* Paris: Marc Bordelet, 1731.

Booth, Wayne C. *The Company We Keep: An Ethics of Fiction.* Berkeley: U California P, 1988.

————. "The Company We Keep: Self-Making in Imaginative Art, Old and New." *Television: The Critical View.* Ed. Horace Newcomb. New York: Oxford UP, 1987. 382–418.

————. "Why Banning Ethical Criticism Is a Serious Mistake." *Philosophy and Literature* 222 (1998): 366–93.

Bordwell, David, and Kristin Thompson. *Film Art: An Introduction.* New York: McGraw-Hill, 2007.

Borges, Jorge Luis. *Labyrinths: Selected Stories and Other Writings.* Trans. Donald A. Yates and James E. Irby. New York: New Directions, 1962.

Bostock, David. "Plato." *The Oxford Companion to Philosophy.* Ed. Ted Honderich. Oxford: Oxford UP, 1995. 683–86.

Bourgeois, René. "Modes of Romantic Irony in Nineteenth-Century France." Trans. Cecilia Grenier. *Romantic Irony.* Ed. Frederick Garber. Budapest: Akadémiai Kiadó, 1988. 97–119.

Boyd, Brian. "Art and Evolution: Spiegelman's *The Narrative Corpse*." *Philosophy and Literature* 32 (2008): 31–57.

Bradbury, Malcolm, and James McFarlane. "The Name and Nature of Modernism." *Modernism.* Ed. Malcolm Bradbury and James McFarlane. London: Penguin, 1976. 19–55.

Bradley, A. C. "Poetry for Poetry's Sake." *Oxford Lectures on Poetry.* London: Macmillan, 1941. 3–34.

Brakke, David. "Parables and Plain Speech in the Fourth Gospel and the Apocryphon of James." *Journal of Early Christian Studies* 7 (1999): 187–218.

Brandis, Christian August. *Handbuch der Geschichte der Griechisch-römischen Philosophie.* 6 vols. Berlin: G. Reimer, 1844.

Brandwood, Leonard. *A Word Index to Plato*. Leeds: W. S. Maney & Son, 1976.

Brecht, Bertolt. *Brecht on Theatre*. Trans. John Willett. New York: Hill and Wang, 1964.

———. *Fünf Lehrstücke*. London: Methuen, 1969.

Breton, André. *Manifestes du surréalisme*. Paris: Gallimard, 1985.

Bricaud, Joanny. *J.-K. Huysmans et le satanisme*. Paris: Chacornac, 1912.

Brooks, Cleanth. "The Heresy of Paraphrase." *The Well-Wrought Urn: Studies in the Structure of Poetry*. New York: Harvest, 1956. 192–213.

———. "Irony as a Principle of Structure." *The Critical Tradition: Classic Texts and Contemporary Trends*. Ed. David H. Richter. Boston: Bedford St. Martin's, 2007. 799–806.

Brooks, Peter. *Reading for the Plot: Design and Intention in Narrative*. Cambridge, MA: Harvard UP, 1992.

Brown, Raymond E., Joseph A. Fitzmyer, and Roland E. Murphy, ed. *The New Jerome Biblical Commentary*. Englewood Cliffs, NJ: Prentice Hall, 1990.

Broyles, Bill Jr. "Flix for Warniks." *On the Media*, NPR, November 4, 2005.

Bultmann, Rudolf. *Existence and Faith: Shorter Writings of Rudolf Bultmann*. Trans. Schubert M. Ogden. Ed. John Marsh. New York: Meridian, 1960.

———. *The History of the Synoptic Tradition*. Ed. John Marsh. Oxford: Blackwell, 1963.

Burke, Edmund. "A Philosophical Inquiry into the Origin of Our Ideas of the Sublime and Beautiful." *Works*. Vol. 1. London: Holdsworth and Ball, 1834. 22–74.

Burlingame, H. J. *History of Magic and Magicians*. Chicago: Burlingame, 1895.

Burnyeat, Myles F. "Socratic Midwifery, Platonic Inspiration." *Essays on the Philosophy of Socrates*. Ed. Hugh H. Benson. Oxford: Oxford UP, 1992. 53–65.

Burt, E. S. "Mallarmé's 'Sonnet en yx': The Ambiguities of Speculation." *Modern Critical Views: Stéphane Mallarmé*. Ed. Harold Bloom. New York: Chelsea House, 1987. 97–120.

Bury, Robert Gregg. *The Symposium of Plato*. Cambridge: W. Heffer & Sons, 1932.

Butler, Lance St. John. *Samuel Beckett and the Meaning of Being: A Study in Ontological Parable*. London: Macmillan, 1984.

Cadoux, A. T. *The Parables of Jesus, Their Art and Use*. London: James Clarke, 1931.

Calder, John. *The Philosophy of Samuel Beckett*. Edison, NJ: Riverrun P, 2001.

Călinescu, Matei. *Rereading*. New Haven, CT: Yale UP, 1993.

Calvin, John. *Institutes of the Christian Religion*. Trans. Ford Lewis Battles. Philadelphia: Westminster, 1960.

Calvino, Italo. *If on a Winter's Night a Traveler*. Trans. William Weaver. New York: Harvest, 1982.

Camp, Elisabeth. "Metaphor and That Certain 'Je Ne Sais Quoi.'" *Philosophical Studies* 129.1 (2006): 1–25.

Carroll, Noël. "Art, Narrative, and Moral Understanding." *Aesthetics and Ethics: Essays at the Intersection*. Ed. Jerrold Levinson. Cambridge: Cambridge UP, 1998. 126–60.

Cavell, Stanley. "Aesthetic Problems of Modern Philosophy." *Must We Mean What We Say?* New York: Scribner, 1969. 73–96.

Chadwick, Charles. "Mallarme's 'Sonnet Allegorique de Lui-Meme': Allegorical of Itself or of Himself?" *Nineteenth-Century French Studies* 31.1 (2002): 104–10.

Chambers, Ross. "Beckett's Brinkmanship." *Samuel Beckett: A Collection of Critical Essays*. Ed. Martin Esslin. Englewood Cliffs, NJ: Prentice-Hall, 1965. 152–68.

Champigny, Robert. "Adventures of the First Person." *Samuel Beckett Now: Critical Approaches to His Novels, Poetry and Plays*. Ed. Melvin J. Friedman. Chicago: Chicago UP, 1970. 119–28.

Charlesworth, James H. *The Historical Jesus: An Essential Guide*. Nashville: Abingdon P, 2008.

Chaucer, Geoffrey. *The Canterbury Tales*. New York: Norton, 1989.

———. *Chaucer's "Canterbury Tales": An Interlinear Translation*. Trans. Vincent F. Hopper. Great Neck, NY: Barron's, 1970.

Chilton, Bruce, and Craig A. Evans, eds. *Authenticating the Words of Jesus*. Leiden: Brill, 1999.

Chisholm, A. R. "Mallarmé and the Riddle of the Ptyx." *AUMLA* 40 (1973): 246–48.

Citron, Pierre. "Ses purs ongles très haut." *Stéphane Mallarmé: Poésies*. Paris: Imprimerie Nationale, 1986. 302–7.

Clarke, Arthur C. *The Nine Billion Names of God: The Best Short Stories of Arthur C. Clarke*. New York: Harcourt, Brace & World, 1967.

———. "Technology and the Future." *Report on Planet Three and Other Speculations.* New York: Harper and Row, 1972. 138–51.

Clay, Diskin. "The Tragic and Comic Poet of the *Symposium.*" *Essays in Ancient Greek Philosophy.* Ed. John P. Anton and Anthony Preus. Albany: SUNY P, 1983. 186–202.

Clément, Bruno. "A Rhetoric of Ill-Saying." Trans. Thomas Cousineau. *Journal of Beckett Studies* 4.1 (1994): 35–53.

Cobb, William S. *The "Symposium" and the "Phaedrus": Plato's Erotic Dialogues.* Albany: SUNY P, 1993.

Cocking, Dean, and Jeanette Kennett. "Friendship and Moral Danger." *Journal of Philosophy* 97.5 (2000): 278–96.

Coetzee, J. M. "At the Gate." *Elizabeth Costello.* London: Penguin, 2004. 193–226.

———. "The Making of Samuel Beckett." *New York Review of Books,* April 30, 2009, 13–16.

Cohn, Robert G. *Toward the Poems of Mallarmé.* Berkeley: U California P, 1979.

Cohn, Ruby. "Beckett Directs: *Endgame* and *Krapp's Last Tape.*" *On Beckett: Essays and Criticism.* Ed. S. E. Gontarski. New York: Grove P, 1986. 291–307.

———. "Philosophical Fragments in the Works of Samuel Beckett." *Samuel Beckett: A Collection of Critical Essays.* Ed. Martin Esslin. Englewood Cliffs, NJ: Prentice-Hall, 1965. 169–77.

———. *Samuel Beckett: The Comic Gamut.* New Brunswick, NJ: Rutgers UP, 1962.

Coleman, Joyce. *Public Reading and the Reading Public in Late Medieval England and France.* Cambridge: Cambridge UP, 1996.

Coleridge, Samuel Taylor. *Biographia literaria.* London: George Bell, 1884 [1817].

Comte, Auguste. *The Catechism of Positive Religion.* Trans. Richard Congreve. London: Kegan Paul, 1891 [1852].

Cook, James. *The Arts of Deception.* Cambridge, MA: Harvard UP, 2001.

Cooper, John. Introduction. *Plato: Complete Works.* Indianapolis: Hackett, 1997. vii–xxvi.

———. "Socrates and Plato in Plato's *Gorgias.*" *Reason and Emotion: Essays on Ancient Moral Psychology and Ethical Theory.* Princeton, NJ: Princeton UP, 1999. 29–75.

Cousineau, Thomas J. *After the Final No: Samuel Beckett's Trilogy.* Newark: U Delaware P, 1999.

Coward, Noël. *Blithe Spirit.* Garden City, NY: Doubleday, 1941.

Cranfield, C. E. B. *The Gospel according to Saint Mark.* Cambridge: Cambridge UP, 1963.

Croce, Benedetto. *Aesthetic as Science of Expression and General Linguistic.* Trans. Douglas Ainslie. New Brunswick: Translation, 1995 [1909].

———. *Guide to Aesthetics.* Trans. Patrick Romanell. Indianapolis: Hackett, 1965.

Crossan, John Dominic. *In Parables: The Challenge of the Historical Jesus.* Sonoma, CA: Polebridge P, 1992.

Currie, Gregory. "Imagination and Simulation: Aesthetics Meets Cognitive Science." *Mental Simulation: Evaluations and Applications.* Ed. Martin Davies and Tony Stone. Oxford: Blackwell, 1995a. 151–69.

———. "The Moral Psychology of Fiction." *Australasian Journal of Philosophy* 73.2 (1995b): 250–59.

———. "The Paradox of Caring." *Emotion and the Arts.* Ed. Mette Hjort and Sue Laver. Oxford: Oxford UP, 1997. 63–77.

———. "Realism of Character and the Value of Fiction." *Aesthetics and Ethics: Essays at the Intersection.* Ed. Jerrold Levinson. Cambridge: Cambridge UP, 1998. 161–81.

Dällenbach, Lucien. *The Mirror in the Text.* Trans. Jeremy Whitely. Chicago: U Chicago P, 1989.

Danto, Arthur. *The Abuse of Beauty: Aesthetics and the Concept of Art.* Chicago: Open Court, 2003.

———. "Philosophy as/and/of Literature." *The Philosophical Disenfranchisement of Art.* New York: Columbia UP, 1986. 135–61.

———. *The Transfiguration of the Commonplace.* Cambridge, MA: Harvard UP, 1981.

Dantzig, Charles. *Encyclopédie capricieuse du tout et du rien.* Paris: Grasset, 2009.

Darwin, Charles. *The Origin of Species.* New York: Signet, 2003 [1859].

Daube, David. *The New Testament and Rabbinical Judaism.* London: Athlone, 1956.

Daugis, Antoine Louis. *Traité sur la magie, le sortilège, les possessions, obsessions et maléfices.* Paris: Prault, 1732.

Davidson, Donald. "What Metaphors Mean." *Inquiries into Truth and Interpretation.* Oxford: Clarendon P, 1984. 245–64.

Davies, Gardner. *Mallarmé et le drame solaire: Essai d'exégèse raisonnée.* Paris: Corti, 1959.

Davies, Paul. "Three Novels and Four *Nouvelles*: Giving Up the Ghost Be Born at Last." *The Cambridge Companion to Beckett.* Ed. John Pilling. Cambridge: Cambridge UP, 1994. 45–66.

Davis, Christina. "An Interview with Toni Morrison." *Conversations with Toni Morrison.* Ed. Danille Taylor-Guthrie. Jackson: U Mississippi P, 1994. 223–33.

de Man, Paul. "Reading (Proust)." *Allegories of Reading: Figural Language in Rousseau, Nietzsche, Rilke and Proust.* New Haven, CT: Yale UP, 1979. 57–78.

de Quincey, Thomas. "The Poetry of Pope." *Collected Writings.* Ed. David Masson. Vol. 11. Edinburgh: A. & C. Black, 1889–90. 51–95.

Dean, Jeffery T. "Aesthetics and Ethics: The State of the Art." *American Society for Aesthetics Newsletter* 22.2 (2002): 1–4.

Deleuze, Gilles. "L'épuisé." *Samuel Beckett: Quad et autres pièces pour la télévision.* Paris: Minuit, 1992. 57–106.

Delon, Michel, ed. *Dictionnaire européen des lumières.* Paris: PUF, 1997.

Descartes, René. *Philosophical Writings.* Ed. Elizabeth Anscombe and Peter Thomas Geach. New York: Macmillan, 1971.

Descaves, Lucien. "Note." *Oeuvres complètes.* Vol. 12. Ed. Joris-Karl Huysmans. Geneva: Slatkine Reprints, 1972. 238–60.

Dewey, John. *Art as Experience.* New York: Penguin, 1980.

Diderot, Denis. "Éloge de Richardson." *Oeuvres complètes.* Vol. 5. Paris: Le club français du livre, 1970 [1762]. 127–46.

———. *Paradoxe sur le comédien.* Paris: Flammarion, 1981 [1773–77].

Dilman, İlham. *Morality and the Inner Life: A Study in Plato's "Gorgias."* London: Macmillan, 1979.

Dodd, C. H. *The Parables of the Kingdom.* New York: Scribner, 1937.

Dodds, E. R. *Plato: "Gorgias."* Oxford: Oxford UP, 1959.

Donahue, John R. *The Gospel in Parable.* Philadelphia: Fortress P, 1988.

Dostoevsky, Fyodor. *The Idiot.* Trans. David Magarshack. London: Penguin, 1956.

———. *Notes from Underground.* Trans. Michael R. Katz. New York: Norton, 1989.

Dover, Kenneth. *Plato: "Symposium."* Cambridge: Cambridge UP, 1980.

Dragonetti, Roger. *Etudes sur Mallarmé.* Gent: Romanica Gandensia, 1992.

Drury, John. *The Parables in the Gospels: History and Allegory.* New York: Crossroad, 1985.

———. "The Sower, the Vineyard, and the Place of Allegory in the Interpretation of Mark's Parables." *Journal of Theological Studies* 24 (1973): 367–79.

During, Simon. *Modern Enchantments: The Cultural Power of Secular Magic.* Cambridge, MA: Harvard UP, 2002.

Dutton, Denis. "The Pleasures of Fiction." *Philosophy and Literature* 28.2 (2004): 453–66.

Eco, Umberto. *The Name of the Rose.* Trans. William Weaver. San Diego: Harcourt Brace, 1994.

———. *The Role of the Reader: Explorations in the Semiotics of Texts.* Bloomington: Indiana UP, 1979.

Edelstein, Dan. "Moving through the Looking-Glass: Deleuzian Reflections on the Series in Mallarmé." *L'esprit créateur* 40 (2000): 50–60.

Eichenbaum, Boris. "The Theory of the 'Formal Method.'" Trans. Lee T. Lemon and Marion J. Reis. *Russian Formalist Criticism: Four Essays.* Ed. Lee T. Lemon and Marion J. Reis. Lincoln: U Nebraska P, 1965. 100–141.

Eisenman, Robert. *James the Brother of Jesus: The Key to Unlocking the Secrets of Early Christianity and the Dead Sea Scrolls.* London: Penguin, 1997.

Eldridge, Richard. *An Introduction to the Philosophy of Art.* Cambridge: Cambridge UP, 2003.

———. *On Moral Personhood: Philosophy, Literature, Criticism, and Self-Understanding.* Chicago: U Chicago P, 1989.

Eliot, T. S. *Selected Prose of T. S. Eliot.* Ed. Frank Kermode. New York: Harcourt Brace, 1975.

Ellison, Ralph. *The Collected Essays of Ralph Ellison.* New York: Modern Library, 1995.

Esslin, Martin. *Samuel Beckett.* New Jersey: Prentice-Hall, 1965.

Eysteinsson, Astradur. *The Concept of Modernism.* Ithaca, NY: Cornell UP, 1990.

Farrell, Frank B. *Why Does Literature Matter?* Ithaca, NY: Cornell UP, 2004.

Feagin, Susan. *Reading with Feeling: The Aesthetics of Appreciation.* Ithaca, NY: Cornell UP, 1996.

Federman, Raymond. "Beckettian Paradox: Who Is Telling the Truth?" *Samuel Beckett Now: Critical Approaches to his Novels, Poetry and Plays*. Ed. Melvin J. Friedman. Chicago: Chicago UP, 1970. 103–17.

Felski, Rita. *Uses of Literature*. Oxford: Blackwell, 2008.

Feuerbach, Ludwig. *The Essence of Christianity*. Trans. Mary Ann Evans [George Eliot]. New York: Harper, 1957 [1841].

Fiard, Jean Baptiste. *De la France trompée par les magiciens et les démonolâtres du dix-huitième siècle, fait démontré par des faits*. Paris: Grégoire, 1803.

Finkelberg, Margalit. *The Birth of Literary Fiction in Ancient Greece*. Oxford: Oxford UP, 1998.

Fish, Stanley. *Doing What Comes Naturally: Change, Rhetoric and the Practice of Theory in Literary and Legal Studies*. Oxford: Oxford UP, 1989.

———. *Is There a Text in This Class? The Authority of Interpretive Communities*. Cambridge, MA: Harvard UP, 1980.

———. "Literature in the Reader: Affective Stylistics." *Reader-Response Criticism: From Formalism to Post-Structuralism*. Ed. Jane P. Tompkins. Baltimore: Johns Hopkins UP, 1980. 70–100.

———. "Why No One's Afraid of Wolfgang Iser." *Diacritics* 11 (1981): 2–13.

Fisher, Philip. *Wonder, the Rainbow, and the Aesthetics of Rare Experiences*. Cambridge, MA: Harvard UP, 1998.

Fisher, Terence. *The Mummy*. London: Hammer Film Productions, 1959.

Fitch, Brian. *Dimensions, structures et textualité dans la trilogie romanesque de Beckett*. Paris: Lettres modernes, 1977.

———. "Narrateur et narration dans la trilogie romanesque de Samuel Beckett: *Molloy, Malone Meurt, L'Innomable*." *Bulletin des jeunes romanistes* 3 (1961): 13–20.

Flaubert, Gustave. *Madame Bovary*. Trans. Francis Steegmuller. New York: Random House, 1992 [1857].

———. "Préface aux *Dernières chansons* [de Louis Bouilhet]." *Oeuvres complètes*. Vol. 12. Paris: Club de l'honnête homme, 1974 [1870]. 37–51.

Fletcher, John. *The Novels of Samuel Beckett*. New York: Barnes and Noble, 1970.

———. *Samuel Beckett's Art*. New York: Barnes and Noble, 1967.

Ford, Andrew. "Katharsis: The Ancient Problem." *Performativity and Performance*. Ed. Andrew Parker and Eve Kosofsky Sedgwick. New York: Routledge, 1995. 109–32.

———. *The Origins of Criticism: Literary Culture and Poetic Theory in Classical Greece*. Princeton: Princeton UP, 2002.

Fowler, Alastair. *Kinds of Literature: An Introduction to the Theory of Genres and Modes*. Cambridge, MA: Harvard UP, 1982.

Francesco, Grete de. *The Power of the Charlatan*. Trans. Miriam Beard. New Haven, CT: Yale UP, 1939.

Frankfurt, Harry. "Freedom of the Will and the Concept of a Person." *Journal of Philosophy* 68.1 (1971): 5–20.

———. "On Bullshit." *The Importance of What We Care About*. Cambridge: Cambridge UP, 1988. 117–34.

Frede, Dorothea. "Out of the Cave: What Socrates Learned from Diotima." *Nomodeiktes: Greek Studies in Honor of Martin Ostwald*. Ed. Ralph M. Rosen and Joseph Farrell, 1993. 397–422.

Frede, Michael. Introduction. *Plato: Protagoras*. Indianapolis: Hackett, 1992a. vii–xxxiv.

———. "Plato's Arguments and the Dialogue Form." *Oxford Studies in Ancient Philosophy*, supp. vol. (1992b): 201–19.

Freud, Sigmund. "The Uncanny." Trans. Alix Strachey and James Strachey. *The Complete Psychological Works of Sigmund Freud*. Vol. 17. London: Hogarth P, 1955 [1919]. 218–52.

Friedländer, Paul. *Plato: An Introduction*. 3 vols. Ed. H. Meyerhoff. Princeton, NJ: Princeton UP, 1973.

Friedrich, Hugo. *The Structure of Modern Poetry: From the Mid-Nineteenth to the Mid-Twentieth Century*. Trans. Joachim Neugroschel. Evanston, IL: Northwestern P, 1974.

Frye, Northrop. "The Nightmare Life in Death." *Twentieth Century Interpretations of "Molloy," "Malone Dies," "The Unnamable."* Ed. J. D. O'Hara. Englewood Cliffs, NJ: Prentice Hall, 1970. 26–34.

Fuchs, Ernst. *Studies of the Historical Jesus.* Ed. Andrew Scobie. Naperville, IL: Allenson, 1964.

Funk, Robert W. *Honest to Jesus: Jesus for a New Millennium.* New York: Harper Collins, 1996.

———. *Language, Hermeneutic and the Word of God.* New York: Harper & Row, 1966.

Funk, Robert W., and Roy W. Hoover, eds. *The Five Gospels: The Search for the Authentic Words of Jesus.* New York: Macmillan, 1993.

Furst, Lilian R. *Fictions of Romantic Irony.* Cambridge, MA: Harvard UP, 1984.

———. "Romantic Irony and Narrative Stance." *Romantic Irony.* Ed. Frederick Garber. Budapest: Akadémini Kindó, 1988. 293–309.

Gadamer, Hans-Georg. *Gadamer in Conversation: Reflections and Commentary.* Trans. Richard Palmer. New Haven, CT: Yale UP, 2001.

———. *The Relevance of the Beautiful.* Cambridge: Cambridge UP, 1986.

Gaiser, Konrad. *Platons ungeschriebene Lehre: Studien zur systematischen und geschichtlichen Begründung der Wissenschaften in der platonischen Schule.* Stuttgart: Klett, 1963.

Gallick, Susan. "Styles of Usage in the 'Nun's Priest's Tale.'" *Chaucer Review* 11.3 (1977): 232–47.

Gardner, Howard, and Ellen Winner. "The Development of Metaphoric Competence: Implications for Humanistic Disciplines." *On Metaphor.* Ed. Sheldon Sacks. Chicago: Chicago UP, 1978. 121–40.

Garinet, Jules. *Histoire de la magie en France, depuis le commencement de la monarchie jusqu'à nos jours.* Paris: Foulon, 1818.

Garnier, Éric. *Commentaire: Le sonnet en X de Stéphane Mallarmé.* Pau: Editions de Vallongues, 2003.

Gauchet, Marcel. *The Disenchantment of the World: A Political History of Religion.* Trans. Oscar Burge. Princeton, NJ: Princeton UP, 1999.

Gendler, Tamar. "The Puzzle of Imaginative Resistance." *Journal of Philosophy* 97.2 (2000): 55–81.

Gentzler, Jyl. "Socrates as Mob Orator: The Sophistic Cross-Examination of Callicles in the *Gorgias.*" *Ancient Philosophy* 15 (1995): 17–43.

Gérard, Alice. "Auguste Comte au purgatoire." *Auguste Comte, qui êtes-vous?* Ed. Edgar Faure. Paris: La Manufacture, 1988. 143–79.

Geulincx, Arnold. *Opera philosophica.* Vol. 3, *Annotata ad ethicam.* Ed. J. P. N. Land. The Hague: Martinum Nijhoff, 1893.

Gibson, Andrew. "Beckett and Badiou." *Beckett and Philosophy.* Ed. Richard Lane. London: Palgrave, 2002. 93–107.

Gide, André. *Paludes.* Paris: NRF, 1920 [1895].

Gill, Christopher. "Dialectic and the Dialogue Form." *New Perspectives on Plato, Ancient and Modern.* Ed. Julia Annas and Christopher Rowe. Cambridge: Cambridge UP, 2002. 145–77.

Ginzburg, Carlo. "Morelli, Freud and Sherlock Holmes: Clues and Scientific Method." Trans. Anna Davin. *History Workshop* 9 (1980): 5–36.

Girard, René. *Deceit, Desire and the Novel: Self and Other in Literary Structure.* Trans. Yvonne Freccero. Baltimore: Johns Hopkins UP, 1965.

Goldschmidt, Victor. *Les dialogues de Platon: Structure et méthode dialectique.* Paris: PUF, 1947.

Gomperz, Theodor. *Greek Thinkers: A History of Ancient Philosophy.* Trans. G. G. Berry. Vol. 2. New York: Scribner, 1905.

"The Gospel of Thomas." *The Nag Hammadi Library.* Ed. James M. Robinson. Leiden: Brill, 1978. 124–38.

Gottschall, Jonathan, and Marcus Nordland. "Romantic Love: A Literary Universal?" *Philosophy and Literature* 30 (2006): 450–70.

Graff, Gerald. "Culture and Anarchy." *New Republic,* February 14, 1981, 36–38.

Grant, Frederick C. "Exegesis of Mark." *The Interpreter's Bible.* Nashville: Abingdon P, 1951.

Grant, Michael. *Jesus.* London: Weidenfeld & Nicholson, 1977.

Greninasca, Jacques. "La semence et le royaume." *Parole-figure-parabole.* Ed. Jean Delorme. Lyon: Presses Universitaires de Lyon, 1987. 103–23.

Griswold, Charles L., "*E Pluribus Unum?* On the Platonic 'Corpus.'" *Ancient Philosophy* 19 (1999a): 361–97.

———. "Irony in the Platonic Dialogues." *Philosophy and Literature* 26 (2002): 84–106.

———. "Le libéralisme platonicien: De la perfection individuelle comme fondement d'une théorie politique." Trans. Jean Dixsaut and Monique Dixsaut. *Contre Platon II: Le Platonisme renversé*. Ed. Monique Dixsaut. Paris: Vrin, 1995. 155–95.

———. "Plato's Metaphilosophy: Why Plato Wrote Dialogues." *Platonic Writings, Platonic Readings*. Ed. Charles L. Griswold, Jr. New York: Routledge, 1988. 143–67.

———. "Relying on Your Own Voice: An Unsettled Rivalry of Moral Ideals in Plato's *Protagoras*." *Review of Metaphysics* 53 (1999b): 283–307.

———. *Self-Knowledge in Plato's "Phaedrus."* New Haven, CT: Yale UP, 1986.

Gumbrecht, Hans Ulrich. *Production of Presence: What Meaning Cannot Convey*. Stanford: Stanford UP, 2004.

———. "Stendhals nervöser Ernst." *Sprachen der Ironie—Sprachen des Ernstes*. Ed. Karl Heinz Bohrer. Frankfurt: Suhrkamp, 2000. 207–32.

Hackforth, R. "Hedonism in Plato's *Protagoras*." *Critical Quarterly* 22 (1928): 39–42.

———. "Immortality in Plato's *Symposium*." *Classical Review* 64 (1950): 43–45.

Hadot, Pierre. *Philosophy as a Way of Life: Spiritual Exercises from Socrates to Foucault*. Oxford: Blackwell, 1995.

Hagberg, Garry. "On Philosophy as Therapy: Wittgenstein, Cavell, and Autobiographical Writing." *Philosophy and Literature* 27 (2003): 196–210.

Halliwell, Stephen. *Aristotle's "Poetics."* Chicago: U Chicago P, 1998.

Halperin, David M. *One Hundred Years of Homosexuality and Other Essays on Greek Love*. New York: Routledge, 1990.

Hamilton, Kenneth, and Alice Hamilton. *Condemned to Life: The World of Samuel Beckett*. Grand Rapids, MI: Wm. B. Eerdmans, 1976.

Harold, James. "On Judging the Moral Value of Narrative Artworks." *Journal of Aesthetics and Art Criticism* 64.2 (2006): 259–70.

Harries, Karsten. "Metaphor and Transcendence." *On Metaphor*. Ed. Sheldon Sacks. Chicago: U Chicago P, 1978. 71–88.

Harvey, Van. "The Historical Jesus, the Kerygma, and Christian Faith." *Religion in Life* 33 (1964): 430–50.

Hayman, David. "Molloy or the Quest for Meaninglessness: A Global Interpretation." *Samuel Beckett Now: Critical Approaches to His Novels, Poetry and Plays*. Ed. Melvin J. Friedman. Chicago: U Chicago P, 1970. 129–56.

Hegel, G. W. F. *Aesthetics: Lectures on Fine Art*. Trans. T. M. Knox. Vol. 2. Oxford: Oxford UP, 1975.

Heidegger, Martin. "The Origin of the Work of Art." Trans. David Farrell Krell. *Basic Writings*. Ed. David Farrell Krell. New York: Harper & Row, 1977. 149–87.

Helms, Randel. *Who Wrote the Gospels?* Altadena, CA: Millennium P, 1997.

Herodotus. *The Histories*. Trans. Robin Waterfield. Oxford: Oxford UP, 1998.

Hesla, David H. *The Shape of Chaos: An Interpretation of the Art of Samuel Beckett*. Minneapolis: U Minnesota P, 1971.

Hill, Leslie. *Beckett's Fiction in Different Words*. Cambridge: Cambridge UP, 1990.

Hills, David. "Problems of Paraphrase: Bottom's Dream." *Baltic International Yearbook of Cognition, Logic and Communication* 3 (2008): 1–46.

Hobson, Harold. "Samuel Beckett: Dramatist of the Year." *International Theatre Annual* 1 (1956): 153–55.

Hoffmann, Heinrich. *Slovenly Peter*. Trans. Mark Twain. New York: Marchbanks P, 1935.

Hofstadter, Douglas. "Reductionism and Religion." *Behavioral and Brain Sciences* 3 (1980): 417–57.

Holbrook, David. "The Nonne Preestes Tale." *The Age of Chaucer*. Ed. Boris Ford. London: Penguin, 1969. 118–28.

The Holy Bible, Revised Standard Version. New York: Thomas Nelson, 1952.

Homer. *The Iliad*. Trans. Richmond Lattimore. Chicago: U Chicago P, 1951.

———. *The Odyssey*. Trans. Richmond Lattimore. New York: Harper, 1975.

Horace. *Satires, Epistles and Ars poetica*. Trans. H. Rushton Fairclough. London: Heinemann, 1970.

Horneffer, Ernst. *Platon gegen Socrates*. Leipzig: Teubner, 1904.

Hume, David. "The Standard of Taste." *Essays Moral, Political, and Literary*. Ed. Eugene F. Miller. Indianapolis: Liberty Classics, 1985 [1757]. 226–49.

——. *A Treatise of Human Nature.* Oxford: Clarendon P, 1960 [1740].

Hunt, Lynn. *Inventing Human Rights: A History.* New York: Norton, 2007.

Hunter, A. M. *Interpreting the Parables.* London: SCM P, 1960.

——. *The Parables Then and Now.* London: SCM P, 1971.

Huysmans, Joris-Karl. *A rebours.* Trans. Brendan King. Paris: Garnier-Flammarion, 1978.

Iersel, B. M. F. van. "Les récits-paraboles et la fonction du secret pour le destinataire de Marc." *Parole-figure-parabole.* Ed. Jean Delorme. Lyon: Presses Universitaires de Lyon, 1987. 189–205.

The Interlinear NIV: Parallel New Testament in Greek and English. Trans. Alfred Marshall. Grand Rapids, MI: Zonervan, 1976.

Ionesco, Eugène. *Le roi se meurt.* Paris: Gallimard, 1963.

Irwin, Robert. Introduction. *Joris-Karl Huysmans, "Là-bas: A Journey into the Self."* Trans. Brendan King. London: Dedalus, 1986. iv–vi.

Irwin, T. H. *Plato's Ethics.* New York: Oxford UP, 1995.

——. *Plato: Gorgias.* Oxford: Oxford UP, 1979.

——. *Plato's Moral Theory.* Oxford: Clarendon P, 1977.

Iser, Wolfgang. *The Act of Reading: A Theory of Aesthetic Response.* Baltimore: Johns Hopkins UP, 1980.

——. *How to Do Theory.* Oxford: Blackwell, 2006.

——. *The Implied Reader.* Baltimore: Johns Hopkins UP, 1978.

Jacobson, Daniel. "In Praise of Immoral Art." *Philosophical Topics* 25 (1997): 155–99.

——. "Sir Philip Sidney's Dilemma." *Journal of Aesthetics and Art Criticism* 54 (1996): 327–36.

Jaeger, Werner. *Paideia.* 3 vols. Trans. Gilbert Highet. Oxford: Oxford University Press, 1939–44.

Jakobson, Roman. "The Dominant." Trans. Herbert Eagle. *Readings in Russian Poetics.* Ed. Ladislav Matejka and Krystyna Pomorska. Cambridge, MA: MIT P, 1971. 82–87.

James, Henry. *The Portable Henry James.* Ed. John Auchard. London: Penguin, 2003.

Jameson, Fredric. "Progress versus Utopia; or, Can We Imagine the Future?" *Art after Modernism: Rethinking Representation.* Ed. Brian Wallis. New York: New Museum of Contemporary Art, 1984. 239–52.

Janvier, Ludovic. *Pour Samuel Beckett.* Paris: Minuit, 1969.

Jefferson, Thomas. *Jefferson's Letters.* Ed. Willson Whitman. Eau Claire, WI: E. M. Hale, 1900.

Jensen, Hal. "Life among the Fixed Stars: Fame and the Distant Progress of Beckett's Late Creations." *TLS,* June 23, 2006, 18.

Jeremias, Joachim. *The Parables of Jesus.* Ed. S. H. Hooke. London: SCM P, 1954.

John, Eileen. "Henry James: Making Moral Life Interesting." *Henry James Review* 18 (1997): 234–42.

——. "Reading Fiction and Conceptual Knowledge: Philosophical Thought in Literary Context." *Journal of Aesthetics and Art Criticism* 56 (1998): 331–48.

——. "Subtlety and Moral Vision in Fiction." *Philosophy and Literature* 19 (1995): 308–19.

Johnson, Barbara. "Les Fleurs du Mal Armé: Some Reflections on Intertextuality." *Lyric Poetry: Beyond New Criticism.* Ed. Chavia Hosek, Patricia Parker, and Jonathan Arac. Ithaca, NY: Cornell UP, 1985. 264–80.

Johnson, Samuel. "Rambler 4." *The Works of Samuel Johnson.* Vol. 4. London: J. Haddon, 1820. 20–27.

Jones, Geraint V. *The Art and Truth of the Parables.* London: Society for Promoting Christian Knowledge, 1964.

Joyce, James. *Ulysses.* New York: Vintage, 1990 [1922].

Julia de Fontenelle, Jean Sébastien Eugène. *Nouveau manuel complet des sorciers; ou, La magie blanche, dévoilée par les découvertes de la chimie, de la physique et de la mécanique, contenant un grand nombre de tours dus à l'électricité, au calorique, à la lumière, à l'air, aux nombres, aux cartes, à l'escamotage, etc.* Paris: Roret, 1837.

Jülicher, Adolf. *Die Gleichnisreden Jesu.* 2 vols. Darmstadt: Wissenschaftliche Buchgesellschaft, 1963.

Kafka, Franz. *Letters to Friends, Family, and Editors.* Trans. Richard Winston and Clara Winston. Ed. Max Brod. New York: Schocken, 1978.

Kahn, Charles H. "Drama and Dialectic in Plato's Gorgias." *Oxford Studies in Ancient Philosophy* 1 (1983): 75–121.

———. *Plato and the Socratic Dialogue: The Philosophical Use of a Literary Form.* Cambridge: Cambridge UP, 1996.

Kahneman, Daniel. "Maps of Bounded Rationality: A Perspective on Intuitive Judgment and Choice." *Les Prix Nobel 2002.* Ed. T. Frangsmyr. Stockholm: Almquist & Wiksell, 2003. 449–89.

Kant, Immanuel. *Critique of Pure Reason.* Trans. Norman Kemp Smith. Edinburgh: Macmillan, 1929 [1781/1787].

———. *Critique of the Power of Judgment.* Trans. Paul Guyer and Eric Matthews. Cambridge: Cambridge UP, 2001 [1790].

———. *Groundwork of the Metaphysics of Morals.* Trans. Mary Gregor. Cambridge: Cambridge UP, 1998 [1785].

Kaufmann, Vincent. *Le livre et ses adresses (Mallarmé, Ponge, Valéry, Blanchot).* Paris: Méridiens Klincksieck, 1986.

Keats, John. *The Complete Poems of John Keats.* New York: Modern Library, 1994.

Keen, Suzanne. *Empathy and the Novel.* Oxford: Oxford UP, 2007.

———. "A Theory of Narrative Empathy." *Narrative* 14 (2006): 207–36.

Kelber, Werner. *The Oral and the Written Gospel.* Philadelphia: Fortress Press, 1983.

Kemp, Gary. "The Croce-Collingwood Theory as Theory." *Journal of Aesthetics and Art Criticism* 61 (2003): 171–93.

Kenner, Hugh. *Samuel Beckett: A Critical Study.* Berkeley: U California P, 1974.

Kermode, Frank. "Hoti's Business: Why Are Narratives Obscure?" *The Genesis of Secrecy: On the Interpretation of Narrative.* Cambridge, MA: Harvard UP, 1979. 23–47.

Kern, Edith. "The Hero as Author." *Twentieth Century Interpretations of "Molloy," "Malone Dies," "The Unnamable."* Ed. J. D. O'Hara. Englewood Cliffs, NJ: Prentice Hall, 1970. 35–45.

Kierkegaard, Søren. *The Concept of Irony, with Continual Reference to Socrates.* Trans. Howard V. Hong and Edna H. Hong. Princeton, NJ: Princeton UP, 1992 [1841].

———. *Concluding Unscientific Postscript.* Trans. Howard V. Hong and Edna H. Hong. Princeton, NJ: Princeton UP, 1992 [1846].

———. *Fear and Trembling.* Trans. Alastair Hannay. London: Penguin, 1986 [1843].

King-Farlow, John. "Self-Deceivers and Sartrian Seducers." *Analysis* 23 (1963): 131–36.

Kissinger, Warren S. *The Parables of Jesus: A History of Interpretation and Bibliography.* Metuchen, NJ: Scarecrow P, 1979.

Klein, Jacob. *A Commentary on Plato's "Meno."* Chapel Hill: U North Carolina P, 1965.

Klosko, George. "The Insufficiency of Reason in Plato's *Gorgias.*" *Western Political Quarterly* 36.4 (1983): 579–95.

———. "The Refutation of Callicles in Plato's *Gorgias.*" *Greece and Rome* 31.2 (1984): 126–39.

———. "Toward a Consistent Interpretation of the *Protagoras.*" *Archiv für Geschichte der Philosphie* 61 (1979): 125–42.

Knox, Bernard. Introduction. *Sophocles: The Three Theban Plays.* Trans. Robert Fagles. New York: Viking, 1982.

Kracauer, Siegfried. "The Mass Ornament." Trans. Thomas Y. Levin. *The Mass Ornament: Weimar Essays.* Ed. Thomas Y. Levin. Cambridge, MA: Harvard UP, 1995 [1927]. 75–88.

Krämer, Hans Joachim. *Arete bei Platon und Aristoteles: Zum Wesen und zur Geschichte der platonischen Ontologie.* Heidelberg: C. Winter, 1959.

Kramnick, Jonathan. "Against Literary Darwinism." *Critical Inquiry* 37 (2011): 315–47.

Kraut, Richard. "Plato." *The Cambridge Dictionary of Philosophy.* Ed. Robert Audi. Cambridge: Cambridge UP, 1999. 709–13.

Krentz, Arthur A. "Dramatic Form and Philosophical Content in Plato's Dialogues." *Philosophy and Literature* 7 (1983): 32–47.

Kundera, Milan. *The Art of the Novel.* Trans. Linda Asher. New York: Harper, 1988.

———. *The Curtain: An Essay in Seven Parts.* Trans. Linda Asher. New York: Harper, 2008.

———. *Testaments Betrayed.* Trans. Linda Asher. New York: Harper, 1996.

Lamarque, Peter, and Stein Haugom Olsen. *Truth, Fiction, and Literature.* Oxford: Oxford UP, 1996.

Lamb, Geoffrey. *Victorian Magic.* London: Routledge, 1976.

Landy, Joshua. "Corruption by Literature." *Republics of Letters* 1.2 (2010), http://arcade.stanford. edu/journals/rofl/files/article_pdfs/Landy_1.pdf.

———. "The Cruel Gift: Lucid Self-Delusion in French Literature and German Philosophy, 1851–1914." PhD diss., Princeton University, 1997.

———. "Music, Letters, Truth and Lies: 'L'après-midi d'un faune' as an Ars Poetica." *Yearbook of Comparative and General Literature*, 1994, 57–69.

———. "The Paradox of Perfection." *Poetics Today* 26.1 (2005): 161–68.

———. "Passion, Counter-Passion, Catharsis: Beckett and Flaubert on Feeling Nothing." *The Blackwell Companion to Literature and Philosophy*. Ed. Garry Hagberg. Oxford: Blackwell, 2010. 218–38.

———. *Philosophy as Fiction: Self, Deception, and Knowledge in Proust*. New York: Oxford, 2004.

———. "Still Life in a Narrative Age: Charlie Kaufman's *Adaptation*." *Critical Inquiry* 37.3 (2011): 497–514.

Lane, Richard, ed. *Beckett and Philosophy*. London: Palgrave, 2002.

Lawrence, Joseph P. "Commentary on Patterson's 'The Ascent in Plato's *Symposium*.'" *Proceedings of the Boston Area Colloquium in Ancient Philosophy* 7 (1991): 215–25.

Lear, Jonathan. "Katharsis." *Phronesis* 33 (1988): 297–326.

———. *Open Minded: Working Out the Logic of the Soul*. Cambridge, MA: Harvard UP, 1999.

Lenaghan, R. P. "The Nun's Priest's Fable." *PMLA* 78 (1963): 300–307.

Lévi-Strauss, Claude. "The Structural Study of Myth." *Myth: A Symposium*. Ed. Thomas A. Sebeok. Bloomington: U Indiana P, 1955. 81–106.

Lewis, David. "Truth in Fiction." *Philosophical Papers 1*. Oxford: Oxford UP, 1983. 261–79.

Livingston, Paisley. *Literature and Rationality: Ideas of Agency in Theory and Fiction*. Cambridge: Cambridge UP, 1991.

Locke, John. *An Essay concerning Human Understanding*. London: Penguin, 1997 [1690].

Loy, J. Robert. *Diderot's Determined Fatalist: A Critical Appreciation of Jacques le Fataliste*. New York: King's Crown P, 1950.

Lukács, Georg. "Realism in the Balance." *Aesthetics and Politics*. Ed. Ronald Taylor. London: NLB, 1977. 28–59.

———. *The Theory of the Novel*. Trans. Anna Bostock. Cambridge, MA: MIT P, 1971.

Lunn, Eugene. *Marxism and Modernism*. Berkeley: U California P, 1982.

Lutz, Mark. *Socrates' Education to Virtue: Learning the Love of the Noble*. Albany, New York: SUNY P, 1998.

Maar, Michael. *Die Feuer- und die Wasserprobe: Essays zur Literatur*. Frankfurt: Suhrkamp, 1997.

MacIntyre, Alasdair. *Three Rival Versions of Moral Enquiry: Encyclopedia, Genealogy, and Tradition*. Notre Dame: U Notre Dame P, 1990.

Mackay, Charles. *Memoirs of Extraordinary Popular Delusions and the Madness of Crowds*. 2 vols. London: Routledge, 1869.

Mackenzie, Mary Margaret. *Plato on Punishment*. Berkeley: U California P, 1981.

Mallarmé, Stéphane. *Correspondance*. Trans. Henri Mondor. Paris: Gallimard, 1959–1985.

———. *Oeuvres complètes*. 2 vols. Paris: Gallimard, 1998 and 2003.

Manning, Stephen. "The Nun's Priest's Morality and the Medieval Attitude toward Fables." *Journal of English and Germanic Philology* 59 (1960): 403–16.

Manson, T. W. *The Teaching of Jesus*. Cambridge: Cambridge UP, 1955.

Marchal, Bertrand. *Lecture de Mallarmé: Poésies, Igitur, Le coup de dés*. Paris: Corti, 1985.

Marcoulesco, Ileana. "Beckett and the Temptation of Solipsism." *The Beckett Studies Reader*. Ed. S. E. Gontarski. Gainesville: U P Florida, 1993. 214–25.

Mariel, Pierre. *Cagliostro: Imposteur ou martyr?* Paris: Culture, Art, Loisirs, 1973.

———. *Dictionnaire des sociétés secrètes en Occident*. Paris: Culture, Art, Loisirs, 1971.

Marson, Eric. *Kafka's Trial: The Case against Josef K*. St. Lucia: U Queensland P, 1975.

McFague, Sallie. *Speaking in Parables: A Study in Metaphor and Theology*. Philadelphia: Fortress P, 1975.

McKay, Nellie. "An Interview with Toni Morrison." *Contemporary Literature* 24 (1983): 418–22.

McKim, Richard. "Shame and Truth in Plato's *Gorgias*." *Platonic Writings, Platonic Readings*. Ed. Charles L. Griswold, Jr. New York: Routledge, 1988. 34–48.

Mele, Alfred R. *Irrationality: An Essay on Akrasia, Self-Deception, and Self-Control.* New York: Oxford UP, 1987.

Mercier, Vivian. *Beckett/Beckett.* New York: Oxford UP, 1977.

Merlan, Philip. "Form and Content in Plato's Philosophy." *Journal of the History of Ideas* 8 (1947): 406–30.

Michaud, Guy. *Mallarmé.* Paris: Hatier, 1958.

Miller, John F. "The Esoteric Unity of Plato's *Symposium.*" *Apeiron* 12 (1978): 19–25.

Miller, Lawrence. *Samuel Beckett: The Expressive Dilemma.* New York: St. Martin's Press, 1992.

Miller, Robert J. *The Jesus Seminar and Its Critics.* Santa Rosa, CA: Polebridge P, 1999.

Mitchell, Robert Lloyd. *A Reading of Plato's "Symposium."* Lanham, MD: UP of America, 1993.

Montefiore, C. G. *The Synoptic Gospels.* London: Macmillan, 1909.

Moran, Richard. "The Expression of Feeling in Imagination." *Philosophical Review* 103 (1994): 75–106.

Morrison, Toni. "Rootedness: The Ancestor as Foundation." *Black Women Writers (1950–1980).* Ed. Mare Evans. Garden City, NY: Anchor P, 1984. 339–45.

Morson, Gary Saul. "Sideshadowing and Tempics." *New Literary History* 29 (1998): 599–624.

Mothersill, Mary. "Make-Believe Morality and Fictional Worlds." *Art and Morality.* Ed. José Luis Bermúdez and Sebastian Gardner. London: Routledge, 2003.

Muecke, D. C. *The Compass of Irony.* London: Methuen, 1967.

Mulhern, J. J. "Treatises, Dialogues, and Interpretation." *Monist* 53 (1969): 631–41.

Mullin, Amy. "Evaluating Art: Morally Significant Imagining versus Moral Soundness." *Journal of Aesthetics and Art Criticism* 60.2 (2002): 137–48.

Murdoch, Iris. "The Sovereignty of Good over Other Concepts." *The Sovereignty of Good.* London: Routledge, 2001 [1970]. 75–101.

Murphy, P. J. "Beckett and the Philosophers." *The Cambridge Companion to Beckett.* Ed. John Pilling. Cambridge: Cambridge UP, 1994. 222–40.

Myers, D. E. "Focus and 'Moralite' in the *Nun's Priest's Tale.*" *Chaucer Review* 7 (1973): 210–20.

Nails, Debra. "Mouthpiece Schmouthpiece." *Who Speaks for Plato? Studies in Platonic Anonymity.* Ed. Gerald A. Press. Lanham, MD: Rowman and Littlefield, 2000. 15–26.

Nehamas, Alexander. *The Art of Living: Socratic Reflections from Plato to Foucault.* Berkeley: U California P, 1998.

——. "An Essay on Beauty and Judgment." *Threepenny Review* 80 (2000): 4–7.

——. Introduction. *Plato: "Symposium."* Ed. Alexander Nehamas and Paul Woodruff. Indianapolis: Hackett, 1989. xi–xxvi.

——. *Nietzsche: Life as Literature.* Cambridge, MA: Harvard UP, 1985.

——. *Only a Promise of Happiness: The Place of Beauty in a World of Art.* Princeton, NJ: Princeton UP, 2007.

——. "Pity and Fear in the Rhetoric and the Poetics." *Essays on Aristotle's "Poetics."* Ed. Amélie Oksenberg Rorty. Princeton, NJ: Princeton UP, 1992. 291–314.

——. "The Postulated Author: Critical Monism as a Regulative Ideal." *Critical Inquiry* 8 (1981): 133–49.

——. *Virtues of Authenticity: Essays on Plato and Socrates.* Princeton, NJ: Princeton UP, 1999.

Nelson, Robert J. "Mallarmé's Mirror of Art: An Explication of *Ses purs ongles.*" *Modern Language Quarterly* 20 (1959): 49–56.

Neumann, Gui. "Diderot précurseur de Beckett: La modernité dans Jacques le fataliste." *New Zealand Journal of French Studies* 4.1 (1983): 43–58.

The New Interpreter's Bible. Vol. 8. Nashville: Abingdon P, 1995.

New Jerusalem Bible. London: Darton, Longman & Todd, 1985.

Nietzsche, Friedrich. *The Gay Science.* Trans. Walter Kaufmann. New York: Random House, 1974 [1882–87].

——. *The Genealogy of Morals/Ecce Homo.* Trans. Walter Kaufmann. New York: Random House, 1969 [1888].

——. "On the Relationship of Alcibiades' Speech to the Other Speeches in Plato's *Symposium.*" Trans. David Scialdone. *Graduate Faculty Philosophy Journal* 15.2 (1991 [1864]): 3–5.

——. *The Will to Power.* Trans. Walter Kaufmann and R. J. Hollingdale. New York: Random House, 1967 [1901].

Nightingale, Andrea Wilson. "Broken Knowledge." *The Re-Enchantment of the World: Secular Magic in a Rational Age*. Ed. Joshua Landy and Michael Saler. Stanford: Stanford UP, 2009. 15–37.

———. *Genres in Dialogue: Plato and the Construct of Philosophy*. Cambridge: Cambridge UP, 1995.

Niznik, Josek, and John T. Sanders, eds. *Debating the State of Philosophy: Habermas, Rorty, and Kolakowski*. Westport, CT: Praeger, 1996.

Noulet, Emilie. *Vingt poèmes de Stéphane Mallarmé*. Geneva: Droz, 1967.

Nussbaum, Martha. "Exactly and Responsibly: A Defense of Ethical Criticism." *Philosophy and Literature* 22 (1998): 343–65.

———. "'Finely Aware and Richly Responsible': Literature and the Moral Imagination." *Literature and the Question of Philosophy*. Ed. Anthony J. Cascardi. Baltimore: Johns Hopkins UP, 1987. 167–91.

———. "Flawed Crystals: James's *The Golden Bowl* and Literature as Moral Philosophy." *New Literary History* 15 (1983a): 25–50.

———. *The Fragility of Goodness*. Cambridge: Cambridge UP, 1986.

———. "Invisibility and Recognition: Sophocles' *Philoctetes* and Ellison's *Invisible Man*." *Philosophy and Literature* 23 (1999): 257–83.

———. *Love's Knowledge: Essays on Philosophy and Literature*. Oxford: Oxford UP, 1990a.

———. "Narrative Emotions: Beckett's Genealogy of Love." *Love's Knowledge: Essays on Philosophy and Literature*. Oxford: Oxford UP, 1990b. 286–313.

———. *Poetic Justice: The Literary Imagination and Public Life*. Boston: Beacon P, 1995.

———. "Reply to Richard Wollheim, Patrick Gardiner, and Hilary Putnam." *New Literary History* 15 (1983b): 201–8.

O'Brien, Michael J. *The Socratic Paradoxes and the Greek Mind*. Chapel Hill: U North Carolina P, 1967.

Oesterley, W. E. *The Gospel Parables in the Light of their Jewish Background*. New York: Macmillan, 1936.

O'Hara, J. D. Introduction. *Twentieth Century Interpretations of "Molloy," "Malone Dies," "The Unnamable."* Ed. J. D. O'Hara. Englewood Cliffs, NJ: Prentice Hall, 1970. 1–25.

O'Neill, Onora. "The Power of Example." *Philosophy* 61 (1986): 5–29.

Olds, Marshall C. "Mallarmé's *glorieux mensonge*.'" *West Virginia University Philological Papers* 30 (1984): 1–9.

Ortega y Gasset, José. "The Dehumanization of Art." Trans. Helene Weyl. *The Dehumanization of Art and Other Essays on Art, Culture, and Literature*. Princeton, NJ: Princeton UP, 1968 [1925]. 1–54.

Ovid. *Metamorphoses*. Trans. Frank Justus Miller. Cambridge, MA: Harvard UP, 1916.

Pagels, Elaine. *The Gnostic Gospels*. New York: Vintage, 1979.

Paige, Nicholas. "Permanent Re-Enchantments: On Some Literary Uses of the Supernatural from Early Empiricism to Modern Aesthetics." *The Re-Enchantment of the World: Secular Magic in a Rational Age*. Ed. Joshua Landy and Michael Saler. Stanford: Stanford UP, 2009. 159–80.

Pascal, Blaise. *Pensées*. Paris: Garnier, 1964 [1669].

———. *Thoughts, Letters and Minor Works*. Trans. W. F. Trotter. New York: P. F. Collier & Son, 1965.

Patterson, Richard. "The Ascent in Plato's Symposium." *Proceedings of the Boston Area Colloquium in Ancient Philosophy* 7 (1991): 193–214.

Paulhan, Jean. *The Flowers of Tarbes; or, Terror in Literature*. Trans. Michael Syrotinski. Urbana: U Illinois P, 2006 [1941].

Pavel, Thomas. *Fictional Worlds*. Cambridge, MA: Harvard UP, 1986.

———. *La pensée du roman*. Paris: Gallimard, 2003.

———. "Naturalizing Molloy." *Understanding Narrative*. Ed. James Phelan and Peter J. Rabinowitz. Columbus: Ohio State UP, 1994. 178–98.

Pearson, Roger. *Unfolding Mallarmé: The Development of a Poetic Art*. Oxford: Oxford UP, 1996.

Penner, Terry. "Socrates on the Impossibility of Belief-Relative Sciences." *Proceedings of the Boston Area Colloquium in Ancient Philosophy* 3 (1987): 263–325.

Perloff, Marorie. "Between Verse and Prose: Beckett and the New Poetry." *On Beckett: Essays and Criticism*. Ed. S. E. Gontarski. New York: Grove P, 1986. 191–206.

Perrin, Norman. *Rediscovering the Teaching of Jesus*. New York: Harper & Row, 1967.

Pilling, John. *Samuel Beckett*. London: Routledge & Kegan Paul, 1976.

Pilling, John, and James Knowlson. *Frescoes of the Skull: The Later Prose and Drama of Samuel Beckett*. New York: Grove P, 1980.

Pillow, Kirk. *Sublime Understanding*. Cambridge, MA: MIT P, 2001.

Pippin, Robert B. "'The Felt Necessities of the Time': Literature, Ethical Knowledge, and Law." *Ars Interpretandi* 7 (2002): 71–90.

———. *Henry James and Modern Moral Life*. Cambridge: Cambridge UP, 2000.

Plant, Bob. "The End(s) of Philosophy: Rhetoric, Therapy and Wittgenstein's Pyrrhonism." *Philosophical Investigations* 27.3 (2004): 222–57.

Plato. *Complete Works*. Indianapolis: Hackett, 1997.

———. *The Works of Plato*. Trans. Thomas Taylor and Floyer Sydenham. Frome: Prometheus Trust, 1996 [1804].

Plutarch. "The Life of Pelopidas." *Lives*. Vol. 5, *Agesilaus and Pompey; Pelopidas and Marcellus*. Trans. Bernadotte Perrin. Cambridge, MA: Loeb, 1917. 341–433.

Poe, Edgar Allan. "The Philosophy of Composition." *Selected Writings of Edgar Allan Poe*. Ed. Edward H. Davidson. Cambridge, MA: Riverside P, 1956 [1846]. 452–63.

———. "The Poetic Principle." *Selected Writings of Edgar Allan Poe*. Ed. Edward H. Davidson. Cambridge, MA: Riverside P, 1956 [1850]. 464–85.

Porton, Gary G. "The Parable in the Hebrew Bible and Rabbinic Literature." *The Historical Jesus in Context*. Ed. Dale C. Allison, Jr., Amy-Jill Levine, and John Dominic Crossan. Princeton, NJ: Princeton UP, 2006. 206–21.

Posner, Richard A. "Against Ethical Criticism." *Philosophy and Literature* 21 (1997): 1–27.

———. "Against Ethical Criticism: Part Two." *Philosophy and Literature* 22 (1998): 394–412.

Poulet, Georges. "Criticism and the Experience of Interiority." Trans. Catherine Macksey and Richard Macksey. *Reader-Response Criticism: From Formalism to Post-Structuralism*. Ed. Jane P. Tompkins. Baltimore: Johns Hopkins UP, 1980. 41–49.

———. *La conscience critique*. Paris: Corti, 1971.

Price, A. W. *Love and Friendship in Plato and Aristotle*. Oxford: Clarendon P, 1989.

Prince, Gerald. *Narrative as Theme: Studies in French Fiction*. Lincoln: U Nebraska P, 1992.

Prioleau, Phoebe. "'I, of Whom I Can't Speak, of Whom I Must Speak': The Search for Self in Samuel Beckett's Trilogy." Honors thesis, Stanford University, 2006.

Prose, Francine. "I Know Why the Caged Bird Cannot Read: How American High School Students Learn to Loathe Literature." *Harper's*, September 1999, 76–84.

Proust, Marcel. *A l'ombre des jeunes filles en fleurs*. Paris: Gallimard, 1988 [1919].

———. *By Way of Sainte-Beuve*. Trans. Sylvia Townsend Warner. London: Hogarth P, 1984.

———. *The Captive/The Fugitive*. Trans. C. K. Scott Moncrieff, Terence Kilmartin, and D. J. Enright. New York: Modern Library, 1992 [1923–25].

———. *Essais et articles*. Paris: Gallimard, 1994.

———. *The Guermantes Way*. Trans. C. K. Scott Moncrieff, Terence Kilmartin, and D. J. Enright. New York: Modern Library, 1992.

———. *Le côté de Guermantes*. Paris: Gallimard, 1988 [1920–21].

———. *On Reading Ruskin*. Trans. Jean Autret, William Burford, and Phillip J. Wolfe. New Haven, CT: Yale UP, 1987.

———. *Pastiches et mélanges*. Paris: Gallimard, 1997.

———. *Time Regained*. Trans. Andreas Mayor, Terence Kilmartin, and D. J. Enright. New York: Modern Library, 1993 [1927].

Pullman, Philip. Introduction. *John Milton, "Paradise Lost."* Oxford: Oxford UP, 2008. 1–10.

Puryear, Martin. *Martin Puryear*. Ed. John Elderfield. New York: Museum of Modern Art, 2007.

Putnam, Hilary. "Literature, Science, and Reflection." *New Literary History* 7 (1976): 483–91.

Quendler, Christian. *From Romantic Irony to Postmodernist Metafiction*. Frankfurt: Peter Lang, 2001.

Quinlan, Michael A. *Poetic Justice in the Drama: The History of an Ethical Principle in Literary Criticism*. South Bend, IN: Notre Dame UP, 1912.

Racine, Jean. "Preface to *Phèdre*." *Britannicus; Phaedra; Athaliah*. Trans. Charles Hubert Sisson. Oxford: Oxford UP, 2001. 75–77.

Radden, Jennifer. "Defining Self-Deception." *Dialogue* 23 (1984): 103–20.

Raeder, Hans. *Platons philosophische Entwickelung*. Leipzig: B. G. Teubner, 1920.

Ramberg, Bjørn, and Kristin Gjesdal. "Hermeneutics." *Stanford Encyclopedia of Philosophy*. Ed. Edward N. Zalta (Winter 2005), http://plato.stanford.edu/archives/win2005/entries/hermeneutics/.

Reginster, Bernard. *The Affirmation of Life: Nietzsche on Overcoming Nihilism*. Cambridge, MA: Harvard UP, 2006.

Renan, Ernest. "De l'activité intellectuelle en france en 1849." *La liberté de penser* 20 (1849): 126–47.

———. *L'avenir de la science: Pensées de 1848*. Paris: Calmann-Lévy, 1890.

Rhees, Rush. *Discussions of Wittgenstein*. New York: Schocken, 1970.

Ricardou, Jean. *Mallarmé; ou, L'obscurité lumineuse*. Paris: Hermann, 1999.

Richard, Jean-Pierre. *L'univers imaginaire de Mallarmé*. Paris: Seuil, 1961.

Richards, I. A. "Metaphor." *The Philosophy of Rhetoric*. New York: Oxford UP, 1965. 89–112.

———. *Principles of Literary Criticism*. New York: Harcourt, Brace, 1959.

———. *Science and Poetry*. London: Kegan Paul, 1926.

Richardson, Brian. *Unlikely Stories: Causality and the Nature of Modern Narrative*. Newark: U Delaware P, 1997.

Ricoeur, Paul. "Biblical Hermeneutics." *Semeia* 4 (1975): 27–148.

———. "La Bible et l'imagination." *Revue d'Histoire et de Philosophie Religieuses* 62 (1982): 339–60.

———. "Life in Quest of Narrative." *On Paul Ricoeur: Narrative and Interpretation*. Ed. David Wood. London: Routledge, 1991. 20–33.

———. "The Metaphorical Process as Cognition, Imagination, and Feeling." *Critical Inquiry* 5 (1978): 143–79.

Robb, Graham. *Unlocking Mallarmé*. New Haven, CT: Yale UP, 1996.

Robert-Houdin, Jean-Eugène. *Confidences de Robert-Houdin: Une vie d'artiste* [2nd ed. of *Confidences d'un prestidigitateur*, 1858]. Paris: Librairie Nouvelle, 1861.

———. *Memoirs of Robert-Houdin*. Trans. Lascelles Wraxall. London: Chapman & Hall, 1859.

Robin, Léon. *La théorie platonicienne de l'amour*. Paris: Alcan, 1908.

Roche, Mark William. *Why Literature Matters in the Twenty-First Century*. New Haven, CT: Yale UP, 2004.

Rorty, Richard. *Consequences of Pragmatism*. Minneapolis: U Minnesota P, 1982.

———. *Contingency, Irony, and Solidarity*. Cambridge: Cambridge UP, 1989.

———. *Critical Dialogues*. Ed. Matthew Festenstein and Simon Thompson. Oxford: Blackwell, 2001.

———. *Philosophy and Social Hope*. New York: Penguin, 1999.

———. *Truth and Progress: Philosophical Papers III*. Cambridge: Cambridge UP, 1998.

Rosen, Stanley. *Plato's "Symposium."* New Haven, CT: Yale UP, 1968.

Rosen, Steven J. *Samuel Beckett and the Pessimistic Tradition*. New Brunswick, NJ: Rutgers UP, 1976.

Rosenblatt, Louise M. "The Poem as Event." *College English* 26.2 (1964): 123–28.

———. *The Reader, the Text, the Poem: The Transactional Theory of the Literary Work*. Carbondale: Southern Illinois P, 1978.

Rousseau, Jean-Jacques. *Emile; or, On Education*. Trans. Allan Bloom. New York: Basic Books, 1979 [1762].

———. *Lettre à d'Alembert sur son article "Genève."* Paris: Garnier-Flammarion, 1967 [1758].

Rowe, Christopher. "Platonic Irony." *Nova Tellus* 5 (1987): 83–101.

Russell, Charles. "The Context of the Concept." *Romanticism, Modernism, Postmodernism*. Ed. Harry R. Garvin. Lewisburg, PA: Bucknell UP, 1980. 180–93.

Ruthven, K. K. *Critical Assumptions*. New York: Cambridge UP, 1979.

Saler, Michael. "At Home in the Ironic Imagination: The Rational Vernacular and Spectacular Texts." *Vernacular Modernism*. Ed. Maiken Umbach and Bernard Huppauff. Stanford: Stanford UP, 2005. 53–83.

———. "'Clap If You Believe in Sherlock Holmes': Mass Culture and the Re-Enchantment of Modernity, c. 1890–c. 1940." *Historical Journal* 46 (2003): 599–622.

Salverte, Eusèbe. *The Occult Sciences: The Philosophy of Magic, Prodigies, and Apparent Miracles.* Trans. Anthony Todd Thomson. New York: Harper, 1847 [1829].

Santas, Gerasimos. *Plato and Freud: Two Theories of Love.* Oxford: Blackwell, 1988.

———. "The Socratic Fallacy." *Journal of the History of Philosophy* 10 (1972): 127–41.

———. "The Socratic Paradoxes." *Philosophical Review* 73 (1964): 147–64.

Sartre, Jean-Paul. *"What Is Literature?" and Other Essays.* Trans. Steven Ungar. Cambridge, MA: Harvard UP, 1988.

Saunders, Trevor J. "Introduction to Socrates." *Plato: Early Socratic Dialogues.* London: Penguin, 1987. 13–36.

Scarry, Elaine. *Resisting Representation.* New York: Oxford UP, 1994.

Schaerer, René. *La question platonicienne: Étude sur les rapports de la pensée et de l'expression dans les dialogues.* Neuchâtel: Secrétariat de l'Université, 1938.

Scheps, Walter. "Chaucer's Anti-Fable: Reductio ad absurdum in 'The Nun's Priest's Tale.'" *Leeds Studies in English* 4 (1970): 1–10.

Schiller, Friedrich von. "Letters on the Aesthetic Education of Man." Trans. Elizabeth M. Wilkinson and L. A. Willoughby. *Essays.* Ed. Walter Hinderer and Daniel O. Dahlstrom. New York: Continuum, 1993 [1795]. 86–178.

Schlegel, Friedrich. "Lyceum Fragments." Trans. Peter Firchow. *"Lucinde" and the Fragments.* Minneapolis: U Minnesota P, 1971. 143–59.

———. "Philosophische Lehrjahre." *Kritische F. Schlegels Ausgabe.* Ed. E. Behler. Vol. 18. Paderborn: Schöningh, 1971. 1–199.

———. "Über Goethes Meister." *Kritische F. Schlegels Ausgabe.* Ed. E. Behler. Vol. 2. Paderborn: Schöningh, 1967. 126–46.

Schleiermacher, Friedrich Ernst Daniel. *Schleiermacher's Introductions to the Dialogues of Plato.* Ed. William Dobson. New York: Arno, 1973.

Schopenhauer, Arthur. *The World as Will and Representation.* Trans. E. F. J. Payne. New York: Dover, 1958 [1818].

Schwab, Gabriele. *Subjects without Selves: Transitional Texts in Modern Fiction.* Cambridge, MA: Harvard UP, 1994.

Schweitzer, Albert. *The Quest of the Historical Jesus.* Minneapolis: Fortress P, 2001.

Scott, Bernard Brandon. *Hear Then the Parable: A Commentary on the Parables of Jesus.* Minneapolis: Fortress, 1989.

Scruton, Roger. "Beckett and the Cartesian Soul." *The Aesthetic Understanding: Essays in the Philosophy of Art and Culture.* Manchester: Carcanet P, 1983. 222–41.

Severn, Bill. *Magic and Magicians.* New York: Van Rees P, 1958.

Sextus Empiricus. "Outlines of Pyrrhonism." Trans. Brad Inwood and L. P. Gerson. *Hellenistic Philosophy: Introductory Readings.* Ed. Brad Inwood and L. P. Gerson. Indianapolis: Hackett, 1988.

Shallers, A. Paul. "The 'Nun's Priest's Tale': An Ironic Exemplum." *ELH* 42 (1975): 319–37.

Shamel, Shafiq. "Seeing Sounds: Reflection, Cause and Effect or Analogy; Understanding Tertium Comparationis." Unpublished manuscript, 2005.

Shelley, Percy Bysshe. "A Defence of Poetry." *Romanticism: An Anthology.* Ed. Duncan Wu. Oxford: Blackwell, 1994 [1821]. 956–69.

Shenker, Israel. "An Interview with Samuel Beckett." *Samuel Beckett: The Critical Heritage.* Ed. Lawrence Graver and Raymond Federman. London: Routledge, 1997 [May 5, 1956]. 146–49.

Sherzer, Dina. "Samuel Beckett, Linguist and Poetician: A View from *The Unnamable.*" *SubStance* 56 (1988): 87–98.

Shields, David. *Reality Hunger.* New York: Knopf, 2010.

Shklovsky, Victor. "Art as Technique." Trans. Lee T. Lemon and Marion J. Reis. *Russian Formalist Criticism: Four Essays.* Ed. Lee T. Lemon and Marion J. Reis. Lincoln: U Nebraska P, 1965. 3–24.

Shorey, Paul. *The Unity of Plato's Thought.* Chicago: U Chicago P, 1968 [1903].

Sidney, Sir Philip. *An Apology for Poetry (or The Defence of Poesy).* Manchester: Manchester UP, 2002.

Simmel, Georg. "The Metropolis and Mental Life." Trans. Helmut Loiskandl, Deena Weinstein, and Michael Weinstein. *On Individuality and Social Forms.* Ed. Donald N. Levine. Chicago: U Chicago P, 1971 [1903]. 324–39.

————. "The Transcendent Character of Life." Trans. Helmut Loiskandl, Deena Weinstein, and Michael Weinstein. *On Individuality and Social Forms*. Ed. Donald N. Levine. Chicago: U of Chicago P, 1971 [1918]. 353–74.

Skinner, Quentin. "Meaning and Understanding in the History of Ideas." *History & Theory* 8 (1969): 3–53.

Smith, B. T. D. *The Parables of the Synoptic Gospels: A Critical Study*. Cambridge: Cambridge UP, 1937.

Smith, S. H. "'Inside' and 'Outside' in Mark's Gospel: A Response." *Expository Times* 102 (1991): 363–67.

Solomon, Philip H. *The Life after Birth: Imagery in Samuel Beckett's Trilogy*. University, MS: Romance Monographs, 1975.

Sontag, Susan. "Against Interpretation." *Against Interpretation and Other Essays*. New York: Picador, 2001. 3–14.

Sprague, Rosamund Kent. "Logic and Literary Form in Plato." *Personalist* 48 (1967): 560–72.

————. "Plato's Sophistry." *Aristotelian Society*, supp. vol. 51 (1977): 45–61.

————. *Plato's Use of Fallacy: A Study of the "Euthydemus" and Some Other Dialogues*. New York: Barnes and Noble, 1962.

Stevens, Wallace. *The Necessary Angel: Essays on Reality and the Imagination*. New York: Vintage, 1951.

Stevenson, Robert Louis. "A Humble Remonstrance." *Selected Writings of Robert Louis Stevenson*. New York: Random House, 1947. 915–25.

Stewart, M. A. "Plato's Sophistry." *Aristotelian Society*, supp. vol. 51 (1977): 21–61.

Stewart, Susan. *Poetry and the Fate of the Senses*. Chicago: U Chicago P, 2002.

Stierle, Karl-Heinz. "Story as Exemplum—Exemplum as Story: On the Pragmatics and Poetics of Narrative Texts." Trans. Charles E. May. *The New Short Story Theories*. Ed. Charles Mayo. Athens: Ohio UP, 1994. 15–43.

Stokes, Michael C. *Plato's Socratic Conversations: Drama and Dialectic in Three Dialogues*. Baltimore: Johns Hopkins UP, 1986.

Stolnitz, Jerome. "On the Cognitive Triviality of Art." *British Journal of Aesthetics* 32.3 (1992): 191–200.

————. "On the Historical Triviality of Art." *British Journal of Aesthetics* 31 (1991): 195–202.

Stow, Simon. "Reading Our Way to Democracy? Literature and Public Ethics." *Philosophy and Literature* 30 (2006): 410–22.

Strauss, David Friedrich. *The Life of Jesus Critically Examined*. Trans. Mary Ann Evans [George Eliot]. Mifflintown, PA: Sigler, 1994 [1835].

Strauss, Leo. *On Plato's "Symposium."* Chicago: University of Chicago Press, 2001.

————. *The City and Man*. Chicago: U Chicago P, 1964.

Svece, Artis. "An Analysis of the Possibility of Deliberate Self-Deception." Master's thesis, Sir Wilfred Grenfell College, Memorial University of Newfoundland, 1996.

Tamen, Miguel. *Friends of Interpretable Objects*. Cambridge, MA: Harvard UP, 2004.

Tanner, Michael. "Morals in Fiction and Fictional Morality." *Proceedings of Mind Supplementary* 68 (1994): 51–66.

Taylor, Charles. *Sources of the Self: The Making of the Modern Identity*. Cambridge: Cambridge UP, 1989.

Tejera, V. "Methodology of a Misreading: A Critical Note on T. Irwin's *Plato's Moral Theory*." *International Studies in Philosophy* 10 (1978): 131–36.

Teloh, Henry. "The Importance of Interlocutors' Characters in Plato's Early Dialogues." *Proceedings of the Boston Area Colloquium in Ancient Philosophy* 2 (1987): 25–38.

Tesanovic, Biljana. *Cohérence formelle et dynamique dans la trilogie de Samuel Beckett*. Paris: Presses Universitaires du Septentrion, 1992.

Thiher, Allen. "Wittgenstein, Heidegger, the Unnamable, and Some Thoughts on the Status of Voice in Fiction." *Samuel Beckett: Humanistic Perspectives*. Ed. S. E. Gontarski, Morris Beja, and Pierre Astier. Columbus: Ohio State UP, 1983. 80–90.

Thucydides. *History of the Peloponnesian War*. Trans. Rex Warner. London: Penguin, 2003.

Todorov, Tzvetan. "Reading as Construction." Trans. Barbara Johnson. *The Reader in the Text: Essays in Audience and Interpretation*. Ed. Susan Suleiman and Inge Crossman. Princeton, NJ: Princeton UP, 1980. 67–82.

Tolstoy, Leo. *Anna Karenina*. Trans. Constance Garnett, Leonard J. Kent, and Nina Berberova. New York: Modern Library, 1993.

Tomashevsky, Boris. "Thematics." Trans. Lee T. Lemon and Marion J. Reis. *Russian Formalist Criticism: Four Essays*. Ed. Lee T. Lemon and Marion J. Reis. Lincoln: U Nebraska P, 1965. 61–98.

Tompkins, Jane P. "The Reader in History: The Changing Shape of Literary Response." *Reader-Response Criticism: From Formalism to Post-Structuralism*. Ed. Jane P. Tompkins. Baltimore: Johns Hopkins UP, 1980. 201–32.

Travis, Peter W. "Reading Chaucer Ab Ovo: Mock-Exemplum in 'The Nun's Priest's Tale.'" *The Performance of Middle English Culture: Essays on Chaucer and the Drama in Honor of Martin Stevens*. Ed. Lawrence M. Clopper, James J. Paxson, and Sylvia Tomasch. Cambridge: D. S. Brewer, 1998. 161–81.

Truffaut, François. *Hitchcock*. New York: Simon and Schuster, 1967.

Tuckett, Christopher, ed. *The Messianic Secret*. Philadelphia: Fortress P, 1983.

Uhlmann, Anthony. "The Ancient Stoics, Émile Bréhier, and Beckett's Beings of Violence." *Samuel Beckett: Endlessness in the Year 2000*. Ed. Angela Moorjani and Carola Veit. Amsterdam: Rodopi, 2001. 351–60.

———. *Beckett and Poststructuralism*. Cambridge: Cambridge UP, 1999.

Valéry, Paul. *Oeuvres*. Vol. 1. Paris: Gallimard, 1960.

Velleman, J. David. "Narrative Explanation." *Philosophical Review* 112.1 (2003): 1–25.

Via, Dan Otto, Jr. "Matthew on the Understandability of the Parables." *Journal of Biblical Literature* 84 (1965): 430–32.

———. *The Parables: Their Literary and Existential Dimension*. Philadelphia: Fortress P, 1967.

Vlastos, Gregory. Introduction. *Plato: Protagoras*. Ed. Benjamin Jowett. Indianapolis: Bobbs-Merrill, 1956. vii–lvi.

———. *Platonic Studies*. Princeton, NJ: Princeton UP, 1973.

———. *Socrates, Ironist and Moral Philosopher*. Ithaca, NY: Cornell UP, 1991.

Vogler, Candace. "The Moral of the Story." *Critical Inquiry* 34 (2007): 5–35.

Walton, Kendall L. "Fearing Fictions." *Journal of Philosophy* 75 (1978): 5–27.

———. *Mimesis as Make-Believe*. Cambridge, MA: Harvard UP, 1993.

———. "Morals in Fiction and Fictional Morality." *Proceedings of Mind Supplementary* 68 (1994): 27–50.

———. "Spelunking, Simulation, and Slime: On Being Moved by Fiction." *Emotion and the Arts*. Ed. Mette Hjort and Sue Laver. Oxford: Oxford UP, 1997. 37–49.

———. "Thoughtwriting—in Poetry and Music." *New Literary History* 42:3 (2011): 455–76

Warner, Martin. "Dialectical Drama: The Case of Plato's Symposium." *Apeiron* 25.4 (1992): 157–75.

Warren, Robert Penn. "Pure and Impure Poetry." *New and Selected Essays*. New York: Random House, 1989. 3–28.

Waterfield, Robin. "Introduction to the *Euthydemus*." *Plato: Early Socratic Dialogues*. London: Penguin, 1987. 297–311.

Watt, Ian. *The Rise of the Novel: Studies in Defoe, Richardson and Fielding*. London: Chatto & Windus, 1957.

Waugh, Patricia. *Metafiction: The Theory and Practice of Self-Conscious Fiction*. London: Methuen, 1984.

Webb, Eugene. *Samuel Beckett: A Study of His Novels*. Seattle: U Washington P, 1970.

Webb, James. *The Flight from Reason*. London: Macdonald, 1971.

Weber, Max. "Science as a Vocation." *Max Weber: Essays in Sociology*. Ed. H. H. Gerth and C. Wright Mills. Oxford: Oxford UP, 1946. 129–56.

Weiss, Johannes. *Die Predigt Jesu vom Reiche Gottes*. Gottingen: Vandenhoeck & Ruprecht, 1900.

Wheatley, Edward. *Mastering Aesop: Medieval Education, Chaucer, and His Followers*. Gainesville: UP Florida, 2000.

White, Nicholas P. "Rational Prudence in Plato's *Gorgias*." *Platonic Investigations*. Ed. Dominic J. O'Meara. Washington: Catholic University of America P, 1986. 139–62.

Wicker, Brian. "Samuel Beckett and the Death of the God-Narrator." *The Critical Response to Samuel Beckett*. Ed. Cathleen Culotta Andonian. London: Greenwood P, 1998. 39–51.

Wieckowski, Danièle. *La poétique de Mallarmé: La fabrique des iridées*. Paris: SEDES, 1998.

Wilder, Amos N. *The Language of the Gospel*. New York: Harper & Row, 1964.

Williams, Bernard. *Ethics and the Limits of Philosophy*. Cambridge, MA: Harvard UP, 1985.

———. Introduction. *The "Theaetetus" of Plato*. Indianapolis: Hackett, 1990.

Wirth, Oswald. *Stanislas de Guaïta: Souvenirs de son secrétaire*. Paris: Editions du symbolisme, 1935.

Witherington, Ben. *The Jesus Quest: The Third Search for the Jew of Nazareth*. Downers Grove, IL: InterVarsity P, 1995.

Wittgenstein, Ludwig. *Culture and Value*. Trans. Peter Winch. Oxford: Blackwell, 1994.

———. *Philosophical Investigations*. Trans. D. F. Pears and B. F. McGuinness. New York: Prentice Hall, 1999.

Wordsworth, William. "Of the Principles of Poetry and the 'Lyrical Ballads' (1798–1802)." *The Prose Works of William Wordsworth*. Ed. Alexander Balloch Grosart. London: E. Moxon, 1876. 79–105.

Wrede, William. *The Messianic Secret*. Trans. J. C. G. Grieg. Cambridge: James Clarke, 1971.

Wright, N. Thomas. "Five Gospels but No Gospel: Jesus and the Seminar." *Authenticating the Activities of Jesus*. Ed. Bruce Chilton and Craig A. Evans. Leiden: Brill, 1999. 83–120.

Zeller, Eduard. *Die Philosophie der Griechen in ihrer geschichtlichen Entwicklung*. 3 vols. Darmstadt: Wissenschaftliche Buchgesellschaft, 1963 [1919–23].

Zeyl, Donald. "Socrates and Hedonism." *Phronesis* 25 (1980): 250–69.

Zunshine, Lisa. *Why We Read Fiction: Theory of Mind and the Novel*. Columbus: Ohio State UP, 2006.

Zurbrugg, Nicholas. *Beckett and Proust*. Gerrards Cross: Colin Smythe, 1988.

INDEX

Adorno, Theodor, 7, 16, 149–50n15, 150n19, 152n34, 153n40, 158n79, 210n9

Agathon, 14, 95, 101–105, 111, 157n71, 186n1, 187n6, 205n106

in elenchus with Socrates, 101–5, 192n32–33, 193n35, 193n39–40, 194n42–46

akrasia, 98–9, 110–11, 117, 189–90n16–19, 190n23, 191n25, 191n27, 197n65, 199n74, 202n89, 203–4n96–97. *See also* Socratic paradoxes

Alcibiades, 95–101, 108, 110, 116–17, 121, 187n3–8, 188n12, 189–90n15–19, 191n27, 192n29, 192n31, 195–6n53–54, 197n65–66, 205n107

as counterexample, 99, 117

allegory, 15, 18, 29, 54–55, 57, 61, 82, 84, 158–59n91, 168n4, 171n45, 173n57, 173n60, 180n45, 181n53, 181n55

Anderson, R. Lanier, 149n11, 158n88, 197n65, 205n110, 219n87

antilogoi, 11–12, 15, 127, 210n15–17

Aristotle, 4, 7, 19, 58, 97, 112, 116, 126, 150n16, 159n93–94, 167n64, 169n9, 186–7n1, 199n74, 210n12, 222n113

ataraxia, 11, 125–27, 129, 135, 138–39, 141–43, 145–46, 208–9n6, 212n28, 216–7n64–65, 220n93

audience partition. *See* elitism

Augustine, 54–55, 72, 218n81

Austen, Jane, 18

Austin, J. L., 9, 154n51, 156n67

Bakhtin, Mikhail, 5, 9, 147n3, 150–51n23, 166n61, 167n68

Barthes, Roland, 5, 151n24, 153n45, 156n68, 185n90

Baudelaire, Charles, 64–68, 83, 148n8, 175–76n87–88, 178–9n32, 182–3n65

Beckett, Samuel, 4, 13, 15–17, 124–46, 151n25, 158n82, 207–24n1–130

as Pyrrhonian skeptic. *See* skepticism

certainty in, 128–30, 212n29, 212–3n31–33

cliché in, 136

Endgame, 90, 92, 158n79, 158n83, 183n69, 184n86, 214n42, 215n48

How It Is, 139, 142, 211n23, 215n48, 216n61, 217n74, 218n81, 218n86, 219n88, 220n95, 222n111–12, 223n115

Molloy, 11, 17, 124–40, 142–43, 145–46, 158n80, 208–9n3–6, 210n17, 212n27, 212n32, 214n41–45, 214–5n47, 215n49, 215n51, 215n53, 216n59–60, 216n62, 216n64, 217n68–70, 217n73, 219n88, 219n91, 220n93, 221–2n109–10, 222n112, 223n117–19, 224n127

Malone Dies, 11, 16, 124, 130–38, 140–41, 143, 158n80, 209n8, 210n10, 211n24, 214n42, 214–5n47, 215n53, 215n56, 216n59, 217n68–72, 217n77, 219n88, 221n105, 222n110, 222n113, 223n125

Murphy, 16, 127, 130, 133–37, 141–42, 158n80–1, 210n9, 210n17, 211n22–23, 214–5n47–48, 217n69, 218n84, 220n97–98, 221n106, 222n110, 222n113, 223–4n127

mutual cancellation in, 127, 145, 211n21–22, 222n113

negative anthropology in, 138, 219n91

Not I, 137, 217n66, 224n127

permutation in, 223–4n127

qualification and refinement in, 128–29, 212–3n32–34

solving and dissolving in, 129–30, 213n40

spiral in, 129, 139–40, 142–44, 146, 220–1n98

Texts for Nothing, 139–40, 143, 210n14, 210n16, 211n26, 212n31, 217n66, 217n73, 218n80, 219n90, 220n94–95, 221n105, 223n121, 224n127

trilogy, 11, 13, 18, 217n75, 219n88. *See also* Beckett (*Molloy*); Beckett (*Malone Dies*); Beckett (*The Unnamable*)

Beckett, Samuel (*continued*)
  The Unnamable, 11, 16, 124, 127, 129–32,
    135–44, 158n79–80, 207n1, 208n4, 209n8,
    210n15–16, 211–2n24–26, 212n29,
    212–3n31–34, 213n38, 213–4n40–42,
    214–5n46–47, 215n50, 215n52, 215–6n57–
    59, 217n65, 217n67, 217n70, 217n73–74,
    217n76, 218n79, 218n84–85, 219n88,
    220n94–95, 220–1n97–99, 221n105,
    221n109, 222n112, 223n115–16, 223n118,
    223n120, 223–4n123–27
  Watt, 126, 129–30, 141, 158n80, 208–9n6, 209n8,
    213n37, 217n73, 220n97, 221n107–8, 223n116
Bible
  Pentateuch, 24, 69–72, 177n15, 172n49
  Prophets, 24, 38, 48, 169n14, 170n27, 170n30,
    170n32, 171n38, 171n45
  New Testament. *See* Gospels; Paul
Booth, Wayne, 4, 30, 38, 154n49, 161n24,
  163–4n38, 164n42, 167–8n69
Boullan, Abbé, 77–8, 178n28–30
Brecht, Bertolt, 17–18, 90, 95, 110, 158n87, 184n86
Bultmann, Rudolf, 47, 57, 60, 156n64, 170n21,
  171n43, 173n55, 173n67

Callicles, 105–11, 113–15, 121, 192n30, 194–5n48,
  195n50–51, 195–6n53, 196n56, 197n66,
  197–98n67, 198n68–69, 198n71, 198–99n72,
  200n82, 200–203n84–92, 204n99, 206n116,
  206–7n120, 207n121
chance, overcoming. *See* contingency
care of the self. *See* self-fashioning
Chaucer, Geoffrey, 3–4, 16–17, 125, 148n7–8
  The Miller's Tale, 23, 26
  The Nun's Priest's Tale, 23–29, 35–37, 39,
    159–60n5–8, 160–61n13–20
  The Wife of Bath's Tale, 28, 160n15
Christianity, 43–63, 69–72, 75–76, 168–75n1–83,
  176n4, 177n14. *See also* Augustine; Gospels;
  Paul
  and magic, 70–2, 176–7n10–15
  early, 47, 50–52, 171n41–43, 172n52
  figurative language in, 56–62, 174n72–76
clarification
  affective, 4–5, 166n62
  cognitive, 5, 8, 9, 37–38, 150–51n21–28,
    155n57, 157n75, 166–7n63, 173n61, 208n2
  sensory. *See* fiction, functions of
  (defamiliarization)
cognitive science, 165n52, 173–4n68, 181n51,
  184n81
constellation, 80–85, 87, 179n34, 181n51, 181n55.
  See also Ursa Major
contemplation. *See* fiction, functions of
content, propositional. *See* messages
contingency (overcome by verse), 82, 85–7,
  182–3n65–67, 183n69
Croce, Benedetto, 6, 7, 151n29, 154n53
Danto, Arthur, 152n31, 153n44, 164n39,
  166–7n63, 175n84, 186–7n1

defamiliarization. *See* fiction, functions of
Descartes, René, 16, 125, 132, 143, 210n9, 215n51,
  215–6n57, 216n60, 218n81
Dickens, Charles, 30, 32–34, 36, 92, 154n47, 167n67
Dickinson, Emily, 64, 175n85
didacticism. *See* messages
Diderot, Denis, 32, 38, 90–91, 150n18, 163n37,
  164n39, 184–5n87, 185n91–92
Diotima, 96–97, 100, 103, 105, 116, 187n6,
  187n8–9, 187–89n11–13, 189n17, 190n19,
  190n21, 191n27, 192n32, 193n38, 194n47,
  205n106
"disenchantment of the world", 16, 69, 176n2–7
disinterestedness. *See* fiction, functions of
  (will-free contemplation)

effects of reading. *See* pragmatics
Eliot, T. S., 5, 7, 15, 150n18, 157n78, 175n84,
  182n62, 207–8n2
elitism, meritocratic, 10, 13, 52–53, 75–77, 117,
  172n50–51, 172n53, 173n56, 175n83, 204n99
empathy. *See* ethical criticism (empathy-based)
enchantment
  metaphysical, 59–60, 70–72, 77–8, 176–7n8–12,
    178n27–31. *See also* faith (religious)
  scientific, 74, 177n19, 177–8n22–23
  secular, 4, 10, 63–4, 74–5, 81–83, 86–9, 92,
    149n12, 177n20, 180n39–42
eschatology, 46, 60–61, 174–5n79–81
"Ethereal Suspension" trick. *See* Robert-Houdin
ethical criticism, 13, 29–39, 149n14, 161–68n21–69
  corruption by, 9, 37, 154n48
  empathy-based, 4, 6, 7, 9, 29, 34, 149n13,
    157n74, 161n21, 161n23, 162n26, 162–3n29–
    31, 163n34, 163n37, 164n42, 164n44
  exemplum-based. *See* exemplarity
  message-based. *See* messages
  training-based. *See* training (of the moral
    imagination)
exemplarity, 6, 7, 10
  positive, 4, 28–29, 144, 148–49n9
  negative, 4, 8, 29, 144, 148–49n9, 160–1n20
exorcism paste, 77, 178n30

faith
  religious, 10, 12, 16, 43, 53–60, 73, 75, 81–2,
    173n63, 174n69, 175n83, 177n21–22,
    180n39–40
  secular. *See* enchantment (secular)
fallacy, 11, 99, 117
  awareness on Plato's part of, 103–5, 193n40,
    199n75, 201n88
  inadvertent *reductio*, 112, 117–8, 203n96
  self-contradiction, 106–7, 117
  undistributed middle, 103–5, 117, 193n37–39,
    193–94n41
fiction
  apologia for, 19
  usage of the term, 3–4, 147–8n4–6, 155n58,
    168n4, 186–7n1

fiction, functions of, 7
  affect-generation, 4–5, 8, 10, 150n17–19, 166n62
  affect-modulation, 4, 8, 150n16, 155n57
  defamiliarization, 6, 10, 152–3n38
  formal modeling, 4, 8, 144, 147n2, 149n12. *See also* self-fashioning
  indirect expression, 6, 82, 125–26, 151–2n28–32, 153n44, 174n74–75
  intimation of utopia, 4, 149–50n15
  knowledge by acquaintance, 6, 10, 152n36
  knowledge of *Zeitgeist*, 6, 152n33–5
  pleasure, 37
  self-clarification. *See* clarification
  simulation, 5, 29, 38–39, 161n22, 161n26
  training. *See* training
  will-free contemplation, 4, 141, 161n23
fiction, ostensible functions of
  intuition-pumping, 35, 165n47–8
  knowledge by revelation, 6, 10, 152n35, 152n37, 173n58, 204–5n104, 207–8n2
  moral improvement. *See* ethical criticism
  propositional knowledge. *See* messages
  zero (other than pleasure), 8, 19, 153n45
figurative language. *See* allegory; metaphor; parable; symbol
fine-tuning of capacities. *See* training
Flaubert, Gustave, 8, 18, 29, 37, 75, 148n8, 153n39, 155n57, 165–6n57, 178n23
fluids, death by, 77, 178n30
formative circle. *See* hermeneutic circle
formative fictions. *See also* training
  affect one soul at a time, 13, 53
  are non-automatic, 12, 13, 38–39, 118–19, 153n45, 155n57, 156n68, 157n75
  are to some extent content-independent, 117–18, 204n102
  contain a manual for use. *See* manual for use
  divide their audiences on meritocratic lines. *See* elitism
  provide interim rewards, 13
  require effort, 53, 64, 172n54
  require pre-capacities. *See* pre-understanding
  take time to have an effect, 12–14. *See also* reading, phases of
  work by means of formal devices, 9, 11, 12, 17–19
  work by means of the process of reading, 9, 12, 19, 154n53

Gadamer, Hans-Georg, 9, 149–50n15, 150n21, 154n54, 156n63
Gendler, Tamar, 30, 162n27–28, 162–3n30
Geulincx, Arnold, 133, 141–42, 145, 209n7, 222n112–13
Gorgias (as character), 33–34, 108–11, 114, 117, 121–22, 196–97n59–62, 197n64, 201n86, 201–2n88, 202–3n92, 206n117, 206–7n120–22, 207n126
Gospels
  Diatessaron, 16, 51
  John, 51, 60
  Luke, 16, 51, 54, 60, 168n4, 169n11, 169n16, 171n37, 172n52, 177n15
  Mark. *See* Mark
  Matthew, 16, 48–51, 56, 59, 168n2, 168n4, 169n7, 169n11, 169n16, 170n31, 171n36, 171n38, 171n40, 173n63, 174n73, 177n15
  Thomas, 60, 168n4, 169n11, 169n13, 172n53, 174n73
gumshoe, scatterbrain, and wallflower, 63

Hadot, Pierre, 194n46, 204n102, 205n109
Hegel, G. W. F., 6–7, 149n11, 152n33, 167n66, 211n20
Heidegger, Martin, 6, 7, 143, 152n35, 152n37, 156n63, 173n58, 207–8n2, 223n120
hermeneutic circle (and formative circle), 12–13, 57–59, 156n63–4
historians, 50, 165n55, 195n49, 200–1n85, 206n118
  polite word to, 16–17, 158n79–84
Homer, 24–26, 36–37, 165n54, 189–90n18, 222n112
Horace, 7, 150n17
Hume, 30, 138, 162–3n30, 215n56, 219–20n93

illusion, 70, 74, 86
  lucid, 12, 75–7, 87–9, 91–2, 155n56, 178n24, 178n26, 183n75, 184n81, 184n83–84
  necessary, 10, 89, 91–2, 184n82, 185–6n94
imaginative inertia, 31, 162–63n29
imaginative resistance, 29–33, 162–3n27–34
instruction. *See* messages
irony, 38
  authorial, 136–38. *See also* irony (Platonic)
  Platonic, 11, 12, 18, 99, 106–7, 110–11, 116–20, 123, 187n6, 189n17, 193n35, 195n51–52, 197n62, 198n68, 204n100, 204n104, 205n109
  Romantic. *See* Romantic irony
  Socratic, 96, 105, 107, 110, 194n44, 195n52, 197n63, 197–98n67, 201–2n88, 202n91, 205n109
Iser, Wolfgang, 7, 150n21, 151n25, 153n44, 154n53, 155n57, 156n62, 157n76, 207–8n2, 219n88

James, Henry, 18, 33–35, 147n2, 152n33, 164n40, 165n49, 165n51, 167n69
Jeremias, Joachim, 169n8, 169n14, 170n20, 170n21, 170n28, 170n30, 171n42, 171n44, 173n55, 174n80
Jesus
  historical, 50–52, 172n46–47
  Mark's. *See* Mark
Jülicher, Adolf, 55, 169n7, 170n21, 171n43, 173n57
Kafka, Franz, 5, 7, 18, 150n20, 154n46, 158–59n91
Kant, Immanuel, 4, 87, 133, 145, 149n14, 215n56, 216n59
  on the sublime, 87, 183n73

Kermode, Frank, 169n15, 171–2n45, 172n51, 173n60
know-how, 10, 38. *See also* training
knowledge. *See also* Beckett (certainty in)
  absolute and limited, 98, 115, 185–6n94, 187n8, 187–8n11
  a priori and empirical, 132–33
  by acquaintance. *See* fiction, functions of
  by revelation. *See* fiction, ostensible functions of
  craft, 109–10, 196n60, 207n126
  instrumental status of (in Beckett), 126, 129, 138–39
  insufficiency of, 55, 92, 144. *See also* Plato
  love of (in Plato), 97
  of ignorance, 127–28, 139, 213n38
  of other minds. *See* fiction, functions of (indirect expression)
  of self. *See* self-knowledge
  of *Zeitgeist*. *See* fiction, functions of
  practical. *See* know-how
  propositional. *See* messages
  sensory. *See* fiction, functions of (defamiliarization)

logic. *See* training (of the capacity for reason)
Lukács, Georg, 7, 152n33, 153n40, 185n93
lyric poetry, 63, 148n8, 150n17, 152n31, 154n47, 155n58. *See also* Baudelaire; Dickinson; Mallarmé
  rhyme in, 78, 83–5, 181–2n54–57, 182–3n64–65

magic. *See also* Christianity
  metaphorical variety, 85
  stage variety. *See* Robert-Houdin
  supposedly real variety, 70, 77–8, 178n28–31
Mallarmé, Stéphane, 10, 12, 13, 15–18, 69–71, 77–92, 127, 151n25, 155n58, 157n77, 177n12, 178–84n32–84, 185–86n94
  Le vierge . . ., 179n36, 180n42, 180n47
  Quand l'ombre . . ., 179n36, 180n47, 182–3n65
  Ses purs ongles . . ., 78–89, 92, 155n58, 179–84n33–80
  Sonnet allégorique de lui-même, 81–82, 179n33–35, 179n37, 181n54–55, 183n76, 184n79
  Une dentelle . . ., 179n35, 182n59
  Un coup de dés, 155n58, 179n36, 180n38, 181n51
manual for use, 12–15, 118, 156n62
Mark, Gospel of, 4, 10, 12, 13, 15–18, 43–64, 72, 125, 148n5, 168–75n1–83
  "messianic secret" in, 48–49, 171n34–36
meaning. *See* semantic dimension
messages, ostensible, 3–6, 8–10, 12, 14–16, 19, 24–29, 43–44, 46, 54–55, 58, 62, 82, 91–2, 119–20, 125–26, 144, 148n8, 151n27, 153n40–41, 153n44, 154n47, 159n2, 161n23, 167n68, 169n7–10, 172n54, 186n95–96, 207–8n2, 208n4
metaphor, 6, 10, 12–14, 16, 18, 45, 56–64, 152n31, 155n58, 156n67, 170n21, 172n54, 173n66, 173–74n68, 174n72–74, 174n76, 175–6n84–88

cognitive theories of, 173–4n68
functions of, 59, 174n74, 175n84
method. *See* training
model for emulation. *See* exemplarity
model, formal. *See* fiction, functions of (formal modeling)
Modernism, 11, 89–92, 185n88, 186n96
Morrison, Toni, 3, 6, 8, 18, 147n2, 159n92, 160n10
motivational conflict. *See* akrasia
mummy movies, 30–31

Nehamas, Alexander, 7, 114, 149n10, 149–50n15–16, 154n47, 154n49, 156n60–61, 157n70, 166–7n63, 182n63, 188n11, 188n13, 189n16, 189–90n18, 191n25–26, 192n34, 193n40, 195n49, 195n51, 195–6n53, 200n82, 200–1n85, 202–3n91–93, 203n94, 204n103, 205n106, 206n115, 219n87
New Testament. *See* Gospels; Paul
Nietzsche, Friedrich, 7, 18, 35, 69–70, 72, 74–75, 82, 86, 92, 147n3, 149n12, 165n50, 176n1, 176n4–5, 180n44, 183n71, 187n5
Nussbaum, Martha, 4, 9, 29–30, 33–34, 37–38, 149n13, 150n16, 156n68, 158n90, 161n21–26, 164n40–41, 164–65n43–45, 165n51, 166n58–60, 167–8n69, 189n17, 193n35, 207–8n2

occasionalism, 16, 133–34, 141–2, 145, 209n7, 216n61–62, 222n112, 223n117
oneiromancy, 24–27, 35–36, 39
oratory. *See* rhetoric
order, imposition of, 82–83, 85–86, 89, 183n70–71
overdetermination, 83–6, 181–2n54–63

parables, 10, 12–13, 15–17, 43–63, 117, 148n5, 153n45, 156n65, 168–75n1–83
  audience partition function of, 52–53, 172n50–51, 172n53, 173n56, 175n83
  definition of, 168n4, 172n54
  didactic theories of, 43–44, 46, 54–55, 62, 169n7–10, 173n57–61
  opacity of, 47–50, 52–53, 169–70n15–17, 170–1n33, 171n40, 171–2n43–45, 173n64
  precursors of in Jewish tradition, 16, 45, 50, 168n3, 171–2n45
  The Good Samaritan, 4, 54, 58, 174n75
  The Sower. See Sower parable
Paul, Saint, 26, 50, 54, 58, 60, 102, 159n6, 192n34
performative utterances, not what this book is about, 154n51, 156n67
Pericles, 15, 95, 105–11, 117–18, 120–23, 148n6, 194–5n48–49, 195n51, 197n63, 198n69, 206n112–13, 206n115, 206n117–19, 207n121
perspective. *See* fiction, functions of (indirect expression)
philosophy
  as a disease, 126–30

as a way of life, 11, 96, 119, 205n109
classical. *See* Aristotle; Plato; Sextus; skepticism
early modern and modern. *See* Descartes;
   Geulincx; Hegel; Heidegger; Hume; Kant;
   Nietzsche; Sartre; Schopenhauer; Wittgenstein
Eastern, 141, 208n2, 222n111
literary devices in. *See* antilogoi; irony
   (Platonic); parables
obtaining expertise in. *See* training (of the
   capacity for reason)
putting an end to, 11, 125–30, 138
Plato, 4, 11–18, 54, 62, 95–123, 125, 148n6,
   151n25, 154n51, 161n23, 165n50, 186–
   207n1–126, 211n20. *See also* irony (Platonic)
   Apology, 105, 118, 195n52, 205–6n111
   Charmides, 195–96n53, 203–4n97
   Crito, 118, 200n81, 203n96
   developmental hypothesis concerning, 96,
      99–101, 117, 190n22, 191n26–27, 203–4n97
   "elenctic certainty" in, 114–5, 202–3n90–92
   Euthydemus, 196n58, 201n88
   Euthyphro, 104, 114, 121, 193n41, 200n80
   Gorgias, 11, 12, 15, 17, 33–34, 95, 105–23,
      148n6, 153n45, 192n30, 193n38, 194–6n48–
      54, 196n56, 196–97n59–64, 197–98n66–69,
      198–99n71–73, 199–203n75–92
   Hippias Minor, 110, 196n58, 203n96
   insufficiency of knowledge in, 100–1, 114–18,
      190–1n24–25, 197n62, 197n65, 197–98n67.
      See also akrasia
   Laches, 121, 203–4n96–97
   Meno, 105, 108, 118, 190n24, 195n49, 196n55,
      196n58, 198n67, 198n70, 202n92, 203n93,
      203n96, 206n114, 207n124
   motivational conflict in. *See* akrasia
   Phaedo, 112–13, 118, 122, 189n14, 191n26,
      193n38, 205n107–8
   Phaedrus, 12, 99–100, 113, 116–18, 186n1,
      188–9n12–13, 190n20–21, 190–1n23–26,
      205n106
   Politicus, 118, 204n102
   Protagoras, 12, 98, 104, 117, 189n15–16, 191n25,
      193n37, 193–94n41, 195n49, 198n67,
      200n82, 200–1n85, 201n87, 202n89,
      203–4n96–97, 205n105, 207n124
   Republic, 100–1, 108, 110, 113, 117, 122,
      188–89n13, 190–1n23–27, 192n29, 193n38,
      196n57–58, 198n68, 198–99n71–72, 200n81,
      201n86, 201–2n88, 203–4n96, 205n108
   Seventh Letter, 116
   Sophist, 118, 193n38
   Symposium, 11–12, 14, 95–105, 111, 116–19, 121,
      157n71, 187–94n3–47, 196n54, 197n65,
      205n106–7
   Theaetetus, 105, 107–8, 122, 192n33, 201n88,
      203n95, 205n106
   theory of Forms in, 97–100, 187n8, 187–8n11,
      189n16
poetry. *See* lyric
Polus, 112–15, 117–18, 121, 199n73, 199n75–76,
   199–200n79, 200n82, 201n86, 201–2n88–
   89, 202–3n91–92, 206–7n120

post-structuralist excesses, 8, 91–2, 126, 129,
   136–7, 139–40, 175n84, 181n52, 186n97,
   209n7–8, 214n43, 219n88
practice-space, fiction as. *See* training
pragmatics of reading, 9–10, 154n50–1, 183n72
pre-understanding (and pre-capacity), 13, 57, 117,
   156n64, 204n99
propositional content. *See* messages
Protagoras (as character), 104, 193n37, 193–94n41,
   196n55, 198n70, 200n82, 201n85, 203n96
Proust, Marcel, 6–9, 18, 35, 59, 84, 90, 130, 136,
   138, 140, 147n3, 149n10, 151n28, 152n31,
   157–58n78, 159n92, 160n10, 175n84,
   182n63, 184n86, 192n30, 210n13, 214n42,
   219–20n93, 221n104
ptyx, 79–80, 84–88, 179n35, 182n64, 183n76,
   184n79–80

reader response theory, 151n25, 153n44, 155n57,
   156n62, 156n68. *See also* Iser
reading
   institutions of, 16, 35–37
   phases of, 12–14, 155n59
reason. *See* training
   abdication of, 127, 210n13
   not always a terrible thing, 157n74
re-enchantment. *See* enchantment
reflexivity. *See* Romantic irony
rereading, 13–14, 89, 155n57, 156n69
rhetoric, 37, 95, 109–115, 118, 123, 195n52,
   196–97n59–61, 198n69–71, 199n79,
   200n80, 206n120, 207n122, 207n126,
   208n4, 212n30
   as craft, 109–11, 114
   as something beneficial to an orator, 109, 111–4
   as something beneficial to others, 109, 111, 114
   in metaphor, 175n84
   in parables (ostensibly). *See* parables (didactic
      theories of)
   of Socrates, 95, 113–15, 200n82–84
   protecting fiction from becoming, 37
rhyme. *See* lyric poetry (rhyme in)
Richards, I. A., 5, 7, 60, 149n11, 151n26, 154n50,
   154n53, 175n84
Ricoeur, Paul, 7, 149n10, 152n37, 155n59, 168n4,
   169n7, 169n9, 172n50, 173n64, 173n66,
   174n74, 174n76
Robert-Houdin, Jean-Eugène, 10, 70–77, 89,
   176n6–8, 177n16–18, 178n26
   Ethereal Suspension trick, 73–75, 177n18
Romantic irony, 11–12, 18, 89–92, 155n58,
   184–86n85–97
   informative hypothesis, 91–2, 186n95–97
   strategic hypothesis, 90–92, 185–6n90–94
   symptomatic hypothesis, 90, 92, 185n89
Rorty, Richard, 4, 29, 149n13, 161n21, 161n23,
   210n9, 211n18, 211n20
Rousseau, Jean-Jacques, 36, 135, 138, 164n39,
   165n53

sanctimonious fictions, 32, 162n27, 163n34,
   167n67

Sartre, Jean-Paul, 7, 35, 152n37, 153n40, 154n53, 156n66, 158n84, 158n91

Schiller, Friedrich, 5, 7, 151n26–27

Schlegel, Friedrich, 91, 184–5n87, 185–6n93–94

Schleiermacher, Friedrich, 12, 156n63, 204n98, 204n104

Schopenhauer, Arthur, 4, 7, 9, 140–43, 145, 149–50n14–15, 175n86, 209n7, 212n28, 219n89, 221n101–2, 221n104, 221n108, 222n110–11, 223n114

self-deception. *See* illusion

self-fashioning, 4, 11, 98, 135–40, 149n11, 189n14, 189n16

selfhood, 130–40
  abolition of, 135–44, 214n42, 219n89
  achievement of, 118–19
  authorial, 82–83, 87, 180–81n48–52
  corporeal, 131–33
  divided diachronically, 130, 214n42
  divided synchronically, 89–91, 184n84, 185n89, 185n91. *See also* akrasia
  doubted, 136
  existent, 136–40, 217–8n79–86
  found in order to be lost, 138–40, 220n94–95

self-knowledge, 136–40. *See also* clarification
  by working back from one's actions, 136, 138–40, 217n78

self-reflexivity. *See* Romantic irony

semantic dimension
  always subordinate to effect. *See* pragmatics
  especially regrettable when reduced to "message". *See* messages
  nonetheless, a role for, 9, 14–16, 157n75, 157–58n77–78
  subdivisions of, 88–89

Sextus Empiricus, 127, 134, 209n7, 211n18–19, 216n63, 224n129

Shakespeare, William, 8, 31, 36, 163n34, 184n85, 186n97

Shelley, Percy, 4, 7, 148–49n9, 149n13, 152n33, 152–3n38

Shklovsky, Viktor, 6, 7, 152–3n38

silence, 87, 126, 137, 139, 145, 183n69, 211n23, 220n95
  as something to be made, 78, 85–86, 127, 178n32, 183n67, 211n23–24, 223–24n127

skepticism, ancient, 11, 15, 17, 116, 126–28, 141, 144, 158n82, 209n7, 212n28. *See also* Sextus

skills. *See* training

Socrates. *See also* rhetoric
  as character, 11, 14–15, 33–34, 95–123, 148n6, 165n50, 186–7n1, 187n4–9, 187–88n11–13, 189–90n15–19, 190–1n21–25, 191n27, 192n29–33, 193n35, 193–96n37–58, 196–97n60–64, 197–203n66–93, 203–4n96–98, 204n101, 204n103, 205n105–9, 205–7n111–21, 207n124–26
  as historical figure, 15, 96–97, 148n6, 187n8, 190n22, 195n51, 200n83
  the paradoxes of, 29, 161n22, 188n11, 190n22, 197n62–63, 197–98n67, 199n79, 204n97

Sontag, Susan, 7, 152–3n38, 157n72

sophists and sophistry, 16, 105, 108, 118, 196n54, 199n75, 201–2n88, 206n120. *See also* Gorgias; Protagoras; rhetoric (of Socrates)

Sower parable, 15, 17, 44–47, 50, 61–63, 168n4, 169n11–14, 169–70n17–22, 172n53, 173n61, 174n75, 175n82
  conflicting interpretations of, 46–47, 170n18–25

spiritual exercise. *See* training

stars. *See* constellations

Straussians, 54, 116, 187n7, 190n22, 203n95
  why I am not one, 204n104

style, as indicator of perspective. *See* fiction, functions of (indirect expression)

sublime, the. *See* Kant

symbol, 10, 57, 59, 87, 214n47

Syrophoenician Woman, 55–57, 59, 61, 173 n62–63

teaching (as against training). *See* messages

therapy, philosophical, 15, 144, 211n18

Thucydides, 165n55, 195n49, 206n118

tragedy, 4, 140, 142, 149n9, 149n12, 150n16, 156n60, 164n39, 167n66, 186n1

training through fiction, 10–14, 17–19, 155n56, 208n4
  of the capacity for emotional disengagement, 18
  of the capacity for faith, 10, 12, 15, 43, 53–63, 173n66, 174n74
  of the capacity for meaning-attribution under conditions of uncertainty, 18
  of the capacity for peace of mind, 11–12, 15, 126–30, 138–46. *See also* ataraxia; antilogoi
  of the capacity for reason, 11–12, 15, 117–20, 204n99–100, 204–5n103–4, 205n106
  of the capacity to impose provisional order, 18
  of the capacity to keep multiple hypotheses in play, 18
  of the capacity to stand back from one's judgments, 17–18
  of the capacity to sustain illusions, 10–12, 15, 86–92, 183n75, 184n83–84
  of the "Machiavellian intelligence", 18
  of the moral imagination, 9, 38–39, 161n23

tranquility. *See* ataraxia

undistributed middle, fallacy of. *See* fallacy

Ursa Major, 80–81, 87, 179n33, 179n36, 180n38, 181n53, 182n60

Walton, Kendall, 30, 32, 150n20, 150n22, 155n57, 156n69, 161n22, 162n27, 163n34, 167n65

Wittgenstein, Ludwig, 3, 147n1, 211n18

Woolf, Virginia, 18

Wordsworth, William, 5–7, 9, 147n3, 150n19

Zunshine, Lisa, 155n57, 158n90, 161n21

Printed in the USA/Agawam, MA
January 11, 2013

571840.021